The
Great Richmond
Terminal
A
Study
in Businessmen
and
Business
Strategy

The Great
Richmond Terminal

A Study in Businessmen
and Business Strategy

Maury Klein

Published for
the Eleutherian Mills–Hagley Foundation

University Press of Virginia
Charlottesville

To Julia,

in remembrance of things past . . .

Preface

PERHAPS no other period of southern history is at once more familiar and more obscure than the post–Civil War era. Indeed the very ease with which the term "New South" and all it connotes come to mind betrays the lack of specialized scholarship on the subject; broad generalizations flourish best where little detailed information exists to contradict them. While much study has been given the postwar period, most of it has concentrated upon either the reconstruction era or upon basic social and political themes. Relatively little attention has been devoted to economic development, even though most historians stress the importance of changing economic patterns in explaining the emergence of the New South.

Especially has the *process* of economic development been ignored. Thomas D. Clark and Albert D. Kirwan's recent volume, *The South since Appomattox,* devotes only a scant chapter to postwar industrial activity, and even C. Vann Woodward's classic *Origins of the New South* allots but two of its penetrating chapters to the subject. The main problem seems to be one of purpose: historians of the period have been interested in economic development not as a problem in itself but rather for the light it sheds upon certain significant changes in other aspects of southern society. Thus, the general impact of economic activity is deemed important and given proper consideration while the process by which it occurred remains outside the pale of most investigations.

Surely this set of priorities can be challenged. The whole notion of a "New" South is at heart an economic concept referring to the gradual movement of the region away from a staple crop economy toward a more diversified (and therefore industrialized) economy. The social, political, and intellectual ramifications of this movement were immense and permeated every aspect of southern life. For that reason the process of industrial development could not help but exert a shaping influence, especially since its basic assumptions and effects often ran counter to southern tradition. The continuous interaction between the process of industrialization and the institutions of a fundamentally agrarian society, if examined closely, can tell us a great deal about the complex adjustments made by the South after its defeat.

In any such study close attention must be paid to the businessmen who gave the South its entrepreneurial leadership. Heretofore the nebulous spirit of the New South has for the most part been identified with its most conspicuous and articulate spokesmen, namely, journalists like Henry W. Grady or the host of politicians who advertised the vast potential of the South and urged its exploitation. Such men were important as propagandists and for the political and legal aid they rendered, but they rarely performed the vital functions of promoting and organizing enterprises and mobilizing the capital needed to carry them out. These and other critical tasks were left to the businessmen, who constitute the key element in the industrialization of the South. Yet little has been written about these businessmen either individually or as a group, and even less has been said about their motives, tactics, and goals. Hence they remain shadowy figures whose activities are by default ascribed to some variation of regional patriotism on one hand or to the Robber Baron syndrome on the other. In truth one can gain a clearer picture of them from literature than from the scholarly investigations that have been made.

The purpose of this study, then, is to illuminate the process of economic development by focusing upon the railroad industry in general and a specific case history, the Richmond Terminal, in particular. Ideally such a study ought to include a detailed examination of the complex interactions between economic activity and all pertinent social and political institutions. Limitations of space and talent, however, compel a more modest objective, namely, the nature of the economic activity itself and the role played by the entrepreneurs who shaped it. The emphasis given this aspect of the problem can be justified by the lack of attention it has received in the past and by the large body of existing literature on other aspects of southern development.

It may be argued that the railroads were not a very representative industry in the southern experience and therefore offer little insight into the general process of economic development. Even if this were true, and I am most unwilling to admit that it was, the railroads would still constitute a logical starting point for any inquiry into southern industrialization. For one thing, they were the first sizable industry to arise in the postwar era and therefore the first to confront the major problems of organization, administration, mobilization of capital, and a host of others. Although the strategies and tactics that evolved in the transportation sector do not precisely fit other sectors, the basic patterns and attitudes learned there did exert considerable influence.

The railroads were a vital sector not only because they came first but because they paved the way for massive investments in other industries and enterprises. On this point a survey of the careers of individual financiers was necessary. As this study will show, most southern rail entrepreneurs either invested in transportation to protect prior interests in other industries or, more commonly, went from the railroads to such sequential investments as mining, cotton mills, real estate, express business, manufacturing, and industrial development of all kinds. In this manner the railroads triggered and fostered industrial activity throughout the South and provided not only transportation but a formidable group of experienced and talented financiers willing to extend their southern commitments.

By the end of the century many of these businessmen had virtually abandoned their railroad enterprises in favor of other and more lucrative sectors. Whatever their individual motives and goals, however, nearly all of them shared one original assumption: that transportation held the key to the South's future economic development and must therefore receive top investment priority. As the study suggests, this original commitment gradually evolved from a developmental to a speculative investment as southern railroads ceased to be profitable enterprises. By that time, however, a basic transportation system had been erected, and new opportunities arose to claim the financier's attention and capital.

The study has been organized to show this basic pattern of development. The first chapter suggests a working hypothetical framework in which the development of southern railroads in general took place during the period from 1865 to 1893. The second chapter presents some biographical sketches of the more important and representative figures connected with the systems that eventually were included in the Richmond Terminal. This background information seems especially important to an understanding of the diversity of interests and motivations that led men to invest in southern transportation; it also seeks to rescue several colorful and fascinating individuals from the oblivion to which they have been consigned by more general surveys.

Chapter III traces the postwar history of the three Terminal systems prior to 1880, a significant turning point in the history of each company. The remaining chapters discuss in detail the rise and fall of the Terminal and its component systems. Throughout the study I have tried to focus upon the process of development as it was shaped by the decisions of individual businessmen. The crucial assumption here is that development occurred by a process of accretion, and that the decision-making process makes no sense unless it is viewed alongside the viable alternatives available at the time. Wherever possible I have discussed these alternatives and the reasons for their ultimate rejection. By examining these entrepreneurial motivations closely it is hoped that a fresh perspective will be thrown upon the whole process of southern industrial development.

In this light it is important to keep in mind that the Richmond Terminal itself constituted one possible response to the problems posed in the transportation sector. To be sure the Terminal has an intrinsic interest of its own. As one of the nation's first pure holding companies it offers a fascinating insight into the evolution of corporate and financial institutions, to say nothing of the social consequences posed by its creation. In this study, however, I am concerned with the Terminal primarily as the most ambitious and spectacular attempt to resolve pressing difficulties in southern transportation. To understand the Terminal's history is to understand the strengths and limitations of the most popular alternative chosen by southern rail leaders during the late nineteenth century.

Nor is the Terminal's significance limited to the past, for the reorganization of 1893 transformed it into the Southern Railway Company, which remains the dominant system in the South. Fairfax Harrison, past president and legal historian of the Southern, once noted that "the territory south of the Ohio and the Potomac, and east of the Mississippi rivers is perhaps more nearly served by the Southern Railway System than is any other territory of like extent served by any other single system." That observation holds true nearly seventy years after its recording.

One final point may be worth making even though it is pursued only implicitly here. In surveying the economic plight of the South in 1865, it is hard to overlook the region's resemblance to more recent emerging and underdeveloped nations. It suffered from a monolithic and somewhat primitive staple economy that had resisted diversification for decades. It lacked capital, skilled labor, technological know-how, and an entrepreneurial tradition, all of which were needed to exploit the untapped resources that were available. Defeat in battle aggravated these difficulties and left the South without credit or even an operating financial system. Emancipation and the ordeal of reconstruction rendered the social and political atmosphere uncertain for more than a decade. Finally, the unmeasurable legacy of bitterness, despair, and frustration wrought by the war threw a constant cloud over the whole process of economic rehabilitation.

There were, of course, many ways in which the South differed from most emerging nations. Despite the deep cultural schism, it shared a common tradition and heritage with its conqueror. It possessed an educated and energetic elite which, though weakened numerically and financially by the war, could provide strong leadership. More important, the war spawned a generation of impoverished but aggressive young men eager to make their fortunes and receptive to the opportunities and rewards of industrialization. And if the traditions of the region resisted surrender to the triumphant industrial order, its natural resources invited exploitation. There existed in the South rich mineral deposits, a large if unskilled labor supply, and easy access to outside markets via water transportation and a rail system that, once recovered from the ravages of war, could service the entire region efficiently. The general postwar poverty and eventual restoration of conservative local government would do much to ensure such inducements as political cooperation, low tax rates, and other concessions.

The effect of these conditions was to lead the postwar South down the now familiar road to economic colonialism. The critical need for capital and experienced entrepreneurial leadership tended to open the control of most major industries to the hands of "outsiders," and the increasing scale of economic activity further hastened the decline of local control. As many historians have pointed out, this process reduced the South to an economic colony of the North, whose financial leaders reaped most of the benefits. In short, economic development of the South followed the same exploitative pattern as took place in the imperial subjugation of foreign countries. To many unreconstructed rebels the North seemed no less a foreign power than Italy did to the Ethiopians, and their resentment ran deep.

This fairly standard description needs two important qualifications, both of which pertain to the process of economic development. First of all, the South's colonial bondage was actually part of a changing economic environment that involved the entire nation. The major issue here may not be northern exploitation of the South so much as the marked decline in local control of firms and industries and the rise of absentee ownership as the scale of operations grew. This trend was in no way unique to the South although conditions there certainly favored it. Secondly, the "northerners" assuming control over southern enterprises often prove at second glance not to be northerners at all but transplanted southerners. As the biographical discussion suggests, the geographical origins of the entrepreneurs appear less important than such factors as individual motivations and training, prior experience, and even generation in explaining the process of economic development.

These are only some of the issues raised by a consideration of the South as an underdeveloped region. To what extent its history can prove helpful in explaining the problems and patterns faced by modern nations remains a controversial question, but one thing is certain: the most satisfactory answer lies in a fuller understanding of the process by which economic development took place and a closer examination of the men who did the job. It is my hope that this volume will provide a helpful step in that direction.

In the last analysis the writing of a book seems to be largely a communal project in which the author serves as chief promoter, organizer, and legman. For the completion of this volume I owe more debts, intellectual and otherwise, than can possibly be repaid in these scant recognitions. The basic ideas and structure of the book were worked out during a year spent at the Harvard Graduate School of Business Administration. As recipient of the Harvard-Newcomen Fellowship in Business History, I gained not only the time to do most of the research but also the wise and generous counsel of Professors James P. Baughman, Ralph W. Hidy, Arthur M. Johnson, Fritz Redlich, and Kozo Yamamura. From their advice came much of what is valuable in this study; for its errors and shortcomings, however, I alone am responsible.

Thanks are due to Senator Claiborne Pell and his aide, Orlando Potter, for putting me in touch with representatives of the Southern Railway Company. In that corporation I am deeply indebted to Frank L. Barton, Milton M. Davenport, and Mahlon D. Edwards for their royal hospitality and their kindness in making pertinent company records available to me. Librarians and archivists throughout the Atlantic Coast region proved uniformly helpful and cooperative. The entire staff of Baker Library filled every request and answered every inquiry promptly and patiently, as did Ruth Walling at Emory University, Joe Howerton at the National Archives, Doris Epps and James A. Fleming at the Virginia Historical Society, Helen Rowland at the Bureau of Railroad Economics, Carolyn Wallace at the Southern Historical Collection at the University of North Carolina, Pollyanna Creekmore at the Lawson-McGhee Library in Knoxville, and Stewart Schneider at the University of Rhode Island.

Completion of the manuscript depended upon the faithful efforts of Kate Sexton, Karen Gesmondi, Eleanor Woodward, and my assistant, Diane DeToro. A special word of thanks goes to David T. Gilchrist of the Eleutherian Mills–Hagley Foundation for his invaluable suggestions, close scrutiny, and prompt handling of the manuscript. A grant-in-aid from the University of Rhode Island expedited the final stages of preparation.

MAURY KLEIN

Kingston, Rhode Island
June 4, 1969

Contents

Maps

Tables

The
Great Richmond
Terminal

A

Study
in Businessmen
and
Business
Strategy

Chapter I

The Lay of the Land

The Geography

THE precise role of geographical factors in the course of southern history remains a moot question. In any consideration of the South's transportation system, however, they become an indispensable starting point. The country roads, the turnpikes, the canals, and the railroads arose from the desire to supplement nature's passageways or to surmount the limitations she imposed. The lay of the land exerted a powerful influence upon the origins of all southern railroads, and for that reason we turn first to a survey of the land itself with its strengths and weaknesses for economic activity.[1]

The contours of southern geography shaped the alternative routes for commerce. The system of waterways flowed southeast to the ocean and southward to the Gulf, where cargoes could be transshipped overseas or to northern commercial centers. As a natural transportation system the rivers were invaluable, but they had severe limitations. The navigable waters of the Atlantic rivers did not reach very far back into the hinterland. Like the rivers reaching the Gulf, they suffered from fluctuating water levels, snags, and other obstructions. The point at which the southeastern rivers ceased to be navigable, known as the fall line, extended roughly from Trenton, New Jersey, to Montgomery, Alabama. There the coastal plain abruptly gave way to a ledge of granite running parallel to the mountains.[2] Along this line all the major rivers had obstructing rapids or falls.

The terrain between the Atlantic seaboard and the Ohio River consisted of several clearly demarcated zones. Along the coast of Georgia and South Carolina stretched an alluvial area of great fer-

[1] Unless otherwise indicated the survey that follows is based upon U. B. Phillips, *A History of Transportation in the Eastern Cotton Belt to 1860* (New York, 1913), 1–20, and Howard Dozier, *A History of the Atlantic Coast Line Railroad* (Cambridge, Mass., 1920), 3–9. The South as a section is usually defined as the geographical entity outlined by the Mississippi River in the west and the Ohio and Potomac rivers to the north.

[2] Cecil Kenneth Brown, *A State Movement in Railroad Development* (Chapel Hill, N.C., 1928), 3.

tility. Transportation for the rice, sea-island cotton, and other products of this region posed no problem, for an intricate network of shallow waterways reached deepwater harbors at Charleston, Beaufort, Savannah, and Brunswick. The people of the coastal lowlands endured a peculiar isolation from the interior, however, for behind them loomed the desolate pine barrens. This sandy, infertile region, thinly settled and broken only by the rivers, extended almost the entire length of the lowland.

The area beyond the pine barrens, the Piedmont plain, dominated southern agricultural activity. At the northern or Virginia end tobacco and cereals flourished. From southern Virginia the great eastern cotton belt, the heart of the South's staple economy, stretched deep into Alabama. Unlike the western cotton belt, which continued on into Texas, the eastern belt suffered from a woefully inadequate waterway network for transporting its lucrative crops. Northwest of the Piedmont, the imposing Blue Ridge and Cumberland mountains walled off the cotton belt from the markets of the Northwest. Across the mountains, in the Cumberland and Shenandoah valleys, thriving crops of grain, livestock, tobacco, and other commodities searched vainly for easy access to commercial outlets. So too did the products of Kentucky and middle Tennessee, whose reliance upon the Ohio, Cumberland, and Mississippi rivers was far from satisfactory.

The rapid extension of the cotton belt and the great influx of settlers into the region beyond the mountains intensified the demand for cheap, reliable transportation. The trend of the southern economy toward specialization in staple crops further accentuated the need. In general the interchange of commodities between the different regions of the South ranged from difficult to impossible. At the center of the problem lay the cotton belt, sandwiched between the mountains and the barrens. U. B. Phillips described the planter's position:

The problem was to send cotton to the coast and to get supplies from across the pine-barrens, on the one hand, or the mountains, on the other. The first system was that of using as main stems the rivers which crossed the barrens, and supplementing them with a network of country roads radiating from the heads of navigation. As regards intercourse with the Northwest, the resort was either to caravans across the mountains or to the circuitous water route of the Mississippi, the Gulf, the Atlantic, and the Carolina and Georgia rivers. The eastern cotton belt confronted by far the most difficult transportation problem in the South; and not only the local planters, but all the world of commerce, were very much concerned with its solution.[3]

By this process a string of important collecting and distributing centers sprang up along the fall line at the points where navigation ceased. On the Atlantic slope these towns included Alexandria, Fredericksburg, Richmond, Petersburg, Fayetteville, Columbia, Augusta, Milledgeville, and Macon, and on the Gulf-bound rivers Columbus and Montgomery. Other important trading centers such as Louisville, Memphis, Nashville, and Knoxville developed at strategic sites along the interior river system.

Together with the port cities, the fall-line towns dominated southern commercial activity.[4] They were the sole passageways to distant markets and for that reason were destined to play an important role with the coming of the railroad. As a solution for the South's transportation problem the railroad could perform four distinct functions: it could provide access to those regions lacking water transportation and thus deprived of trade on any large scale; it could supplement existing waterways by connecting the hinterland to the fall-line and port towns; it could supplant inadequate or unreliable water routes by furnishing more direct lines parallel to the rivers or diagonally away from them toward a more favorably situated port; and it could replace dependence upon water altogether by creation of a long-haul overland line.

In broad terms there existed three basic routes over which southern trade might flow. The first and most obvious of these ran north-south from the Ohio River to the Gulf via either an all-rail or all-water route. The most vital artery here was of course the Mississippi River, which dominated north-south traffic until the last quarter of the nineteenth century.[5] As the continent's most extensive water system, the Mississippi naturally stimulated the construction of supplemental rail lines. At the same time its navigational drawbacks prompted the building of two railroads parallel to the river, one terminating at New Orleans and the other at Mobile.

[3] *History of Transportation,* 2–3.

[4] The term "port cities" here includes both deepwater ports such as New Orleans, Mobile, Savannah, and Wilmington and river towns like Columbus and Augusta, which provided quick access to the sea.

[5] William H. Joubert, *Southern Freight Rates in Transition* (Gainesville, Fla., 1949), 198–205; Albert Fishlow, *American Railroads and the Transformation of the Antebellum Economy* (Cambridge, Mass., 1965), 275–98.

As the territorial border and only natural transportation route linking the South and West, the Mississippi River system afforded the north-south route a powerful advantage in both inter- and intraregional traffic.[6] To secure a part of the rapidly expanding western traffic in grain and other commodities, alternative trade routes would have to offset the superior position of the north-south system, and that is precisely what happened. Even before the Civil War the northern east-west trunk lines and rail-canal routes began to cut heavily into the river traffic. But these routes by-passed the South and therefore became deadly rivals to southern commercial aspirations. They played an essentially negative role in southern development except to the extent that their success spurred the growth of competing interregional lines in the South.

The second basic route ran northwest-southeast. Creation of an interior system from the upper Mississippi and Ohio rivers to the South Atlantic seaboard offered several possibilities. It would breach those two formidable barriers, the mountains and the pine barrens, open up the isolated mountain valleys, and permit easy exchange of intraregional traffic. For the coastal and river ports it would provide access to hitherto unexploited markets in the hinterland. To the upper river cities such as Cincinnati, Louisville, Cairo, and Memphis it offered direct connection to the southeastern cotton belt instead of transshipment from New Orleans. In terms of through traffic it meant alternative outlets via rail-water connections. In short, a northwest-southeast rail system running perpendicular to the Mississippi and Ohio rivers would open up a major portion of that territory most deprived of natural transportation facilities.

But the route had its disadvantages as well. It would be both difficult and expensive to build. To sustain itself it would have to charge higher rates than river transportation and thus subject itself to a treacherous competition with its water-based rivals. Since capital resources were limited, the route would be built in segments as local enterprises. The various roads would have to depend upon local traffic as their primary source of support, since through business would not become an important factor until after the Civil War. But the value of local traffic varied considerably from one region to another. The companies reaching the At-

---

[6] As Fishlow, *American Railroads*, 277, 279–88, has suggested, the importance of intraregional traffic has been neglected and deserves detailed investigation.

lantic coast, for example, would have to build many miles through the barrens, from which no important income could be expected.

Despite these and other handicaps the northwest-southeast route became a reality before the Civil War.[7] By 1860 rail connections linked Louisville, Memphis, Cairo, Hickman, Kentucky, and indirectly, Cincinnati with Charleston and Savannah. Along this line lay such important interior cities as Nashville, Chattanooga, Atlanta, Macon, and Augusta. The inclusion of Chattanooga and Atlanta in such a list marked a significant by-product of railroad development: the rise of prominent commercial centers at strategic points along the rail network. The particular triumph of Atlanta and Chattanooga was no accident, for both were located just at the crossroads of the northwest-southeast route and its third competitor.

This third basic route, going northeast-southwest, simply followed the cotton belt parallel to the mountains. It would enjoy the advantage of prime local territory throughout most of its length. Grades would be easier because the mountains could be avoided, although much bridging of waterways would have to be done. For long hauls it would form the most direct route northward and the only one without transshipment.

Several variations on the route were possible, all of which reached fruition by the late nineteenth century. A coastal line could extend from New Orleans through Mobile, Savannah, Charleston, Wilmington, Richmond, and points north. An interior line from Greenville or Vicksburg on the rivers could split the heart of the piedmont via Montgomery and Atlanta or Macon to Richmond. Such a chain of roads would in fact perform the logical task of stringing together the trading centers along the fall line. Or the line from the Gulf ports might veer more sharply northward toward Chattanooga and traverse the valleys through the Blue Ridge into Richmond or Norfolk. On a smaller scale roads could be built between Gulf and Atlantic ports. Like the northwest-southeast route, these overland roads would be costly to build and would arise as a string of separate local roads.

Around these three basic trade routes the major southern rail-

[7] See the summary in Fairfax Harrison, *A History of the Legal Development of the Southern Railway Company* (Washington, D.C., 1901), 3–18. For an excellent map of the southern rail system as of April 1, 1861, see George R. Taylor and Irene Neu, *The American Railroad Network, 1861–1890* (Cambridge, Mass., 1956), map III.

road systems would evolve. The early through lines, composed of several local companies, catered to the primary need of exploiting the territory served by each road; hence they did not follow the most direct or efficient course for interregional or even intraregional traffic. As long as through traffic remained subordinate to local business, through lines would continue to consist of a conglomeration of somewhat meandering roadbeds. When, shortly after the Civil War, railroad managers began to perceive the importance of through business, new construction followed more direct lines to short-cut the older polyglot roads.

The frenzy of railroad construction in the late nineteenth century did not divert the flow of commerce from these three basic routes. Rather the new roads intensified competition both among and within the three alternative channels. Using a slightly different conceptualization, Fairfax Harrison concluded that "all the railroads which have since been opened [after 1860] have served no greater purpose than to parallel existing lines and partition their traffic in the interest of individual communities or as branches to open to such communities the advantages of rail connection with the rest of the world." [8]

Geographical factors, then, imposed significant conditions and limitations upon the development of southern railroads. But it would be extremely misleading to dismiss that development as the product of geographical determinism. Like most human activity the creation of railroads resists easy interpretation or simple causal relationships. Although the physical environment did indicate some locations as more favorable for railways than others, it did not call the railroads into existence. Mere desirability alone could not mobilize capital and other resources. Neither could it organize an enterprise or ensure its success upon completion.

What the geography did was to provide a framework within which decision makers sifted alternatives and formulated their strategies. Like artists working within the restrictions of a given medium, they managed not only to surmount their limitations but even, on occasion, to utilize them as well.

[8] *Southern Railway,* 15. Harrison describes southern rail developments in terms of five trunk lines rather than basic channels of trade, but his approach fits well into the one suggested here. Two of his trunk lines traverse the northwest-southeast route, with one originating on the Mississippi and the other on the Ohio River. One follows the north-south route between the Ohio and the Gulf. The other two follow the northeast-southwest route, one through the mountain valleys and the other along the Atlantic seaboard.

The Men

The men who ruled the major southern railroads during the late nineteenth century fall into two broad groups differentiated by generation, sociological background, and business training. As a result they differ strikingly in their basic ideas and values, their perception of problems, their goals, and the strategies by which they sought to attain those goals. This section will analyze the characteristics and values of each group, while the next will consider the strategies they evolved.[9]

The handful of systems that came to dominate southern transportation by 1893 emerged as the offspring of about ten parent roads. All had been completed before the war. As the oldest and most established roads they played a role far out of proportion to their size relative to the South's total mileage. The men who managed them during the first two postwar decades possessed forceful personalities and considerable administrative ability. They make up the first group of southern rail leaders and are listed in Table 1 along with their companies.[10]

A survey of biographical data for these and other southern railway managers of the same period reveals some significant similarities. Most of them belonged to the same generation. They matured at just about the time when the railroad began to demonstrate its effectiveness as a means of transportation. Most of them played some role in ante-bellum railroad development, as promoters, financiers, investors, or engineers. The southern states, lagging somewhat behind the rest of the nation, did not embark upon their

---

[9] The analysis given here is based largely upon my "Southern Railroad Leaders, 1865–1893: Identities and Ideologies," *Business History Review*, XLII (Autumn, 1968) , 288–310.

[10] The omission of three other major roads deserves explanation. The Western & Atlantic, being state-owned, did not develop the same pattern of leadership, and its history falls somewhat outside this discussion. The lines between Cairo and New Orleans that eventually became the Chicago, St. Louis & New Orleans fell under the control of a nonsouthern railroad, the Illinois Central. Hence its management belongs in a slightly different context. The Mobile & Ohio, though an important road, has certain unique characteristics that make it difficult to treat within this analysis. It was a federal land-grant road and much longer than other *original* southern roads. Consequently its financial and expansion policies pursued a different course. Or, to put it a different way, it was conceived as a trunk line rather than a local road, and this rendered its development significantly different from that of other southern roads.

most extensive construction until the 1850's.[11] By that time all these leaders except John M. Robinson had gone into business, and the outbreak of war found every one of them well established in some career.

The nature of their business activity deeply affected their attitude toward railroad promotion and development. Economic functions had not yet become overly specialized, and businessmen pursued a variety of interests. Merchants displayed a special diversity of talents, often acting as bankers, brokers, factors, shipowners, insurance men, and primary investors in mining, manufacturing, and real-estate development. In the coastal and river ports and fall-line towns they became the center of commercial activity and capital mobilization.[12]

But if individual businessmen ranged far and wide in their in-

[11] See the figures in Henry V. Poor, *Manual of the Railroads of the United States for 1873–74* (New York, 1874) , xxviii–xxix.

[12] A superbly succinct statement of merchant capitalism and its relationship to railroad development can be found in Taylor and Neu, *American Railroad Network,* 3–5.

TABLE 1. Selected southern railroads and their presidents, 1865–1880

Road	Length (miles)	Terminals	Year opened
1. Richmond & Danville	141	Richmond Danville	1856
2. East Tennessee, Virginia & Georgia [a]	242	Chattanooga Bristol, Tenn.	1855–56
3. Georgia	171	Augusta Atlanta	1845
4. Central of Georgia	295	Macon Savannah	1843
5. Louisville & Nashville	185	Louisville Nashville	1859
6. Nashville & Chattanooga	151	Nashville Chattanooga	1854
7. Seaboard & Roanoke	80	Roanoke Portsmouth	1851
8. Wilmington & Weldon	164	Wilmington Weldon, N.C.	1840
9. Atlantic, Mississippi & Ohio [b]	428	Norfolk Bristol	1852–57
10. Atlantic & Gulf [c]	237	Savannah Bainbridge, Ga.	1858

TABLE 1 (*cont.*)

Name	Road	Born	Tenure as president	Primary occupation
1. A. S. Buford	R. & D.	1826	1866–83, 1885–86	RR man politician
2. Richard T. Wilson	E.T.V. & G.	1831	1871–79	banker
3. John P. King	Georgia	1799	1841–78	RR man manufacturer
4. William M. Wadley	Central	1813	1866–82	RR man
5. James Guthrie	L. & N.	1792	1860–68	politician RR man
H. D. Newcomb	"	1809	1868–74	merchant RR man
E. D. Standiford	"	1831	1874–80	physician banker
6. Vernon K. Stevenson	N. & C.	1812	1848–65	merchant RR man
Edwin W. Cole	"	1832	1869–79	RR man
7. John M. Robinson	S. & R.	1835	1867–93	RR man
8. Robert R. Bridgers	W. & W.	1819	1865–88	RR man lawyer
9. William Mahone	A.M. & O.	1826	1865–76	RR man
10. John Screven	A. & G.	1831	1859, 1862–80	RR man planter

SOURCES: Henry V. Poor, *Manual of the Railroads of the United States* (New York, 1869–94). Biographical data taken from standard biographical dictionaries and obituaries. See also the biographical sketches in chap. 2 below.

    ª This road was originally two roads, the East Tennessee & Virginia (Knoxville to Bristol) and the East Tennessee & Georgia (Knoxville to Chattanooga), which were consolidated in 1869.

    ᵇ This road was originally three roads, the Norfolk & Petersburg, the Southside (Petersburg to Lynchburg), and the Virginia & Tennessee (Lynchburg to Bristol), which were consolidated in 1870.

    ᶜ This road was originally intended as part of a through line to Mobile, but it was opened only to the small town of Screven by 1858. Extension to Bainbridge was completed in 1867.

terests, their focus remained strongly localized. They lived in an age lacking substantial political, social, and economic centralization or integration. Success or failure of their enterprises hinged largely upon the prosperity of their community. As coastwise commerce and trade with the interior increased after 1815, a vigorous duel for commercial superiority commenced between leading southern ports and interior distributing centers. In the ensuing struggle it was only natural for businessmen to identify their own interests with those of their community and region.

In this struggle the railroad was destined to play a major role. For the railroad leaders, then, the importance of their "settled" position must not be overlooked. Not all the men were native southerners and less than half still lived in his native state in 1860, but all had established strong local ties. Being essentially of the same generation, they may reasonably be assumed to have had a fairly common fund of experiences, ideas, attitudes, and ambitions.[13] They belonged to the generation that built the early railroads; as presidents they represented powerful commercial and financial interests in the territory drained by the road and especially its key terminal city. The roads themselves had been built as local enterprises. Their stock tended to be widely distributed among a large number of holders, with the largest lots belonging either to the state or to prominent merchants and bankers of their main terminus.[14]

Since the presidents' economic horizon rarely extended beyond the terminal city, they naturally assumed a provincial attitude toward the road's function. They conceived it primarily as their most potent weapon in the growing commercial rivalry. For the interior towns, deprived of suitable water transportation, the railroad appeared to be an indispensable instrument for effective competition. Not surprisingly, then, local interest groups regarded the railroad more as a servant to their region than as a part of some larger coordinated network. This prevailing attitude, by no means unique to the South, has been well summarized by George R. Taylor and Irene Neu:

[13] There would seem to be evidence that the two groups discussed here may be considered as "coevals," as described by Fritz Redlich in his *History of American Business Leaders* (Ann Arbor, Mich., 1940) , I, 23–30. Certainly the analysis given here suggests that the members of each group perceived their problems and responded to them in quite similar fashion. In this vein it is interesting to note that the youngest and least "settled" of the group, Robinson, proved the most adaptable and enduring in his role as president.

[14] The testimony given by various southern railroad presidents in U.S., Congress, "Southern Railroads," *House Reports*, 40 Cong., 2d sess., 1868, No. 3, I, 1–130, makes this pattern of local control abundantly clear. For more specific examples of stock distribution, see the stockholder lists in the *Annual Reports of the Central of Georgia Railroad & Banking Company*, 1869–81, and the Annual Report of the Wilmington & Weldon, 1867–68. See also the list of Danville stockholders for 1869 in the Virginia State Library, Richmond. The L. & N. provides an example of a large block of stock being owned by the city of Louisville; see *Commercial and Financial Chronicle*, XXIX (1879) , 41. For the Georgia Railroad, see *Railway World*, XXIV (1880) , 482.

The first railroads in the United States were built, as were most of the early turnpikes and canals, to serve nearby and local needs. . . . As the possibilities of railway transportation became more clearly recognized, the roads were looked upon by the business groups in each large city chiefly as devices for forwarding their own interests. Rival groups therefore encouraged the building of lines which widened their own market areas, while they carefully avoided any development which might benefit the merchants of another city.[15]

In formulating policy the presidents sought to achieve three basic goals: long-term investment profit, localization of traffic at the principal terminus, and development of the economic resources of the region tributary to the road. The pursuit of these goals gave rise to the concept loosely described as "local control." It meant keeping the company out of the hands of "outsiders," northern or southern, whose economic interests were not directly related to the road's territory. "Foreign" investors and bondholders would be tolerated, even cultivated, so long as they acquiesced in the policy of localizing as much traffic as possible at the chief terminus. But outside parties with interests in rival lines or cities were anathema. Time and again railroads rebuffed attempts by an enemy to absorb it; thus the Raleigh & Gaston in 1871 disdainfully rejected an offer by the Danville to buy 7,500 shares of its stock, fearing that "outside" influence might divert traffic from Raleigh to Richmond.[16]

On each road prominent local merchants and bankers dominated the board of directors. Often they were virtually the same group that had run the road before the war, and many of them had been instrumental in building the line.[17] These men formed the power base upon which the president retained his position. However strong-willed or domineering the president, he well understood his role as spokesman for directors and stockholders whose desires and interests extended well beyond the railroad itself.

Under these circumstances it should not be surprising to find the presidents developing strong personal ties not only to the com-

[15] *American Railroad Network*, 4–5.

[16] *Annual Report of the Raleigh & Gaston Railroad*, 1871, 12. Similar examples abound in the reports of other roads, and the language suggests the bitterness of the contest for business.

[17] This continuity of management is made clear by a survey of boards of directors for the period 1855–70 and by the testimony given in "Southern Railroads," *passim*.

munity but to the company as well. Ten of the thirteen men had some railroad experience prior to the war, and at least eleven of them had been associated in some capacity with the road they were to dominate after Appomattox. Edwin W. Cole, William Mahone, William M. Wadley, and Robinson all had practical railroad experience; Robert R. Bridgers, James Guthrie, John P. King, H. D. Newcomb, and Vernon K. Stevenson played significant roles in the promotion or construction of their roads; and John Screven inherited the presidency of the Atlantic & Gulf from his father, who had been the leading figure in it from its inception. Virtually everyone in the group had external investments in local enterprises, so that their railroad work became a logical extension of their other financial interests.[18]

During the postwar era the presidents devised policies consistent with their role as representatives of local interests. Indeed their general policies differed little from those practiced before the war. In the language of Arthur M. Johnson and Barry E. Supple, their approach was "developmental" rather than "opportunistic." [19] Such an approach required that profits and development be conceived as long-term goals, that the company be run to satisfy investors rather than speculators, and consequently that the stock be tightly held and protected from rapid turnover and fluctuation in value. This last goal was made substantially easier to achieve in those cases where the state held a sizable portion of the outstanding equity.

By the early 1880's, for reasons soon to be explained, most of the presidents had given way to representatives of a new generation. In contrast to their predecessors, the second group tended to be "opportunistic" in their approach. They are summarized in Table 2.

The second group, with the partial exception of Henry B. Plant, constituted a distinct change from the former presidents and their developmental approach. Their ideas and values bore the stamp of a different age, and their previous experience instilled within them expectations and visions distasteful to their predecessors. Nearly all had been uprooted by the war before they had developed careers. Hence they emerged from combat somewhat at loose

[18] To cite some examples: King was deeply involved in cotton manufacturing in Augusta; Newcomb was a prominent Louisville merchant; and Cole, Stevenson, and Wilson all had extensive mining and real-estate interests in Tennessee.

[19] For explication of these terms, see Johnson and Supple, *Boston Capitalists and Western Railroads* (Cambridge, Mass., 1967), 8–10, 181–91, 333–46.

TABLE 2. Dominant personalities in selected southern railroads, 1880–1893

Name	Road [a]	Born	Tenure as president	Primary occupation
1. William P. Clyde	R. & D.	1839	none	steamships financier
John H. Inman	"	1844	1890–92	financier cotton broker
George S. Scott	"	1837	1884, 88–89	financier
2. George I. Seney	E.T.V.&G.	1826	none	banker
Calvin S. Brice	"	1845	none	financier lawyer
Samuel Thomas	"	1840	1882–90	financier industrialist
3. Harry B. Hollins	C. G.	1854	none	banker
John C. Calhoun	"	1843	none	financier
Patrick Calhoun	"	1856	none	financier lawyer
4. H. Victor Newcomb	L. & N.	1844	1880 (9 mos.)	financier
C. C. Baldwin	"	1830	1881–84	financier merchant
Eckstein Norton	"	1831	1886–91	banker
5. Clarence H. Clark	Norfolk & Western [b]	1833	none	banker
6. Henry B. Plant	Savannah, Florida & Western [c]	1819	1880–99	financier

SOURCE: Annual reports of each company.
[a] Four roads included in Table 1 are omitted here for the following reasons: 1) S. & R. retained same president until 1893; 2) Bridgers of the W. & W. died in 1888 and was succeeded by Benjamin F. Newcomer, who had been involved with the road since the end of the war; 3) N.C. & S.L. was acquired by the L. & N. in 1880; 4) Georgia was leased jointly by the Central and L. & N. in 1881.
[b] This was a reorganization of the A.M. & O. in 1881.
[c] This was a reorganization of the A. & G. in 1879.

ends, ripe for whatever opportunities happened along and eager to make their fortunes in an environment extremely congenial to individual action. Their essential business training took place in the immediate postwar era with its emerging industrialism, rampant individualism, and extreme emphasis upon material values. Thrust into an environment stalked by commercial tigers ever bent on new prey, they learned the art of tooth and claw well.

Not one of the new leaders possessed practical railroad experience. Most were financiers, and in fact their accession marked the beginning of a trend to separate the functions of financial and operational control. Many of them did not even become president but exercised their influence through the board. Unlike the first group, the financiers usually held, in conjunction with their friends, a majority of the company's stock and therefore a commanding voice in policy making. In these cases the president became merely the operational head. Even on those roads where the financier assumed the presidency he tended to leave operations in the hands of a vice-president especially appointed because of his practical railroad experience. A specialization of functions wrought by changing conditions had begun to emerge.

The most striking difference in the new group lay in their distinct lack of local, regional, or personal ties. It was no accident that many of them, soon after gaining control of a road, made its stock more accessible by listing it on the New York Stock Exchange. Unfettered by the provincialism of the old presidents, they conceived of their roads not as distinct entities serving particular towns or ports but as mere components of much larger systems spanning the entire section and free from dependence upon any one commercial center as an outlet. For them the railroad constituted but one of many diversified and often interdependent financial interests. William P. Clyde, for example, moved to railroads as an extension of his interests in shipping, and Plant did likewise from his involvement in the express business. John H. Inman, Samuel Thomas, and Calvin S. Brice held extensive investments in southern coal, iron, and real estate. The bankers and brokers all did a considerable business in southern railroad securities. None of them made the railroad his exclusive business, and none localized his outside investments nearly as much as the old presidents and their supporters had done. The new leaders were, in the parlance of the era, "men of large affairs."

The reign of the financiers proved short and in many ways detrimental. They were poor builders, unwise (and largely uninterested) administrators, and on occasion fraudulent manipulators. They differed most significantly from their predecessors in that they pursued their opportunities for short-term profits rather than long-term investment. They came not to build and patiently develop profits out of operations but to make transactional fortunes through construction of new lines, speculation in and manipulation of securities, and investment in areas affected by the railroad. Whether the systems they created prospered or failed over the long run seemed of little concern to them, for they profited chiefly from the transactions involved in the act of creation and could usually withdraw from management as easily as they had entered.

In retrospect it seems clear that the era of the financiers comprised a transitional bridge between the earlier small companies dominated by strong-willed individuals and the later systems whose management had become impersonalized and functionally specialized. The mere accession to power of financiers in place of railroad men suggested the extent to which the environment and the problems posed by it had changed. Growth of the larger systems, so dependent upon the energy and strategic planning of individual personalities, rendered continuation of that personal con-

TABLE 3.   Growth of selected southern railroad systems as measured by total assets (in 1,000's)

System	Total assets 1865	Total assets 1893
1. Louisville & Nashville	$13,519	$136,634
2. Chesapeake & Ohio	10,315 [a]	126,234
3. Norfolk & Western	26,411 [b]	119,229
4. East Tennessee, Virginia & Georgia	7,430 [c]	99,346
5. Richmond & Danville	7,302	35,167
6. Central of Georgia	8,422	30,658

SOURCE: Annual reports of each company.
[a] Figure for 1870.
[b] Figure for 1871.
[c] Figure for 1869.

trol impossible. The figures in Table 3 illuminate the extent of company growth for selected systems.

The policies and strategies of the financiers took their contours from this rapidly changing economic environment. Their performance in meeting this challenge varied considerably. At their best they were conscientious financiers genuinely interested in erecting a sound transportation empire; at their worst they were rapacious freebooters bent on speculative fortunes. To the dismay of the historian they were often a complex mixture of both. C. C. Baldwin and Clyde, for example, both acquired unsavory reputations for speculating in their company's stock, yet Clyde made important and original contributions to the steamship industry. Inman, Brice, and Thomas all made fortunes centered around dubious transactions within their companies, but all played important roles in developing the coal, iron, and steel industries of the South.

For all their flaws, the financiers made genuine contributions to the development of southern transportation. Most important, they possessed a breadth of vision usually lacking in the older presidents. By transcending regional loyalties they freed southern roads from their basically local orientation and helped integrate them into a national network. However poorly they built, they left the South a coherent and fairly complete rail system. Their ultimate failure lay in their inability to organize and administer efficiently what they had built. Though virtually all of them acknowledged the importance of the task, few displayed either the heart or the talent for it in practice.

As early as the mid-1880's, when Baldwin was forced out of the L. & N., the financiers began departing the scene. The Panic of 1893 hastened their exit and paved the way for a third group of railroad leaders. The new group, all of them trained, practical railroad men, would reorganize and regroup the systems and give them the most efficient administration of their short histories. But they would no longer dominate their companies and would leave financial policy primarily to the bankers and financial representatives on the board. From their efforts would come the unified systems of the twentieth century, and their accession to power marked the end of what might be called the "adolescent" period of southern railroads.[20] To understand the process by which that adolescence groped toward maturity, it is necessary to consider the strategic thinking behind it.

The Strategy

It has already been suggested that the goals and policies of the two groups of southern railroad leaders can be characterized as "developmental" and "opportunistic." In like fashion the strategies employed by each group can be conceptualized within a different but complementary framework as "territorial" and "interterritorial." Examination of these strategic concepts sheds considerable light upon the interaction between the decision makers and the rapidly changing environment that confronted them.[21]

It is important to note that all the roads in Table 1, each one the nucleus of a future system, lay along one of the three basic

[20] For definition of this term, see Jan Kimenta and Jeffrey Williamson, "Determinants of Investment Behavior: United States Railroads, 1872–1941," *Review of Economics and Statistics*, XLVIII (May, 1966), 172–81.

[21] This analysis is based upon my "The Strategy of Southern Railroads, 1865–1893," *American Historical Review*, LXXIII (April, 1968), 1052–68.

channels of trade mentioned earlier.[22] While this choice location served the companies well throughout the period under discussion, it became especially important to them in an era of proliferating competition. They possessed the widest range of alternative strategies to pursue and choices to make. For that reason it is not surprising to find the more vigorous and perceptive entrepreneurs gravitating into their management.

The deep-rooted provincial loyalty of the railroad managers expressed itself clearly in their strategic thinking. From this localized perspective emerged the territorial concept that guided policy making before and after the war. The road existed to service its key terminus and the region tributary to it. The welfare of city, territory, and company alike required that all concerned realize their mutually dependent relationship and the need to perpetuate it. Basic to this realization was the tenet of one road for one territory. The region drained by the road constituted its realm of control, much like a feudal barony, with boundaries determined roughly by the line's terminals and connecting points. The description of western territorial strategy by Julius Grodinsky applies equally well to southern conditions:

> To serve a territory with no railroad competition was the ambition of every railroad operator. . . . An exclusively controlled local territory, was a valuable asset, as long as it lasted. A monopoly of this kind was perhaps the most important strategic advantage of a railroad, provided, of course, the monopolized area either originated valuable traffic or served as a market for goods produced in other areas. Territory thus controlled was looked upon as "natural" territory. It belonged to the road that first reached the area. The construction of a line by a competitor was an "invasion." Such a construction, even by a business friend of the "possessing" road, was considered an unfriendly act. The former business friend became an enemy.[23]

[22] Here again the absence of north-south lines is worthy of comment. It may be suggested that the north-south route possessed peculiar limitations that hampered the growth of large systems such as took place along the other routes. Obviously sequential construction could not be undertaken since the original lines already connected waterways to the north and south. Lateral construction, except on a very local basis, could only divert traffic flow from the main north-south channel and thus defeat its purpose. In addition, the extreme western location of the north-south routes prevented their being developed as "hubs" of lines reaching along several trade routes. The limitations of the north-south route compared to the east-west axis for western railroads are discussed in Johnson and Supple, *Boston Capitalists*, 186–91, 222–40, 340–42, and *passim*.

[23] *Transcontinental Railway Strategy, 1869–1893* (Philadelphia, 1962), 104–5.

In the ante-bellum period prevailing conditions nurtured territorial strategy. Competition within the skeletal southern network scarcely existed for through traffic and was virtually absent at the local level. The predominance of local traffic with its higher non-competitive rate structure permitted many roads to achieve financial stability, retire part of their debt, and pay regular dividends. The strategy of stressing long-term goals by protecting the territory, constructing short feeder lines into yet untapped corners, maintaining the road by plowing earnings back regularly, and still paying dividends consistently had become both plausible and remunerative. The spurt of construction during the 1850's posed some threats to the territorial concept, but none serious enough to warrant rethinking of the strategy.

Had the war not intervened, it might be supposed that continued construction would eventually have forced modification of the territorial strategy. The impact of the South's defeat, however, caused an immediate derangement in the economic environment. The cost of rehabilitation disrupted ante-bellum policies by saddling the roads with additional debt and enlarged fixed costs. To service this extra burden the roads would require more traffic at higher rates, but both proved difficult to obtain in the impoverished postwar South. The old reliance upon patient development of local traffic continued but obviously could not provide immediate relief to pressing financial needs. For most managers the only feasible alternative lay in securing more through traffic to augment local income.

The desire for increased through traffic involved a host of problems. Unlike local traffic, it brought distant and once neutral roads into fierce competition for an uncertain traffic at considerably lower and wildly fluctuating rates. Since through lines consisted of separate connecting roads, command of through traffic also demanded a high level of cooperation. Competition for through tonnage could only be cutthroat and treacherous, and the returns extremely unstable.

Most managers seemed reluctant to touch the problems involved, but the economic circumstances forced a shift in strategy.[24] The old dependence upon local traffic would not suffice in the South's prostrate condition. The need for immediate earnings to service the cost of reconstruction and the slowness of returns from

---

[24] For an illustration of this reluctance, see the *Annual Report of the Seaboard & Roanoke Railroad*, 1867, 14–15.

local development made a new source of income seem imperative. The fluctuation of staple crops in the overwhelmingly agricultural South further unsettled earning expectations, and later the advent of state railroad commissions helped depress local as well as through rates. Under conditions that promoted uncertain traffic and steadily falling rates, there seemed no feasible alternative but to adopt a policy stressing a heavy increase in tonnage carried.

The gradual shift in emphasis from local to through traffic constitutes the most significant factor in southern railway strategy. It would have a profound effect upon the development of large integrated systems, which evolved not from coherent planning but through a process of piecemeal expansion based upon momentary needs. It gave rise to the rapid expansion and consolidation movements characteristic of the 1870's and 1880's. The economic factors behind it affected policy decisions in every company and often resulted in bitter fights for control. Perhaps most important, the financial difficulties created by its pursuit lay behind the change in profit motivations from developmental to opportunistic. In 1860 most managers sought to realize profits through efficient operation and development of the property. By about 1880, however, the operation of most southern roads had ceased to be profitable.[25] The source of individual rewards lay instead in manipulation of the road's financial structure, usually to the detriment of the company.

In concrete terms the change in strategic thinking manifested itself most clearly in expansion policy. The need to assure stable through routes forced managers to reconsider the territorial concept. As an integral part of traditional policy they could not easily disavow it, nor did they wish to. In Joseph Schumpeter's terms they were prisoners of their pasts: "Past economic periods govern the activity of the individual. . . . All preceding periods have, furthermore, entangled him in a net of social and economic connections which he cannot easily shake off. They have bequeathed him definite means and methods. . . . All these hold him in iron fetters fast in his tracks." [26] Unable to abandon the old strategy entirely, they tended to recast it into the notion of an enlarged territory suitable for controlling a through line but still capable of being sealed off from encroaching rivals. To achieve this end three alternative tactics seemed possible: cooperation, construction, and con-

[25] For a quantitative study reaching this conclusion, see Maury Klein and Kozo Yamamura, "The Growth Strategies of Southern Railroads, 1865–1893," *Business History Review*, XLI (Winter, 1967) , 358–77.

[26] *The Theory of Economic Development* (Cambridge, Mass., 1961) , 6.

solidation. The applicability of each for a given road depended upon its individual circumstances, but most managers attempted some combination of all three.

Cooperation assumed many forms. On the simplest level it involved agreements with connecting lines to promote through traffic at common rates. Sometimes the alliance sought to provide the road with entry into hitherto untapped territory, but more often it aimed at uniting several companies into a competitive through line.[27] Later in the period, protection of their mutual territories might prompt several roads to ally against invading lines and competing routes.[28] On a grander scale the managers attempted cooperation in two vital areas: fast freight service and rate maintenance. The first took place with formation of the Green Line in 1868 and the second with the founding of the Southern Railway and Steamship Association in 1875.[29]

While the Association proved to be the most successful major railway pool, it could not completely stifle rate cutting and other abuses. Nor could it eliminate competition. As commercial rivalry, aided to some degree by reconstruction politics, spurred construction of new lines, managers quickly realized that cooperation alone was too tenuous a foundation for defense of the territory. Alliances once made could be quickly unmade if better opportunities arose. The temptation to eschew long-term stability for short-run profits became especially irresistible to the hungrier roads. The opening of a new and "invading" line tended to alter existing relationships dramatically and cause a shuffling of alliances. And the stakes were high. Loss of a vital connector meant serious diversion of business and even a fatal blow to the company.[30]

Fearful of isolation, managers naturally resorted to securing

[27] *Annual Report of the East Tennessee, Virginia & Georgia Railroad,* 1870, 14; *Central of Georgia Report,* 1880, 7. Such alliances also extended to river and coastal steamers; see the *Annual Report of the Southwestern Railroad,* 1868, 574.

[28] *Chronicle,* XXX (1880), 384, 542, XXXIII (1881), 357; *Railway World,* XXV (1881), 980, XXVII (1883), 1072.

[29] For background on the Green Line and the Association, see Joubert, *Southern Freight Rates,* chap. 2; *Report of the Industrial Commission* (Washington, D.C., 1900–1902), IX, 626–27; Henry Hudson, "The Southern Railway and Steamship Association," *Quarterly Journal of Economics,* V (October, 1891), 70–94.

[30] For laments over such losses, see *Chronicle,* XX (1875), 501, XXII (1876), 180, XXXII (1881), 576–77; *Raleigh & Gaston Report,* 1873, 18; *Annual Report of the Richmond & Danville Railroad,* 1879, 204.

their vital connections on a more permanent basis. Hence began the growing reliance upon construction and consolidation as methods of achieving stability. Heretofore expansion had been conceived mainly as the construction of small lateral feeder lines to develop local resources; now it came to be seen as the building or acquisition of larger roads to ensure through connections. The timetable of growth naturally varied, but no major road remained unaffected by the need. The potential dangers raised by the activities of rival lines spurred even the most reluctant manager to enlarge his domain.

The strategy of territorial expansion, either by construction or consolidation, proved expensive. It often meant passed or reduced dividends and therefore required considerable justification to the stockholders. The most striking aspect of the expansion rationale was its essentially defensive nature. Most managers conceded freely that new acquisitions would not be a source of direct profit for some time.[31] They had acted from necessity rather than choice, and they sought mainly to protect instead of expand. Additions to the system drained precious capital and usually brought more headaches than benefits to the company, but they were needed to survive.

The strategy of territorial expansion had already drawn southern roads into fierce conflict by 1873, but panic and depression brought matters to a crisis. Only a steady growth of business could alleviate the financial burdens of restoration and expansion, the cost of which left even the strongest roads little margin for withstanding adversity. Policy makers had presumed that their efforts would create some stability among the roads, but the economic contraction hit them like a thunderclap. Unable to survive the blow, weaker roads tumbled rapidly into default and receivership.[32]

The failure of so many roads aggravated an already bad situation. Rates declined steadily as the bankrupt roads, freed from payment on their debt, undercut their solvent competitors ruthlessly to get whatever business was available. More important, foreclosure made the purchase of many key roads cheap and easy for the rival companies. And since many of the defaulted lines had

[31] See, for example, *East Tennessee Report,* 1877, 12; *Danville Report,* 1874, 229; *Chronicle,* XIX (1874) , 118.

[32] Figures on the number and mileage of roads in default can be found in John F. Stover, *Railroads of the South, 1865–1900* (Chapel Hill, N.C., 1955) , 123–25.

themselves pursued expansion by acquiring stock and bonds in connecting roads, purchase of the parent company often meant control over subsidiary lines as well.[33] The old defensive fears reasserted themselves in earnest after 1873. Managers of solvent roads, though struggling to keep their own companies afloat, could not resist the temptation to snatch up foreclosed roads to prevent rivals from doing so. By the late 1870's a new race toward consolidation had begun.

In reaffirming their dependence upon expansion the managers sealed their own doom. Clinging faithfully to the territorial concept and reluctant to expand their economic horizons, they tried once more to isolate their domains. But their very efforts to preserve the territorial concept created the seeds of its destruction. Their attempts at defensive expansion under depression conditions deeply antagonized many stockholders. Conservative investors resented the sacrifice of dividends to the acquisition of insolvent roads and prophesied inevitable bankruptcy; younger, impatient holders generally approved expansion but opposed the grudging, piecemeal approach of the older managers. Severe clashes over policy erupted on many boards. One by one the first group of managers fell victim to age, organized opposition, and obsolete policies as their roads passed into the hands of a new generation.

The territorial strategy failed because it became increasingly inapplicable to the economic environment. A major cause of its demise, however, rested with the managers themselves and their inability to perceive the logical consequences of their policies. Expansion had proved ineffective as a defensive strategy. It could not succeed because it fed upon its own impetus. In trying to seal off their territories the managers only further exposed them by enlargement. The process of building new lines or acquiring old ones brought previously neutral companies into direct confrontation, with each branding the other an "invader." Territories that had once seemed distinct now developed overlapping zones of conflict, especially as rival companies pushed into hitherto untapped regions or sought entrances into more distant markets. The result was not protection but increased warfare, not stability but competition at more places and on a grander scale.

One astute observer, Joseph Nimmo, Jr., sensed what was taking place not only in the South but in the nation as a whole: "There is reason to believe that the managers of certain of the great railroad

---

[33] *Railroad Gazette,* XIII (1881), 586–87.

organizations of the country, in attempting to carry out their ambitious policy of railroad extension, failed to foresee the fact they
were erecting competitive agencies more rapidly than they were
gaining control over commerce." [34] To be sure, the fast-departing
managers were not unaware of their plight. They recognized their
dilemma only too well but were helpless to find effective solutions.
A. S. Buford of the Danville summarized their discomfort well in
1880:

This work amidst the extension, completion and reorganization of railroad lines now regarded as essentially necessary for their successful
operation, has, by common consent, been found . . . one of the most
difficult features of railroad management. . . . Experience is daily demon-
strating some of the requisites to the only safe policy in this regard, based
upon an intelligent recognition of the just rights of each line of road, as
well as those of the public, whenever conflicts of interest and competition
naturally or circumstantially exist. The best methods of securing these
important objects are yet, to a certain extent, experimental.[35]

The limitations of vision common to the older managers did not
bind their successors. The territorial concept held neither meaning
nor relevance for the younger men. They thought rather in terms
of vast systems reaching into every corner of the South and vying
for traffic at every important market. To put it another way, they
sought to compete in more than one of the basic trade channels instead of limiting themselves to the one along which the parent
road lay. Coming to power just at the return of national prosperity, they had no fear of expansion. Indeed their major concern was
that growth proceed rapidly enough for them to capture waiting
markets. In their hands expansion became both an offensive and
defensive weapon.

The most significant aspect of this change in strategic thinking
was the rapid growth of interterritorial competition. It constituted
the logical alternative to the territorial concept: if a monopolistic
territory could not be protected from invaders then the best hope
for increasing business lay in expanding the field of battle. The
key to survival appeared to be a diversification of outlets for both
through and local traffic. At the local level the old policy of developing local resources along the enlarged lines would provide the
company with a reliable base for traffic growth. Meanwhile, participation in the struggle for through traffic on a larger scale seemed

[34] *First Annual Report on the Internal Commerce of the United States*
(Washington, D.C., 1877), 59.
[35] *Danville Report*, 1880, 413.

to offer better opportunities for stabilizing over-all earnings. The new strategy promised greater flexibility. It would take time for new local traffic to develop sufficiently to turn a profit, and only a system large enough to cover losses in one territory with gains in another seemed able to buy that time.

The renewed expansion spawned by the receiverships of the 1870's furnished the impetus for the development of the major interterritorial systems. With a startling speed the parent roads, nearly all of them under new management, increased the mileage under their control. The L. & N. jumped from 966 miles in 1878 to 3,231 in 1883, the Danville from 448 to 2,503, the East Tennessee from 272 to 1,389 and the Central of Georgia from 861 to 1,754.[36] By 1881 contemporary observers, impressed by the swiftness of southern consolidation, could list seven companies as dominating southern traffic: 1) the Danville, 2) the Savannah, Florida & Western, nucleus of a system being formed by Henry B. Plant, 3) the East Tennessee, 4) the Norfolk & Western, 5) the Louisville & Nashville, 6) the Central of Georgia, and 7) the Chicago, St. Louis & New Orleans, southern subsidiary of the Illinois Central.[37]

The confrontation of major roads wrought by interterritorial expansion also fostered consolidation at a higher level. The clash of rivals over disputed ground often led to a fitting Darwinian climax, with one company absorbing the other. Thus Victor Newcomb, thwarted by the equally ambitious schemes of Edwin "King" Cole of the Nashville, Chattanooga & St. Louis, proceeded to buy his adversary's company out from under him in 1880.[38] The following year the L. & N. joined the Central in removing a powerful competitor by leasing the Georgia Railroad.[39] In 1881, too, the Danville shut the Baltimore & Ohio out of the South by purchasing the Virginia Midland.[40] The culmination of this movement came in 1888 when the Richmond Terminal gained control of three major systems.

The desire to penetrate new territories provided a powerful impetus for the consolidation activities of the 1880's. So too did it spur the impressive record of new construction during the same

[36] These figures include lines directly and indirectly controlled and are based upon mileage figures in Henry V. Poor, *Manual of the Railroads of the United States for 1878* (New York, 1878) and *Manual of the Railroads of the United States for 1883* (New York, 1883).

[37] *Railroad Gazette*, XIII (1881), 586–87.

[38] Stover, *Railroads of the South*, 225–26.

[39] *Central Report*, 1881, 9–10; *Annual Report of the Louisville & Nashville Railroad*, 1881, 11.

[40] *Danville Report*, 1881, 501–2.

period.[41] Growing systems generally built new lines for one or more of three reasons: to open new territories or reach new markets; to form new through connections with other systems; and to parallel an existing rival enjoying monopoly status. Though the amount and type of construction naturally varied, no system remained aloof lest it lose ground to competitors.

Interterritorial competition naturally produced friction and resentment, and the scope of its rivalries led to renewed efforts at cooperation. As in the previous period, alliances rose and flourished at least for a time. Perhaps the most ambitious attempt involved the formation of the Associated Railways of Virginia and the Carolinas in 1885. Composed of the roads controlled by the Danville, the Atlantic Coast Line, and the Seaboard Air-Line, the Association reached agreement on the following provisions: joint management of all traffic; harmonizing of competition; no independent soliciting of traffic; common auditors to examine all accounts; mutual aid and protection when attacked by other lines; interchange of traffic wherever possible; establishment of an arbitration board to settle disputes; and specific arrangements for apportioning traffic.[42]

The basic tactics of cooperation, construction, and consolidation utilized by the earlier managers continued to serve their successors. They differed primarily in the scale of operations and in the desired goals. The first resulted from the shift in strategic thinking from territorial monopoly to interterritorial supremacy. The second concerned the changing emphasis between developmental and opportunistic motivations. The financiers who created the large systems derived little personal return from operations. Their profits came instead from such varied sources as construction of new lines, speculation in securities associated with the company, transactions involved in the acquisition of other lines (in which they often held personal interests), and such external investments influenced by the railroad as real estate, mineral lands, express business, manufacturing, and industrial development.

Because the financiers tended to think in short-term rather than long-term profits, they evinced little concern for the swollen capitalizations produced by their policies. The financial effect of interterritorial strategy was to burden every system with considera-

[41] Specific examples of the consolidation process and figures for the rate of new construction can be found in Stover, *Railroads of the South*, chap. 9.

[42] A copy of the agreement, dated August 1, 1885, can be found at the Bureau of Railroad Economics, Washington, D.C. See also *Railroad Gazette*, XV (1883), 628–29.

bly enlarged fixed costs that required additional earnings to service. During the 1880's, when general prosperity seemed to bless every enterprise, a constant expansion of business seemed inevitable to the financiers. Moreover, the centralization born of consolidation promised reduced administrative costs and increased operational efficiency.

By the end of the decade, however, serious flaws in the interterritorial strategy had begun to appear. The assumption that business would increase proved correct, but steadily declining rates prevented earnings from increasing in like proportion. Nor did the absorption of rival roads entirely reduce competition. The large systems expected to contend with each other, especially for through traffic, but they also faced unforeseen rivalry for local business. Besides its positive effect upon interterritorial expansion, the prosperity of the 1880's stimulated construction of smaller local lines as well. As a result the giants confronted an invasion of gnats, each capable of making severe inroads into local traffic. The attempt to stifle or at least centralize competition failed, and the policy of penetrating every available territory created new weaknesses as well as new markets.

The pursuit of interterritorial strategy led nearly all southern roads into grave financial difficulties. Many of them toppled into receivership after 1893. But the old strategy did not die easily. The problems that had called it into existence remained unsolved, and the decade of the 1890's witnessed further consolidation and construction.[43] An 1893 journal report predicting control of the South by only two systems proved exaggerated in degree but not in kind.[44] The change in strategic thinking that evolved around 1880 ensured that, for better or worse, southern railroads would proceed steadily down a course of further concentration and amalgamation. The fruit of this activity was the development of a rail network unwelcome to some of its creators, unplanned in any over-all sense, but ultimately enduring.

The Patterns

In this brief outline of southern railroad development two conceptual frameworks have been utilized. One relates the process of ex-

[43] Developments during the period 1890–1900 are treated in Stover, *Railroads of the South*, chap. 12.

[44] New York *Indicator*, June 7, 1893.

pansion and development to important shifts in strategic thinking, differentiated here by the terms territorial and interterritorial. The other attempts to explain entrepreneurial goals and profit motivations by categorizing them as developmental or opportunistic. Of course these conceptualizations will not fit any specific case precisely. Neither companies nor individuals follow one simple pattern of behavior over time, and their over-all characteristics cannot be neatly pigeonholed without some distortion. The usual

FIGURE 1. Comparison of broad developmental patterns for western and southern railroads, 1840–1893. A, western railroads; B, southern railroads

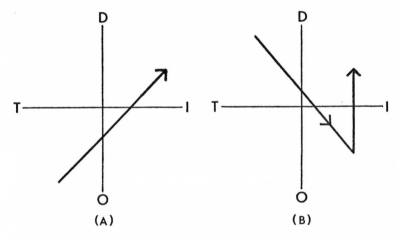

(A)   (B)

limitations to generalizations apply to this hypothetical framework no less than to others like it.

Despite these standard reservations, the concepts suggested here can serve as a valuable guide for understanding the development of southern and other railroad systems. Moreover, by use of a simple Cartesian diagram to combine the two approaches, some helpful intersectional comparisons on the patterns of development can be made. Figure 1 furnishes an interesting example.[45] Let T represent territorial, I interterritorial, D developmental, and O opportunistic. Diagram A represents the broad pattern of development for western railroads as described by Johnson and Supple,[46] while

[45] The use of this diagram was suggested by Professor James P. Baughman, to whom I am deeply indebted.

[46] *Boston Capitalists, passim.*

diagram B represents the pattern for southern railroads as given here.

The diagrams seem to indicate that railroad development within the two areas proceeded along significantly different patterns. The reasons for this divergence are worthy of a careful study in themselves and can only be hinted at here.[47] Geographical considerations comprise one factor. At one level the southern systems could expand along two important trade routes by radiating auxiliary lines out in all directions. Western lines, however, could engage in significant sequential construction only along the east-west axis since north-south lines, like their southern counterparts, soon ran into water at either end. This affected both the investment process and competitive positions, since the possible patterns of development tended to influence the motivations behind it.

More important, the roads of both sections differed in the source of their original capital. Southern roads arose primarily as local roads built with local capital to serve local needs under local management. They were therefore naturally inclined to be territorial and developmental. Only when changes in the economic environment prompted the development of through lines and integrated systems did local resources prove inadequate and territorial strategies become obsolete. The growing need for outside capital to forge interterritorial systems produced a climate conducive for opportunistic investment.

The financial problems created by this process and the withdrawal (or conversion) of the opportunists left their successors with an obvious choice. They could either abandon the troubled property and their investment in it or they could pick up the pieces and try to unify them into a sound transportation system. In choosing the latter course as more feasible they committed themselves to a return to developmental policies stressing long-term goals—but as an interterritorial system rather than a local road.

Western roads, on the other hand, drew upon outside capital from the very beginning. They originated as territorial roads not just to serve local needs (local interests in fact did not control them), but because the outside investors wanted a maximum return on as small a capital outlay as possible. Then, when changing conditions frustrated this original design, investors faced the difficult choice of withdrawing or commiting further resources to the

---

[47] Generalizations on the western roads are derived primarily from *ibid.*

project. Those who chose the second alternative had to pursue an essentially developmental policy which led to the creation of inter-territorial systems.

The pattern of development for southern railroads, though often similar in appearance to that of the West, followed its own individual course and deserves individual attention. Within that pattern there arose a variety of alternative policies, techniques, and strategies to cope with the multitude of problems confronting railway managers. The Richmond Terminal represented one possible and novel solution to these problems. As the most ambitious and audacious attempt it merits especially close study, for its history illuminates not only railroad development but southern economic development as well.

Chapter II

The Players

(in alphabetical order)

Calvin S. Brice (1845–1898). Born in Denmark, Ohio, the son of a Presbyterian minister, Brice spent his youth in schooling and the Civil War. When the war interrupted his studies at Miami University in Oxford, Ohio, he managed to get into the Union army but returned to school after three months. Upon graduating in 1863, he recruited a company for the 180th Ohio and served as its captain until July, 1865. He then studied law at Michigan, gained admittance to the bar in 1866 in Cincinnati, and opened an office in Lima, Ohio.

Within a short time Brice developed a flourishing practice as a corporation lawyer. His brilliance in protecting business interests naturally drew him closer to men deeply involved in railroad promotion, notably Charles Foster, a Republican congressman. Gradually his interests shifted from the law to business enterprise. Becoming legal counsel for the Lake Erie & Louisville (later Lake Erie & Western), he went to Europe in 1870–71 to help obtain a loan for the road. His growing involvement in the company brought him into contact with Samuel Thomas and other Ohioans with whom he would long be associated. Shortly after his return from Europe he moved to New York but retained an office in Cleveland.

Brice's success with the Lake Erie confirmed his abandonment of the law. He soon plunged into numerous other projects culminating in the New York, Chicago & St. Louis or "Nickel Plate" road. That venture gave Brice his first large fortune; before its completion he had been worth about $200,000. It also resulted in formation of the Brice-Thomas-Seney syndicate destined to play an important role in the East Tennessee and Richmond Terminal companies. With a growing reputation for entrepreneurial talent, Brice branched quickly into a host of other projects, including the Pacific Mail Steamship Company, the Chicago & Atlantic, Cincinnati Northern, Chicago, Indianapolis & Louisville, and Cleveland, Akron & Columbus railroads, Chase National Bank, Metropolitan Bank, Southern Trust Company, United States Express Company,

and several other rail, industrial, and real-estate project
years he extended his investments to Chinese railroads through the
American Development Company, known popularly as the Brice
Chinese Syndicate.

Despite his extensive business career, Brice delved deeply into
politics as well. He served as a Democratic elector in 1876 and
1884 and became chairman of the national committee during
Cleveland's 1888 campaign. In 1890 he won election to the Senate
from Ohio. Although he continued to live in New York for business reasons, Brice remained steadfastly loyal to his native state.
He always listed his legal residence as Lima, Ohio, and became an
ardent member of the Ohio Society of New York. On the Senate
floor he never failed to wear a red carnation, the state flower, in
his buttonhole. His devotion to the state and its economic interests
won him wide popularity there.

Short, slight, but broad-shouldered, Brice masked his square features with a closely trimmed sandy beard. Talkative, genial, generous, and energetic, he pursued the simple principle that politics
existed primarily for the protection of personal financial interests.
His deep roots in Wall Street led opposition editors to caricature
him by printing his name as "Calvin $ellars Brice." [1]

ALGERNON S. BUFORD (1826–1911). A native of Rowan County,
North Carolina, Buford moved to Virginia at an early age. Despite
an early education in agriculture, he determined first to teach and
then to study law. After graduating from the University of Virginia in 1848, he opened an office in Pittsylvania County. As his
practice grew he moved to Danville, where he also became owner
and editor of the Danville *Register*. The twin occupations of editor and lawyer naturally drew Buford into politics, and he served
one term (1853) in the Virginia legislature.

After Sumter, Buford promptly enlisted as a private in the Confederate army. That same fall, however, he gained election to the
Virginia House of Delegates and held that seat until the war's end,

---

[1] *Dictionary of American Biography*, III, 31–32; *National Cyclopedia of
Biography* (New York, 1898–1963), XXVII, 75; Taylor Hampton, *The Nickel
Plate Road* (Cleveland, 1947), 40–42; Henry Clews, *Twenty-Eight Years in
Wall Street* (New York, 1887), 554; New York *Times*, New York *Tribune*, and
New York *Sun*, Dec. 16, 1898; Lima, Ohio, *Times-Democrat*, Dec. 16, 19, 20,
1898; W. Ten Eyck Hardenbrook, *Financial New York* (New York, n.d.),
267–75; Dun & Bradstreet Reports, Ohio, III, 280; *Biographical Dictionary of
the American Congress, 1774–1961* (Washington, D.C., 1961), 596.

his military glory going no further than a commission as lieutenant colonel of militia. When the war ended Buford returned to Danville, intending to resume his legal and political career. An unexpected call to the presidency of the Richmond & Danville took him to Richmond, where he remained for the rest of his life. During his tenure as Danville president, he continued to mix in state politics, largely on behalf of his company.

Tall and slender, the handsome Buford epitomized the Virginia gentleman. His striking features, white hair, and erect carriage reminded one associate of Julius Caesar. Stern and reserved during the transaction of business, he lapsed into merriment and an easy gallantry in social circles. Above all he prized his reputation for integrity and loyalty. One acquaintance noted that "he never breaks nor avoids a contract and adheres to every promise he makes. . . . [He is] a good man, honest, truthful and frank and every lineament of his face bespeaks his true character."

After leaving the Danville, Buford returned to politics and the law. He served one term (1888) in the Virginia legislature and ran unsuccessfully for governor in 1893. Long an active member of the Virginia Agriculture and Mechanics Society, he served four years as its president.[2]

JOHN C. CALHOUN (1843–1918). A grandson of the great statesman, John Calhoun traced his heritage deep into the roots of South Carolina aristocracy. After local schooling he attended South Carolina College until leaving in 1861 to join the Confederate cavalry. Four years of war destroyed his home, ruined his family fortune, and left him with no prospects for the future. Turning to planting, he formed a plan with James R. Powell in 1866 to colonize Negroes on cooperative plantations in the Yazoo Valley, Mississippi. So well did the venture work out that a year later Calhoun sold out to Powell for $10,000 and went to Chicot County, Arkansas, to repeat the enterprise on a larger scale.

The Arkansas plantations worked out equally well, and Calhoun gradually recouped his fortune. He personally supervised operations and was credited with draining over 5,000 Negroes into the Mississippi Valley from the South Atlantic seaboard. In time, however, he aspired to bigger things. He sold his Arkansas hold-

[2] David Schenck Diary, April 1, 1883, May 15, 1884, Schenck papers, Southern Historical Collection, University of North Carolina, Chapel Hill; *Railroad Gazette*, XVI (1884), 367; L. G. Tyler (ed.), *Encyclopedia of Virginia Biography* (New York, 1915), V, 701–2.

ings in 1884 and went to New York. There he immersed himself in Wall Street affairs and developed some reputation as a manipulator. A newcomer to financial circles, he dealt cautiously and diversified his interests. Among other enterprises he controlled the Baltimore Coal Mining and Railway Company and invested heavily in New Brunswick coal fields. To this latter project he sent his eldest son as manager.

Genial, courteous, and somewhat grave, Calhoun lacked the fiery temper and natural brilliance of his younger brother. More than once he restrained Pat's impetuosity with his careful, balanced judgment. The two brothers complemented each other well and often entered new ventures together.[3]

PATRICK CALHOUN (1856–1943). Like his brother, Pat Calhoun was born in Fort Hill, South Carolina. His father, one of the largest cotton planters in the ante-bellum South, died when Pat was only nine. Too young to fight in the war, he went in 1871 to study law with his grandfather, Duff Green, in Dalton, Georgia. He gained admittance to the bar in 1875 and moved the next year to St. Louis, where he opened a practice. A short time later his health failed, forcing him to leave St. Louis and join John in Arkansas.

In 1878 Calhoun settled in Atlanta to resume his legal career. By specializing in corporation law he quickly acquired a lucrative practice and a wide circle of business contacts. He became senior partner of the firm Calhoun, King & Spaulding in 1877, but his indomitable energy and ambition led him into a wide range of business interests as well. He organized the Calhoun Land Company to raise cotton in the Mississippi Valley and acquired extensive properties in South Carolina, Georgia, and Texas. His enterprises included planting, real estate, oil, railroads, street railways, manufacturing, and mining. Youngest of the men involved in the Terminal, he remained active in business until 1913.

Unlike his somewhat staid brother, Pat became known for his flamboyant personality and hot temper. A precociously brilliant lawyer, he could be aggressive to the point of arrogance. An inability to curb his temper often made him reckless of consequences. Once in 1889 he challenged a business adversary who had called him a liar and insisted that the duel be carried out despite all legal obstacles. Yet, when in control of his temper, Calhoun could be

---

[3] *National Cyclopedia*, XIII, 506; *Who Was Who in America, 1607–1896* (Chicago, 1963), 184; Savannah *Morning News*, Jan. 3, 1887.

charming and gracious. His impeccable demeanor and sharp wit made him a favorite at social gatherings. In business affairs he often relied upon the counsel of his brother to stabilize his own sometimes erratic judgment.[4]

WALTER S. CHISHOLM (1836–1890). Several Georgia lawyers achieved more state and national prominence than Walter Chisholm, but few achieved greater professional distinction or exerted more influence in business circles. Born in Columbus, Chisholm lost both his parents by the age of twelve. After early schooling in Liberty County he attended the University of Georgia, graduating in 1855. Two years later he gained admittance to the bar in Savannah and commenced practice there. In 1863 he was elected judge of the Savannah city court, a position he maintained for fifteen years. It proved to be the only public office he ever held.

Though Chisholm had limited military experience during the Civil War, his chronically poor health forced him to accept a post as head of a military examining board. After the war he resumed his Savannah practice and extended his corporate work into the burgeoning railroad field. In 1877 he became general counsel for the bondholders of the bankrupt Atlantic & Gulf. That position eventually brought him into close association with Henry B. Plant, who reorganized the Savannah-based road into the Savannah, Florida & Western. As Plant enlarged his railroad empire through his Plant Investment Company, Chisholm became his general counsel and vice-president of the system. He also served as counsel for Plant's Southern Express Company.

Chisholm's growing involvement with Plant's affairs ultimately led him into the Terminal, where he served essentially as the latter's spokesman and watchdog. Increasingly his business activities concentrated in New York. Plagued constantly by ill health, he nevertheless left Savannah in 1885 to be nearer the center of his affairs. Five years later he died in New York after a short illness.

In addition to his work for Plant, Chisholm ranged into other Georgia enterprises. He maintained close contacts with the Central of Georgia and owned considerable real estate in the Savannah

---

[4] *National Cyclopedia*, XXXIV, 231; *Who Was Who in America, 1897–1942* (Chicago, 1942), II, 97. For the duel, see *Railroad Gazette*, XXI (1889), 652; Charleston *News and Courier*, April 5, 1964; Atlanta *Constitution*, August 11, 1889.

area. Dignified, reliable, and astute, he was highly regarded even by his business adversaries.[5]

WILLIAM P. CLYDE (1839–1923). Of all the personalities involved in the Terminal none except perhaps John Inman proved more enigmatic and elusive than William Clyde. As the son of Thomas Clyde, a wealthy Philadelphia shipowner, he had every advantage during childhood. He entered Trinity College in 1860 but left to fight with the "Philadelphia Grays" and served until the war's end. Upon discharge he joined his father in the Clyde Steamship Company. Later he organized his own firm, W. P. Clyde & Company, as well.

As a ship builder and operator Clyde earned a reputation for daring innovation. Although he built and owned all types of steamships, he always displayed a preference for the relatively new screw propeller. He worked unceasingly with new designs and made genuine technical improvements. In 1871 he built the first compound engine ever made in the United States and installed it in the *George W. Clyde*. Fifteen years later he developed the first large triple-expansion engine in this country and put it into the first American commercial steel steamer. By the age of forty he had become recognized as an authority in the field.

Clyde's precocity extended into the realm of management as well. In 1873, at the age of thirty-four, he assumed the presidency of the Pacific Mail Steamship Company. Within a short time he became the dominant figure in New York–San Francisco shipping. His enterprises included the Panama Railroad, which he linked to San Francisco and Central America via steamships. He also controlled an eastern line from New York to Aspinwall. Even after he branched into domestic railroad investments, the coastal steamers remained Clyde's first love. In the long run his rail activities appeared to be little more than extended speculations.

Despite his youth and intense ambition, Clyde won fast friends easily. Capable of ruthlessness to the point of treachery, he outwardly exuded warmth and charm. Tall, sinewy, and handsome, he radiated an infectious enthusiasm. His unfailing optimism and self-confidence rendered him bold and decisive in everything he

[5] *National Cyclopedia*, II, 358; Dun & Bradstreet Reports, Georgia, I, 98. For his Central of Georgia contacts, see the Raoul to Chisholm letters in the William Raoul Letter Books, Emory University, Atlanta.

took up. A slight acquaintance once described him as "warm hearted, genial, generous and true. Though a millionaire he is wholly unostentatious and simple in his manners. . . . No one meets him without feeling a friendship for him."

Clyde's ability to make quick and lasting impressions proved an invaluable asset in an environment heavily dependent upon personal relationships. No better example of his charm can be given than an observation by David Schenck. In comparing Clyde with George Perkins, a New York banker, he noted simply, "I like this man, and respect him very much, but I have an affection for Mr. Clyde." [6]

HUGH M. COMER (1842–1900). A native of Jones County, Georgia, Comer personified an important transition in southern business life. The son of a prominent cotton planter and state senator, he received his education at Auburn and East Alabama Male colleges. After the war, however, he saw no future in planting and turned instead to the manufacturing end of the cotton industry. He operated a cotton-milling firm, Drewry & Comer, in Eufaula, Alabama. When that enterprise failed to satisfy his ambitions, he moved to Savannah in 1868 and founded the cotton commission house of Bates & Comer. Within a short time the firm became one of the strongest and most reliable in the region.

Comer remained active in the firm for the rest of his life, and in a real sense his subsequent business activities became an extension of his deep involvement in cotton. In 1876 he founded the Bibb Manufacturing Company, a cotton mill, in Macon. Later he opened two mills in Columbus and branched into fertilizer production as well. His involvement in Georgia railroads merely confirmed their importance to the cotton industry. He joined with two close associates, W. W. Gordon and William G. Raoul, to support local control and conservative management policies for the Central of Georgia as advocated by William M. Wadley. But powerful as he became in state railroad affairs, he never switched his primary business allegiance to them. He accepted the Central's presidency in 1892 with obvious reluctance, and prior to that he did not hesitate to promote the rival Seaboard Air-Line in hopes of lowering rates in the state.

In all his business activities Comer exemplified the power and

[6] *National Cyclopedia*, XX, 57; David Schenck Diary, Oct. 1, Dec. 15, 1881; New York *Times*, Nov. 19, 1923; Boston *Transcript*, Nov. 18, 1923.

rationale of local interests. Although he invested in a Texas ranch during the 1886 cattle boom, his economic commitments remained firmly entrenched in Savannah and Georgia. For that reason he bitterly opposed every rail combination that took control of the state's roads outside the region.[7]

WILLIAM W. GORDON (1834–1912). Another representative of local interests, Gordon was a native of Savannah. His father had served as the first president of the Central of Georgia, but young Gordon had no immediate interest in the road. After graduating from Yale in 1854, he joined the cotton firm of Tison & MacKay as a clerk. Two years later the firm reorganized as Tison & Gordon and gradually developed a statewide reputation for reliability and integrity. Specializing in sea-island and upland cotton, it had already become a powerful house before the war.

Gordon's career in cotton suffered a typical interruption in 1860. He left the firm to join the Confederate cavalry. His service extended the duration of the war and included riot duty afterward. Though not a professional soldier, Gordon learned quickly enough to carve out a distinguished military record. Like many an ex-Confederate, he loved nothing better than to recall his war exploits in later days. Unlike most of them, however, he was able to return to active duty as brigadier general of volunteers during the Spanish-American war.

In 1878 Tison died and Gordon changed the firm to W. W. Gordon & Company. As the power and influence of his house grew, he turned to other enterprises. For six years, 1884 to 1890, he sat in the Georgia legislature. He served as president of the Savannah Cotton Exchange from 1876 to 1879. After 1890 he moved into banking as vice-president of the Merchants National Bank.

As a cotton dealer Gordon naturally maintained a close interest in the Central. His role in the company sharpened around 1880, when the Wadley regime appeared in danger of losing power. Over the next decade Gordon steadily deepened his commitment, especially after the Central fell into the hands of the Terminal. By 1892, when the Central succumbed to receivership, Gordon had developed an obsession to follow in his father's footsteps. He wanted the Central presidency above all else and nearly broke with his lifetime friend William Raoul when he thought Raoul

[7] *National Cyclopedia*, XXI, 295; Dun & Bradstreet Reports, Georgia, XXVIII, 200, XXIX, 540.

had deliberately blocked his ambition. Tough, wiry, and spritely, Gordon enjoyed his reputation of being something of an eccentric and a superb storyteller. Needless to say, he specialized in tales of the war.[8]

HARRY B. HOLLINS (1854–1938). A freewheeling financier from the start, debonair Harry Hollins cut an impressive swath through Wall Street at a startlingly early age. Born in New York City, he was educated there before entering the firm of Levi Morton & Company in 1870. During the next three years he worked as clerk for D. P. Morgan & Company and cashier for Oakley & Company and John D. Prince & Company. His education in finance well launched, Hollins left shortly after the Panic of 1873 for an extended world tour. When he returned in 1875 he opened an insurance brokerage firm, Grundy, Hollins & Martin. Three years later he left to form his own Hollins & Company.

Hollins's meteoric rise in financial circles derived in part from his own brilliance and in part from his influential contacts. He early became a favorite of the Vanderbilts and by 1880 was referred to popularly as "the Vanderbilt's broker." In banking he was an original founder of the ill-fated Knickerbocker Trust Company and served as director for North American Safe Deposit, Corporation Trust, and various other financial institutions. In 1888 he went into the Bank of Mexico as well. Like most of his peers he branched into numerous other enterprises, including Metropolitan Ferry, Central Union Gas, and Havana Tobacco Company.

By 1890 Hollins had become a millionaire several times over, but misfortune dogged his enterprises. Several of his rail ventures turned out poorly though he himself profited handsomely. The Knickerbocker Trust collapsed in the panic of 1907, and Hollins's own firm went bankrupt in April, 1914. Despite his abundance of personal charm and ability, his career seemed tarnished in retrospect. He proved a cunning financier but a poor builder.[9]

JOHN H. INMAN (1844–1896). No man played a more important or less understood role in the Terminal than John Inman. Blessed

[8] *National Cyclopedia*, XV, 217; New York *Times*, Sept. 12, 1912; *Who Was Who, 1607–1896*, 471. For the near break with Raoul, see chap. 9 below.

[9] New York *Times*, Feb. 25, 1938; J. W. Leonard (ed.), *Who's Who in Finance, 1911* (New York, 1911), 600. For the Hollins & Company bankruptcy, see New York *Times*, April 1, June 5, June 9, June 23, Dec. 23, 1914, Nov. 18, 1915.

with great financial abilities, vast personal magnetism, and boundless energy, he attained great pinnacles of wealth and influence only to suffer a nervous disorder and an early death at the age of fifty-two. From his home in Jefferson County, Tennessee, Inman migrated to Georgia at age fourteen. He eschewed schooling in favor of becoming assistant cashier in his uncle's bank. He was there less than two years when the war began. Upon turning eighteen Inman promptly enlisted in the Confederate army and served until 1865. Discharged, broke, and jobless, Inman had no desire to return to strongly unionist East Tennessee. With less than a hundred dollars in his pocket he went to New York, where he found work in a cotton house. His diligence and ability to learn quickly impressed his employers, and in 1868 he became full partner in the reorganized firm of Austell & Inman. Two years later he joined with an employee of the firm and fellow Tennessean, James Swann, in founding his own firm, Inman, Swann & Company.

In short order Inman mastered the intricacies of finance and launched a busy career as capitalist and promoter. He helped organize the New York Cotton Exchange and long remained associated with it. Without relinquishing his cotton activity he involved himself in various New York banks, his deepest commitment being to the Fourth National Bank. Later he moved into insurance as well, serving as director for American Surety, Home and Liberty Insurance, Home Insurance, Liberty Insurance, and the Royal Insurance Company in England. In a city crowded with financial titans and self-made men, Inman took a back seat to no one. He was a millionaire several times over by age thirty-five and had ascended into the best of New York society.

For all his success, however, Inman could not sever his ties to the South. Intrigued by the industrial potential of the region, he turned his capital and energies in that direction. For fifteen years he was the foremost promoter of investment in the South; in later years he claimed to have influenced the flow of over $100,000,000 in northern capital to the region. In addition to the Terminal he helped organize Tennessee Coal & Iron and numerous other mineral enterprises. He bought extensive tracts of coal and iron land, including a large parcel in the Sequatchie Valley, and invested in various secondary industries. In later years he went into the American Cotton Oil Company and American Pig Iron and Storage Company.

In most of his southern enterprises Inman leaned heavily upon the advice of his older brother Samuel, whose prudence tempered the younger man's impulsiveness. Tall, lithe, and athletic, Inman radiated charm and energy. He attracted the attention of men in high places and as a lifelong Democrat vigorously supported the administrations of Grover Cleveland. In all his activities he relied heavily upon oblique tactics and personal diplomacy to achieve his ends. He won an early reputation for his shrewd intractability and deft manipulation around a table of hard bargainers.

Inman's enthusiasm for the South's potential proved a worthy if fickle harness for his considerable talents. At the height of his career in the 1880's he had become associated in the public mind with the image of the "New South." But the reversals in fortune that culminated with the fall of the Terminal in 1892 led to his undoing. He had just begun to erect an impressive new mansion on Fifth Avenue when his enterprises began to crumble. The Panic of 1893 left him distraught and pressed for funds. In desperation he attempted to recoup his losses in a familiar fashion: speculating in cotton. The effort led to a nervous collapse and secret confinement in a sanitarium in Connecticut. There in 1896 he died, leaving a scattered and hopelessly tangled legacy to his wife and six children. Not until 1913 was Inman's estate finally sorted out. Its taxable value was appraised at $918,576.[10]

EDWARD T. LAUTERBACH (1844–1923). In an age that boasted a wide array of specialized legal talents, few achieved the prominence and distinction of Edward Lauterbach. A native of New York City, he attended City College and received his degree in 1864. After gaining admittance to the bar in 1866 he helped organize the firm of Morrison, Lauterbach & Springarn. Devoting itself to the increasingly complex needs of the transportation and communication industries, the firm prospered steadily until Springarn's death in 1887. Lauterbach then joined with George Hoadley, a former governor of Ohio, and Edgar M. Johnson to form the new firm of Hoadley, Lauterbach & Johnson.

Throughout his long career Lauterbach concentrated his practice in the railroad, telegraph, and maritime industries. Brilliant of mind and facile of speech, he possessed a genuine talent for re-

---

[10] *D.A.B.*, IX, 484–85; *National Cyclopedia*, II, 443, X, 423; New York *Times*, Nov. 6, 1896, March 7, 1913; New York *Tribune*, Nov. 7, 1896; New York *Sun*, Dec. 10, 1889; Knoxville *Journal*, Nov. 6, 1896. Some correspondence from Inman can be found in the Grover Cleveland papers, Library of Congress. The items are mostly formal acknowledgments, and only a few have information of any interest.

organization that revealed itself especially in his work with the Terminal and the Philadelphia & Reading Railroad. He played an important role in shaping New York's railroad statutes. In another area, he assumed the vice-presidency of the Pacific Mail Steamship Company in 1882 and promptly immersed himself in a study of the maritime industry and its problems. In governmental and financial circles alike he won wide respect for his erudition and abilities.

A man of considerable personal charm and grace, Lauterbach enlivened his dignified demeanor with a dry wit. In politics he remained a devout Republican throughout his life.[11]

EMANUEL LEHMAN (1827–1907). The career of Emanuel Lehman typified a familiar pattern of his age. Born in Bavaria, he completed his high-school education there before migrating to the United States in 1847. He settled in Montgomery, Alabama, where his older brother Henry had opened a general commission business three years earlier. During the next decade three other Lehman brothers arrived to join the firm, to the head of which Emanuel succeeded upon Henry's death in 1855.

The Lehmans pursued a business increasingly dominated by cotton. During the ante-bellum period the firm's growing role as factors convinced the brothers of a need for a northern office as well. After Henry's death Emanuel left his brother Mayer in charge of the Montgomery house and opened a branch office in New York in 1856. Interrupted by the war, the New York house resumed operations in 1865 and soon extended its interests to sugar, coffee, and other commodities. That same year the brothers also opened a branch in New Orleans under the name Lehman, Newglass & Company.

In each of these enterprises the Lehman brothers gained spectacular results. Led by Emanuel, they demonstrated sound judgment and a fine regard for detail. Diversity did not weaken any of the houses but on the contrary strengthened all largely because the brothers carefully divided managerial responsibility. The Montgomery house became one of the richest, most reliable, and most powerful in the South. Investing heavily in real estate from the beginning, the brothers reaped their reward when industrial development began to swell property values. One knowledgeable ob-

[11] *National Cyclopedia*, XXVI, 227; *Who Was Who, 1897–1942*, 709; New York *Times*, March 5, 1923; Boston *Transcript*, March 5, 1923.

server noted in 1879 that the Lehmans "own more RE [real estate] in the different counties in this immediate vicinity than any other 15 men in them."

Success in the commission business naturally turned Emanuel toward investment banking. The Alabama firm played an active role in financial affairs even before the war and had long served as fiscal agent for the state. In the New York house Emanuel increased the scope of investment activity by promoting railroad construction, iron and steel furnaces, coal mining, and other related industries. As always he bought heavily in real estate wherever his investments ventured. Unlike other merchants-turned-bankers, however, Emanuel never abandoned his interest in cotton. On the contrary, the Lehmans plunged deeply into manufacturing and owned large mills in both Montgomery and New Orleans.

In New York, Emanuel immersed himself thoroughly in the city's financial and social activities. He took part in such ventures as the Metropolitan Ferry and Third Avenue Railroad and became associated with several banks. Outside of business he cultivated a modest reputation for philanthropy and showed a natural preference for various Jewish charities. Handsome in appearance and elegant in manner, his swarthy complexion brightened by a neatly trimmed grey goatee, he maintained an air of shrewd imperturbability. The hard glint of his dark eyes convinced more than one associate that a genius for cold appraisal lay behind them.[12]

THOMAS M. LOGAN (1840–1914). Of all the men associated with the Terminal, Logan seemed least likely for the role. A product of the tidewater aristocracy, he was born in Charleston and graduated from South Carolina College in 1860. He served as a volunteer during the bombardment of Sumter and was later elected a lieutenant in Hampton's Legion. Promoted to captain after Bull Run, he embarked upon a distinguished military career that earned him the rank of brigadier general in 1865. After recovering from wounds suffered during the Seven Days campaign, he fought with distinction at Antietam, Chickamauga, and several other engagements.

A month after surrendering at Durham Station, Logan borrowed five dollars to marry the daughter of a Virginia judge and

[12] *National Cyclopedia*, XXV, 98; New York *Times*, Jan. 11, 1907; Dun & Bradstreet Reports, Alabama, XIX, 326, 333.

settled in that state to study law. Eager, intense, and ambitious, he soon neglected law in favor of the more promising opportunities in railroad promotion and politics. After achieving some success in small mining and manufacturing enterprises around Richmond he concentrated in 1878 upon the task of developing the Danville beyond its previous role as a territorial road.

In thrusting himself into the jungle of railroad promotion and finance, Logan proved adroit at weathering the shifting fortunes of the game. Through it all he never lost his loyalty to his adopted state. He resisted the temptation to move to New York and continued to reside in Richmond. The strength of his roots in Virginia and his proud war record made him an invaluable bridge between the more provincial and conservative Richmond investors and the "outside" financiers who joined forces to develop the Danville. During the great bear raid on both Danville and Terminal stock in the mid-1880's, Logan threw in one and a half million dollars of his own money to support both securities. Through patient effort and a fortunate association with John D. Rockefeller, he later disposed of his shares at a profit nearly equal to his original investment. Within a short time he began to range beyond the South. In 1890 he bought control of the Seattle, Lake Shore & Eastern and sold it for a large profit to the Northern Pacific.

Few of his peers rivaled Logan in personal charm and graciousness. Slight of build, with blonde hair and clear blue eyes, he tended to observe much and say little. Although reflective by nature, he by no means lacked audacity. His prudent decisiveness greatly impressed his associates, one of whom said of him: "His mind is comprehensive and clear, and when he concludes upon anything, he is bold and fearless in its execution. . . . I regard him as one of the ablest and strongest men I ever met, and if he lives he will be one of the master spirits of this great practical age." [13]

CHARLES M. McGHEE (1828–1907). Despite increasingly diverse business interests that prompted him to move to New York about 1887, McGhee never lost sight of his native Tennessee. Born in Monroe County, he graduated from East Tennessee College (now the University of Tennessee) in 1846 and entered upon a career as merchant and banker in Knoxville. During the war he served as colonel in the Confederate Commissary. Afterward he resumed his

---

[13] David Schenck Diary, Dec. 15, 1881; *D.A.B.*, XI, 367–68; *National Cyclopedia*, I, 472; Ezra J. Warner, *Generals in Gray* (Baton Rouge, La., 1959), 189–90; Richmond *Times-Dispatch*, August 12, 1914; New York *Times*, August 12, 1914.

business interests in Knoxville, where he became an advocate of state and regional interests for nearly two decades. He served as president of the Peoples Bank and held a seat in the state legislature for one term. While there he once entered a resolution to grant free railroad transportation to college students to and from Knoxville. Fiercely loyal to his alma mater, he became a trustee and served for a time as secretary-treasurer. On one occasion he bailed the school out of serious financial difficulties.

McGhee's concern for and large investment in Knoxville's commerce naturally interested him in the railroads serving the city. The financial weakness of those roads led him, together with R. T. Wilson and Joseph Jaques, to advocate consolidation of the East Tennessee roads. Later they enlisted the support of Thomas A. Scott and the Pennsylvania Railroad and bought the state's interest in several of its roads. In all his Tennessee interests McGhee remained basically a developmental investor. Reluctantly taking an active role in the management of the Memphis & Charleston, the East Tennessee, and finally the Terminal itself, he did so primarily to protect his extensive investments not only in the railroad but in the resources of the region as well. As his surviving financial records reveal, he did not hesitate to speculate for short-term profits, but the size of his over-all commitment made the strength of his long-term interest clear.

By the 1880's McGhee had moved to New York and expanded his investment horizons. Retaining his close friendship with Wilson, he joined that financier in such enterprises as the Texas & Pacific Railroad, Pacific Mail Steamship, American Cattle Trust, and Western Union Beef. His investments in Tennessee included Tennessee Coal & Iron, East Tennessee Iron & Coal, Roane Iron Company, Knoxville Woolen Mills, and a host of other projects, some of which were run by members of his family. He retired from business about 1897 and thereafter devoted much of his time to civic enterprises.[14]

JOHN G. MOORE (1847–1899). The son of a Maine sea captain, Moore received an education in private schools before entering his uncle's lumber business in New York. In only three years he did well enough to start his own firm in lumber and railroad ties and

[14] Charles M. McGhee papers, Lawson-McGhee Library, Knoxville, Tenn.; *D.A.B.*, XII, 48; *National Cyclopedia*, XII, 198; Knoxville *Journal*, May 6, 1907; Knoxville *Tribune*, May 6, 1907; New York *Times*, May 6, 1907.

soon developed a large trade in neighboring states as well. Then, in partnership with John O. Evans, he formed the firm of Evans & Moore to engage in government construction. The company prospered and eventually became the National Dredging Company.

In 1880 the two partners organized Mutual Union Telegraph Company for the purpose of leasing lines to private firms by day and newspapers at night. Connecting New York, Boston, Philadelphia, and Washington, the company did well enough to begin extending its lines. Evans died before completion of the lines, leaving Moore to face the hostility of an aroused Western Union. After a bitter battle for supremacy, Western Union relented and leased Mutual Union at a huge profit for Moore and his associates. The victory won him considerable respect in financial circles and a seat on the board of Western Union for the rest of his life.

After an extended vacation abroad Moore plunged into financial affairs more vigorously than ever. Taking a new partner, Grant B. Schley, he founded the house of Moore & Schley in 1885. The next year he bought a seat on the New York Exchange and acquired control of the Chase National Bank. In short order the house earned a reputation as "market movers" and opened branches in Washington and Philadelphia. Prominent clients of the firm included, among others, the Rockefellers, the Havemeyers, and W. C. Whitney. Moore personally negotiated the series of deals by which the New Haven Railroad gained control over most of New England's lines. He also conducted important transactions for such roads as the Erie and the Northern Pacific.

A devoutly conservative Republican, Moore in 1894–95 instituted the first proceedings to test the constitutionality of the income tax. For relaxation he preferred travel and yachting. He lived well and was known as a genial host. In business his friends and adversaries alike respected his foresight, his even temperament, and his acute judgment of character.[15]

WILLIAM G. RAOUL (1843–1913). A lifelong advocate of local "conservatism," Raoul did not inherit his Georgia roots by birth. Born and raised in Livingston Parish, Louisiana, he remained there until the outbreak of war. After Sumter he enlisted in one of Louisiana's proudest units, the Washington Artillery, and served in the field for two years. His mechanical abilities caught the alert

[15] *National Cyclopedia*, XXII, 293; New York *Times*, June 24, June 27, June 29, Dec. 3, 1899.

eye of William M. Wadley, who had resided in Louisiana before the war. Then superintendent of transportation for the Confederacy, Wadley had Raoul promoted and placed in charge of car construction.

The wartime experience launched Raoul into a railroad career, and the association with Wadley proved deep and enduring. The tie became personal when Raoul married one of Wadley's daughters. Professionally they shared many attitudes in common, and Wadley would remain the younger man's mentor for nearly two decades. Immediately after the war Raoul joined his father, brother, and Wadley in founding the Southern Car Works in Independence, Louisiana. Within a short time Wadley was called to the presidency of the Central; the Raouls stayed with the firm until its failure a few years later.

Dejected, broke, and without prospects, Raoul moved to Georgia to join his father-in-law in April, 1871. He accepted a job with the Central a year later and began a distinguished career with that system. He became roadmaster for the Central in 1874, superintendent of the Southwestern in 1876, and general superintendent of the Montgomery & Eufaula in 1879. The following year the sick and aging Wadley persuaded his board to create the new post of vice-president and tendered Raoul the position. During the last year of Wadley's presidency he was so incapacitated that Raoul virtually assumed all the practical responsibilities of his office.

Although his personal connection to Wadley undoubtedly aided Raoul's rise within the Central's management, there is no question that his own talent played a more important part in his success. He won a reputation as an outstanding practical railroad man, and even his severest critics conceded his administrative and technical abilities. Devoted to the policies advocated by his father-in-law, he won the support of the latter's friends and succeeded to the presidency in 1883. He held the office for four years, and even after his departure from active management he maintained a close interest in the company. Afterward he became president of the Mexican National Railway and involved himself in numerous other projects. His loyalties never left the Central, however, and he devoted considerable attention to protecting the property (especially the Southwestern) from what he considered unwise and rapacious management by the Terminal interests.

Grave and dignified in his demeanor, Raoul could be arbitrary and abrupt in his dealings with directors and stockholders alike.

Though recognizing the inevitability of the trends toward consolidation and regulation, he deplored the practical effects of both and wrote extensively against them. To the end of his life he remained an advocate of local control and blamed the Central's failure upon the loss of its management to impersonal "outside" interests.[16]

ISAAC L. RICE (1850–1915). A native of Bavaria, Rice came to the United States at the age of six. After private tutoring in this country he went to Paris in 1866 to study literature and music. He returned three years later, wrote and taught to support his studies, and published in 1875 a treatise entitled *What is Music?* His interest then turned to law, and in 1880 Rice received a degree in that field from Columbia, where he fell under the influence of John W. Burgess.

Soon after opening his practice, Rice turned his attention to corporate law. His brilliantly analytical mind and skill at unraveling legal complexities won him a prominent clientele and led to his participation in several important cases. He served as counsel for several railroads involved in reorganization, including the Texas & Pacific and the St. Louis & Southwestern. In addition to his role in the Terminal, he played a leading part in the formation of the Reading Company and figured prominently in the reorganization of the Philadelphia & Reading.

Despite his crowded legal and financial career, Rice's intellectual pursuits never lapsed. In 1886 he founded *Forum* magazine, patterned after several contemporary English reviews, and ran it at a heavy financial loss. Long an avid chess player, he played expertly enough to fashion an original variation on the King's Knight's Gambit widely known as Rice's Gambit. In business he was no less an innovator, being an early promoter of numerous electrical inventions such as the storage battery. In that area his business enterprises included the Quaker City Chemical Company.

In his tastes and appearance Rice remained the fashionable cosmopolitan. Suave and urbane, studious and thoughtful, he pos-

---

[16] The best source for biographical material on Raoul are his letter books and other personal papers in the Emory University Library, Atlanta. A brief autobiographical sketch can be found in Raoul to C. W. Brewster, June 2, 1890. The Savannah *Morning News* and *Evening Press* for Jan., 1883, contain considerable biographical information; see also *Railroad Gazette*, LIV (1913), 188.

sessed a sharp tongue and ready wit. He bore a slight resemblance to Sigmund Freud and was considered by many of his less polished and educated associates as something of an eccentric.[17]

GEORGE I. SENEY (1826–1893). In speculative circles Seney was regarded as a late bloomer. He seems in retrospect to have lived two lives, with the dividing line between them falling around 1879. Born in Newton, Long Island, the son of a Methodist preacher, Seney graduated from the City University of New York in 1847 and went immediately into banking. His mother's relatives obtained for him a position with the Gallatin bank; later he moved to the Bank of North America and then, in 1853, to the Metropolitan Bank. There he rose steadily to the office of president and developed a reputation for strong and conservative leadership. Originally organized by dry goods merchants for their own convenience, the Metropolitan became a state bank in 1851 and a national bank in 1865. Under Seney's leadership it became one of the most respected institutions in New York.

During the first postwar decade Seney prospered both financially and socially. He lived in a fashionable Brooklyn neighborhood and kept close company with E. H. R. Lyman, John T. Martin, and Alexander T. White, all wealthy merchants. He gave freely of his time and money for civic and charitable enterprises. He donated large sums to his native church, endowed the Seney Hospital in Brooklyn, and apparently enjoyed his growing reputation as a philanthropist. At the same time he built up a sizable art collection.

After 1879 the image of Seney as a staid, somewhat phlegmatic banker changed abruptly. He first distinguished himself during a speculative frenzy that year. Shortly afterward he plunged into a variety of railroad projects including the East Tennessee, Nickel Plate, Ohio Central, and Rochester & Pittsburgh. Virtually the same syndicate, headed by Seney, handled each of these ventures, and in each of them Seney charted what banker Henry Clews called "an original course . . . in speculation—so original, in fact, as to stamp the enterprises with which he became identified with his name."

The Seney technique featured a lavish watering of stocks, a promotion of the securities in glowing terms, and a vigorous support

[17] *D.A.B.*, XV, 541; *National Cyclopedia*, XI, 447; *Who's Who in Finance, 1911*, 664; New York *Times*, Nov. 3, 1915; *American Chess Bulletin* (Dec., 1915).

of them by "washed sales." Into these enterprises Seney poured not only his own resources but those of his bank and certain other financial institutions connected with it. The Panic of 1884 brought sudden disaster to the whole affair. The Metropolitan suspended and eventually closed its doors, and its fall carried a Brooklyn bank and an insurance company down with it. Most of the railroads involved plunged into receivership. Seney resigned the bank presidency and pledged his personal fortune, including the Brooklyn mansion and the art collection, toward his obligations. Though seemingly ruined, he managed to recoup his fortune in fairly short order. Clews hinted that Seney had actually lost little in the crash and therefore cared little about the bank disaster.

Despite his bent for philanthropy, Seney was considered a cold fish by some of his peers. It became notorious that many of his associates failed while Seney's own fortunes flourished, and that he evinced little sympathy for used-up friends crushed by his schemes. That personal ruthlessness came back to haunt him in 1884. With sardonic relish Clews recorded that

Seney gave his money away, and it was placed in the wrong quarters for any tangible return. He was a great patron of the churches and religious institutions. If he had studied the life of Daniel Drew, he might have discovered that investments in such enterprises as these were not particularly profitable. In his financial difficulties, Seney was left high and dry without friends who would come to the rescue.[18]

ALFRED M. SULLY (1841–1909). To many acquaintances Sully seemed more a literary man than a financier. Like many of his peers, he came to finance by way of the law. A native of Ottawa, he migrated to Ohio and graduated from Cincinnati Law School in 1862. He then moved to Davenport, Iowa, where he developed a thriving corporate practice over the next decade. One of his partners, Austin Corbin, moved to New York in 1872 and went into banking. Corbin invited Sully to join him but the latter, still pondering a literary career, declined. Instead he gave up his practice and traveled extensively through the South and Southwest. Finally, in 1876, he went to New York and became chief counsel and

[18] *D.A.B.*, XVI, 583–84; *National Cyclopedia*, I, 520; Clews, *Twenty-Eight Years*, 162–67; Hampton, *Nickel Plate Road*, 33–36; New York *Times*, April 8, 1893; Brooklyn *Daily Eagle*, April 8, 1893; New York *Tribune*, April 8, 1893. There is a biographical sketch of Seney in the Ingraham Genealogical Papers, Library of Congress.

manager for the New York & Manhattan Beach Railroad, of which Corbin was president.

The position marked the beginning of a long and profitable relationship with Corbin. The two men eventually bought the entire Long Island system of roads from J. P. Morgan and put it on its feet, with Sully assuming the presidency of some of the branches. In addition Sully invested in the Indiana, Bloomington & Western, Ohio Southern, Central Iowa, and several other midwestern roads. In each case he realized substantial transactional and developmental profits. The Long Island venture absorbed most of his attention, however, until 1885, when he and Corbin took on their biggest project. They bought into the financially moribund Philadelphia & Reading, with Sully becoming a major holder and banker for its president, F. B. Gowen. There ensued a bitter fight for control with Drexel, Morgan that lasted for nearly a year and ended in a victorious compromise. At its conclusion Corbin became president of the company while Sully went onto the board and executive committee.

Shortly after the Reading fight, Sully shouldered the complex problem of the Terminal. His unhappy experience with that company doubtless prompted his virtual retirement from business after leaving the presidency in 1888. Having lost his wife in 1882, he became something of a recluse and devoted much of his time to literature. Tall, slender, and sensitive in appearance, he appeared somewhat ascetic in contrast to some of his more epicurean associates on Wall Street. His reserved, unassuming manner and deep, thoughtful eyes belied a tremendous nervous energy and restlessness. The long, square contours of his features reminded Henry Clews of William M. Evarts.[19]

SAMUEL THOMAS (1840–1903). Unlike many of his peers, Thomas moved to railroads from an early career in the iron industry. He was born in South Point, Ohio, but spent his childhood in Marietta. At seventeen he joined the Keystone Iron Company as a junior clerk and swiftly worked his way to the second position in the firm while studying law, geology, mining, chemistry, and metallurgy on the side. When the war broke out he enlisted in the 27th Ohio and was elected lieutenant in August, 1861. He served in the field until 1863, when he was promoted to captain and detailed to

[19] *National Cyclopedia*, III, 365; *Who Was Who, 1607–1896*, 1204; Clews, *Twenty-Eight Years*, 553–54. The brief biographical sketch in *Railroad Gazette*, XIX (1887), 184, incorrectly states that Sully was born and raised in Iowa.

organize troops. He helped form the 63rd and 64th United States Infantry and became colonel of the latter regiment.

For a time Thomas served as provost marshal while the regiment protected the Mississippi River between Helena and Natchez. For his efforts he earned a brevet commission as brigadier general. After Appomattox he was assigned as assistant commissioner to the Freedman's Bureau in Mississippi. In May, 1866, he returned to serve as assistant adjutant general for O. O. Howard, but six months later he left the army to become assistant manager of the Zanesville Iron Works. He remained there until 1872, when former governor William Dennison called him to take charge of the construction and operation of new rolling mills and blast furnaces in Columbus. While undertaking this task he involved himself in state politics as well.

The Columbus assignment launched Thomas into a brilliant career as industrialist and capitalist. After building the Columbus works he played a major role in combining extensive Hocking Valley coal and iron properties into the Hocking Valley Coal and Iron Company. The development of these works, and especially his large interests in rolling mills, led him naturally into railroads. In 1875, with his Columbus mills idled by the depression, he joined with several of his stockholders, who included some of Ohio's most prominent men, to build the Columbus & Toledo Railroad. By securing contracts for the road's rails Thomas managed to keep his mills going despite hard times. His Ohio properties were considered among the soundest in the state, a status Thomas achieved by excellent management and a proclivity for making good contacts.

During the 1880's Thomas joined the migration of the ambitious toward Wall Street, where he dealt himself shrewdly into an impressive variety of enterprises including the Nickel Plate, Ohio Central, Lake Erie & Western, South Shore & Atlantic, and many others. He did not limit his activity to railroads but went into banking and contracting as well. From an estimated worth of about $250,000 in 1877 he amassed a fortune of several million dollars in little over a decade. The breadth of his business interests can only partially be reflected by some of the firms for which he served as director: Western Union Beef, Pacific Mail Steamship, Pacific Steel, Tennessee Coal & Iron, Metropolitan Dredging, American Pig Iron Storage Warrant, and the Cuba Company.

As early as 1878 Thomas became convinced that the South and West held the key to profitable investment. Here as in his earlier enterprises he utilized the railroads to realize opportunistic profits and made his major long-term commitments to such sequential investments as coal and iron, manufacturing, mining, banking, and real estate. Few of his associates could match his sharp mind and shrewd instincts. Tall, solidly built, and affable, he lived in fine style and pursued his interest in art, literature, and especially science. In typical fashion he clung to the sentimental vestiges of his childhood and, like Brice, took a deep interest in the Ohio Society. He also belonged to the Southern Society, the Union League, and the Republican Club. Durable and energetic, he weathered every crisis without seriously threatening his carefully won fortune. One acquaintance characterized him well by noting that "he won't go into any thing he can't see his way out of." [20]

WILLIAM M. WADLEY (1813–1882). No one better epitomized the American vision of the self-made man than William Wadley. Born in Brentwood, New Hampshire, he was apprenticed to the blacksmith's trade at an early age. From his mastering of this trade emerged a genuine talent in metalworking and a robust constitution with such strength that in later years it was said he could twist an iron horseshoe with his bare hands. In 1834 he migrated to Savannah in search of his fortune. Working first as a common laborer and then, as his superior mechanical and executive abilities became apparent, as a supervisor, Wadley held jobs with a number of young railroads including the Central, Western & Atlantic, New Orleans, Jackson & Great Northern, Southern Railroad of Mississippi, and Vicksburg, Shreveport & Texas.

Wadley's nomadic career did not derive from dissatisfaction with his work. On the contrary, he had by 1860 become acknowledged as a railroad expert and the New Orleans road paid him the incredible salary of $10,000 a year. By that date he had become a southerner, at least in style. He married a Savannah girl of good family by whom he had seven children, acquired some land and slaves, and fought for the South in the war. On December 3, 1862, he was appointed colonel and superintendent of transportation for the Confederate army. In that demanding and exceedingly frustrating office Wadley gave a superb account of himself against insuperable obstacles until his abrupt dismissal in the spring of 1863.

[20] *National Cyclopedia*, XXV, 31–32; New York *Times*, Jan. 12, 1903; *Who Was Who, 1897–1942*, 1230; Clews, *Twenty-Eight Years*, 554–55; Hampton, *Nickel Plate Road*, 38–43; Dun & Bradstreet Reports, Ohio, LXV, 340.

The reasons for his mysterious fall have never been made clear, and in later years Wadley himself shed no light on the matter.

Penniless and distraught over the South's defeat, Wadley considered emigrating to South America after the war. The Vicksburg road, of which he had been president, was bankrupt and in ruins, and his connection with it was severed by questionable means. At that nadir in his career the Central, ravished by war and leaderless, summoned him to the presidency. The restoration of the Central and the guiding of its destiny through the difficult postwar years became his lifework. Though his achievement was not without its shortcomings, he succeeded in making the Central the most powerful corporation in Georgia and one of the finest railroad properties in the South. In honor of his service and devotion a large statue was erected opposite the Union Station in Macon, and two towns, one in Georgia and one in Louisiana, bear his name.

Throughout his career Wadley dominated his enterprises with an intensity and genius that inspired both affection and fear among his subordinates. For all his southern inclinations he retained the strength and solidity of the Yankee smith. Gruff, laconic, and demanding, he had no sympathy for those who did not meet his own high standards. Imperious to a fault, he nevertheless maintained a scrupulously impartial honesty that won him the respect even of his adversaries. He valued power above wealth and never speculated in his company's stocks; partly for that reason he died a relatively poor man. His bluntness of manner doubtless grated upon southern sensitivities. As Robert R. Black has so succinctly put it, "if he never lost himself in the fabled southern penchant for verbosity, he equally failed to absorb the southern flair for diplomacy and tact." A contemporary observer, commenting upon Wadley's financial integrity, aptly summarized his entire character: "A No. 1 anyway you take him." [21]

RICHARD T. WILSON (1831–1910). Long associated with the commercial activity of eastern Tennessee, Wilson was actually born in Habersham County, Georgia. After rudimentary schooling he mi-

[21] Sarah L. Wadley, *A Brief Record of the Life of William M. Wadley, Written by His Eldest Daughter* (New York, 1884) ; T. B. Catherwood (ed.), *The Life and Labors of William M. Wadley* (Savannah, 1885) ; *National Cyclopedia*, I, 201; Dun & Bradstreet Reports, Georgia, XXVIII, 137, XXIX, 577. An excellent account of Wadley's wartime service can be found in Robert R. Black, III, *The Railroads of the Confederacy* (Chapel Hill, N.C., 1952), 107–23; see also *Central of Georgia Magazine*, XLIII (April, 1933), 4.

grated to Tennessee and became a merchant in Loudon. During the war he served with the Confederate Commissary and on one occasion went to Europe to dispose of cotton for the government. Unlike many of his acquaintances, Wilson managed to preserve at least part of his wealth at the war's end. He chose not to revive his Loudon firm but went instead to New York immediately after the fighting stopped.

In New York, Wilson established the general commission firm of Wilson, Callaway & Company, his partner being a fellow Tennessean deeply interested in the railroads of the region. When Callaway died in 1870 the firm became R. T. Wilson & Company, and in common with many other merchants Wilson drifted more and more into banking. Despite his removal from Tennessee he maintained a strong personal and financial interest in the state. In close alliance with Callaway, McGhee, and Joseph Jaques he mobilized a considerable amount of capital for the development of railroads, mining and other industries, manufacturing, and real estate. Through his own efforts and those of the Southern Railway Security Company, Wilson persistently sought to unify and harmonize the South's railroads. He played a major role in developing the East Tennessee in the first years after its formation.

In typical fashion Wilson's activities expanded in scope and shifted westward as new opportunities opened up. Although his firm prospered from the transactional profits that derived from its investment activities, it remained a conservative company noted for its willingness to stick with a property. For Wilson as for many of his peers, the making of money proved eminently compatible with the mission of developing his native region. Starting with the East Tennessee and other nearby properties, he moved into the growing system of Huntington-controlled roads west of Tennessee. Gradually he involved himself in some roads west of the Mississippi and, together with McGhee, Thomas, Brice, and others, went into Western Union Beef and other cattle enterprises. He served on the boards of numerous banks and industrial firms and retired from business about 1906.[22]

[22] *National Cyclopedia,* XXIII, 360; Boston *Transcript,* Nov. 26, 1910.

Chapter III

The Twilight of Territorial Strategy

ALL three roads that would form the nucleus of the Richmond Terminal emerged from the war with similar problems of rehabilitation and finance. Worn-out equipment had to be renovated or replaced and new rolling stock purchased. Bonded interest accrued during the conflict had to be paid. Capital had to be raised to service both these needs at a time when the companies could market their paper only at a severe discount. Traffic patterns disrupted by wartime needs had to be restored. New sources of business had to be developed from an impoverished southern economy that promised little immediate hope of supporting its reviving railroads. To the men in charge of the companies the prospects looked anything but encouraging.

The Richmond & Danville

As the connecting link between two major centers the Danville prospered from the moment it opened in 1856.[1] It drew a rich traffic in tobacco and other agricultural products from the region adjacent to its line. The state owned 60 per cent of its stock and Richmond investors most of the remaining 40 per cent. Considered one of the most important roads in Virginia, it soon acquired a reputation for sound management and commanded excellent credit throughout the late 1850's.[2] During the ante-bellum period it functioned entirely as a local road with no connections south of Danville. A 48-mile gap separated the Danville from Greensboro, North Carolina, where the North Carolina Railroad and Charlotte & South Carolina Railroad provided through lines to Colum-

[1] Charles Turner, "Virginia Railroad Development, 1845–1860," *The Historian*, X (Autumn, 1947), 50–52; Harrison, *Southern Railway*, 80–89.
[2] "Southern Railroads," 3–4; Dun & Bradstreet Credit Reports, Virginia, XLIII, 126.

bia. Attempts to close the gap had been thwarted by two groups: Danville interests fearful of losing their status as a terminal city and becoming a mere way stop on the longer through route, and North Carolinians anxious to localize trade within the state via a projected east-west railroad. The closing of this gap would mean completion of a north-south through route that would draw traffic to Virginia outlets instead of North Carolina ports.[3]

The exigencies of war dramatically altered the situation. Confederate transportation needs demanded construction of the line and stilled even the virulent North Carolina protests. In 1862 the Danville-controlled Piedmont Railroad Company received a charter from the state and began construction. Shortages of labor and material seriously hampered the work, and the road did not open until 1864.[4] Its completion marked a crucial moment in the Danville's history, for possession of through connections preferred new opportunities and new problems. Once free of abnormal wartime conditions, it would require a careful rethinking of strategy.

During the war the Danville provided the Confederacy with invaluable service and paid a dear price for its efforts. Impossible traffic demands caused rapid deterioration of rolling stock, roadbed, and other equipment for which replacements simply could not be obtained. However lucrative the business, the overtaxed road could not bear the strain. By 1865 wartime attrition had reduced the road to virtual ruin and a bleak future. Capital to rehabilitate the road would have to be found, and the prostrate South was in no condition to supply it. Future earning capacity seemed limited in an atmosphere dominated by physical and economic exhaustion, and the uncertain political situation did nothing to clarify the picture.[5]

Under these trying circumstances the company needed strong leadership. In seeking a president it naturally turned first to the large supply of competent and now jobless military heroes. General Joseph E. Johnston became the most prominent candidate and seemed certain of election. Then Governor Francis Pierpont, anxious for a speedy reconciliation with the North, intervened. Suggesting delicately that Johnston's election might create the

---

[3] Brown, *State Movement*, 22–23, 65–68, and "A History of the Piedmont Railroad Company," *North Carolina Historical Review*, III (1926), 198–222.

[4] Black, *Railroads of the Confederacy*, 148–53, 206; Harrison, *Southern Railway*, 89–92, 113–15.

[5] For the Danville's wartime performance, see Harrison, *Southern Railway, passim,* and the annual reports of the company for the period.

wrong impression in the North, he persuaded the stockholders to elect instead A. S. Buford of Danville.[6]

The decision proved a wise one. Tall, slender, and courtly, Buford's manner personified the southern country gentleman. He possessed sound judgment and a genuine talent for administration.[7] In trying to formulate policy for the company Buford faced five immediate problems: rehabilitating the road; securing capital for restoration and other needs; devising means of developing local traffic; evaluating the importance of through traffic to the company's future needs; and evolving tactics for obtaining connections for through service on the best possible terms.

Restoration and mobilization of capital necessarily came first. The process of reconstruction inevitably gave rise to a large floating debt carried at high interest rates. Unwilling to see the company dependent upon the uncertain whims of the money market and fearful that its credit might be jeopardized by unforeseen pressures, Buford gained approval to convert the floating debt and existing funded debt into a new consolidated mortgage. He paid dearly (and willingly) to dispose of the debt, selling $760,500 worth of the new bonds in 1868 at prices averaging between 64 and 70. With that sacrifice he buttressed the company's credit and maintained its reputation as a reliable investment even though it paid no dividends for sixteen years.[8]

The development of local resources remained, as before the war, the basic source of income for the Danville. To stimulate increased business along the line Buford resorted to several devices. He encouraged immigration into the untilled acreage of southern Virginia, built small feeder lines to service infant coal, iron, and quarry industries, and bought additional waterfront property on the James River to provide facilities for handling industrial traffic. To attract new capital into the region and coax more business out of existing shippers, he steadily pared down the Danville's high rates, cutting them 28 per cent in 1867 and reducing them further in 1871. In the latter year he introduced a new uniform local rate schedule. By 1872, he could proclaim that

this company for several years past has been boldly prosecuting a policy of development. A necessity—the necessity of self-preservation, and of

[6] H. J. Eckenrode, *The Political History of Virginia during Reconstruction* (Baltimore, 1904), 32. Buford was elected in Oct., 1865.

[7] David Schenck Diary, April 1, 1883.

[8] *Annual Report of the Richmond & Danville Railroad,* 1868, 278–79; Dun & Bradstreet Reports, Virginia, XLIII, 126, 180.

fulfilling faithfully its highest duties to its own interests as well as to the public—required it. . . . The result will be that which always follows well-meant and well-directed labor and enterprise, faithfully and honestly and manfully adhered to—success. And if the measure of it be small at first, and its progress slow, its continuance is the more assured, and the benefits and blessings to those who have labored and waited for it, only the more permanent.[9]

The very slowness of that development, however, forced Buford to reconsider his attitude toward through traffic. Though it remained secondary to local business as a source of income, it gradually assumed a role of increasing importance in his strategic planning. The reasons were obvious. It offered immediate if unstable returns at a time when the Danville (like other roads) sorely needed cash. Investment in development of local resources required patient waiting before the harvest, and even then the harvest could not always be relied upon. Buford himself admitted the drawbacks of overdependence upon local business:

The conditions of the country on which your road is dependent for earnings, in common with other sections of the Southern States, is anomalous and difficult, and its business consequently variable in character and reduced in amount; indeed altogether incapable at present of its ordinary maximum production. . . . The industrial prostration prevalent throughout the eastern and southern portions of the State, in which seasons more or less unpropitious for agricultural productions, concurring with other well known social and political causes, had served greatly to depress enterprise and thus correspondingly to effect local business both of tonnage and travel.[10]

The logic of through business involved other compelling factors as well. The monopoly enjoyed by the Danville over its territory might not last indefinitely. Indeed, the more prosperous the business, the more likely an "invading" road might be tempted to seize a portion of it. Through traffic would then come to be increasingly important, but control over it depended upon having reliable connections at both terminals. Efforts to stabilize those connections had proved exasperating and frustrating as each company shifted its policy to maximize immediate opportunities. Suppose these lines discovered it more profitable to throw their through business to routes other than the Danville. By refusing to make competitive joint rates they could effectively isolate the Danville.

---

[9] *Danville Reports*, 1867, 191; 1871, 580, 584–85; 1872, 5–7, 10–12.
[10] *Ibid.*, 1868, 281; 1869, 367.

And what if rival roads gained control over the Danville's connectors? The result would be the same: to freeze the Danville out of the fight for through traffic.[11]

Such claustrophobic thoughts spurred Buford and his directors to action. They must not neglect through traffic; indeed, they had to foster its growth by guaranteeing permanent connections. To do this would necessitate large expenditures and considerable risk; but not to do it might mean eventual isolation and reduction to a local road. The Danville lay along the northeast-southwest trade route passing through the piedmont region of the South Atlantic states. Potentially it could become part of a through line running from Chesapeake Bay to the Gulf at Mobile or even New Orleans. Much of this route remained unbuilt, but the growing activity in railroad construction seemed to promise early completion of the line.

Under these circumstances the Danville could ill afford delay or hesitation. By 1867 Buford had outlined a program to provide the company with the most efficient through line in its territory. The plan involved five other roads: the Richmond & York River; Piedmont; Charlotte, Columbia & Augusta; Atlanta & Richmond Air-Line; and North Carolina. The York River road held the key to northern connections. It reached the Chesapeake Bay steamers via the York River at West Point but had suffered complete destruction during the war. In 1867 only 24 of its 38 miles had been rebuilt, and it did not connect with the Danville in Richmond. After some difficulty Buford obtained the right to build a connector road, but financial problems delayed completion of the road. The road finally reopened in 1869.[12]

Looking southward, Buford faced a formidable task. The Piedmont remained firmly in the Danville's possession and provided entry into Greensboro.[13] Connections south of that point depended upon the North Carolina Railroad, which traversed a crude arc between Goldsboro and Charlotte. Dependence upon that road for northbound through traffic did not look promising. It was more lucrative for the North Carolina not to interchange

---

[11] *Ibid.*, 1867, 190; 1869, 371; 1871, 581–83; 1873, 123.

[12] *Ibid.*, 1867, 190; 1868, 282–83; 1869, 370; 1871, 583–84; *Chronicle*, XV (1872), 252; "Southern Railroads," 2; Harrison, *Southern Railway*, 237–41. A map showing the gap between the two roads in Richmond can be found in Taylor and Neu, *American Railroad Network*, 47. The Danville apparently did not contribute any direct aid to completion of the York River road.

[13] *Danville Report*, 1867, 190.

traffic with the Danville at Greensboro but rather to make the longer haul to Raleigh or Goldsboro. From those points the company could reach the sea via the Raleigh & Gaston, Seaboard & Roanoke, and Wilmington & Weldon railroads. The desire of North Carolinians to localize traffic at state ports also mitigated against northbound shipments to "foreign" Virginia outlets via the Danville. In addition, a difference in gauge further complicated traffic interchange between the two roads.[14]

Cooperation alone obviously could not assure the Danville's entrance into Charlotte. On that premise Buford labored to bring the North Carolina to terms, first by threatening construction of a parallel line and then by offering to lease the road instead. Bitter controversy over a similar proposal by the Raleigh & Gaston deferred all action for two years. Finally on September 11, 1871, Buford got his way. Unable to obtain only the track between Greensboro and Charlotte, the Danville leased the entire North Carolina road for 30 years at $260,000 per annum.[15] Immediately Buford moved to change the North Carolina's gauge from its standard 4 feet 8 inches to the 5-foot gauge of the Danville. He had two reasons: it would facilitate traffic interchange and it would help divert traffic from the rival roads (all of them standard gauge) that connected with the North Carolina at Raleigh and Goldsboro. In desperation the competing roads filed suits seeking injunctions against the gauge change and the lease itself. The fight dragged on until March, 1875, when the courts sustained the Danville's position in both cases.[16]

From Charlotte, Buford might go in two directions: southwest to Atlanta and southward via Columbia to Augusta. The 1869 consolidation of two roads into the Charlotte, Columbia & Augusta under a management friendly to the Danville assured the latter connection.[17] The first project waited upon completion of the 268-mile Atlanta & Richmond Air-Line. The two companies engaged in its construction consolidated in 1870 to push work forward. At

[14] The strategic situation is described in detail in Brown, *State Movement*, 155–60.

[15] *Ibid.*, 160–73; *Chronicle*, XIII (1871), 402; Harrison, *Southern Railway*, 124–34. The Danville also agreed to pay all taxes up to $10,000 a year on the road.

[16] *Chronicle*, XVI (1873), 652, XVII (1873), 156, XX (1875), 267; *Danville Report*, 1871, 581–82; 1872, 8–9; 1873, 121–22; 1874, 229; 1875, 325–26; Brown, *State Movement*, 179–81. See also the *Annual Report of the Raleigh & Gaston Railroad*, 1871, 10–11; 1873, 18.

[17] *Danville Report*, 1868, 283; 1869, 371–72.

first the Danville offered little more than encouragement, but when progress lagged it assumed a more active role. In 1872 Buford extended his company's credit to guarantee the last stages of construction, and friends of the Danville purchased stock and bonds in the Air-Line company. When the road finally opened on September 28, 1873, it used rolling stock provided by the Danville.[18]

By September, 1873, Buford had achieved his goal. The 547-mile road from Atlanta to Richmond, soon known as the Piedmont Air-Line, lay securely within the Danville's grasp. In his report Buford heralded the triumph:

This Company has been for years shut up to the alternative of a continued subjection to competing interests, with an indefinite prospect of unprofitableness, or a struggle for development, outgrowth and future prosperity. The latter has been considered by the Company as more in accord with the original objects of its organization, and more promising to its future prospects.[19]

Creation of the through line proved too expensive a task for the Danville to undertake by itself. A significant change in the company's ownership made its continued growth possible. In 1871 the state of Virginia authorized the sale of all state-owned railroad stocks, including the 24,000 Danville shares. After complex negotiations the stock passed, with the Danville board's approval, into the hand of the Southern Railway Security Company on August 31, 1871. Organized in 1871, S.R.S.C. was probably the first important pure holding company. Its stockholders consisted of men interested in the Pennsylvania Railroad, New York bankers and firms holding either long-term southern railroad securities or short-term notes for rails and other equipment, Baltimore merchants, two Englishmen, and three Tennesseans deeply involved in the railroads of their state.[20]

Throughout its short existence S.R.S.C. was dominated by the Pennsylvania and its gregarious vice-president Thomas A. Scott. A

[18] *Ibid.*, 1868, 283–84; 1871, 585–86; 1872, 9–10; 1873, 122–23; Henry V. Poor, *Manual of Railroads for 1891* (New York, 1891), 462; Harrison, *Southern Railway*, 195–203.

[19] *Danville Report*, 1873, 123, 126.

[20] C. C. Hall (ed.), *Baltimore: Its History and People* (New York, 1912), III, 165–69; New York *Times*, March 31, 1901; Harrison, *Southern Railway*, 93–94. A list of S.R.S.C. stockholders in 1872 can be found in *Proceedings of the Stockholders Convention in the Memphis & Charleston Railway Company*, Jan. 17–19, 1872, Baker Library.

man of bold schemes and restless energy, Scott envisioned a vast Pennsylvania-dominated system of southern roads. If well integrated and run efficiently such a system might enrich the Pennsylvania and also thwart the southern ambitions of the rival Baltimore & Ohio. Backed by the resources of Scott's powerful corporation, S.R.S.C. quickly acquired control of eight southern roads: the Danville; East Tennessee, Virginia & Georgia; Charlotte, Columbia & Augusta; Wilmington & Weldon; Northeastern of South Carolina; Wilmington, Columbia & Augusta; Richmond & Petersburg; and Cheraw & Darlington. The swiftness of the company's growth inevitably aroused fear and resentment among other southern rail managers, especially in Virginia, where considerable animosity developed between the Pennsylvania, the B. & O., and the Atlantic, Mississippi & Ohio Railroad dominated by William Mahone.[21]

At first glance the advent of Pennsylvania control might be expected to signal a radical change in Danville policy. Prior to the state's sale of its stock Virginians had owned nearly all the company's stock, and only one man held more than a thousand shares. Some sixteen individuals or firms owned blocks of 200 or more shares, with their total holding amounting to but 7,694 of 40,000 shares.[22] Loss of local control might well have provoked a reaction, but none occurred, mainly because no fundamental change in policy took place. The ambitions of the S.R.S.C. men proved compatible with those of the Danville's local interests, and their presence on the board caused little friction or deflection of purpose. Buford urged his stockholders to realize that S.R.S.C. wished only to form a mutually profitable partnership and did not want to exploit the Danville for purely selfish purposes:

In the Pennsylvania Railroad Company as your co-proprietor, you have a friend—not an enemy—identified by large interests with every movement in your history . . . a partner who has, and can have, no interest but that which is common to the smallest owner, the success, thrift and usefulness

---

[21] Nelson M. Blake, *William Mahone of Virginia* (Richmond, 1935), chaps. 4–5; Harrison, *Southern Railway*, 475–97. For more detail on the Pennsylvania's involvement in S.R.S.C., see Stover, *Railroads of the South*, chap. 6, and George H. Burgess and Miles C. Kennedy, *Centennial History of the Pennsylvania Railway Company* (Philadelphia, 1949), 279–81. A list of S.R.S.C. holdings in March, 1872, can be found in *Chronicle*, XIV (1872), 386, and a list of officers for 1873 in *ibid.*, XV (1872), 794.

[22] Calculated from the stockholders list for 1869 in the Virginia State Library, Richmond.

of your line of road, and the magnified prosperity of the communities and sections who use it.[23]

That friend was badly needed, especially after 1873. The Panic and its ensuing depression hit the Danville at a most inopportune time. The company had seriously extended itself in completing the Atlanta and Charlotte road, pushing construction on smaller feeder lines, and leasing the North Carolina. The Air-Line could hardly be expected to do much business in depression conditions and in fact succumbed to receivership in November, 1874. The North Carolina, plagued by litigation over the change of gauge, could not earn its rental and soon began losing heavily. Nor did the main stem escape unscathed. Increased competition precipitated by stagnating business conditions drove rates steadily downward. The opening of the Virginia Midland Railroad between Lynchburg and Danville in 1874 cut heavily into the company's local business there.[24]

Inevitably contraction of the money market saddled the company with a troublesome floating debt, as Table 4 suggests. Finding itself cramped for ready cash, the Danville sought relief from its proprietors. It received no sympathy from S.R.S.C., for the holding company had already decided to retrench. By 1873 it controlled thirteen major roads totaling 2,131 miles, few of which paid any dividends even before 1873. Feeling the pinch of contraction, S.R.S.C. began to dispose of its properties, selling off its last important holdings in 1876. Sale of these roads further weakened the Danville's competitive position. The Charlotte, Columbia & Augusta, once in new hands, immediately diverted through traffic from the Danville to the Wilmington, Columbia & Augusta.[25]

The dissolution of S.R.S.C. left only the Pennsylvania as a possible ally. That company's stockholders, too, had grown critical of the unprofitable southern program and demanded retrenchment. The Pennsylvania in 1873 charged off the entire southern investment to profit and loss, but it did not abandon the Danville. Taking over S.R.S.C.'s stock in the road, it relieved Buford's immediate financial burden by taking most of the Danville's floating debt

[23] *Danville Report*, 1874, 227. For more detail on S.R.S.C.'s policy-making role, see my "Southern Railroad Leaders," 299–301.

[24] *Danville Report*, 1874, 227–28; 1875, 324.

[25] *Ibid.*, 1878, 204–5; *Chronicle*, XXIII (1876), 576; *Railroad Gazette*, V (1873), 474–75, VIII (1876), 540. The list of roads controlled by S.R.S.C. can be found in Stover, *Railroads of the South*, 118.

at prices below the current market rates. By 1875 it had helped convert much of the short-term debt into permanent securities by taking $1,092,000 of the Danville's bonds at the price of 80 for the whole lot. Finally, the Pennsylvania canceled outright certain collateral obligations given it by the Danville for construction of the Atlanta-Charlotte line.[26]

Grateful for the Pennsylvania's support, Buford imposed a rigid austerity program upon the road. He slashed all salaries 10 per cent and eliminated all but the most necessary expenditures.

TABLE 4.   Richmond & Danville floating debt, 1867–1880

Year	Amount	Year	Amount
1867	$ 758,417	1874	$1,120,802
1868	173,870	1875	548,102
1869	121,907	1876	385,391
1870	229,374	1877	387,527
1871	353,458	1878	324,610
1872	573,343	1879	169,413
1873	1,100,830	1880	208,620

SOURCE: Calculated from *Annual Reports of the Richmond & Danville Railroad Company*, 1867–1880.

Slowly and erratically conditions improved. By the summer of 1876 the financial crisis had passed, and credit ceased to be a problem. The decline in earnings touched bottom in 1877 and would soon begin a period of steady growth. Creation of the Southern Railway & Steamship Association in 1875 helped alleviate the thorny rate problem, but the general competitive situation remained uncertain and potentially explosive. By the decade's end Buford had guided the Danville safely through a critical period to a position of prominence among southern roads. But the company's future direction had not yet been marked out. Much depended upon the inclinations of the Pennsylvania, whose directors were known to be willing to part with their last southern holding.

[26] *Danville Report*, 1874, 224–26; 1875, 329; 1876, 17; 1878, 213; *Railroad Gazette*, VI (1874), 91, 376; *Chronicle*, XVIII (1874), 14. Acceptance of the Danville's bonds at 80 would seem to have been a good deal for the company. The powerful Louisville & Nashville Railroad, a consistent dividend payer with total assets nearly four times those of the Danville, had to take slightly under 80 for bonds sold in 1874 (see *Annual Report of the Louisville & Nashville Railroad*, 1875, 6).

The Danville's future rested precariously in the hands of unknown parties with unfathomable ambitions.[27]

The East Tennessee, Virginia & Georgia

The strength and weakness of the East Tennessee lay in its peculiar isolation. Wedged in between the Clinch and Great Smoky Mountains, it traversed the narrow valley from Dalton, Georgia, to Bristol, Virginia, uncrossed by any other line—an advantage it would retain until the 1880's. The original line consisted of two separate companies, the 131-mile East Tennessee & Virginia between Bristol and Knoxville and the 111-mile East Tennessee & Georgia between Knoxville and Dalton. A 30-mile extension from Cleveland, Tennessee, completed the route into Chattanooga.

The very isolation of the valley region had prompted construction of the roads. Farmers and merchants eager to reach commercial outlets had commenced work from Knoxville south late in 1836. They hoped to connect with the projected system of roads in Georgia, but delays and financial difficulties postponed all work beyond grading for a dozen years. By 1848 the Western & Atlantic, Georgia, and Central of Georgia roads had been completed, and the Tennessee enterprise, aided by state funds, revived. To the north three Virginia roads forming a through route from Norfolk to Bristol offered an outlet to the sea if the gap between Knoxville and Bristol could be closed. That task became the work of the East Tennessee & Virginia Company, which enjoyed close relations with its southern connection from the beginning.[28]

By 1856 both Tennessee roads had been completed, and within a year the through line to Norfolk opened. The new markets for Tennessee produce in the Georgia cotton belt brought unaccustomed prosperity to the mountain valleys, although the heavy debt incurred by construction delayed the paying of dividends on the road itself. During the late 1850's both roads continued to develop their traffic. The onset of war thrust an intolerable load of business upon them. The line between Chattanooga and Norfolk constituted the most direct (and most exposed) route between the western Confederacy and the Virginia front. For two years the East

---

[27] *Danville Report*, 1874, 224; Dun & Bradstreet Reports, Virginia, XLV, 139.

[28] Phillips, *History of Transportation*, 372–75; James W. Holland, "The East Tennessee and Georgia Railroad, 1836–1860," *Publications of the East Tennessee Historical Society*, III (1931), 89–107; Harrison, *Southern Railway*, 641–63.

Tennessee roads did a flourishing business limited only by their lack of rolling stock. Then, in September, 1863, the Union army seized the East Tennessee & Virginia and severed the link. For the rest of the war both companies functioned under federal control.[29]

Not until August 28, 1865, did the reorganized companies receive their property from the federal government. The problems confronting the management seemed enormous. The roads had been run down, the rolling stock dilapidated, and equipment and supplies exhausted by federal use. The treasuries were empty and credit standings impaired. Unpaid interest on state and company bonds totaled $347,970 on the East Tennessee & Georgia alone. To begin operations the roads had to purchase their rolling stock back from the government, giving in exchange a two-year bond at 7.3 per cent interest. Attempts to offset this charge by claims against the government for war damages and usage led to prolonged litigation and compromise settlements.[30]

Despite these handicaps the roads resumed normal operations in a surprisingly short time. Earnings exceeded the most sanguine expectations although the heavy cost of rehabilitation severely reduced net income. The amazing recovery of the two companies owed much to its unique location. The East Tennessee remained a vital link in the most direct northeast-southwest rail route between Mobile and the Atlantic seaboard. The only alternative rail route east of Atlanta consisted of the meandering coastal line via Augusta, Charleston, and Wilmington. As long as these conditions prevailed the company could count upon reasonably steady growth, but significant changes were already in the wind. The East Tennessee roads depended heavily upon through traffic just when other companies were coming to realize its importance. The result would be increased competition, construction of new through lines, and consequently an important shift in existing traffic flows. Important decisions would have to be made about future strategy and development.

The leading figure in the two roads, Thomas Callaway, recog-

[29] Black, *Railroads of the Confederacy*, 68–70, 106, 225–26; *American Railroad Journal*, XL (1867), 25, 536–37.

[30] *American Railroad Journal*, XL (1867), 25, 536–37, XLII (1869), 1295; *Railroad Gazette*, V (1873), 114. See also Carl R. Fish, "The Restoration of Southern Railroads," *University of Wisconsin Studies in the Social Sciences and History*, No. 2 (Madison, Wis., 1919), 8–27, and *Annual Report of the East Tennessee, Virginia & Georgia Railroad*, 1870, 4. For resolutions and correspondence on the consolidation, see *Annual Report of the East Tennessee & Virginia Railroad*, 1869.

nized the potential menaces before him. A prominent businessman in eastern Tennessee, Callaway had been one of the original promoters of the East Tennessee & Georgia and served for a time as its president. After the war, he returned to the office and directed the road's restoration. Experience soon convinced him that consolidation of the companies was necessary for their survival. In 1868 he gained the presidency of both roads and within a year persuaded the two boards to unite their interests. On November 26, 1869, the two roads formally consolidated into the East Tennessee, Virginia & Georgia Railroad. Callaway assumed the presidency, but his health failed and he died less than a year later.[31]

His successor, Richard T. Wilson, had long been a close associate of Callaway. After the war he had gone to New York and founded the banking house of Wilson, Callaway & Company. He retained interests in East Tennessee, however, and as president relied heavily upon two cohorts, Charles M. McGhee and Joseph Jaques. When the state disposed of its 4,225 shares of East Tennessee & Georgia stock, Wilson and McGhee bought most of it and added holdings in the Virginia road as well. Once in control of the road they directed its policy for ten years.[32]

Wilson, McGhee, and Jaques did not maintain personal control over the road for very long. Sensing the power of the newly formed S.R.S.C. and the possibilities it offered for future development, the trio, acting on behalf of the holding company, arranged to sell 10,000 shares of East Tennessee, a majority, to the Pennsylvania. Later it would be charged that the three pocketed large personal profits by selling at par stock they had purchased for 30 to 60 cents on the dollar. In the process Wilson, McGhee, and Jaques all became stockholders in S.R.S.C. Wilson gained a seat on the board, and operating control of the East Tennessee remained in their hands. For that reason the change in ownership occasioned no important shift in management or policy.[33]

Like most of his peers, Wilson devoted much of his attention to the development of local resources. In his first year as president he stated the policy he would reiterate every year:

[31] *East Tennessee Report,* 1870, 4–5, 9–10; *Chronicle,* XI (1870), 338; *American Railroad Journal,* XLI (1868), 1283, XLII (1869), 288, 1399.

[32] Harrison, *Southern Railway,* 664–65; *Chronicle,* XI (1870), 401.

[33] *Chronicle,* XIII (1871), 604, XIV (1872), 386; *Railroad Gazette,* II (1870), 391, IV (1872), 506, V (1873), 244; *Stockholders Convention . . . Memphis & Charleston Railway,* 6. Prior to S.R.S.C. control, most of the East Tennessee stock resided in local hands (see "Southern Railroads," 96, 115).

It has been the intention and desire of the officers of your Road to foster and encourage the agricultural, manufacturing and mining interests of East Tennessee and to develop the resources of the Country in every particular. . . . We have been prompted to this course by a sense of justice, as well as by a knowledge of the fact that in the building up of East Tennessee the interest of your road is promoted. . . . We fully appreciate the fact that the interests of East Tennessee and the interest of your Company are inseparably connected.

The resources were there to be tapped. The mountain regions adjacent to the road contained rich deposits of iron, coal, copper and other ores, and marble. With considerable success Wilson helped attract capital into mining and quarry enterprises, building short feeder branches when necessary. At one point he hired a geologist to collect information on all available mineral resources and offered the findings to interested investors. He encouraged the growth of manufacturing as well, especially in finished iron products. In time he envisioned the rise of an integrated iron and steel industry and claimed that Bessemer pig could be produced as cheaply along the East Tennessee line as anywhere in the country.[34]

Returns from local traffic increased steadily but at a disappointingly slow pace. The need for immediate income drove Wilson to a careful consideration of the East Tennessee's position as a through line. The road's monopoly of the short route to the northeast had received two severe jolts. First, the three Virginia roads between Bristol and Norfolk had been consolidated by William Mahone in 1870 under the name Atlantic, Mississippi & Ohio. That should have greatly expedited the handling of through traffic, except that Mahone savagely opposed S.R.S.C. and Pennsylvania influence among southern roads. It was he who charged that Wilson, McGhee, and Jaques had profited unduly from the Pennsylvania transaction, and in November, 1872, he carried his fight to the East Tennessee's annual meeting in Knoxville. He had already offered to buy the company's entire stock at par. Few took his offer seriously, but no one doubted that he wanted the road. His attempt to unseat the managerial triumvirate met a decisive defeat, but his continued hostility rendered eastern connections unstable for several years.[35]

---

[34] *East Tennessee Report,* 1870, 14–15, 17; 1871, 10, 12–13, 16–17; 1873, 7–10; 1874, 23–24; 1878, 20–21; R. T. Wilson to Charles M. McGhee, August 7, 1878, McGhee papers.

[35] *Chronicle,* XV (1872), 659, 692; *Railroad Gazette,* IV (1872), 506; Blake, *William Mahone,* chaps. 4–5.

The second problem concerned the ambitious expansion of the Danville. Completion of the Atlanta-Charlotte road would end the East Tennessee's unchallenged supremacy as a northeast through line. The new Piedmont Air-Line into Richmond would be 123 miles shorter than the East Tennessee's precarious route into Norfolk. The two roads virtually paralleled each other on opposite sides of the Blue Ridge Mountains and would compete for overland through traffic east of Atlanta. The results of that competition could not be foreseen, but the prospects offered little encouragement to the East Tennessee. The Panic of 1873 helped cripple the efficiency of the new rival, but it also fomented a sharp competition for through traffic that tempted shippers to use more roundabout routes.[36]

Unwilling to rely solely upon the northeast route, Wilson and his colleagues sifted the alternatives. The company already possessed connections to the South Atlantic ports via the various Georgia roads. For through traffic, however, these roads were of little use and in fact harmed the East Tennessee by offering an alternative rail-water route for shippers on the southern portion of the road's line. Two roads, the Selma, Rome & Dalton and the Alabama & Chattanooga, furnished promising connections into the heart of Alabama and Tennessee. Both, however, suffered from financial anemia and soon went bankrupt. During the long and tangled litigation over foreclosure, Wilson could do little more than watch helplessly and bemoan the loss of business caused by the proceedings. In 1878 the court finally detached that part of the Selma road between Dalton and the Alabama state line and reorganized it as the Georgia Southern. Wilson hurried to buy controlling interest in the new company.[37]

To the west the East Tennessee drew traffic from the Memphis & Charleston Railroad running between Memphis and Stevenson, Alabama, near Chattanooga. This highly touted road, opened in 1858, had long been considered one of the South's premier arteries. It served as a natural feeder from its Mississippi River terminus to both through routes converging at Chattanooga: the northeast all-rail route via the East Tennessee or the southeast rail-water route via the Georgia roads and coastal steamers. Despite the strategic location, however, it never lived up to expectations. War damage,

[36] For Wilson's complaint over heightened competition, see *East Tennessee Report*, 1873, 7–8.

[37] *Ibid.*, 1870, 15–16; 1873, 7; 1874, 10; 1878, 13–14; Harrison, *Southern Railway*, 775–811. The Alabama & Chattanooga connected Chattanooga with Meridian, Mississippi.

newly built competitors, and frequent sieges of yellow fever at Memphis all marred its earning capacity.[38]

Nevertheless, the East Tennessee management considered the Memphis road an indispensable connection. In March, 1872, S.R.S.C. leased the road and thus assured its cooperation with the East Tennessee, but the arrangement scarcely lasted two years. The Memphis & Charleston could not pay its way, and the retrenchment policies adopted by S.R.S.C. after 1873 caused the holding company to seek some way out of the lease. On April 30, 1874, it succeeded in canceling the lease, and the burden of decision fell upon the East Tennessee. Wilson and his friends controlled enough securities to retain control of the Memphis & Charleston management, but the arrangement left them uneasy. In 1877, somewhat reluctantly, he persuaded the East Tennessee board to lease the road for twenty years. By then the line had accrued a deficit of $344,191 and still required heavy expenditures for improvements. Wilson admitted candidly to his stockholders that "it will not be a source of any direct profit to your Company," but he saw no feasible alternative.[39]

Two other closely related projects also attracted Wilson's attention. The first involved construction northward from Knoxville to the Kentucky state line to meet a proposed extension of the Louisville & Nashville's Lebanon branch. The second concerned the building of two alternative roads southeast of Knoxville, one through South Carolina to Charleston and the other into North Carolina via the long-delayed Western North Carolina Railroad. Completion of these projects would fulfill a dream of long standing: the creation of a through line from Louisville or Cincinnati to Charleston.[40]

To the northern project Wilson offered profuse encouragement but no direct aid. The Knoxville & Kentucky Railroad, with state aid, reached Caryville, 39 miles from Knoxville, in 1869 before de-

[38] *Chronicle,* III (1866), 486–87; *Report of the Chief Engineer of the Memphis & Charleston Railroad Company,* Jan. 15, 1851, Baker Library; *Annual Reports of the Memphis & Charleston Railroad,* 1866–70, *passim.*

[39] *Chronicle,* XIII (1871), 808, XV (1872), 353–54, XVII (1873), 380, XVIII (1874), 297, 376, 488, XXV (1877), 255; *East Tennessee Report,* 1877, 4, 11–12; 1879, 7–11, 17–20; Harrison, *Southern Railway,* 751–56. The Memphis & Charleston actually agreed to the lease to avoid bankruptcy. For details, see Stuart Daggett, *Railroad Reorganization* (Cambridge, Mass., 1908), 148–49.

[40] For early efforts to complete this line, see Phillips, *History of Transportation,* 168–220, 375–80. For background of the Knoxville & Ohio, see Harrison, *Southern Railway,* 861–75.

faulting on its state bonds. Reorganized in 1871 as the Knoxville & Ohio, the company made no further progress, and the L. & N. refused to press its work without some guarantee that the southern link would be finished. By 1873, however, the project of constructing an independent road south from Cincinnati had revived. Wilson and McGhee journeyed to Cincinnati to discuss the project, and the board passed resolutions to encourage it, but ultimately the city chose instead to build directly to Chattanooga.[41]

Progress to the south proved no less frustrating. Here Wilson chose to take a more active role. In 1872 he purchased the 39-mile Cincinnati, Cumberland Gap & Charleston Railroad (thereafter known as the Morristown branch) and a controlling interest in the Western North Carolina Railroad. He planned to extend the Morristown road to Asheville, where it would meet the yet unfinished Western North Carolina and provide access to both the Carolinas. Completion of the Spartanburg & Union Railroad would carry the line another major step toward Charleston, and the prospect of this network might in turn entice the Cincinnati Southern to build to Knoxville. It also promised new markets for Tennessee produce, coal, and other products.[42]

Wilson's efforts to reorganize the Western North Carolina met strong resistance from a minority of his own stockholders. Resentful of expansion policy in general and S.R.S.C. control in particular, they filed suit to prevent use of East Tennessee funds in another state. When the Tennessee Supreme Court upheld their complaint, Wilson tried to get the North Carolina Railroad to absorb the Western and complete construction. With Buford's approval the North Carolina consented and tried to obtain the necessary legislation. Unfortunately the destiny of the Western and the state's huge investment in it had become a fiercely controversial issue in North Carolina politics. The proposal to consolidate the North Carolina and the Western North Carolina touched off a furious debate.[43]

On December 23, 1873, the consolidation act passed the legisla-

[41] *East Tennessee Report,* 1870, 18; 1873, 8, 11; 1874, 4; Poor, *Manual for 1891,* 147, 198; *Louisville & Nashville Reports,* 1866, 47–50; 1869, 6–7; 1873, 10. For the Cincinnati project, see E. M. Coulter, *The Cincinnati Southern and the Struggle for Southern Commerce, 1865–1872* (Chicago, 1922), and Charles Hall (ed.), *The Cincinnati Southern Railway* (Cincinnati, 1902).

[42] *East Tennessee Report* 1870, 18; 1873, 8; 1874, 10–11; *Railroad Gazette,* V (1873), 114.

[43] A detailed account of the complex Western episode and the Danville role in it can be found in Brown, *State Movement,* 188–226.

ture, only to be enjoined by certain bondholders. The tortuous lit-igation that followed prevented the North Carolina from making any progress on the road and threw Wilson and Buford into de-spair. Finally, in June, 1875, the road went up for sale and was re-purchased by the state. Wilson relinquished his equity holdings to the state but kept a sizable number of Western bonds. The state agreed to push construction to Paint Rock, where it would join the extended Morristown branch. But the rugged terrain rendered progress painfully slow, and the road did not even reach Asheville by the end of the decade.[44]

In plotting the East Tennessee's expansion Wilson had proved a cautious tactician. He offered hearty encouragement to any worth-while project, and the board cheerfully passed resolutions to that effect, but he was slow to commit the company to any major outlay of funds. Indeed his entire financial policy had been conservative. After extinguishing the state debt in 1870 he issued few new bonds, increasing the company's funded debt from $3,581,400 in 1871 to only $4,186,000 in 1880. At the same time he took great pride in keeping the floating debt consistently low, thereby avoid-ing any ill effects from the tight money market in 1873. After 1873 he paid regular dividends except in 1877, but he kept them low and diverted most of the earnings into improvements and other fin-ancial needs. To those stockholders clamoring for larger dividends he replied that "time will show that it was a wise policy to apply the income to the improvement of your property instead of divid-ing it. . . . There can be no question . . . about the expediency of continuing the expenditure of money as rapidly as our finances will permit, and thus sustain its character as a first-class road." Throughout most of the 1870's East Tennessee bonds commanded prices between 90 and 100.[45]

Not everyone applauded Wilson's policies. The fight over the Western North Carolina revealed one circle of hostile critics, and they were not alone. Wilson's cautious approach had preserved the company during a trying period, but he had failed to define clearly the company's strategy for the future. While the development of

[44] *Ibid.*, 216–26; *East Tennessee Report,* 1876, 11; 1877, 11–12; *Railroad Gazette,* VII (1875) , 389; Harrison, *Southern Railway,* 258–95.

[45] *East Tennessee Report,* 1870, 12–14; 1873, 5, 13–15, 20; 1874, 8–9, 17; 1876, 9; 1877, 6, 9–10; 1878, 11–13; 1879, 15–16; *Chronicle,* XXI (1875) , 275. For complete debt figures, see Appendix III. For movement of the company's stock and praise of its strength, see Dun & Bradstreet Reports, Tennessee, XVIII, 20, 142.

local resources proceeded nicely, the road's future as a through line remained as ambiguous as ever. Except for the bleeding Memphis & Charleston and the Georgia Southern, Wilson's expansion efforts had produced no tangible results. The East Tennessee still depended upon its somewhat unstable northeastern connection and had done little either to ensure its connection or to seize alternative routes capable of competing for traffic hitherto beyond its reach.

And competitors were not standing still. Ambitious new through lines blossomed all around the East Tennessee. Even though the depression had lifted, the struggle for through traffic would get worse instead of better. Rates declined relentlessly beneath increased competitive pressures and the advent of state regulation. Despite its apparent financial healthiness, the East Tennessee's earning power had stagnated. Gross earnings had peaked in 1873 and declined steadily thereafter. Not once after 1875 did gross earnings equal those of 1869, the first year of consolidated management.[46]

Wilson could ill afford to sit idle, and he well knew it. The close of the decade found him casting hopefully about for a workable strategy that would give the East Tennessee new direction. Inevitably that strategy would involve further expansion.

The Central of Georgia

During the ante-bellum years the Central enjoyed a reputation as one of the strongest and most prosperous roads in the South.[47] Its origins derived from the desire of Georgians to funnel the state's commerce through the port of Savannah and especially to prevent the new Charleston & Hamburg Railroad from directing traffic eastward through Augusta to Charleston. The Central was but one of several projected roads designed to provide the state with an efficient transportation system. Chartered in 1833, it struggled through the depression years after 1837 to complete its main line by 1843. A thriving business came immediately to the new line. Within a decade it became the strongest corporation in the state and paid consistently high dividends ranging from 5 to 15 per

[46] See the figures in Appendix III.

[47] The origins and early development of the Central are splendidly treated in Phillips, *History of Transportation*, chap. 6. The account given here, unless otherwise indicated, is drawn from Phillips.

cent. It possessed unquestioned credit, and its stock was considered the best and safest investment in the state. Both of the Central prewar presidents, William W. Gordon and R. R. Cuyler, were men of unusual ability who gave the company excellent administration. One enthusiastic observer labeled it the "best managed road in the world." [48]

The Central's main line, designed to embrace a maximum of local business with the gentlest possible grades, swept a graceful arc from Savannah to Macon. It achieved northern connections via the Macon & Western (completed in 1846) into Atlanta and the state-owned Western & Atlantic (completed in 1851) to Chattanooga. The Southwestern Railroad from Macon to Albany, with branches projected westward to Columbus and Eufaula, Alabama, on the Chattahoochee River, gave the Central access to the rich cotton counties southwest of Macon. Only one line, the powerful and well-managed Georgia Railroad (completed in 1837) between Atlanta and Augusta, competed directly with the Central. The two roads paralleled each other for nearly 100 miles at a distance of only 40 to 50 miles apart. Competition for the local business in the region between the roadbeds naturally produced sparks, and the attempt by either company to build feeder lines aroused vehement protest from the other. Both vied for southbound through traffic from the Western & Atlantic at Atlanta, with the Georgia apparently having the upper hand.

Mindful of the Georgia's strength, President Cuyler concentrated upon developing the region south and west of Macon for the Central. As the company grew richer he found it possible to pay the usual dividends, maintain the road in top condition, and still contribute heavily to other projects. Believing firmly that a region should not build more railroads than it could support, his strategy was to monopolize for the Central the territory bound by the Georgia Railroad to the north and the Chattahoochee River on the west. To that end he persuaded his board to subsidize construction of those feeder lines deemed necessary to render this territory tributary to Savannah.[49]

In systematic fashion the Central pursued this policy. It contributed a total of $327,300 to the Southwestern and, together with the

[48] Dun & Bradstreet Reports, Georgia, XXVIII, 161. Phillips, *History of Transportation,* 263, notes that the road cost only $13,000 per mile to build, about half that of most roads in the United States.

[49] Cuyler's strategy is clearly explicated in the *Annual Reports of the Central of Georgia Railroad & Banking Company,* 1843–60, *passim.*

city of Savannah, proved decisive in the completion of that line. Realizing the road's pivotal importance to the Central, Cuyler further unified the interests of the two companies by becoming president of the Southwestern in 1855. In that position he encouraged construction of the branch to Columbus on the Chattahoochee. Beyond the river he funneled Central money into two connecting roads, the Montgomery & West Point and the Mobile & Girard. On the Central's main line he aided various smaller branches. Despite opposition from the Georgia and certain Augusta businessmen, Cuyler helped build a 54-mile road from the Central's Millen depot to Augusta and immediately leased it to the Central. To ensure water connections with New York he brought five steamships under company control.[50]

Cuyler's territorial strategy had its defensive aspects as well. In the fight for through traffic the Georgia gained valuable ground in 1853 when it finally bridged the Savannah River and connected with the road to Charleston.[51] The duel for local traffic had lost none of its intensity by the 1850's, when the Georgia threatened to upset the prevailing delicate balance by building a road from Warrenton on its main line to Macon. Such an extension would cut deeply into the Central's local traffic and could divert some through business from Savannah to Augusta and Charleston. Outraged by the proposed "invasion" Cuyler thundered against it in his annual reports. When the Georgia formally committed itself to the project in 1860, Cuyler took up the challenge:

This Board cannot view with indifference the renewed hostility manifested towards the Central of Georgia Road, and must, ere long, put forth such power as it may possess to counteract the mischief of a road leading direct from Macon to Warrenton. . . . This Company earnestly desires to avoid all disturbance of the general railroad system, built up by the people of Georgia at so great cost; and with that view, to forego the building of lines to connect the Central with the Georgia Road, but if we are to be disturbed . . . it will become our duty, in self defense, to augment our revenues by lines from Eatonton to Madison, and from Davisboro, by Sparta to Union Point, designed by a system of low rates, to draw produce from the whole interior *directly* to Savannah, and to carry return merchandise directly from Savannah to the interior.[52]

[50] *Ibid.*, 1859, 126–27. A list of the Central's investments in other companies by 1859 can be found in *ibid.*, 1859, 136.

[51] See Phillips, *History of Transportation*, 162–63, 207–8, 216. For background on the Georgia Railroad, see *ibid.*, chap. 5.

[52] *Central Report*, 1860, 163–65. See also *ibid.*, 1856, 52–55.

The Georgia did not constitute the only threat. New railroad projects, most of them in south Georgia, threatened the territories of both older companies. Promoters of these roads drew much of their strength from shippers who resented the high local tariffs of the older lines. To help finance their projects they petitioned the legislature for state aid. The thought of the state lending its support to a rival road infuriated Cuyler. He argued that the Central, Georgia, Western & Atlantic, and the roads west of Atlanta with all their branches gave the state a near-perfect rail system. Bluntly he accused the state of betraying its trust:

The policy . . . was for the State to build part, and the private Companies part of a great Railroad line from the north-western section of Georgia to the south-eastern section at Savannah . . . and also lines to Columbus and Augusta, uniting with the navigable streams which bound the State on the west and on the east . . . thus was begun and established the basis of a *Railroad system* for Georgia. . . . It may well be asked if the Companies between Savannah and Atlanta, and between Augusta and Atlanta, would have been able to accomplish their work if it had been imagined that the State would ever in coming time, grant aid to build railroads as rivals or competitors with their lines. And it may truly be answered that they never could.[53]

The most dangerous proposal, construction of a road from Macon to the port of Brunswick, became an issue on which the feuding Central and Georgia could unite. The projected road would split the inverted bowl formed by the Central and Southwestern lines right down the middle. It could seriously injure the Central's local business and threaten the through traffic of both companies. As the two strongest corporations in the state the Central and Georgia wielded considerable political power, and they used all their influence to block passage of any aid bill. Largely because of their efforts no such measure passed the legislature during the 1850's.

Then came the war. Although old problems did not disappear, they were submerged beneath the pressures of military necessity. Like other southern roads the Central depreciated steadily under the strain. It could not replace worn equipment, its shops were diverted to making gun carriages and other ordnance materiel, and part of its rolling stock had to be sold to other lines. The worst blow came in 1864 when Sherman's advancing army left much of

[53] *Ibid.*, 1857, 77–80. See also the *Reports* for 1858–60.

the Central's main line in total ruin. By December, 1865, the re-organizing company could assess its loss. Much of the roadway had been devastated, along with bridges, depots, water tanks, pumps, and other equipment. Most of the locomotives had been run off or crippled by both armies, and rolling stock was scattered all over the Confederacy. The shops and other buildings suffered heavy damage, and many of the company's records had been destroyed in the hasty evacuation of Savannah.[54] Cuyler himself had died during the year, leaving the company leaderless.

Under a pall of gloom and pessimism the board elected as new president William M. Wadley, former superintendent of the line. The problems confronting him were many and difficult. Foremost among them, of course, was restoration of the road, and to do that he had to find capital. For a start Wadley had $337,028 received in settlement for the steamships owned by the Central. These had been sold in 1862 and the money retained in London.[55] To meet immediate needs Wadley negotiated the sale of slightly over $700,000 in mortgage bonds at 85. He used short-term notes to purchase rails and other equipment in New York and England. With relentless energy he drove the work forward. The vigor and competence of his management quickly restored confidence in the company's securities. On June 12, 1866, the main line finally resumed operations along its entire length. Wadley estimated the cost of rehabilitation at between one and two million dollars. The rolling stock remained dilapidated, the motive power inadequate, and the roadbed and equipment shabby, but these could be improved gradually.[56]

Once past immediate needs Wadley faced the difficult task of formulating strategy. The aftermath of war had wrought significant changes in the Central's position. Though still the most

[54] *Central Report*, Dec. 1, 1865, 273–80; Black, *Railroads of the Confederacy*, 60, 88–90, 125–27, 132–33, 252, 259–60, 269, 290–91.

[55] *Central Report*, 1862, 220–21; Dec. 4, 1866, 309–10. Stover, *Railroads of the South*, 53, quoting Robert Somers, credits the Central with investing large portions of its earnings in London. I can find no evidence to support this claim. Most likely he confused the steamship sale money with the reserved earnings.

[56] *Central Report*, March 1, 1866, 288–96; Dec. 4, 1866, 303–6; "Southern Railroads," 40. Stover, *Railroads of the South*, 53, suggests that the Central's vigorous recovery was due in part to its connection with the bank. This may be doubted, for the Central's bank lacked sufficient capital and had nearly $600,000 in outstanding notes to redeem. For its difficulties, see *Central Report*, Dec. 4, 1866, 307, 311.

powerful corporation in Georgia, it no longer wielded its former influence. In the turmoil of reconstruction politics the Central's voice in legislative affairs lost its authority. Specifically it could no longer bar the construction of new roads. Despite extensive lobbying by the Central and other roads, the legislature in December, 1866, agreed to endorse the bonds of the Macon & Brunswick. By 1872 it had endorsed the bonds of six other roads, at least half of which threatened to alter the Central's existing flow of traffic. In addition, the vital through artery to the north, the state-owned Western & Atlantic, fell victim to the Republican regime of Governor Rufus Bullock. After 1868 corruption and mismanagement marred operation of the road.[57]

The flowering of new competition came at a most unfortunate time for the older roads. Local business remained depressed until the state's exhausted economy could recover. Reduced business coupled with the financial burden of rehabilitation made it more difficult than ever for the carriers to earn a profit. They hoped to recoup some of their losses through higher rates, but the construction of rival lines forced a decline in rates and division of an already inadequate traffic. The need for increased revenues compelled managers to seek more through traffic to augment local income, and that in turn drew them into an even more fiercely competitive situation aggravated by the uncertainties of existing connections.

Wadley's response to these problems was both prompt and predictable. His basic goals and attitude differed little from those of Cuyler, from whom he doubtless inherited some of his ideas. He wished to preserve for the Central control of the territory rightfully belonging to it. Unlike his predecessor, he could no longer fend off the encroachers who sought to preempt the Central's through and local business. Perceiving that he confronted two different threats, he evolved a strategy to fit each one. At the local level he would continue the traditional policy of developing local resources. He would also provide superior service by maintaining the road in first-class condition, keeping rates as low as practicable, and offering special inducements like the bargain rate on fertilizer introduced by Cuyler in 1858 to foster increased productiveness.[58]

---

[57] For the general picture of Georgia railroads during Reconstruction, see C. Mildred Thompson, *Reconstruction in Georgia, 1865–1872* (New York, 1915), 229–54, 310–24, and Stover, *Railroads of the South*, 79–88. For background of the Macon & Brunswick, see Harrison, *Southern Railway*, 834–47.

[58] *Central Report*, 1858, 102–3.

When necessary he would build new feeder lines into untapped regions to prevent rivals from doing so. As early as 1866 he warned his stockholders of the contest to come:

We should fail in our duty were we to ignore the construction of other lines, that seek to divide the business now passing over yours. The policy of building competing lines of Railway, when *one* is capable of doing promptly all the business offering, we regard as mischievous. . . . Notwithstanding our view of the effect of opposition lines, we presume they will nevertheless be built; and it, therefore, behooves you to prepare for the contest should it come. One of the most important matters to be attended to then, is the condition of your Road.[59]

The through traffic situation involved problems of greater complexity and magnitude. Prior to the war the Central had enjoyed a role as one of the prime rail-water routes. Eastbound through traffic converging at Chattanooga could either take the all-rail route via the East Tennessee roads or choose between the rail-water routes over the Western & Atlantic to Savannah via the Macon & Western and Central or to Charleston via the Georgia and South Carolina roads. Traffic could also move, of course, down the Mississippi to New Orleans or southward to Mobile via the Mobile & Ohio. In the years after the war, however, the increasing importance of through traffic spurred the completion of new lines along both trade axes. These included the Danville's line from Atlanta to Richmond, an alternative Atlanta-Richmond route via Augusta, Columbia, and Wilmington, completion of a route (composed of several companies) from Louisville to Mobile and New Orleans, and completion of a similar line from Cairo, Illinois, to New Orleans. Other companies, notably the Chesapeake & Ohio, were hurrying construction to join in the fight for through business.[60]

As these new competitive conditions unfolded before Wadley's eyes, the weakness of the Central's position alarmed him. Despite the diversity of securities in other roads held by his company, vital connections to the north and west of Macon remained tenuous. Control over the Savannah-based steamships, a vital link in the Central's through traffic, had been lost. Conditions north of At-

[59] *Ibid.*, Dec. 4, 1866, 308–9. One short line involved a connection to the Central's wharfs for Wadley's own sawmill company (see *ibid.*, 1874, 13–14).

[60] An incomplete listing of through routes and the companies embraced in them can be found in Harrison, *Southern Railway*, 15–18. See also chap. I above.

lanta promised to be uncertain as long as the state road remained a political football. And when its status finally changed, who would gain control of it? West of Atlanta a series of roads had finally reached New Orleans, but the Georgia controlled the crucial Atlanta & West Point Railroad. Beyond the Chattahoochee the Central's bid for the business of south Alabama could only be termed ephemeral and incomplete.

To preserve the Central's territorial integrity and protect the primacy of Savannah, Wadley resolved upon a policy of expansion. He began in 1869 by leasing the Southwestern on terms that would later provoke controversy within the Central. To secure this invaluable road he agreed to pay Southwestern holders an 8 per cent dividend for every 10 per cent declared for Central stockholders and a minimum 7 per cent dividend whether the Central declared one for itself or not. The lease would last indefinitely, and the Central would pay all fixed and current charges on the Southwestern.[61] Two years later he solidified entrance into Atlanta by leasing the Central's northern connector, the Macon & Western. Control of that road brought with it a majority interest in the Savannah, Griffin & North Alabama Railroad, soon to be completed from Griffin to Carrollton. Opponents of the Central attempted to block the lease, but Wadley carried the case to the supreme court and won.[62]

With his northern connection secure Wadley took up the water problem. It seemed essential to him that the Central own its steamships if it wished reliable sea connections. Accordingly, in 1872 he purchased six steamers plying the coastal route to New York. In explaining the acquisition he stressed the urgency of establishing the Central's position in the quest for through traffic:

New York is, and will continue to be, the great commercial centre of the country. This being recognized, and the fact that there are numerous land routes from the South and Southwest terminating at New York, the question to be settled is whether an all rail or rail and ocean transportation is the cheapest. This contest is upon us, and without the absolute control of ships, it would be quite out of our power to make the issue, which it is believed, must ultimately be decided in our favor.

[61] For the provisions in detail, see *Central Report,* 1869, 7–10.
[62] *Ibid.,* 1871, 7; *Chronicle,* XII (1871), 721, XVIII (1874), 374. For background on the Macon & Western, see Phillips, *History of Transportation,* 264–72, 296–302, and Thompson, *Reconstruction in Georgia,* 314–15.

That the Central's charter did not permit it to own ships directly did not deter Wadley. In 1875 he created an independent corporation, the Ocean Steamship Company, with himself as president and other Central directors as officers. The Central transferred its ships to Ocean in exchange for $795,000 of Ocean's $800,000 stock, which then became an asset of the parent company.[63]

Western expansion proved more difficult. Anxious for the Central to plant itself firmly in eastern Alabama, Wadley was forced to extend himself further than he wished. The key road proved to be the Western Railroad of Alabama, an 1870 consolidation of the Montgomery & West Point and Western of Alabama companies. The main line from Montgomery to West Point, completed in 1856, drew traffic eastward to Atlanta. The branch between Selma and Montgomery (opened in 1870) furnished the last link in a through line east from Vicksburg. Another branch from Opelika to Columbus, Georgia (opened in 1854), offered connections to the Southwestern's Columbus branch. The Western's strategic location made it a valuable feeder for the Georgia, South Carolina, and Central, and all three roads had been interested in it before the war. Despite the merger, however, the Western failed consistently to pay its way. Unable to withstand the Panic of 1873, it defaulted quickly and headed toward receivership.[64]

Mindful of the Western's sensitive location, Wadley had for some time been trying to get the Georgia and South Carolina roads to help him sustain its solvency. The Georgia's president, John P. King, proved amenable, but the financially weak South Carolina refused to commit itself. King joined Wadley on the Western's board in 1873, and both began acquiring the road's bonds in anticipation of a default. After lengthy negotiations the two presidents agreed to purchase the road at foreclosure sale and operate it jointly. On April 19, 1875, Wadley and Georgia's vice-president James Davies obtained the road for $3,286,257. The expensive investment provoked bitter criticism within King's board and resulted in an injunction. After a heated contest at the Georgia's annual meeting the sale was confirmed on May 26. By agreement the Central would control the Columbus to Opelika route,

---

[63] *Central Report*, 1872, 7–8; 1873, 11–12; 1874, 7; *Chronicle*, XVIII (1874), 459; Catherwood (ed.), *Wadley*, 11. One authority notes that the rail-water route remained predominant until 1886 (Joubert, *Southern Freight Rates*, 69).

[64] Henry V. Poor, *Manual of the Railroads of the United States for 1874–75* (New York, 1875), 143–44.

the Georgia would have the West Point-to-Opelika line, and the remaining portion from Opelika to Selma would be shared. To manage the Western, Wadley brought in the brilliant and talented E. Porter Alexander, a man destined to loom large in the Central's future affairs.[65]

Possession of the Western gave the Central an important foothold in Alabama. To supplement it Wadley acquired as feeder lines the Vicksburg & Brunswick and Montgomery & Eufaula. He tightened the Central's grip on the Mobile & Girard and extended the Southwestern deeper into western Georgia to meet the Central's Alabama roads across the river. He admitted the branches would not be profitable in themselves but justified their cost by the business they would bring to the main line.[66]

In all his expansion activities Wadley's tactics were obviously defensive. He wished not to expand but to protect. To that end he savagely fought construction of state-supported roads. In 1869 he joined other roads in an unsuccessful injunction to block completion of the Brunswick & Albany. Though he could not stop the Macon & Brunswick, he reduced it to a local road by his leasing of the Macon & Western. When the Macon & Brunswick went bankrupt in 1873 its president blamed the failure upon the road's being completely blocked at Macon. Later Wadley tried to purchase both the Brunswick & Albany and Macon & Brunswick, but his efforts were invalidated under a section of the new state constitution of 1877 that prohibited the legislature from authorizing any corporation to "buy shares, or stock, in any corporation in this state, or elsewhere, or to make any contract, or agreement whatever, with any such corporation which may . . . defeat or lessen competition, or to encourage monopoly." [67]

Despite the constitutional restrictions Wadley got much of what he wanted. The Panic of 1873 with its avalanche of receiverships and cutthroat rate wars redoubled his efforts to protect the Cen-

[65] *Central Report*, 1869, 11–12; 1874, 9; 1875, 8–9; Mary G. Cumming, *The Georgia Railroad and Banking Company, 1833–1945* (Augusta, Ga., 1945), 84–85; Henry V. Poor, *Manual of the Railroads of the United States for 1876–77* (New York, 1877), 359; *Railroad Gazette*, V (1873), 515, VI (1874), 145, VII (1875), 57, 167, 188, 231, 236, 360, 388; *Chronicle*, XVIII (1874), 456, XX (1875), 398; Alexander Lawton to E. P. Alexander, April 10, 1875, Edward Porter Alexander papers, Southern Historical Collection.

[66] *Central Report*, 1871, 9–10; 1879, 7–8; *Chronicle*, XVIII (1874), 374, XXIII (1876), 549.

[67] *Central Report*, 1878, 7; *Railroad Gazette*, X (1878), 278, 566; *Chronicle*, IX (1867), 300, XIV (1872), 422, XX (1875), 130, 501, XXII (1876), 304.

tral. He had acquired the Western partly because he feared it might fall into the hands of a dangerous rival such as the Louisville & Nashville, which had begun to penetrate Alabama from the north. In procuring the Montgomery & Eufaula he paid more than the road was worth in order to outbid the L. & N. His justification of that expensive purchase bore an unmistakably defensive stamp: "That road is so situated that if in the hands of parties whose interests were in antagonism with this company our interest could not fail to suffer seriously." [68] In a similar vein he approved every attempt to ameliorate the constant slashing of rates and threw his full support behind the work of the Southern Railway & Steamship Association.

Inevitably, Wadley's expansion policy brought with it a sharp increase in the Central's obligations. The funded debt, which had been only $786,000 in 1869 when the Southwestern was leased, rose to $3,617,000 by 1879. The change in debt position alone did not offer an accurate picture of the Central's obligations because of Wadley's expansion techniques. Leases, bond endorsements, and even the purchase of securities in other roads would not be directly reflected in the funded debt. In addition to its own bonds the Central had by 1874 assumed liability as endorser for $1,492,500 in the bonds of other roads. But the price of growth revealed itself most clearly in the company's total payment for interest and rentals on leased roads. In 1869 that figure had been $141,943; by 1879 it reached $712,040.[69]

To provide for these spiraling costs Wadley retrenched with ruthless efficiency. Spartan in his own habits and dedicated to the Central's long-term welfare, he expected directors and stockholders alike to follow suit. Since 1867 he had cheerfully paid dividends of 10 and 12 per cent. Feeling the pinch of the company's extended obligations, he declared no dividend in 1873 and only 4 per cent in 1874. After that he paid nothing for five years except 2.5 per cent in 1878. By devoting all earnings to betterments and obligations he maintained an impeccable credit standing during the harsh depression years and despite his expensive acquisitions. But the stock suffered dearly. At one time before the Panic it had reached 130; the curtailment of dividends, however, drove it steadily downward

[68] *Central Report*, 1872, 15; 1873, 22; 1879, 7; *Chronicle*, XXIII (1876), 498, XXV (1877), 430; *Louisville & Nashville Report*, 1873, 10–12; 1876, 12; *American Railroad Journal*, LII (1879), 381–82.

[69] Poor, *Manual for 1881*, 401–3; *Central Report*, 1873, 10–11. For the figures, see Appendix V.

to a low of 32 in March, 1877. On the same date Central bonds were being quoted at par.[70]

As might be expected, Wadley's financial policies did not draw applause from all his directors and holders. Nor did his dictatorial methods win him friends even among his supporters. Those who objected to his personal domination of company affairs he dismissed with imperious disdain and an ill-concealed temper. Edward C. Anderson, a long-time supporter of the president, recorded his disgust at a typical convening of the Ocean Steamship Board: "the meeting was a farce as all the business we had been called together to transact had been decided and acted upon beforehand by Wadley." On another occasion he noted with relish that "the meeting of the Directors . . . today knocked the conceit out of Wadley." [71]

The personality conflict inflamed natural divisions over policy. The high cost of expansion manifested itself most glaringly in the Southwestern lease as stockholders of that road continued to receive their guaranteed dividend while Central holders went hungry. Resentment over dividend policy brought severe clashes within the management and in 1875 led to the successful ouster of two dissident directors.[72] Part of the trouble lay in the changing ownership of Central stock. From the beginning Central stock had the reputation of being widely scattered and tightly held, with much of it belonging to small investors. While this condition continued to prevail, a small but significant change had begun to take place. The renowned New York merchant Moses Taylor, who had served as trustee for the Central's bond issue in 1866, became the company's largest single stockholder and joined the board in 1874. William Garrison of New York, who had sold the steamships to Wadley and served as agent for Ocean, also moved onto the board that year. Other prominent bankers such as D. Willis James and Junius S. Morgan acquired sizable blocks of the stock, which was not listed on the New York Exchange but had to be bought and sold mostly in Savannah. The presence of Taylor caused Wadley little uneasiness, for he steadfastly supported the president's pol-

[70] *Chronicle,* XVII (1873), 834, XXVII (1878), 382; Dun & Bradstreet Reports, Georgia, XXVIII, 160–61. The stock and bond prices for this entire period have been culled from the Dun & Bradstreet reports and from various issues of the *Chronicle.* For the quotations given here, see *Chronicle,* XXIV (1877), 201.

[71] Edward C. Anderson Diary, March 14 and Sept. 22, 1877, Edward C. Anderson papers, Southern Historical Collection.

[72] *Ibid.,* Dec. 30, 1874, Jan. 2, and Jan. 4, 1875.

icies. But the gradual coalescing of the Central's stock into significant blocks could be dangerous should organized and determined opposition arise.[73]

By 1879 the Central seemed fixed in an economic environment quite unlike that envisioned at the close of the war. The effects of rehabilitation, depression and financial stringency, proliferating competition, declining rates, political turmoil, and a growing public hostility to the railroads had all conspired to make the goals of prosperity, stability, and territorial integrity more elusive than ever. In the quest for these goals Wadley had nearly exhausted his prodigious energy. Now sixty-six years old, his leonine mane heavily streaked with grey and his craggy features etched with worry and fatigue, the former blacksmith was a sick man. The battles grew daily more difficult to fight and the victories fewer and smaller.

But he could find no rest. The Central was his life, and he would not quit. As the decade closed the company retained its reputation as one of the South's wealthiest corporations and the stock had climbed back to 72. New prospects and fresh dangers clamored for his attention. Within the company his adversaries hatched new schemes to bring him to bay and were rumored to be soliciting the support of New York financiers. Outside the company ambitious rivals, especially the powerful L. & N., were seeking entrance into Georgia. It was known for certain that L. & N. interests had begun to buy Central stock.[74]

The most pressing business of all, however, concerned the Nashville, Chattanooga & St. Louis Railroad and its colorful president, Edwin "King" Cole. At a hastily summoned board meeting on January 5, 1880, Wadley informed his directors that Cole had offered to lease the Central for twenty years, with a guaranteed dividend of 6 per cent for the first seven years and 7 per cent thereafter. The startled directors seemed in favor of accepting, and Wadley so notified Cole. For the first time in its history the Central appeared destined to become merely a part of a larger system.[75]

---

[73] *Central Report,* 1866, 288–89; 1874, 95, 99, 103; and 1879, 101–2; "Southern Railroads," 39–43. In 1879 Taylor held 4,020 shares, while Wadley himself owned only 75. For stockholder lists, see the *Central Reports* for 1873–81.

[74] Dun & Bradstreet Reports, Georgia, XXIX, 542, 668; Savannah *Morning News,* Feb. 24, 1880.

[75] Anderson Diary, Jan. 5, 1880; *Railroad Gazette,* XII (1880), 21; *Chronicle,* XXX (1880), 43.

Chapter IV

The Tail and the Dog

Transformation of the Danville, 1880–1886

Entrance of the Clydes

THE uncertainty surrounding the Danville's future reached a momentous climax in the spring of 1880. The Pennsylvania had at last decided to dispose of its last southern holdings, and after prolonged negotiations sold its Danville stock to a syndicate headed by Thomas and William Clyde of Philadelphia. The new owners actually comprised three distinct groups, each with its own motives and ambitions for the Danville. The first group consisted of former S.R.S.C. men such as Wilson, McGhee, B. F. Newcomer, W. T. Walters, and Plant. Their interest in the Danville survived the shifting fortunes of the investment company and owed its tenacity to the Danville's position as a competitor to the East Tennessee. The long-delayed completion of the Western North Carolina remained a bone of contention between the Danville and the East Tennessee. Wilson and McGhee wished to protect the future of this important connection by ensuring cooperation of the Danville. In addition, of course, the change in ownership promised a bullish movement in Danville stock and possible short-term profit.[1]

The second faction included several prominent Richmond bankers, merchants, and other interested parties, among them General Thomas M. Logan, John and Daniel Stewart, John and Thomas Branch, A. Y. Stokes, W. H. Palmer, Joseph Bryan, and James H. Dooley. While regarding the Danville as a profitable investment, they had more at stake in terms of long-run development. Richmond's future as a commercial center hinged largely upon the Danville's fate in the growing competition for traffic. The Pennsylvania's withdrawal would leave the Danville's territory open to invasion by such eager adversaries as the B. & O. If the stock fell into the wrong hands the road—and Richmond's fu-

---

[1] H. W. Schotter, *The Growth and Development of the Pennsylvania Railroad Company* (Philadelphia, 1927), 110–11; *Railway World*, XXIV (1880), 610–11; *Chronicle*, XXX (1880), 249, 651. See also *Danville Report*, 1880, 406–7.

ture—might be irreparably damaged. The presence of the Richmond investors worked two ways: it protected the city's commercial aspirations, and it made the transition of ownership more palatable to local interests. Largely for that reason, and the retention of Buford as president, the Richmond *Dispatch* hailed the new combination as presenting "to this city . . . great possibilities —great opportunities." [2]

The key to the deal, however, lay with William Clyde and his father. They had become interested in the Danville through their steamship operations. In addition to the Clyde Steamship Company, they controlled the Philadelphia and New York Transportation Company, running three ships between those cities. Early in the 1870's Thomas Clyde saw great possibilities in tapping lower Chesapeake Bay if he could secure rail connections. To that end he purchased the crippled Richmond & York River road in 1873 and arranged to complete the connection with the Danville in Richmond. Soon afterward the Clydes formed the Baltimore, Chesapeake and Richmond Steamboat Company to run a regular service between Baltimore and West Point. To cement the rail-water relationship they obtained from the Virginia legislature an act authorizing the reorganized Richmond, York River & Chesapeake Railroad to hold stock in the steamship company.[3]

Transfer of the stock to the railroad company assured through connections to Baltimore. Inevitably the Clydes drew closer to their vital artery, the Danville. A traffic agreement followed in April, 1875, by which the York River Line, as it came to be known, became part of the Piedmont Air-Line. When the Charlotte, Columbia & Augusta left S.R.S.C. control and immediately disrupted its traffic arrangements with the Danville, the Clydes stepped in to help purchase control of the road.[4] By 1880 they had made sizable commitments to their southern operations. A change in Danville ownership could not help but force difficult questions of strategy upon them. The decision to extend their investments to the Danville appeared logical under the circumstances, especially considering William Clyde's penchant for risk taking. His presence in the syndicate provided it not only with aggressive leadership but with confidence as well. His magnetic personality and indomitable energy would do much to shape the company's destiny.

[2] June 21, 1880.
[3] Harrison, *Southern Railway*, 245–47; *Chronicle*, XVI (1873), 661.
[4] *Danville Report*, 1879, 203–5; *Chronicle*, XXVII (1878), 280.

Interterritorial Expansion

The accession of the Clydes marked an important milestone in the Danville's history. The pattern of growth inaugurated under Buford could not be reversed. The aging president's desire to preserve his road's territorial integrity seemed to approach fruition with the formation of the Piedmont Air-Line, but in fact it did not. Operation of the new line only involved the Danville more intensely in competition with rival routes, and new opponents armed with grand schemes appeared on every flank.

To the extent that he sought to free the Danville from its status as a merely local road Buford had been entirely successful. What he failed to realize, however, was that the very nature of his triumph defeated the purposes of territorial strategy. The company's new position rendered it vulnerable to more competitors at more places. The process of growth diluted the strong personal and local loyalties that had once characterized the corporation. Enlargement also made close personal supervision over all aspects of management increasingly difficult and unsatisfactory. And the end was not yet in sight. The Danville's territory had not been sealed off but rather expanded. It had not stifled competition and could therefore expect continued conflict on a greater scale, especially with neighboring roads expanding under similar pressure.

The Clyde regime confirmed the Danville's new role as a regional carrier rather than a local road. Unlike Buford they possessed no strong local ties and no particular desire to emphasize the primacy of Richmond. Nor did they respect any notion of territorial strategy. Instead they would meet intensifying competition with further expansion and centralization of control. That Buford remained in the presidency suited their purposes nicely. The Clydes and their colleagues were not railroad men and cared little for operational problems. Buford would continue to preside over the road's operation, and his presence would help preserve the loyalty of Richmond interests. But he would no longer play a significant role in financial policy or strategic planning.

The company's new interterritorial status also forced administrative changes. The system was becoming too unwieldy for the simple, personal structure of its management. The mere separation of operational and financial functions proved inadequate to cope with the complex problems arising from interterritorial competition. As a result the new owners instituted in 1881 a group of

standing committees on finance, the road, real estate, and inciden-
tal business, and an executive committee. These committees assumed the policy-making responsibilities formerly held by a handful of officers and the board.[5]

While still in the process of reorganizing the Danville's management, Clyde launched a policy of aggressive expansion. Such a policy was but the logical extension of the decision to acquire the
Danville. An efficient working of the Piedmont Air-Line required
that local rivals be neutralized or harmonized. Survival in interterritorial competition demanded that alternative routes reaching
new markets be developed. Already several rival systems had
begun to penetrate the territories served by the Danville. The B. &
O. still searched for connections south of its Virginia Midland, the
L. & N. under Victor Newcomb had launched its quest for southeastern markets, and the Atlantic Coast Line had begun to coa-
lesce the loose string of roads along the seaboard into an effective
through line. Ever mindful of these pressures, the Danville syndicate justified its strategy in plain language:

The effect of this combination will be to give greater economy of
operation and increased efficiency of service than has heretofore been
possible under the old condition of things where the roads were independent and disconnected. While it secures to the owners greater protection from competition, it also affords the public better and cheaper
facilities.[6]

To fashion their expansion plans the syndicate needed a special
legal instrument. They had clearly earmarked the Danville as the
center of their envisioned network, but the company's charter denied it the right to lease or control any road that did not connect
directly with it. In an effort to skirt this annoying obstacle the syndicate, apparently at Logan's suggestion, established the Richmond & West Point Terminal Railway and Warehouse Company.[7]

---

[5] *Danville Report*, 1881, 505–6. The evolution of formal and more elaborate
administrations took place in virtually every growing southern system. Their
experience seems to offer additional support for the Chandler thesis that
structure follows strategy (see Alfred D. Chandler, Jr., *Strategy and Structure*
[Cambridge, Mass., 1962]).

[6] *Railway World*, XXIV (1880), 610–11.

[7] Most sources attribute the origin of the Terminal to Logan although one
correctly notes that "Mr. Clyde was the moving spirit in procuring this
charter" (see New York *Times*, August 28, 1892; Baltimore *Sunday News*, July
24, 1892; and David Schenck Diary, Dec. 15, 1881).

Birth of the Richmond Terminal

The act incorporating the Terminal passed the Virginia legislature on March 8, 1880, or more than three months before news of the Clyde syndicate's activities became widely publicized. The following list of the original subscribers to the Terminal's stock makes the syndicate's domination clear:

William P. Clyde	250 shares	John Stewart	100 shares
Thomas Clyde	100 "	Joseph Bryan	100 "
Thomas M. Logan	100 "	F. R. Scott	50 "
James H. Dooley	100 "	John Branch	100 "
W. H. Palmer	100 "	D. K. Stewart	100 "
F. F. Milne	100 "	A. Y. Stokes &	
Reuben Foster	50 "	Co.	100 "
A. S. Buford	100 "	R. T. Hubard	60 "
		Total	1,510 shares [8]

The stock remained in private hands because the Danville could not legally hold it.[9] William Clyde assumed the presidency of the company, and his father became a director along with Logan, Bryan, Buford, and J. N. DuBarry of the Pennsylvania Railroad.[10]

The Terminal functioned as a pure holding company from the very first, and never in its bizarre history did it actually operate a single railroad. The key to its purpose rested in section 8 of its charter:

The said company is hereby authorized to subscribe to the capital stock of any railroad company chartered by the State, or by North Carolina, South Carolina, Tennessee, Kentucky, Georgia, Alabama or Mississippi which may have been constructed, or may hereafter be constructed. It is also authorized to acquire, by purchase or otherwise, stock or bonds of any such railway company.[11]

---

[8] Minutes of the Annual Meeting of the Richmond & West Point Terminal Railway & Warehouse Company, 1880, archives of the Southern Railway Company, Washington, D.C.

[9] In preparation for assuming control of the holding company, the Danville authorized purchase of $500,000 of Terminal stock as soon as any Terminal-controlled road connected with the Danville (*Danville Report*, 1880, 404–5).

[10] DuBarry resigned in June, 1881, and was replaced by W. H. Palmer (Minutes of the Directors' Meeting of the Richmond & West Point Terminal Railway and Warehouse Company, June 21, 1881, archives of the Southern Railway Company).

[11] *Charter of the Richmond and West Point Terminal Railway and Warehouse Company, March 8th, 1880 and Acts Amendatory Thereof* (Richmond, 1889), 5.

Two years later the Terminal succeeded in having its charter amended to broaden these already generous powers. Capital stock, originally limited to $5,000,000, could now be increased indefinitely at the discretion of the directors. Additional provisions for the acquisition and consolidation of railroads were granted, and the states of Florida, Louisiana, Arkansas, and Texas were added to the territory covered by the charter.

Possession of the Terminal enabled the Danville to expand with astonishing rapidity. Clyde sold his own interest and that of the Pennsylvania in the Charlotte, Columbia & Augusta to the holding company.[12] In collaboration with the East Tennessee interests in the syndicate, the Terminal secured control of the unfinished Western North Carolina and announced its intention to complete the road.[13] To the south the company also acquired the reorganized 164-mile Greenville & Columbia and three short tributary roads totaling another 131 miles.[14] Four smaller roads also fell under Terminal domination: the Asheville & Spartanburg (50 miles), Northeastern of Georgia (39 miles), Knoxville & Augusta (16 miles), and Richmond & Mecklenburg (31 miles).

The most ambitious project of the Terminal was its construction of the long-delayed Georgia Pacific Railroad. Known originally as the Georgia Western, the road had been conceived in 1854 as an important artery linking the Georgia and Alabama systems. It would run westward from Atlanta toward Tuscaloosa or Jacksonville. The onset of war delayed the undertaking and attempts to revive it in the 1870's led to bankruptcy and foreclosure. The penetration of northern Alabama by the L. & N., however, rekindled interest in the moribund company. Seeking access to Atlanta and the southeastern seaboard, the L. & N. management outbid the equally concerned East Tennessee to acquire the Georgia Western franchise in 1879.[15]

For over a year L. & N. president Victor Newcomb threatened to build a road from Birmingham to Atlanta. Using the charter as a

<hr/>

[12] Terminal Directors' Minutes, June 21, 1881.

[13] *Ibid.*, August 26, 1881; Harrison, *Southern Railway*, 295–305. For details see the relevant correspondence in the Alexander Boyd Andrews papers, Southern Historical Collection. A year after the purchase the former holder of the franchise, William J. Best, tried to regain the road. For this controversy, see David Schenck Diary, August 12, 1881; and *Chronicle*, XXXIII (1881), 385–86, 581.

[14] Harrison, *Southern Railway*, 28, 311–29. The three smaller roads were the Blue Ridge, the Laurens, and the Spartanburg, Union & Columbia.

[15] *Ibid.*, 407–25; R. T. Wilson to C. M. McGhee, Dec. 16, 1879, McGhee papers.

club, he wrung important concessions from the Georgia roads and promptly lost interest in the Georgia Western. On February 26, 1881, he sold the franchise to John B. Gordon, the soldier-turned-politician, for $50,000. Gordon planned to build from Atlanta across the Mississippi to a connection with the Texas & Pacific at Texarkana. In this arrangement he agreed to give the L. & N. entrance into Atlanta. Scarcely had the ink dried, however, when Gordon sold a half interest in the Georgia portion of the projected road to the East Tennessee for $50,000.[16]

Lacking the resources to construct his road, Gordon opened negotiations with the Terminal and signed a formal agreement on July 30, 1881. The road would be built from Atlanta to Greenville, Mississippi, on the river. Charters were obtained in Georgia, Alabama, and Mississippi and consolidated under the name of Georgia Pacific Railroad Company. To do the work the Terminal officers chartered the Richmond & Danville Extension Company in New Jersey and retained 51 per cent of its stock in the Terminal treasury. The date of that charter, May 28, 1881, marked the beginning of the Georgia Pacific, a road destined to loom large in the Terminal's affairs.[17]

Expansion drew its impetus from overtly defensive pressures as well. Control of the vital Piedmont Air-Line seemed tenuous to the Clyde regime, especially since the B. & O. continued its efforts to invade the territory south of its Virginia Midland road. The B. & O. management tried first to wrest control of the Atlanta & Charlotte Air-Line from the Danville. At the same time they talked of extending the Midland southward through Danville to Spartanburg.[18]

Alarmed by these threats, Clyde moved swiftly. He secured the northern connection by leasing his York River road to the Danville in perpetuity. After resolving differences within the Air-Line he executed a similar lease for it, though the B. & O. countered with a suit disputing its validity.[19] But Clyde and his supporters re-

[16] For more detail on the East Tennessee's motive, see chap. 5 below.

[17] Terminal Directors' Minutes, July 30, August 26, 1881; Harrison, *Southern Railway*, 426–42. A copy of the agreement with Gordon can be found in the archives of the Southern Railway Company along with an informative prospective on the resources along the projected road.

[18] *Chronicle*, XXXII (1881), 437, and *Danville Report*, 1881, 507. Such a line would have paralleled the Danville through North Carolina.

[19] *Danville Report*, 1881, 499–502, 515–16; Harrison, *Southern Railway*, 203–10, 247; *Chronicle*, XXXII (1881), 367. See also the unidentified clipping in the William P. Palmer Scrapbook, 58, Virginia Historical Society.

alized that a permanent solution could be achieved only by forcing the B. & O. out of the region entirely. Discouraged by their setbacks and unwilling to make further investments, the B. & O. chose to withdraw by disposing of the Midland. By late August agreement had been reached, and the Terminal took over the 405-mile road through central Virginia.[20]

Clyde's vision had swiftly become a reality. By 1883 the Danville owned or controlled 847 miles of road and the Terminal 1,657 miles for a total of 2,504 miles.[21] The enlarged system had cemented its basic route from Atlanta to Richmond but no longer relied upon it exclusively. Construction of the Georgia Pacific pushed westward and reached Birmingham by November, 1883.[22] At the same time the Western North Carolina penetrated the mountains to complete its connection with the East Tennessee in January, 1882.[23] Possession of the Midland provided access to Washington while acquisition of the lines south of the Danville gave the company a firm grip on traffic in the Carolinas. The impact of the proliferating system caused a Columbia newspaper to bewail the "great combination . . . which rumbled beneath our feet without our knowing where the earth would yawn and what section of the South on the Atlantic board would fall into the great railroad crater and be passed on . . . to the Northern centres." [24]

In many ways the Clyde regime pursued what appeared to be developmental policies. The management under Buford continued to emphasize the development of local resources, and many large Danville holders branched out into related industries. In 1881 Buford, Logan, Branch, and Stokes founded the Virginia Mining and Manufacturing Company to search out and exploit iron, coal, and other mineral deposits adjacent to the company's road. Other enterprises of a like nature soon followed. In anticipation of in-

[20] Terminal Directors' Minutes, July 30, August 26, 1881; Harrison, *Southern Railway*, 494–500; *Danville Report*, 1881, 504, 515–16; *Chronicle*, XXXIII (1881), 256; Thomas Logan to Isaac Carrington, Nov. 4, 1881, Isaac Carrington papers, Duke University, Durham, N.C. For more detail on the political ramifications of this fight, see Blake, *William Mahone*, chaps. 4–5.

[21] Henry V. Poor, *Manual of Railroads for 1884* (New York, 1884), 398.

[22] For progress of the Georgia Pacific, see *Chronicle*, XXXIII (1881), 201, 491, XXXVI (1883), 195, XXXVII (1883), 563; *Railway World*, XXVI (1882), 783.

[23] Harrison, *Southern Railway*, 301; *Chronicle*, XXXIV (1882), 550.

[24] Columbia *Register*, July 2, 1881.

creased through traffic the Terminal and Danville joined in constructing additional wharfage, warehouse, cotton compressing, and shipping facilities at West Point. To demonstrate the Danville's new stature the directors in 1881 commenced paying regular quarterly dividends, and that same autumn the company's stock went on the New York Stock Exchange for the first time.[25]

Speculation and the Ironclad Pool

The listing of Danville and Terminal stock on the New York Exchange suggested more than the company's rise to national prominence. It betrayed another and equally important role played by Clyde: that of speculator. Despite his substantial investment, Clyde indulged in a considerable amount of opportunistic manipulation. This apparent contradiction can best be explained by the unique status of the holding company. As a mere auxiliary to the Danville the Terminal's stock tended naturally to become a speculative plaything. An investor might go into Danville with every intention of pursuing conservative developmental goals. His caution need not extend to Terminal stock, however, for as long as the Danville held slightly more than half the Terminal issue there was no danger of losing control.

Largely for that reason speculation ran rife in Terminal stock, both among "insiders" and investors outside the company who had little or no knowledge of its affairs. The Terminal in fact became notorious for the shroud of mystery that cloaked its affairs.[26] Interested investors, particularly those outside New York, could uncover little information on the company's machinations. This veil of secrecy, coupled with its natural appeal to speculators, rendered Terminal stock especially susceptible to rumor and panic. These characteristics all came to the fore during a sensational speculation that climaxed in the winter of 1882.

To cement their grip upon the Danville, Clyde and his associates hit upon the idea of a stock pool. On June 1, 1881, about a year after assuming control, the syndicate signed an "ironclad" pool agreement. The pool included the following investors:

[25] Dun & Bradstreet Reports, Virginia, XLVI, 40; *Danville Report,* 1881, 517; 1882, 15, 19; *Chronicle,* XXXIII (1881), 461; *Railway World,* XXV (1881), 1028.

[26] See, for example, William P. DeSaussure to T. M. Logan, May 1, 1882, Thomas M. Logan papers, Southern Historical Collection.

Ironclad pool June 1, 1881

John Stewart	4,000 shares	James T. Gray	426 shares
W. P. Clyde	5,000 "	T. M. Logan	2,313 "
Joseph Bryan	2,000 "	G. W. Perkins	2,715 "
James H. Dooley	1,500 "	A. S. Buford	1,650 "
Thomas Branch &		Minor lots	2,880 "
Co.	4,000 "		
W. H. Palmer	737 "		

27,221 shares

Total of 40,000 shares outstanding

The stock was to be assigned to an executive committee composed of Clyde, Perkins, Bryan, Palmer, Logan, Dooley, and John Branch. They in turn deposited it with the Central Trust Company where, the committee agreed, it would remain for the ten-year term of the pool. Since possession of the Danville stock carried with it a majority of Terminal stock, that company also remained in the hands of the syndicate.[27]

While the pool lasted it had the beneficial effect of binding together the Richmond and New York interests. There is little doubt that the latter group, led by Clyde and George W. Perkins, a drab but quietly efficient banker, dominated the syndicate. By removing a majority of the stock from the market, the agreement also tended to dampen speculation and promote long-term investment goals. But signs of conflicting purposes emerged within a few months. Most (but not all) of the Virginians were developmental investors seeking stability and a regular return on the stock. The New Yorkers, however, unencumbered by local loyalties and large investments in businesses related to the railroad, took a more opportunistic view of the situation. They desired a flexibility in their investment which, they soon realized, the pool provisions denied them.

Predictably the New Yorkers soon chafed under the restrictions of the agreement. The pool certificates were not admissible upon the New York Exchange. They could not be used as collateral for loans or for delivery on sale. In late October the New Yorkers forced a significant and ultimately fatal modification of the pool agreement: that any holder of pool certificates could present them at the Central Trust Company within ninety days and receive his stock in exchange. The amendment immediately spawned a flock

---

[27] *Railway World*, XXV (1881), 738; *Railroad Gazette*, XIII (1881), 421; John S. Bryan, *Joseph Bryan: A Memoir* (Richmond, 1935), 246.

of rumors: the New York stock would be withdrawn and the Richmond holdings retained intact; the purpose of the modification was to allow Perkins to form a new syndicate; or, most seriously, the breaking of the pool would be but the prelude to a general dumping of the stock.[28]

The uncertainty produced by the rumors coupled with other forces, including an increase in capitalization by the Terminal, touched off a wild speculative streak in both stocks. On a generally declining market Terminal common soared from 122 in November to 263 in February, 1882, and Danville from 99½ to 250 during the same period. In March the bubble burst. Terminal cascaded to 100, Danville to 110, and even some of the insiders suffered heavy losses. These spectacular price gyrations, which saw Danville fall 130 points in one day, gave rise to charges that Clyde and a few intimates had used Terminal money to push prices up and then unloaded to break the market.[29]

The charges against Clyde remained unproved and therefore open. The wildcat streak left a bad taste in the mouths of many investors and confirmed the Terminal's reputation on Wall Street as a speculative issue. For all his personal charm, Clyde could not erase the damage done to his own image and that of his company. Both stocks continued to decline in active trading for some months. Meanwhile the Clyde regime faced more serious problems of fashioning a viable financial policy to handle the enormous cost of expansion.

The Financial Woes of Expansion

Once having determined upon a strategy of interterritorial expansion, the Clyde management had to confront difficult problems of finance. The cost of expansion began with the price of acquisition, but by no means did it end there. Newly acquired roads were often in sorry shape, with shabby facilities and decrepit equipment.

[28] *Railroad Gazette*, XIII (1881), 610, 641; Richmond *State*, Oct. 24, Nov. 5, 1881.

[29] *Railway World*, XXV (1881), 1235; *Railroad Gazette*, XIV (1882), 385, XIX (1887), 162–63; Bryan, *Joseph Bryan*, 247; New York *Times*, August 28, 1892. Not all the insiders profited from the speculation. Joseph Bryan, who was on the executive committee of the pool, bought into both stocks at their peak and lost heavily. All stock prices unless otherwise indicated are taken from the *Chronicle* and the semiannual *Handbook of Railway Securities* published by the *Chronicle*.

Funds would be needed to refurbish the roadbed and to provide additional facilities, rolling stock, motive power, and numerous other necessities. Investment in a new road, especially one with a history of poor earning capacity, thus required considerable capital beyond the initial purchase price and was not to be taken lightly. Not surprisingly, the Danville found that its rapid accumulation of new properties imposed a severe strain upon its resources.

To be sure the Terminal shouldered much of the cost of expansion, but this burden fell equally upon the Danville. To raise money for its purchases the Terminal increased its capital stock three times in nine months, going to $3,000,000 in June, 1881, $5,000,000 that same December, and $15,000,000 in March, 1882. In each instance the Danville had to take half the new issue to retain its control over the holding company. After paying cash for the first lot the company resorted to a $4,000,000 issue of debenture bonds, offered to Danville holders at 45, to pay for the second issue. For the third issue the Danville increased its own capital stock by $1,000,000 to $5,000,000 and paid for the remainder in cash.[30]

Despite all efforts the burden of new acquisitions produced troublesome floating debts in both companies. Much of the Danville's difficulty involved advances to the Extension Company for work on the Georgia Pacific. Clyde found it necessary to skip the last quarterly dividend in 1882. This action added new fuel to rumors, vigorously denied by Buford and other officials, that the Danville was borrowing at exorbitant rates. Shortly afterward the Terminal took steps to alleviate its burden by arranging to sell off certain stocks. When more money was needed to complete the Virginia Midland transaction, the Terminal borrowed $2,000,000 on collateral trust notes given at 90. The loan cost the company 11 per cent per year at real rates, but this was considered by one observer as "probably as low a rate as could be expected on the security offered." [31]

[30] Terminal Directors' Minutes, June 21, Dec. 28, 1881, May 6, 1882; Terminal Annual Meeting Minutes, March 30, 1882; *Danville Report*, 1881, 504–5, 515–16; 1882, 6–7, 16–17; *Railroad Gazette*, XIV (1882), 16, 216, 419; *Railway World*, XXVI (1882), 60, 325. A copy of the deed to secure the debenture issue can be found in the Virginia Historical Society.

[31] Terminal Directors' Minutes, Jan. 8, 1883; *Railroad Gazette*, XV (1883), 52, 84; *Chronicle*, XXXV (1882), 457, 577, XXXVI (1883), 56, 109, 141. As part of the security for the notes the Terminal promptly pledged the Midland stock it had just purchased.

Continuing financial problems and brisk movements in both Danville and Terminal stock portended significant changes in the company's future. The sharp fluctuations in price indicated a rapid turnover that was in fact taking place. Many of the Richmond investors, uneasy over the gyrations, sold out their holdings. The aging and infirm James Stewart alone disposed of 5,000 shares or 10 per cent of the Danville's entire issue. Rumors abounded as to who had been purchasing the Richmond stock. Most of it apparently went to New Yorkers and some into the hands of John D. Rockefeller, whose representative, Robert Harris, joined the Danville and Terminal boards late in 1882 along with two other New York financiers, John A. Rutherfurd and M. Bayard Brown.[32]

The whole spectacle bewildered Buford. Wearily he watched control of the Danville slip further from the Richmond interests and into the grasp of unknown financiers. Though he guarded his public remarks carefully, his dissatisfaction with the course of Danville affairs occasionally bobbed to the surface. In one interview he admitted his regret that the stock had ever been put on the New York Exchange, where no track could be kept of its purchasers. But the turnover had only begun.

A New Syndicate and "the First National Crowd"

The manifold activities of the Terminal could not help attracting the attention of other financiers. The liberality of its charter intrigued the imaginative capitalist, as did the tight nature of its relationship to the Danville. The discordance within its management offered possibilities for gaining easy access to the company, and the selling off by the Richmond interests made securities readily available at low prices. By July, 1883, Danville had dropped to 55 and Terminal to 28. An annoying floating debt persisted in both companies, and earnings, though improving, could not be stretched far enough to meet all demands.

A new syndicate soon coalesced to take advantage of the situation. At its center remained Clyde, whose position and talents were indispensable to the newcomers. His unrivaled knowledge of Terminal affairs and large personal holdings rendered him too formi-

[32] Terminal Directors' Minutes, April 10, 1883, and Annual Meeting Minutes, Dec. 14, 1882; *Chronicle*, XXXV (1882), 405, 457; *Railroad Gazette*, XIV (1882), 654; Henry V. Poor, *Manual of the Railroads of the United States for 1882* (New York, 1882), 385, and *Manual for 1883*, 955.

dable to be alienated. For his own part, Clyde needed new allies and fresh capital to combat the deteriorating financial situation within the Danville and Terminal companies. Moreover, the sale of so much Danville stock threatened to dilute his command of the situation, especially if the securities fell into antagonistic hands.

In addition to Clyde the new syndicate comprised two distinct factions, each with its own goals. The first consisted of the trio who had recently bought control of the East Tennessee: George I. Seney, Calvin S. Brice, and General Samuel Thomas. In developmental terms they wished to neutralize the sharp competition between their system and the Danville and promote a greater interchange of business between them. On a short-term basis they also saw ample opportunity for speculative profits in the transactions of securities among the companies involved. On this score they joined forces with George S. Scott, a New York banker who eventually came to hold the largest single block of Danville stock.

The second faction consisted of what came to be known as "the First National crowd"—men associated with the First National Bank of New York.[33] Headed by George F. Baker and Harris C. Fahnestock, this group included several other bankers such as Samuel Shethar and John McAnerney, who also had close ties with Seney and his Metropolitan Bank. They constituted an important source of new capital and entered the syndicate primarily for the business it promised to offer them. None of them were railroad men, and only McAnerney, who had run a rolling mill and railroad supply firm in Poughkeepsie until he failed in the 1870's, had any sizable indirect involvement in the business.[34] Lacking any deep commitment to transportation, they naturally concentrated upon transactional profits and played an essentially passive role in strategy and management.

During the summer of 1883 Scott and Clyde quietly bought Danville on behalf of the syndicate until they cornered a majority of the stock. Scott preferred to move in secrecy but early in August the talkative Brice, to Scott's annoyance, admitted to a reporter that the syndicate had gained control:

Yes, the report is true that a syndicate in which I am interested has bought control of the . . . Danville road. We have the strongest combina-

[33] See Charles Leonhardt to Calvin M. McClung, March 15, 1892, McGhee papers. Leonhardt was McGhee's private secretary.

[34] For information on McAnerney (1838–1928), a Rhode Islander who went south and fought for the Confederacy, see New York *Times,* March 23, 1928.

tion that has ever been formed to take hold of southern railroads. We have secured about 28,000 of the 50,000 shares. . . . Our purpose is to confine all our railroad and steamship lines under one management, and equip and operate the system in the best possible manner.[35]

The syndicate's maneuvers did not go unchallenged. As their scheme unfolded the remaining Richmond interests and the New Yorkers outside the syndicate united to block the takeover. Late in July the Danville directors had voted to issue an additional $2,000,000 in stock to relieve the floating debt and purchase badly needed new equipment. Since the new issue would complicate the syndicate's efforts to acquire control, Scott and Clyde joined forces against it. By corralling a majority of Danville stock before the September 12 annual meeting, they managed to defeat the directors' resolution. Rutherfurd then persuaded the directors to file suit against Clyde, Logan, and Bryan to recover $987,000 of Terminal funds lost by them as a committee in sustaining the company's stock during the crash in February, 1882. With the syndicate in control, however, the suit had no chance of gaining stockholder approval.[36]

Confident of his position, Scott himself had demanded the September 12 meeting. At both the directors' and general meetings everything went smoothly. Thomas, Fahnestock, and McAnerney joined Scott, Brice, Baker, and Seney on the Danville board. On the Terminal board Logan resigned and Clyde promptly nominated Scott to replace him. Robert Harris left in favor of Shethar. When Bayard Brown and Rutherfurd refused to resign, Clyde pushed through a resolution to oust them. In their place came Baker and Brice. Walter G. Oakman, a close friend of Clyde's, replaced Logan as vice-president, while Clyde himself retained the presidency. On the Danville, Buford kept his office, but his tenure would be limited. The general meeting approved all changes, and at the regular Terminal annual meeting in December no further changes occurred.[37]

The decisive victory of the new syndicate produced a sweeping change in management, but it did not still dissension within the two companies. The Richmond and New York investors who lost

[35] *Chronicle*, XXXVII (1883), 100, 111–12, 128; *Railroad Gazette*, XV (1883), 520; *Railway World*, XXVII (1883), 831.

[36] *Railroad Gazette*, XV (1883), 488, 520, 614. In Oct. one Terminal holder filed suit privately against the trio to recover $200,000 in damages (see *ibid.*, 682).

[37] Terminal Directors' Minutes, Sept. 12, Oct. 3, 1883; Terminal Annual Meeting Minutes, Sept. 12, Dec. 13, 1883; *Railroad Gazette*, XV (1883), 846.

the contest found themselves relegated to the status of minority holders, but they continued to scrutinize every move of the new officers. Buford himself resigned on May 3, 1884, and was replaced by Scott. Perhaps no other single event better dramatized the transformation of the Danville in less than a decade. In an era of interterritorial systems the aging president's localized orientation had become obsolete. Uncomfortable with the new problems that confronted him and displeased with the policies of the new owners, he found his position untenable. Still he kept his post until Scott announced that the Danville's headquarters would be moved to New York. This severing of local identity proved unendurable for Buford. Of his departure a member of the company's legal staff noted sadly that "there is not an employee nor officer of the whole system . . . who does not feel a pang of sorrow and regret at the retirement of so good and true and faithful a man." [38]

Serious problems of financial policy and general strategy faced the new management. The persistent floating debt exceeded a million dollars even before the election. Earnings within the enlarged system continued to increase but not fast enough to match spiraling fixed charges. Preaching a doctrine of strict economy, the Scott regime tried to cut expenses. For a time the directors thought of abolishing the New York office; instead they elected to close the Richmond office and centralize general headquarters in New York. [39]

Despite loud protests the management passed the October interest on the 1882 debenture bonds. To increase net earnings they slashed improvement expenditures drastically. The operating ratio, which had averaged 60.2 per cent over the previous decade, fell to 48.3 per cent during 1883 and 1884. At the cost of running down the system physically, the management succeeded in increasing net earnings by 25.9 per cent during those two years even though gross earnings increased by only 11.7 per cent. But even this improvement did not suffice to meet all needs. By 1885 they managed to cut the floating debt in half, but the funded debt increased from \$5,903,550 in 1882 to \$9,384,500. [40]

Having failed to make any appreciable improvement in the company's finances, the Scott management fared no better in the

---

[38] David Schenck Diary, May 15, 1884. Buford did remain on the Terminal board.

[39] *Railway World*, XXVII (1883), 999; *Railway Gazette*, XVI (1884), 386.

[40] *Railroad Gazette*, XV (1883), 664. Percentages calculated from data in Appendix II. The debenture bonds were 6 per cent cumulative income bonds payable if earned. For more detail, see *Chronicle*, XXXVII (1883), 373.

field of strategy. To improve general operation of the system Scott surrendered his seat on the Terminal board to Frederic W. Huide-koper, a man with impressive credentials in railway management.[41] In broad terms the major task was to establish a favorable relationship with other developing interterritorial systems. The union of interests with the East Tennessee helped abate competition, but the financial panic of 1884 hurt business in both systems. To the south and west, the L. & N. and Georgia roads remained potential threats to future expansion, with the latter competing directly for eastbound traffic out of Atlanta.

The presence of Walters and Newcomer, who held large interests in the Atlantic Coast Line, in the original Clyde syndicate had served to ameliorate the rivalry between the Danville and its most direct competitor. Although their influence waned after the accession of the Scott syndicate, the two systems continued to pursue a policy of reasonable cooperation. During the summer of 1885 this policy bore fruit. Drawing the equally ambitious Seaboard & Roanoke system into their circle, the three systems signed an agreement forming the Associated Railways of Virginia and the Carolinas. The pact included the roads listed in Table 5.[42]

The Association provided a valuable supplement to the larger existing pool, the Southern Railway & Steamship Association, in that several of the Association members did not belong to the pool. As an essentially defensive alliance, however, it could not satisfy the Danville's need to rethink its strategy. The momentum of consolidation coupled with the management's largely opportunistic motivations ensured that further expansion would play a major role in the Danville's future. As the Georgia Pacific pressed closer to the Mississippi the alternatives for growth widened. Should the company continue to build westward across the river or be content to rely upon connecting roads? Should it attempt to build an elaborate system of feeders in the newly occupied territory west of Atlanta or attempt to acquire roads already there? Or should it work instead to strengthen its already powerful position on the South Atlantic seaboard by acquiring more lines in that region? Perhaps it might even move into the Georgia roads south of Atlanta to get a share of the traffic moving via the rail-water routes.

[41] Terminal Directors' Minutes, Feb. 19, 1885.

[42] A copy of the agreement, dated August 1, 1885, can be found in the Bureau of Railroad Economics. For the basic provisions of the pact, see chap. 1 above.

The Scott regime did little to answer these important questions. Their hesitancy derived in part from the company's strained financial situation and in part from continued division within the management. Two examples illustrate their uncertainty. The growing importance of through traffic uncovered a serious weakness in the Danville system: the lack of a suitable major port for transshipment. Despite all efforts to develop it, West Point remained far too small and inadequate a facility to serve a major system. Meanwhile Baltimore to the north and Norfolk to the south continued to flourish, and Collis Huntington was busily engaged in trying to make Newport News into a first-class port to service his burgeoning Chesapeake & Ohio system. Failure to procure an adequate water outlet could severely hinder the Danville's growth, and the search for a solution to this problem should have received more priority than it did.

TABLE 5. Component systems in the Associated Railways of Virginia and the Carolinas

Road	Miles
Piedmont Air-Line	
Richmond & Danville	755
Virginia Midland	362
Columbia & Greenville	296
Charlotte, Columbia	
& Augusta	373
Western North Carolina	274
Total	2,060
Atlantic Coast Line	
Richmond & Petersburg	23
Petersburg	61
Wilmington & Weldon	199
Wilmington, Columbia	
& Augusta	189
Cheraw & Darlington	40
Northeastern of South	
Carolina	102
Total	614
Seaboard Air-Line	
Seaboard & Roanoke	80
Raleigh & Gaston	97
Raleigh & Augusta	108
Columbia Central	242
Total	527
Grand total	3,201

SOURCE: Figures taken from Poor, *Manual for 1886.*

By the mid-1880's it had become clear that natural limitations would prevent West Point from ever achieving equal distinction with Baltimore or even Norfolk. The obvious alternative was to secure entrance into one of the major port cities to compete with the roads serving those outlets. Opportunities for reaching both Norfolk and Baltimore actually materialized. As early as 1883 certain merchants of Norfolk had petitioned the Danville to build a branch to their city and offered to subscribe part of the necessary capital. Though much discussion followed, the Danville never took up the project. To be sure it would have been bitterly opposed by the Norfolk-based roads, notably the Norfolk & Western and the Seaboard & Roanoke, but every proposed extension encountered opposition from interests likely to be affected adversely.[43]

The Baltimore project reached a higher stage of development. The withdrawal of the B. & O. from its southern activities left the city with no adequate rail connection to vie for southern trade. To remedy this situation representatives of the Baltimore Merchants & Manufacturers Association drew the Danville officers into lengthy negotiations. Their offer was relatively simple. The city of Baltimore would loan the strapped Danville $2,000,000 on favorable terms. In exchange, the Danville would extend the Virginia Midland to Baltimore and, most important, devise a differential rate structure favoring Baltimore on all freight. To protect the city's investment, three seats on the Danville board and eight on the Midland would be given to its representatives.[44]

The project would in effect have made Baltimore the Danville's main terminus and destroyed the last vestiges of its purely territorial origins. The Scott regime's reaction appeared to be mixed, though they kept negotiations going for some time. Clyde could not have been happy, since the new connection would cripple his steamer business at West Point. The Baltimoreans delivered their end of the bargain. The Maryland legislature passed a bill authorizing the city to make the loan, though hedging it with restrictions. The Virginia legislature responded no less decisively. When the Danville took the first step of seeking a bill to approve consolidation of the Midland with the Danville, the state senate handed it a stinging defeat. One observer noted that "the opposition to it was entirely local, and had its origin in the fear of the Richmond people that much of the business . . . might be diverted to

[43] *Railroad Gazette*, XV (1883), 628–29.   [44] *Ibid.*, XVI (1884), 120, 290.

Baltimore." [45] This local opposition plus continued inability to agree upon the rate differential finally caused abandonment of the project.

In terms of clarifying the company's strategy, the Scott regime had made little headway by 1885. Money remained in short supply, especially after the 1884 panic, and future prospects seemed nebulous. The bankers in the syndicate and the opportunistic investors had more to cheer about. Transactional profits continued firm as the First National and its allies handled much of the financial business for the Danville and most of its subsidiary roads.[46] In March, 1885, an allied firm destined to leave its mark upon the Terminal's history made its first appearance when the Terminal agreed to sell $350,000 in Asheville & Spartanburg bonds to Inman, Swann & Company.[47]

The over-all situation, however, remained unsatisfactory. The brief depression after 1884 caught the East Tennessee right in the midst of a precariously financed expansion program and dealt it a mortal blow. In January, 1885, the company plunged into bankruptcy and receivership. Its difficulties not only complicated traffic relationships but created further dissension within the Danville syndicate as well. The East Tennessee interests there needed funds to save their system. The squeeze for cash left the Danville interests unwilling to offer anything beyond sympathy. Their own austerity program, which had already eroded the road's once fine physical plant, could not be prolonged without disastrous effects. Expenditures for long-delayed improvements would have to be made and the belt tightened elsewhere. In their quest for economy the Scott regime hit upon a simple scheme: they would do away with the Terminal.

Dumping the Terminal

The holding company actually cost little to run. It had no earnings beyond dividends and interest from the stocks and bonds it held, and few expenses beyond administrative costs and interest on the notes issued in 1883. But as a front the Terminal often meant

[45] *Ibid.*, 214.

[46] For a typical example, see Terminal Directors' Minutes, April 2, 1884, where Clyde, Scott, Baker, and Brice passed a resolution to deliver to the First National $2,000,000 in Western North Carolina bonds at 75.

[47] *Ibid.*, March 17, 1885. The price was 80 less 2½ per cent commission.

delay and sometimes unfortunate complications in Danville policy. Moreover, its earnings had to be shared with outside stockholders, and the need to purchase half of its constantly accelerating equity proved a burden to the Danville. Most important, it had outlived its usefulness. Late in 1884 the Scott regime had secured authorization from the Virginia legislature for the Danville to hold stock in railroads that did not connect with it. Acquisition of that power rendered the Terminal an unnecessary appendage.[48]

Once possessed of that power, the Scott regime devised a plan, authored by Clyde, that was at once simple and profitable. The Danville would transfer the Terminal's main holdings to itself, paying for them with Terminal stock held by the Danville. Having emasculated the holding company, the syndicate could then dump their remaining Terminal stock on the market before outside investors realized what had happened. A profit could be made on this sale, the Danville would have firm control of its subsidiary roads, and the Terminal would be cast adrift.

At the Terminal annual meeting on December 9, 1885, the syndicate began to implement its plan. It passed a resolution calling for a union of interests between the two companies to find "the simplest and most economical administration attainable." By casting its scheme in the form of a merger, the syndicate managed to disguise its real intentions for a time. The plan presented by Clyde at a directors' meeting on April 15, 1886, however, did not exactly smack of subtlety. It called for the Danville to lease directly certain of the Terminal's roads and then to acquire the securities held by the Terminal in the leased roads. For these securities the Terminal would receive $2,500,000 in its own stock. The interlocking directorates of the two companies made approval of the plan a mere formality.[49]

Within short order the Danville leased the Midland, Western North Carolina, Charlotte, Columbia & Augusta, Columbia & Greenville, and Northeastern of Georgia, leaving only the Georgia Pacific and some minor roads in Terminal control. Still the syndicate camouflaged their plot by encouraging rumors of an exchange of stock between the two companies. With the leases in hand Scott briskly wrapped up the loose ends. He announced the Danville's intention to take from the Terminal all its choice securities in the roads being leased by the former, and he arranged the transfer of

[48] *Railroad Gazette*, XVI (1884), 876.
[49] *Ibid.*, XVII (1885), 815, XVIII (1886), 138; *Chronicle*, XLII (1886), 488; Terminal Directors' Minutes, April 15, 1886.

the Danville's stock in the holding company. After completing this transaction the syndicate dumped its remaining Terminal stock on the market at low prices. Scott resigned his seat on the Terminal board and prepared to yield control of the Terminal gracefully.[50]

At first glance the coup seemed to have been carried off brilliantly. The Danville now controlled all major subsidiary roads except the Georgia Pacific. The stock dumping realized nearly $2,000,000 in market sales, and for its $2,500,000 in Terminal stock the Danville acquired the securities listed in Table 6 with a nomi-

TABLE 6. Securities acquired by Danville from Terminal in dumping operation, 1886

Road	Security	Amount acquired
Western North Carolina	2nd-mortgage bonds	4,110
" " "	preferred stock	31,680
" " "	common stock	31,680
Columbia & Greenville	preferred stock	10
" "	common stock	10,000
Knoxville & Augusta	1st-mortgage bonds	100
" "	common stock	1,000
Charlotte, Columbia & Augusta	common stock	13,024
Richmond & Mecklenburg	common stock	3,000
Asheville & Spartanburg	common stock	3,680
Oxford & Henderson	—	entire interest

SOURCE: *Chronicle*, XLII (1886), 728–29.

nal value of $22,000,000 and a market value of $11,000,000. The transactions also boosted the price of Danville stock, which rose from 75 to 149 during the spring. By June, Scott prepared to move the Danville's general offices from Richmond to Washington, while observers wrote obituaries for the Terminal. One writer predicted that the holding company "will probably be wound up and disappear altogether."[51]

As might be expected, the whole affair enraged minority Terminal holders, especially those like Logan and Rutherfurd who had been ousted in the 1883 turnover. Their company had been stripped bare and its stock driven down by the dumping maneuver. Early in the fight they formed a committee, with Robert Har-

[50] *Railroad Gazette*, XVIII (1886), 285, 291, 323, 479, 484; *Chronicle*, XLII (1886), 519, 604; David Schenck Diary, Dec. 18, 1886; Terminal Directors' Minutes, May 23, 1886.
[51] *Railroad Gazette*, XVIII (1886), 434, 479; *Chronicle*, XLII (1886), 683.

ris as chairman, to protect their rights. Once aware of the syndicate's tactics, they obtained an injunction on April 26 to block transfer of the Terminal's securities to the Danville. Scott replied smugly that "our proceedings have been strictly legal and fair, and will be sustained beyond a doubt." [52]

He spoke too soon. The bitterness of the public dispute did not fully reflect the fierce contest taking place within the Terminal. With Scott gone Clyde was left to bear the stockholder committee's wrath. On May 3 the committee, consisting of Harris, Logan, Rutherfurd, D. Willis James, G. E. Kissell, and H. R. Garden, appeared before the directors' meeting and submitted a list of inquiries about the recent Danville-Terminal transactions. When discussion produced no satisfactory answers the committee prepared to withdraw. Clyde stopped them to ask about the pending litigation. If they would only be patient, he promised, complete information would be forthcoming. Appeased by his apparent promise, the committee left to await further word. [53]

At this point Clyde tacked evasively. He had received two letters from the committee demanding answers to the following questions: Has any lease between the Danville and Midland been executed? Has *any* contract between the two companies been made? Has any contract been made between the Danville and the Terminal to transfer certain securities of the latter to the former? Was the alleged lease of the Midland a part of this transfer or dependent upon it in any way? The committee wanted not only answers but copies of all pertinent contracts and resolutions or actions by the boards of all companies involved. [54]

The May 3 meeting had been arranged because no reply to the letters had been forthcoming. Shortly after that session Clyde phrased a careful reply. He admitted the Midland had been leased as of April 15 and furnished a list of the Terminal securities transferred to the Danville. He conceded further that the Midland lease was an integral part of the transfer package, "without which it would have not been made." He attached a statement of the Terminal's financial obligations in the deal but declined to furnish copies of any contracts or resolutions. [55]

Clyde's reply left the committee unmoved. On May 10 they wrote a sharp rebuke in which they accused Clyde of evading the

[52] *Railroad Gazette*, XVIII (1886), 306; *Chronicle*, XLII (1886), 575, 728–29.
[53] Terminal Directors' Minutes, May 3, 1886.
[54] *Ibid.*, Oct. 18, 1886. The committee letters were dated April 20 and 28, 1886, and are reprinted in their entirety here.
[55] *Ibid.*

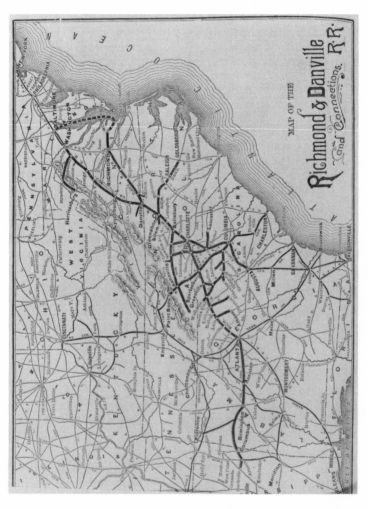

Richmond & Danville System, 1885. From *Investor's Supplement, Commercial and Financial Chronicle* (Feb., 1886), 79

inquiries. Again they demanded copies of all resolutions pertaining to the Midland lease and all information and contracts on the transfer of securities:

Since the first letter . . . we understand that the Danville and yourself have made a contract involving a complete change of ownership of some of the most important properties of the Terminal, and that the Danville has leased the C C & A, the C & G, and the W N C. As to those leases you were perfectly silent in our conference Monday though we learned they had been executed, and you have still declined to give us a copy of the contract between Danville and Terminal providing for a transfer of the securities of the latter company.

The committee also accused Clyde of misinterpreting its prior leniency and of misleading it about the Western North Carolina during the conference.

Most important, the committee denounced the whole securities transfer scheme. In so doing they went right to the heart of the matter: Clyde's dual role as president of the Terminal and agent of the Danville. How could he possibly protect the rights of his stockholders? For the first time the crucial anomaly of the holding company relationship lay exposed; Clyde served only one management but two masters. In formulating policy suitable to the Danville he had come into conflict with minority holders not interested in the Danville and anxious to make the Terminal itself a going concern. He could not please both masters, and in outright collision one would have to be sacrificed to the other.

The committee recognized this anomaly only too well. They knew that the split over policy was irreconcilable, that the Danville and Terminal could never again attain what little harmony existed in the old relationship. The alternative, then, was to effect a new relationship favorable to the Terminal minority holders. Moreover, they edged closer to accusing Clyde outright of betraying his trust as president. Perceptively and acidly they called attention to his board's untenable position:

We are aware that a contract between yourselves and the Danville can only be annulled or modified by the concurrence of both, but as you have made the contracts between yourselves as Danville directors on the one side with yourselves as Terminal directors on the other, we presume you can in the same double capacity make any correction.[56]

The charges stung Clyde. Dropping his natural mask of geniality, he resorted to bluster. On May 13 he dismissed the committee's

[56] *Ibid.*

demands as arrogant and dictatorial and accused its members of trying to derange the Terminal's credit and slander its directors. Of the charges proper he said only that

it is possible that in the discharge of what we have believed to be our duty we may have erred in legal technicalities, but we certainly cannot be reasonably expected to exhibit our records and intentions . . . to a self constituted committee of gentlemen who seem much more intent . . . in finding flaws and technical errors in our mode of procedure than in endeavoring by cooperation, approval, or suggestion to assist us in our efforts.

In frigid tones Clyde informed the committee that "unless the tone and temper of your communications are changed, . . . further correspondence must prove fruitless." Two weeks later he warned them that further accusations would lead holders of large demand loans to call them in early and seriously embarrass the Terminal. "Therefore," he concluded loftily, "if serious financial embarrassment of this company should follow continued agitations by your committee, the responsibility must rest with you and not with the directors of this company." [57]

The war of words dragged on through the hot, fitful summer. Despite the injunction the Danville remained confident of ultimate victory, and the Scott regime continued to tidy up its financial structure. In autumn the management issued a new 5 per cent consolidated first mortgage to consolidate all outstanding debt, especially the unpaid debentures.[58] On November 1 the company even leased a new road, the 50-mile Washington, Ohio & Western.[59] But all eyes remained focused on the Terminal minority holders. No one expected them to accept defeat gracefully, but their tactics remained obscure.

In actuality the minority plan had become perfectly clear. They realized the futility of relying upon the injunction alone to salvage their investment. The only feasible alternative lay in acquiring control of the expiring Terminal and reviving it. Since this required considerable capital, the tireless Logan took upon himself the task of organizing a new syndicate. Once again he attempted to weave a combination of local and Wall Street interests. Several influential Richmonders led by James B. Pace, a wealthy banker, wished to return the company's offices to Richmond and threw

[57] *Ibid.*
[58] For terms of the offer to debenture holders, see *Railroad Gazette*, XVIII (1886), 517.
[59] *Ibid.*, 768.

their support behind Logan. In New York the former rebel general enlisted the aid of a coterie of talented financiers including Emanuel Lehman, Isaac L. Rice, George F. Stone, and Alfred Sully.[60] Nearing the end of his labors to reorganize the Philadelphia & Reading, Sully agreed to join Logan in heading the new combination.[61]

The Danville's dumping of Terminal stock made control relatively easy to acquire. As the price of Terminal slowly gravitated upward, however, Clyde and his cronies guessed what was happening. By summer's end Sully's group neared a majority of Terminal stock, but the real struggle had only begun. At a directors' meeting on October 19 Clyde's board passed resolutions calling for a general meeting on November 19 and asking that the existing injunction against the stock transfer be vacated. Three weeks later the board approved the sale of 25,000 shares of Terminal by Clyde at 42 or above. They would concede the Terminal to the new combination; a battle had been lost, but the war went on.[62]

The situation approached a dangerous stalemate. Possession of the Terminal alone did the Sully syndicate no good. Most of its choice properties now belonged to the Danville under lease, and the latter also held $620,000 of the Terminal's $800,000 floating debt. To put pressure on the Danville, the Sully syndicate filed new suits asking cancellation of the leases on grounds of fraud, but litigation consumed precious time. Nor could the Danville syndicate afford a prolonged impasse. Debts continued to mount, and the Terminal's credit grew weaker daily. The general meeting had been called to seek some compromise solution, but only the most optimistic held out any hope of success.[63]

The crisis apparently produced a split between the Scott–First National crowd and Clyde and his friends. The latter proposed to continue the fight by issuing $3,500,000 in new collateral trust bonds to take up the floating debt and the old 1883 notes. The former made no specific offer but expressed willingness to take over

[60] Stover, *Railroads of the South*, 244–45, ignores the Richmond faction and assigns a prominent role to such men as Henry M. Flagler and Robert K. Dow. It appears that these and other financiers supported the new syndicate but took little active part in it. The accounts in Stover and in Daggett, *Railroad Reorganization*, 159–61, are based upon essentially superficial sources and contain numerous errors of fact and sequence.

[61] David Schenck Diary, Dec. 18, 1886.

[62] Terminal Directors' Minutes, Oct. 19 and Nov. 8, 1886; *Railroad Gazette*, XVIII (1886), 749.

[63] David Schenck Diary, Dec. 18, 1886; *Chronicle*, XLII (1886), 487–88.

all the Terminal property, operate it, and turn the net earnings
over to the Terminal holders. If both plans failed, some Danville
holders said they favored severing all relationships with the Terminal.[64]

Clyde's position had become deceptively weak. He had lost control of the Terminal, and possession of a majority of Danville resided in the hands of the First National group. If they elected to
sell out to the new syndicate, his downfall would be a mere formal-
ity. Sully's group grasped this fact. They came to the conclusion
that to salvage their investment in the Terminal they must gain
control of the Danville. They offered to buy the First National's
majority by exchanging two shares of Terminal for one of Danville, but Scott refused disdainfully. Attempts to go into the market succeeded only in running Danville up past 200 in early November. The facts soon became uncomfortably transparent: the
First National crowd wielded a solid majority and would sell only
on their own terms. If these were not accepted, then the bitter
fight might go on indefinitely.[65]

The syndicate had no choice. Prolonging the conflict would succeed only in tearing both companies to shreds. In November the
negotiations began. Rice presided at the November 19 Terminal
meeting and had it postponed until November 26. Next day the
two sides struck an agreement. By its provisions Scott, Baker, and
Fahnestock agreed to sell Sully, Pace, and Logan, on behalf of the
Terminal, 25,000 shares of Danville stock on the following terms:
the price would be $5,000,000 cash and $1,500,000 in Terminal
common at par which figured out to $200 cash and $30 in Terminal common per share of Danville; that sum would be paid in
three installments, thirty, sixty, and ninety days from the agreement date; the Danville agreed to secure the resignations of at
least three of the five Terminal directors and its president, these
positions to be filled by the purchasers; the new Terminal board
would move to purchase the Danville stock from the Sully syndicate; to make this purchase, the Terminal would increase its capitalization from $15,000,000 to $24,000,000.[66]

The increased capitalization held the key to the agreement and
warrants further explanation. Of the $9,000,000 new common,

[64] *Ibid.*

[65] *Ibid.* Terminal stock had gone as high as 77⅛ during the fight.

[66] Terminal Annual Meeting Minutes, Nov. 19, 1886; David Schenck Diary,
Dec. 18, 1886. A copy of the agreement, dated Nov. 20, 1886, is in the Southern
Railway archives.

$1,500,000 would go to the First National group as part of the purchase price. In addition, $5,000,000 in new preferred stock paying 5 per cent cumulative dividend over the common would be created. This preferred and the remaining $7,500,000 of new common could be used to obtain the $5,000,000 cash needed for the Danville stock. The 25,000 shares of Danville would be pledged as much as legally possible to guarantee the cumulative preferred dividend.[67]

In effect, then, the Sully syndicate paid an exorbitant price for the Danville, added a substantial amount for their own troubles, and tossed the entire burden into a swollen capitalization for the Terminal. They bought more than property: they sought to buy harmony. But so extensive an increase in the Terminal's securities did not bode harmony. Rather it offered extra leverage for discordant elements within the company to use. The higher the capitalization the more difficult it became for any single faction to dominate the company. As long as the Danville, with its relatively small capitalization, controlled the Terminal, power could be tightly and effectively wielded. But to reverse the relationship and make the Terminal the center of power seemed to invite the very sort of factional sniping the Sully syndicate wished to eradicate.

If any of the participants foresaw these problems they kept their qualms to themselves. The directors' meeting approved the transaction, and the general meeting followed suit on November 26. Only Clyde and his cohorts remained somewhat at loose ends. Mindful that his tenure was near its end, he drew one last reward for his labors. At directors' meetings on November 17 and 18 the outgoing Terminal board approved a resolution to compensate Clyde for his services as president. He received a $6,000 annual salary retroactive to 1880, when he first assumed office. Pocketing the $42,000, Clyde withdrew the next day from active participation in the Terminal's management. He would await a better day.[68]

All changes went according to plan. On November 20 Sully assumed the presidency of the Terminal, and Logan, Rutherfurd, Stone, and Rice became directors. Four days later the new management released a circular to the stockholders explaining the Danville transaction and offering the new preferred stock for sale.

[67] Besides the agreement itself, see Terminal Directors' Minutes, Nov. 20, 1886, and New York *Times*, August 28, 1892.

[68] Terminal Directors' Minutes, Nov. 17 and 18, 1886. Clyde himself apparently voted on the resolution, which included a warm memorial to his "generous and unmeasured devotion."

Each holder of 100 shares could subscribe to the new issue to the extent of one-third the par value of his holdings. For that third he would receive 33⅓ shares of the new preferred and 50 shares of the new common. The November 26 meeting ratified all agreements and transactions. At the regular annual meeting on December 8, Rice passed a motion to increase the number of directors from five to thirteen, exclusive of the president. The new board consisted of Sully, Logan, Stone, Rutherfurd, Rice, Lehman, Henry M. Flagler, Robert K. Dow, John Inman, John G. Moore, Simon Wormser, John Wanamaker, Pace, and E. D. Christian, the last two being Richmonders.[69]

On December 13 the Terminal made its first payment and took formal possession of the Danville.[70] The long-drawn-out battle seemed finally resolved, or did it? As Wall Street put it, the tail now wagged the dog: the Terminal controlled the Danville. But the real nature of the holding company remained an enigma even to its possessors, and its very unfamiliarity continued to intrigue active imaginations. It had suddenly assumed a role never intended for it, and its possibilities were many. The financiers had not yet mastered the form and to a large extent would have to feel their way. And one vital faction of the old syndicate remains to be accounted for: the Brice-Thomas-Seney trio. Their role in the Terminal's dramatic evolution depended upon events unfolding within the management of the East Tennessee.

[69] *Ibid.*, Nov. 19, 20, and 30, 1886; Terminal Annual Meeting Minutes, Nov. 26, Dec. 8, 1886; *Railroad Gazette*, XVIII (1886), 804, 822, 825, 857; *Chronicle*, XLIII (1886), 608, 635. Copies of the Notice to Stockholders, dated Nov. 24, 1886, and the Preferred Stock Trust Agreement, dated Dec. 6, 1886, can be found in the Southern Railway archives.

[70] *Railroad Gazette*, XVIII (1886), 880.

Chapter V

The Perils of Expansion
The East Tennessee Experience, 1880–1886

The Beginnings of the Cart-Wheel Expansion

THE quest of the East Tennessee management for a viable strategy impaled it upon the horns of a familiar dilemma. The sheltered location of the road rendered it impervious to any serious competition for most of its local business. As long as it remained content to rely upon local traffic and eschew the burdens of growth on a large scale, the future seemed secure if not spectacular. But the changing economic environment would not allow so complacent a policy. Despite all of Wilson's efforts, the stagnation in earnings threatened to linger on and worsen unless positive steps were taken to arrest it. By 1880 the question was no longer whether or not to expand but in what direction to expand.

Here again the East Tennessee confronted an embarrassment of choices. The company could go north toward Cincinnati, eastward to the Carolinas via the Morristown branch, or to the southeast and southwest by acquiring various bankrupt roads in those regions. Potential allies or enemies crowded the East Tennessee on each of these flanks: the Danville to the east, the Georgia roads to the south, the Erlanger roads to the southwest, and the L. & N. to the north and west. The L. & N. posed an especially serious threat. It had begun a policy of aggressive expansion that reached its peak in 1880 when Victor Newcomb doubled the system's mileage. "Newcomb's Octopus," as it had come to be known, reached Chattanooga and searched impatiently for an outlet to the seaboard. So far the Georgia roads had thwarted his ambitions, but the blockade was crumbling. Other roads hastened to strengthen themselves against the L. & N.'s growing powers. This rapid escalation of expansion could not help influencing the East Tennessee's considerations.[1]

A close look at the formulation of strategy by Wilson sheds much light on the delicacy of the problems involved. Construction of the Cincinnati Southern had revived the L. & N.'s desire to com-

[1] For more detail on the L. & N.'s strategy, see Stover, *Railroads of the South,* chap. 10.

plete the Lebanon branch connection to the East Tennessee. During the autumn of 1879 the L. & N. management offered again to build to the state line if Wilson would guarantee to meet it there. The project had more appeal for Wilson now even though it meant buying control of the Knoxville & Ohio. To his thinking, however, the connection meant little unless the East Tennessee could finish the Morristown branch at the same time. If the Western North Carolina met the Morristown branch at the Tennessee–North Carolina border, that would open a new through line to the northeast via the Danville. It would also draw the L. & N., East Tennessee, and Danville closer together to protect their mutual interests.

By Wilson and McGhee's estimates the project could be financed by bonding the Morristown branch for $1,600,000. Of this amount $500,000 would be exchanged for K. & O. bonds and another $1,000,000 sold at 90 to raise $900,000 in cash. The bonds would add $90,000 a year to fixed charges. Net earnings of the K. & O. would provide about $35,000 of this, leaving $55,000 needed from the new business to be produced by the connection. Wilson felt sure a syndicate could be raised easily on these terms. "If the North Carolina people were ready to join us," he noted, "I would have no doubt about the propriety of our making the move. . . . I have pretty well made up my mind that it is proper for us to do so anyway, as it cannot be long before the North Carolina connection will be made." [2]

But the North Carolina situation remained nebulous, and meanwhile new problems arose. In 1877 the ill-fated Georgia Western, building westward from Atlanta, underwent bankruptcy and foreclosure. By 1879 the franchise had become available to the highest bidder. McGhee saw in it an excellent opportunity for the East Tennessee to enter the region southwest of Chattanooga. He urged Wilson to acquire the franchise, but the latter demurred. The step would involve numerous problems. It would disrupt existing good relations with the Western & Atlantic and Atlanta & West Point roads, upon which the East Tennessee depended for much of its through passenger business. These roads would surely see the Western as a threat even though it could not handle its passenger service.

In addition, the move would raise serious problems with the Nashville, Chattanooga & St. Louis system. The East Tennessee co-

[2] R. T. Wilson to W. T. Walters, Oct. 29, 1879, McGhee papers.

operated with that road in its through line to Nashville via the Virginia & Tennessee Air-Line. Moreover, the Memphis & Charleston used N.C. & S.L. trackage to reach Chattanooga from Stevenson, Alabama. Any attempt to build the Western might well disrupt these two arrangements with grave consequences for the East Tennessee. And the capital required for the project would doubtless prohibit the company from undertaking any of its other proposed extensions. Despite these reservations, Wilson agreed to bid on the franchise.[3]

His efforts soon met powerful opposition. The L. & N. wanted the franchise more urgently than Wilson. Its management wished to use the proposed road as a club to bludgeon the recalcitrant Georgia roads into concessions. At the sale they outwitted Wilson's agent to claim the franchise, and Wilson hastened to seek an alliance with them. The experience once again demonstrated the inadequacy of the East Tennessee's capital to accomplish the ends necessary for its survival. Quietly Wilson tried to draw new interests into the company, among them Morris K. Jesup, a wealthy banker who already had large holdings in southern railroads; Henry B. Plant, whose domination of the Southern Express Company led him into rail enterprises; and W. T. Walters.[4]

With the help of these financiers Wilson sought to draw the L. & N. into an alliance to harmonize potential threats raised by the Western and to assure both companies of stable connections west of Memphis.[5] The first issue lapsed when Edward H. Green, a large New York holder in L. & N., assured Wilson that the company had no plans to build at the moment. The key to the second objective lay in the financially moribund Memphis & Little Rock Railroad. Possession or domination of that road could guarantee connections to the Iron Mountain road or, more important, to the expanding Texas & Pacific, in which Wilson and McGhee were becoming involved.

The problem with the Memphis & Little Rock was its sorry earning power. As Wilson expressed it, "There is no immediate promise of the Road being able to earn anything over what will be required to go into it, for at least three years to come; and it really takes a courageous party to buy bonds on a road of such a history as it has." Nevertheless, it remained a vital connection to western

---

[3] Wilson to McGhee, Oct. 31, 1879, *ibid.*   [4] *Ibid.*, Dec. 16, 1879.

[5] The L. & N. also reached Memphis and therefore had much interest in trying to stabilize connections there. For the importance of an independent connection west of Memphis, see *Railroad Gazette*, XVI (1884), 855.

traffic. To minimize risk Wilson proposed a joint syndicate consisting of the East Tennessee, L. & N., Little Rock & Fort Smith, and perhaps the people building the Texarkana branch of the Texas & Pacific to share the cost of purchasing and maintaining the road.[6]

While these enterprises hung fire, Wilson had to resolve the situation to the south. Within a year two important roads came up for sale: the Selma, Rome & Dalton and the Macon & Brunswick. Though both of these roads had exceedingly poor performance records, Wilson and McGhee agreed that possession of them was vital to the East Tennessee. Wilson already owned controlling interest in the Georgia portion of the Dalton. When the Alabama line came up for sale on June 14, 1880, he bought it as well. The purchase extended the East Tennessee's southern terminus to Selma and boded possible conflict with the L. & N. and Central of Georgia in that region.[7]

The Macon & Brunswick posed more formidable problems. That sorry line had been operated by a receiver on behalf of the state of Georgia since lapsing into bankruptcy in 1873. An attempted sale in 1875 forced the state to reclaim the road to prevent heavy sacrifice. Seeing that the road would always remain worthless unless it could reach Atlanta, the legislature tried a new tack in 1879. It authorized sale of the road on condition that the buyer extend the line to Atlanta. Acquisition by the East Tennessee would mean extending beyond Atlanta to Rome, where it would connect with the Dalton and form a new through line to the seaboard.[8]

Wilson pondered the intricacies of the problem. To undertake the project would require heavy commitments for highly uncertain returns. Moreover, the undeveloped port of Brunswick was decidedly inferior to Savannah or Charleston, and much of the road traversed the unproductive pine barrens. Construction of the Atlanta-Macon line would directly parallel the powerful Central of Georgia and doubtless cause a savage competition. On the other hand, it would give the East Tennessee its long-desired outlet to the seaboard and, together with the Dalton, provide alternative sources of new business. And completion of the link between Chattanooga and Atlanta would end forever the East Tennessee's de-

[6] Wilson to McGhee, Oct. 31, Dec. 27, 1879, McGhee papers. Ultimately Wilson decided against the Memphis & Little Rock, and the Iron Mountain acquired the road (see *Chronicle*, XXX [1880], 142, 466).

[7] Harrison, *Southern Railway*, 808–12; *Chronicle*, XXX (1880), 434, 651.

[8] Harrison, *Southern Railway*, 834–47.

pendence upon the Western & Atlantic. To be sure, it would also transform a friendly relationship into a bitter rivalry.

The temptation proved irresistible even to the cautious Wilson. Enlisting the support of Plant and other allies, he formed a syndicate to purchase the Brunswick in February, 1880. Legal and title disputes ensnared the transaction in controversy, however, and the matter dragged on for several months.[9]

The accelerating growth of the East Tennessee soon began to affect its management. The demands of the system and his own proliferating interests outside the road made the presidency an intolerable burden for Wilson. After conferring with McGhee he resigned his post in the spring of 1880 and was replaced by Edwin "King" Cole. Fresh from the loss of his Nashville, Chattanooga & St. Louis system to the wily Newcomb and the L. & N., Cole stepped energetically into his new office. McGhee continued as vice-president, and Wilson served only as financial director.[10]

Wilson's gradual withdrawal from active participation in East Tennessee affairs proved a harbinger of further change. After some hesitation he had launched the company into a kind of cart-wheel expansion, with lines fanning out in every direction much like spokes from a hub. He had come to believe that the road's position rendered it unfeasible to rely upon one basic route for future growth. Rather it must reach out to compete in as many distant fields as possible. But fulfillment of that strategy would require considerably more capital than the company could muster. New money could only be mobilized outside the East Tennessee, and the suppliers of it were destined to leave a deep imprint on the company's history.

Entrance of the Seney Syndicate

Like so many crucial corners of the Terminal's history, the precise origins of the Seney syndicate remain obscure. The exact motives that prompted a circle of prominent northern capitalists to plunge suddenly into southern railroads can only be surmised here. The key intermediary seems to have been the colorful Edwin Cole. As president, Cole threw himself wholeheartedly into the expansion

[9] Wilson to McGhee, Feb. 3, 1880, McGhee papers; *Chronicle*, XXX (1880), 169, 192, 248, XXXI (1880), 559.

[10] *Chronicle*, XXX (1880), 567; *Railway World*, XXIV (1880), 535.

program. He renewed negotiations for the K. & O. and agreed with Wilson to build a short but vital connector from the Chattanooga arm to the Dalton arm of the Y-shaped road. This eleven-mile line, known as the "Ooltewah cutoff," enabled northbound traffic to reach Chattanooga without taking the long swing via Cleveland. To ensure peace in the new territories reached by his lines and to protect his homeground, Cole participated in talks seeking the formation of a giant rail pool to include the East Tennessee, Cincinnati Southern, Kentucky Central, Chesapeake & Ohio, South Carolina, and Erlanger roads.[11]

In bestowing the presidency upon Cole, Wilson unleashed a veritable tiger. The furies of expansion, once uncaged, tended to feed on their own impetus anyway, but Cole's influence could only quicken the pace. His record with the Nashville road had been one of swift growth, daring maneuver, and unpredictable behavior. His flamboyant style could not have endeared him to the conservative Wilson, and his grandiose schemes must have left the guardian of the purse strings uneasy. In coming reluctantly to an expansion policy Wilson had husbanded his resources carefully. Cole's ambition, however, required massive transfusions of capital in short order. The conflict could only have produced friction and accentuated Wilson's growing concern about the East Tennessee as a safe investment. It also sent Cole northward in search of less reticent financiers willing to supply Cole with the capital he needed. That search led him to Seney and his associates.[12]

Cole's appeal caught the syndicate at a delicate time. Its leader, George I. Seney, president of the Metropolitan Bank, had pursued a banking career described by fellow financier Henry Clews as "slow and phlegmatic, without manifesting any special parts that indicated superior brilliancy as a financier." [13] Having made no name for himself on Wall Street until the speculative upheaval in 1879, he had come only recently to rail enterprises. By 1880 he had formed a syndicate to control the Lake Erie & Western Railroad

[11] *Railway World,* XXIV (1880), 565. Although specific proposals came out of the talks, no pool was formed. For the proposal, see *Chronicle,* XXXII (1881), 121.

[12] This analysis is admittedly based upon circumstantial and largely indirect evidence. Cole's role, however, is confirmed by a public letter written by Thomas in protest of state regulation. Addressing it to Cole, he noted that "it was due to your exertions and representations solely that the Seney people engaged in railroad building in Georgia" (unidentified clipping in William G. Raoul Scrapbook, I, 21).

[13] Clews, *Twenty-Eight Years,* 163.

and build extensions for it. At the same time plans were made to construct a road from Buffalo to Cleveland. By the winter of 1881 this project had become the genesis of the New York, Chicago & St. Louis or "Nickel Plate" road.[14]

On February 2 and 3, 1881, Seney summoned a group of his associates to his office at the Metropolitan Bank. Those present included Calvin Brice, Samuel Thomas, Edward H. R. Lyman of the tea import house, A. A. Low & Brothers, merchant and storage dealer John T. Martin, and several other men. All were involved in the Lake Erie & Western, Ohio Central, and Peoria, Decatur & Evansville Railroads. At the February 3 meeting the syndicate agreed to form the New York, Chicago & St. Louis Railway Company with an authorized capital of $16,000,000. Their reasons for taking on the project remain unclear. Since the new road paralleled the Vanderbilt Lake Shore and Michigan Southern roads, it has been argued persuasively that the venture had the speculative goal of forcing Vanderbilt to buy his new competitor off at an inflated price. On the other hand, sound defensive reasoning lay behind the project. The Lake Erie's traffic arrangements with the Vanderbilt lines had virtually sealed it off from western traffic. Threatened with possible ruin, the Lake Erie syndicate may also have been prompted by the desire to protect their investment.[15]

Whatever the priority of motivations, the Seney syndicate had committed itself to a sizable project by February, 1881. Apparently Cole approached the group shortly afterward with his plans for the East Tennessee. By early spring he had aroused enough interest to lure Seney, Brice, Thomas, Lyman, and Martin into a second substantial commitment. Early in May word leaked out that the syndicate had subscribed $16,000,000 to purchase the East Tennessee and use it as the nucleus of a vast southern system.[16] Here, too, the syndicate's reasoning is hard to fathom. Perhaps they entered the project as an entirely separate venture. More likely, however, they envisioned large short-term profits needed to support the more important Nickel Plate enterprise. On the surface their motives appear to have been purely opportunistic. But, as often happened, once in they found it difficult to get out easily.

[14] For more detail, see Hampton, *Nickel Plate Road*, chaps. 2, 15. The Lake Erie road connected Sandusky, Ohio, and Bloomington, Ill.

[15] For the defensive argument, see John A. Rehor, *The Nickel Plate Story* (Milwaukee, 1965), 13–17. The evidence in hindsight would seem to favor speculation as the primary but not exclusive motivation.

[16] *Railroad Gazette*, XIII (1881), 284; *Chronicle*, XXXII (1881), 522; *East Tennessee Report*, 1881, 8.

Transformation of the East Tennessee

Although Cole retained the presidency of the system, Seney, Brice, and Thomas dominated the company from the beginning. The willingness of the syndicate to incur the burden proved a great relief to Wilson, who disposed of most of his holdings and withdrew entirely from the company. The *Chronicle*, noting his departure in sorrow, praised him as "the author and creator of this system." In lauding his policies the paper added that "it is proper to state that the results mentioned were achieved, not through any stock-jobbing manipulations, but wholly through good business management."[17]

The Seney management took a radically different tack. To mobilize the capital needed for their schemes the syndicate completely reorganized the East Tennessee and endowed it with a liberal outpouring of new securities. In little over a year the company's total assets soared from $10,321,338 to $82,500,000, capital stock (now in common and preferred) from $1,967,074 to $44,000,000, and funded debt from $4,186,000 to $38,500,000. Here, as in the Nickel Plate, Seney unveiled a technique hitherto unsuspected in his financial repertory: the lavish watering of a reorganized company from the very outset. The audacity of his methods astonished and outraged veteran Wall Street operators. With fine relish Henry Clews recalled Seney's impact:

There was nothing mean or niggardly about his method of free dilution . . . the stocks were strongly puffed, and as they were so thoroughly diluted their owners could afford to let them get a start at a very low figure. The future prospects of the properties were set forth in the most glowing colors, the public took the bait, and the stocks became at once conspicious among the leading active fancies of the market.[18]

Not surprisingly, East Tennessee securities went onto the New York Exchange shortly after the syndicate gained control.[19]

In exchange for this capital the syndicate acquired in short order the East Tennessee, the Dalton, the K. & O., the Brunswick, and various smaller branches, in addition to the continuing lease on the Memphis & Charleston. The aggregate totaled some 1,183 miles. For his pains Wilson received a nice profit on those lines still held in his name. Other large East Tennessee holders re-

[17] XXXIII (1881), 553.   [18] *Twenty-Eight Years*, 164.
[19] *Railway World*, XXV (1881), 760.

warded themselves by selling off large parcels of the stock at inflated prices before the new issues drove them down. In June, McGhee unloaded $36,000 in East Tennessee stock at around 200. When the expanded issue first went on the New York Exchange in August it was quoted at 33. Nor did the syndicate overlook the news media in their promotion. Through Cole the ambitious but financially strapped Henry Grady subscribed to a sizable block of East Tennessee stock for himself and for his paper. Thereafter the Atlanta *Constitution* tended to view the Seney syndicate's operations with a favorable eye.[20]

In general the Seney management pursued a fairly simple strategy. They moved quickly to weld together the sprawling, disjointed lines into an effective interterritorial system. Immediately after consummating the long-delayed Brunswick transaction Cole began work on the missing links between Macon and Atlanta, and Atlanta and Rome. Completion of the 161-mile road in October, 1882, provided the company with its outlet to the sea at Brunswick.[21] To the southwest, the syndicate extended the Dalton westward by purchasing the 95-mile Alabama Central, which reached Lauderdale, Mississippi, from Selma. From there rental of Mobile & Ohio trackage provided entrance into Meridian, and plans abounded for later expansion to the Mississippi River.[22]

Since this aggressive expansion inevitably alarmed neighboring roads, the East Tennessee coupled its growth with a search for peace treaties. To the north Cole signed an agreement with Collis Huntington by which the East Tennessee could reach Cincinnati over the latter's yet unfinished system of roads.[23] More important, Cole formed a new working agreement with the Norfolk & Western and Shenandoah Valley roads that promised to stabilize the vital eastern connection. The tripartite pact, signed September 28, 1881, seemed to interlock the destiny of both major systems on a permanent basis. The terms forbade each road from building a rival line against the other and guaranteed the East Tennessee access to Norfolk, Baltimore, Philadelphia, and New York. In expli-

20 *East Tennessee Report,* 1881, 7–14; Wilson to McGhee, June 29, 1881, McGhee papers; Henry W. Grady, "Cash Account Book 1881," 10, 184–86, Henry W. Grady papers, Emory University. This account book indicates that Grady also speculated in Danville stock early in 1881 and owned about $20,000 in the Danville Construction Company for the *Constitution.*

21 *Chronicle,* XXXIII (1881), 100, XXXV (1882), 430; Harrison, *Southern Railway,* 847–51. The project was incorporated as the Cincinnati & Georgia Railroad and then leased to the East Tennessee upon completion.

22 Poor, *Manual for 1882,* 452, 480.   23 *Chronicle,* XXXIII (1881), 303.

cating the pact Cole noted that "the contract was for a consolidation of business interests . . . for the protection of the roads. . . . The location of these roads is such that competition and rival builders will have great difficulty in seriously affecting the property." The roads would thereafter become known as the Virginia, Tennessee & Georgia Air-Line.[24]

In Alabama, Cole came at least temporarily to terms with the powerful L. & N. The two companies agreed to exchange Montgomery business at Calera, where their lines crossed. The L. & N. would prorate all Montgomery business in return for the East Tennessee's promise not to build any new road in the Montgomery district for the ten-year duration of the contract. As part of the bargain the L. & N. agreed further to grant the East Tennessee access to New Orleans and Mobile and to prorate on all business to those points.[25]

The traffic agreements left the southern and northern spokes of the road in relative peace for the moment. Serious trouble arose on the western spoke, the burdensome Memphis & Charleston. Despite the lease, the inability of the two companies to ameliorate their difference grew worse instead of better. The East Tennessee regarded the Memphis road as a necessary if expensive evil. Net earnings on the road seldom covered its fixed charges, and improvement expenditures left a perpetual deficit. Minority holders on the Memphis road, however, viewed matters differently. They accused the East Tennessee of manipulating accounts to deprive them of dividends. In addition, the road was coveted by other growing systems in the region despite its notoriously poor earning record. For other roads as for the East Tennessee, the Memphis road bore the reputation of so many southern lines: weak ally but powerful enemy.

Early in the 1880's parties hostile to the East Tennessee acquired substantial amounts of Memphis & Charleston stock. At the 1881 annual meeting they passed resolutions directing the board to take legal action to annul the lease. By March, 1882, however, nothing had been done, and it was rumored that the East Tennessee had bought off the dissidents. The impending change in management apparently complicated the deal, for that summer the minority renewed the attack. At the annual meeting in August, 1882, the stockholders declined a proposal to consolidate with the East Ten-

---

[24] *Ibid.*, 357; *Railway World*, XXV (1881), 947, 980.
[25] *Railroad Gazette*, XIII (1881), 577; *Chronicle*, XXXIII (1881), 468.

nessee. Instead they authorized the directors to appoint a committee to negotiate a settlement for the lease. At this point the East Tennessee seemed willing to surrender its albatross; Thomas assured the meeting that an offer of $400,000 for the lease would be accepted.[26]

By November the details had been worked out. The Memphis line would pay $800,000 for improvement costs incurred by the East Tennessee. Of this $306,000 would be in first-mortgage bonds and the rest in cash. The company elected a new board with none of the familiar East Tennessee personnel and announced itself ready to operate without the lease. But word soon leaked out that the Memphis road, once free of the old contract, had arranged for a lease to the Erlanger system. The news provoked second thoughts among the Seney syndicate, who now saw an invidious Erlanger-inspired plot behind the whole affair. When the Memphis road could not raise the necessary cash by the allotted date, Brice and Thomas suspended negotiations for over a month on the plea of prior commitments. To the protests from the Memphis holders they replied only that the lease would not be surrendered unless the money was handed over on the spot, a palpable impossibility.[27]

Outraged and frustrated, the Memphis holders escalated the struggle. They persuaded Drexel, Morgan & Company to lend them the $1,313,000 necessary for cancellation of the lease. At a February, 1883, conference Brice and Thomas first agreed to the new terms and then resorted again to stalling tactics. In desperation the Memphis holders applied for a receiver only to find themselves outflanked once more. Before the courts could act Thomas quietly formed a syndicate to acquire a majority of the road's stock. Taking most of the stock himself, he announced in August that the company had changed ownership and all opposition to the lease would be dropped. The two roads retained their separate organizations, East Tennessee personnel returned to the Memphis board, and the dispute evaporated.[28]

By the fall of 1883 the fractious problem on the Memphis & Charleston had been settled, though by no means permanently.

[26] *Railroad Gazette*, XIV (1882), 156; *Chronicle*, XXXV (1882), 212, 236.

[27] *Chronicle*, XXXV (1882), 431, 516, 602, XXXVI (1883), 81, 108. To unify their holdings the Memphis holders formed a stock pool on Sept. 6, 1882. A copy of the agreement is in Baker Library.

[28] *Chronicle*, XXXVI (1883), 170, 196, XXXVII (1883), 234, XXXVIII (1884), 61.

Minority holders remained to protest their treatment by the East Tennessee. Lacking equity strength on which to resist, they would resort instead to the courts. The entire episode prophesied a serious problem within every growing system and one that would constantly plague the Terminal: the clash of interests between the parent system management and security holders in roads absorbed by expansion. The objectives of each proved radically different and often irreconcilable. Too late did rail entrepreneurs discover that mere consolidation alone did not bring unity of interests. But more of that in later chapters.

The Shifting of Power and Alliances

While the East Tennessee worked to strengthen its position as an interterritorial system, noticeable signs of strain began to show within its management. The liaison between Cole and the Seney syndicate, never entirely comfortable, deteriorated rapidly. Cole, an individualistic empire-builder, had assumed the syndicate would provide him with capital and, preoccupied with its numerous other affairs, give him free rein to run the system. But Seney and his associates would grant no such license and insisted on participating actively in policy making. The friction revealed itself especially in financial policy. Cole thought primarily in terms of the system itself and its needs. The syndicate, however, regarded the company as but one of many interests and weighed its demands carefully in the balance with the claims of other projects. Neither had any strong personal or regional loyalty to the system, but Cole could devote himself more completely to its welfare. In that sense his ties to the East Tennessee were largely personal while those of the syndicate were almost purely financial.

The clash of wills and viewpoints could not long continue. Seney had put a majority of his supporters on the board, including Brice, Thomas, Samuel Shethar and H. L. Terrell, two financial associates, Nelson Robinson, his son-in-law, Robert Seney, his brother, and George McGourkey, cashier of the Metropolitan Bank. McGhee and a fellow Knoxville capitalist, E. J. Sanford, had also grown close to Brice and Thomas and supported the syndicate's policies. Finding himself opposed at every turn, Cole finally resigned in May, 1882. Thomas shed some of his minor responsibilities and replaced him as president. Henry Fink, brother of Albert Fink and a capable railroad man in his own right, assumed the vice-presidency in charge of operations.[29] The change crystallized a growing separation of financial and operational control. The financiers had little knowledge or interest in operational details. Their willingness to delegate much of their authority and concentrate instead upon broad questions of strategy marked the first step toward a more sophisticated administration.

Shortly after Thomas took office the syndicate wound up its Nickel Plate enterprise. The road opened for traffic on October 23, 1882, after much difficulty. The enormous cost had strained the syndicate's resources and forced Seney to seek capital in London. At the height of their troubles in July, 1882, the syndicate had been forced to throw a sizable chunk of East Tennessee stock on an already depressed market. Their action drove the stock's price down from 21⅜ to 8½. But a timely loan from the house of Seligman salvaged the project, and three days after the new road opened the syndicate sold it to representatives of William H. Vanderbilt. The handsome profit realized on the transaction enabled the syndicate to buttress their investment in the East Tennessee.[30]

While still grappling with the Memphis & Charleston problem the Seney syndicate had to undertake a major reassessment of strategy. Two important changes in the over-all situation, one west of the Mississippi and one east of the Blue Ridge, demanded immediate attention. Conditions in the West had coalesced suddenly after 1877, when Jay Gould's purchase of the Missouri Pacific inaugurated a strategy of rapid consolidation by the master manipulator. Both the Texas & Pacific and the Iron Mountain fell into his hands, and the hapless but strategic Memphis & Little Rock, after Wilson abandoned his grand design, drifted into receivership by 1882. Meanwhile Gould found himself locked in combat with Collis Huntington.[31]

In carrying his fight east of the Mississippi, Gould went hunting for potential allies capable of hurting Huntington's eastern lines. The East Tennessee seemed a likely prospect. It could greatly disturb Huntington's connections south of Kentucky. Moreover, it badly needed a strong western ally to provide the Memphis road with new traffic and the management, practical financial men all,

---

[29] *Railroad Gazette*, XIV (1882) , 276.

[30] For detailed account of the Nickel Plate episode, see Hampton, *Nickel Plate Road,* chaps. 2–11.

[31] For background to the Gould-Huntington fight, see Grodinsky, *Transcontinental Railway Strategy,* chaps. 8–14.

could be amenable to negotiation. Gould could not have over-looked the fact that Seney and his associates had recently nicked Gould's old enemy, William Vanderbilt, in the Nickel Plate trans-action. By the winter of 1883 rumors of the proposed alliance abounded, and some reports hinted at large purchases of East Ten-nessee stock by Gould's agents.[32]

Seney and his associates were in fact considering the possibilities of an alliance or outright sale to Gould, but the second situation complicated these deliberations. Conditions within the Danville management had also changed rapidly. A new syndicate was being formed to take over the system, and the Seney syndicate found an opportunity to enter it. Participation in the Danville maneuver-ing, however, would immediately arouse the suspicion of the Nor-folk & Western and disturb the infant Virginia, Tennessee & Geor-gia Air-Line. The tripartite pact, while only a working agreement, looked to the ultimate consolidation of all the roads involved. While little had been done toward that goal, rumors of an im-pending merger revived in the spring of 1883.[33] But certainly the East Tennessee could not involve itself in both the Danville and the Norfolk at the same time. The competitive situation would not tolerate it.

In the spring of 1883, then, Seney and his associates confronted a series of delicate, closely intertwined choices. No decision could be made in a vacuum. Each would have repercussive effects on the others, and any choice would upset the fragile existing balance of relationships. An alliance with Gould would alienate Huntington, who might close off the connection to Cincinnati. It would also alarm the L. & N. and, incidentally, the Central of Georgia, an-other potential candidate for traffic interchange with the Missouri Pacific. Rejection of the alliance might antagonize the powerful Gould and destroy any hope of an effective western connection. Participation in the Danville would doubtless affect the Virginia, Tennessee & Georgia Air-Line adversely, while merger with the Norfolk would drive the Danville into opposition. Nor should the negative pressure be overlooked. Failure to act on any of these op-tions might leave the East Tennessee system helpless to affect the rapidly changing competitive environment. Events were moving fast; indecision could leave the company overshadowed by vast new combinations and alliances.

To provide for any eventuality Thomas summoned a special stockholders' meeting for June 23. At the meeting the syndicate

---

[32] *Railroad Gazette*, XV (1883), 273.   [33] *Ibid.*, 288.

had resolutions passed investing them with sweeping powers to build or buy any branches or extensions, or acquire lines of other companies needed to perfect the system. To do this they were authorized to increase the common stock from $27,500,000 to $35,000,000 and the preferred from $16,500,000 to $25,000,000. In addition they could issue another $10,000,000 in 6 per cent bonds. The resolutions did not specify the project for which these funds were allocated. The going rumor suggested a three-step plan: consolidating the Memphis & Charleston, extending the Georgia Division from Brunswick to Jacksonville, and forming an alliance with Gould either by lease or agreement.[34]

Less than two months after the meeting, however, the Gould negotiations died a sudden and mysterious death. At the same time interest in the Danville deal warmed noticeably.[35] Though the evidence is sketchy, it seems reasonable to assume a connection between the two decisions. In broad terms two possibilities come to mind. Developmentally the syndicate may have decided to strengthen their position at home before striking alliances beyond the region. Perhaps they feared Gould's influence and reputation for swallowing systems whole. Some of the syndicate, notably Brice and Thomas, were getting in too deep to get out easily. They had begun to invest heavily in such outside projects dependent upon the railroad as real estate, ore fields, mining, and related industries. Given the size of their commitment, they might well be reluctant to surrender control of the system to the unpredictable Gould.

Secondly, it seems probable that the Danville deal promised higher opportunistic profits than did the Gould alliance. Once having sold out to Gould, even at a fat profit, the Seney syndicate would be out of the game. Participation in the Danville purchase, however, would not only leave them in the game but broaden the possibilities as well. In this respect the syndicate deviated markedly from its Nickel Plate strategy. Whatever their original intentions, the financiers did not get out quickly. The combination of sequential investments and short-term transactional profits not only kept them in but led to a substantial deepening of their commitment. In view of the alternatives available to them one must conclude that they found their southern enterprises rewarding.

By early August the Danville deal had been consummated.

---

[34] *Ibid.*, 435; *Chronicle*, XXXVI (1883) , 731.
[35] *Railroad Gazette*, XV (1883) , 519.

Within a short time Seney, Brice, and Thomas took seats on the Danville board, Brice joined the Terminal board, and Baker, Fahnestock, and Scott came to the East Tennessee board. Lyman and Martin also moved onto the latter in place of McGourkey and another "dummy" director. The consequences of the change became evident at once. Late in the year the East Tennessee board resolved that a certain amount of eastbound traffic then going via the Norfolk & Western should be sent instead over the Morristown branch to the Danville. To slake the Norfolk's anger the directors appointed a committee to meet with the Virginia road's officers to discuss a proposed consolidation of the Air-Line companies. That no such merger would take place, however, had already become a foregone conclusion.[36]

The decision to unite with the Danville merits close examination because of its later repercussions. In retrospect it illustrates clearly the conflict between personal desires and corporate needs. Geography, logistics, and the best strategic interests of the East Tennessee system dictated continuation of the alliance and a probable merger with the Norfolk and Western. The combined systems offered the most favorable route to all northern outlets and, as would later become painfully apparent, Norfolk possessed unmistakable advantages over West Point as a port. Through traffic moving via the Norfolk road would have a comparatively long haul over the East Tennessee. In contrast, the shifting of this same traffic flow would utterly swamp the inadequate facilities at West Point.

The alliance between the two systems did open one new possibility. The opening of the Morristown branch and completion of the K. & O. to a connection with the L. & N. and Kentucky Central formed the first and only northwest-southeast trade route between the Ohio Valley and the southeastern seaboard. Traffic could now flow from Cincinnati to the Carolinas and to the ports of Charleston, Port Royal, Wilmington, and Morehead City without going via the established Chattanooga-Atlanta route. But even in this case the East Tennessee would have a short haul, and the Danville would receive most of the benefits. Small wonder that a contemporary observer noted skeptically, "it is a little difficult to understand what purpose is to be accomplished by uniting the system with the Richmond & Danville, and it is also not easy to see from what direction the large increase in the net earnings of both systems,

[36] *Ibid.*, XVI (1884), 17; *Chronicle*, XXXVII (1883), 719.

spoken of by Mr. Brice as certain to result from the union, is to come." [37]

The plain fact was that the East Tennessee and Danville systems paralleled each other to an embarrassing degree. In virtually every instance they could not avoid competing with each other for through traffic. Completion of the Georgia Pacific to Greenville would extend the parallel right to the Mississippi River's edge. No amount of consolidation or unity could alter the physical situation. Most likely the result could only be dissension within the two managements as each faction sought to favor that system in which it had the largest investment. This clash of interests would occur again and again until reaching its climax within the structure of the Terminal. Under these circumstances it seems most unlikely that the Seney syndicate chose to enter the Danville for reasons of strategy or developmental necessity. Rather they went in because the deal suited their personal opportunistic goals at the expense of a company to which they had no real personal loyalty.

The Seney syndicate did not rest on its oars after the Danville transaction. Having rejected Gould they hastened to solidify the Cincinnati connection. Brice ensured the key Kentucky Central link by purchasing the road jointly with Huntington. An agreement with the Plant system gave the East Tennessee access to Jacksonville over the former's roads, and on October 12, 1884, the East Tennessee ran its first train from Cincinnati to Jacksonville.[38] Nor had the notion of buying out the Erlanger roads been dropped. In March, 1884, an East Tennessee committee went to London to negotiate a lease of the system.[39]

But money was running low and financial conditions had deteriorated during 1883. The East Tennessee remained squarely in the midst of its buoyant expansion program. Any sudden contraction of the skittish money market could prove disastrous. Without much warning, it came and it did.

Collapse and Reorganization

By 1884 the East Tennessee had firmly established its position as a cart-wheel system. Its steel tentacles stretched westward to the Mis-

[37] *Chronicle,* XXXVII (1883), 111–12. Daggett, *Railroad Reorganization,* 150–51, overstates the value of the Western North Carolina connection between the two systems.

[38] *Chronicle,* XXXVIII (1884), 619, XXXIX (1884), 409.

[39] *Railroad Gazette,* XVI (1884), 123.

sissippi, southeastward to the South Atlantic coast, and deep into the Alabama and Mississippi interiors. Completed through lines carried its traffic to Cincinnati, Norfolk and points north, and eastward to the Carolinas. Its lines exceeded 1,400 miles, and the management talked of further growth. But the cost of that growth had been enormous and the operational returns negligible. Most damaging of all were the financial methods behind the expansion. Seney's "front ending" technique of loading the property with heavily watered securities at low prices proved fatal. In 1884 the system hovered precariously on the brink of collapse and needed only a slight shove to topple it. That shove came in good measure with the panic of 1884.

The data make clear the system's sickly state. The original 272-mile road had been capitalized at $7,232 in stock and $15,000 in bonds per mile. Annual interest charges ran about $283,000 or $1,040 per mile. Leaving aside the leased Memphis & Charleston, the Seney syndicate had acquired about 800 miles of new road with a capitalization of $80,000 stock and $25,000 bonds per mile and an annual interest charge of about $1,400,000 or $1,750 per mile.[40] To service this additional debt, a healthy increase in net earnings would be required. As Table 7 indicates, however, no such increase occurred. Gross earnings grew but not rapidly enough to cover mounting interest costs. Net earnings lagged behind despite all efforts to manipulate the operating ratio.

The erratic behavior of the earnings data in Table 7 can be largely explained by consideration of the operating ratio. During the period 1869–80 the East Tennessee operated at an average of 66.7 per cent of gross earnings. In four years under Seney management the ratio dropped to 58.1 per cent, and for three of those years it stayed at the same figure: 59.2. Such stability could not have been maintained except by design. The over-all decrease cannot be justified by increased efficiency simply because expansion itself necessitated large expenditures for new equipment and rolling stock to refurbish acquired lines and finish new ones. Much of the capital to meet these extraordinary expenditures would normally have appeared under operating expenditures; yet the operating ratio actually declined during the period! The logical conclusion, and one born out by later findings, is that the Seney management pursued the same policy as the Clyde syndicate: it pared improvement and other capital expenditures to the bone in order to boost

40 *Ibid.*, 884.

TABLE 7. Selected data on operations of the East Tennessee system, 1877–1884

Year	Gross earnings (1000's)	Rate of increase in gross earnings (%)	Net earnings (1000's)	Rate of increase in net earnings (%)	Ratio of net to gross earnings (%)	Interest payments (1000's)	Rate of increase in interest payments	Ratio of interest payments to net earnings (%)	Operating ratio (%)
1877	$1,010	—	$ 341	—	33.5	$ 284	—	83.3	66.2
1878	1,022	.011	410	.202	40.1	287	.011	70.0	59.9
1879	988	-.033	368	-.102	37.5	280	-.024	76.1	62.5
1880	1,213	.228	436	.185	35.9	283	.011	64.9	64.1
1881	2,117	.745	955	1.190	45.1	386	.364	40.4	54.9
1882	3,145	.486	1,283	.343	40.8	1,283	2.324	100.0	59.2
1883	3,776	.201	1,318	.027	40.8	1,501	.170	113.9	59.2
1884	4,173	.105	1,700	.290	40.8	1,403	-.065	82.5	59.2

SOURCE: Calculated from data in Appendixes III and IV.

net earnings. As the table shows, even this tactic did not suffice to meet the obligations imposed by expansion. Without it the deficit would have been greater. As it was, the system's physical plant gradually deteriorated under the Seney regime despite florid claims to the contrary.[41]

The systems growing physical debility pointed up a glaring flaw in Seney's methods of finance. No provision had been made for raising capital to finance needed improvements. Interest and other obligations swallowed virtually all net earnings, and Seney's glutting of the market with East Tennessee securities made the resort to additional stock or bonds impossible. The company's securities had declined steadily during 1884. By December preferred stood at 7½, common at 4¼, general-mortgage fives at 52, and income bonds at 13.[42] Yet these improvement expenditures offered the only hope for future success. As Stuart Daggett put it, the new roads were "a group of poorly equipped, unprofitable lines located in a keenly competitive territory." [43] Survival depended upon ability to meet that competition effectively, which in turn meant acquiring the facilities to provide efficient, even superior service. Seney's extravagant financing of the system's expansion ruined any hope of obtaining those facilities under existing conditions.

Fate did little to ease the growing crisis within the system. For all its attempts to develop the resources along its lines and thus diversify its traffic, the East Tennessee still depended heavily upon cotton. Both the 1883 and 1884 seasons produced light crops that crippled the system's earnings during otherwise favorable years on most southern roads. Savage competition drove rates so low at Memphis that the Memphis & Charleston actually withdrew from the market for a time. Strict rate regulation by the Georgia and Alabama state commissions prevented the company from covering some of their losses by raising tariffs, and the need for long-delayed improvements grew daily more urgent. To meet its obligations the company came to depend increasingly upon short-term loans.[44]

The money panic of May, 1884, proved a mortal blow to the tottering system. In buttressing his rail enterprises Seney had deeply involved the Metropolitan Bank, which held a sizable number of

[41] See Henry Fink's remarks in "Receiver's Report, East Tennessee Virginia & Georgia Railroad Company, January 7th to June 30, 1885," 11–14, Bureau of Railroad Economics.

[42] *Railroad Gazette*, XVI (1884) , 884.

[43] *Railroad Reorganization*, 151.

[44] *Railroad Gazette*, XVI (1884) , 884; *East Tennessee Report*, 1884, 4–5.

East Tennessee securities as collateral for loans. When the money market contracted, neither the bank nor Seney personally could meet their overextended obligations. The once proud bank suspended that same month, leaving Seney without resources to bail out the East Tennessee. The Metropolitan's fall severely aggravated the crisis, and only Seney's resignation enabled the institution to reopen temporarily in an attempt to calm the panic.[45]

Brice and Thomas, who had been gradually drawing away from Seney over matters of policy, made little effort to ease his predicament. They moved quickly, however, to aid the East Tennessee, which suddenly could find no short-term money. To carry the floating debt and meet interest payments due June 1, they assembled a small syndicate within the company and subscribed an issue of $1,200,000 in 6 per cent debenture bonds at full face value. Their prompt action in maintaining the company's credit and taking the bonds without discount drew praise from the *Chronicle*, which noted dryly that "the action of the directors was so unique in this respect—it happening so seldom that members will apply their own resources to sustain the property with which they are identified." [46]

The debentures staved off immediate default, but the situation grew no better. As autumn waned it became clear that the January interest payments could not be met. Thomas resolved to let matters slide no further. He appointed a funding committee consisting of himself, Lyman, Shethar, and George Sheldon, who had just joined the board. On December 30 the committee issued a circular to the bondholders in which it fully admitted the seriousness of the situation. In fairly explicit terms the circular set forth the reasons for the dilemma: construction of new roads had exceeded estimates, large sums were needed for improvements, and no provision had been made for them. For the next two years an estimated $1,117,217 would be required for construction, equipment, and betterments.[47]

Net earnings could not provide these funds, nor could they even cover fixed charges. The committee estimated total interest payments and other fixed obligations for 1885–86 at about $1,750,000 per year. Assuming a 60 per cent operating ratio and a continued

---

[45] *Chronicle*, XXXVIII (1884), 581–82. The East Tennessee transferred its trust business to Central Trust Company.

[46] XXXVIII (1884), 706, XXXIX (1884), 168–69, XL (1885), 4–5. General-mortgage bonds were selling at about 50 at the same time.

[47] For the circular, see *ibid.*, XL (1885), 29–30.

decline of 10 per cent in gross earnings, the net earnings for 1884–86 would average only about $1,400,000 a year or $350,000 short of meeting fixed charges. In all the committee concluded that $2,250,000 would be needed to cover deficits through 1886 and provide the necessary improvements and equipment.

To raise this money it ruled out temporary loans as unwise and issued four recommendations, listed here in abbreviated form: 1) holders of consolidated fives should fund four coupons by depositing them with the Central Trust Company in exchange for 6 per cent funded coupon bonds; 2) holders of the $2,000,000 Cincinnati & Georgia Division first-mortgage sixes should fund four coupons on the same terms given to consolidated fives; 3) holders of the debentures should extend those bonds falling due in 1885–86 for ten years and accept similar debentures in lieu of interest for those two years; and 4) holders of series A car trust certificates should extend all principal payments falling due in 1885–86 for ten years. Under these provisions the total amount extended would be $2,280,600.

In stressing the perilous condition of the company the committee did its security holders a good service. The Thomas plan won guarded approval in some quarters, but it had little chance of success.[48] The committee had not acknowledged any need to reform the company's top-heavy capital structure. They appeared to perceive the basic problem as a temporary difficulty induced by hard times rather than a fatal flaw within the structure itself. As a result they offered a palliative rather than a cure.[49] The plan pleased virtually no one within the company and soon led to a vigorous struggle for power between the Brice-Thomas faction, the Seney faction, and the foreign bondholders, who constituted the largest single bloc of minority holders. The wide disagreement of the factions promised a long and bitter fight.

The Lawsuits Descend

The two major factions entered combat with opposing centers of power. Seney's associates controlled a majority of the equity while the Brice-Thomas group possessed a substantial portion of the outstanding debt. Despite his recent misfortunes and shriveling empire, Seney refused to surrender. Upon learning of Thomas's ap-

---

[48] See *ibid.*, 4–5.
[49] Daggett, *Railroad Reorganization*, 154, makes the same point.

peal to the bondholders, he promptly resigned as director but managed to replace three opponents on the board with his own men. To protect the company from unfriendly litigation the board asked that the property be placed in receivership, and on January 6 Henry Fink took charge of the system. The bondholders continued to complain. Two major holders, the Metropolitan Bank and the New York Clearing House Association, which held a large amount of the bonds as collateral on a loan to the bank, accepted the Thomas funding scheme. Their acquiescence seemed to indicate that all would go smoothly for the plan.[50]

But such was not the case. The receivership itself touched off a veritable blizzard of litigation. The Georgia division already had several suits pending against it when Fink took office. Shortly after his appointment a band of Georgia creditors filed suit for and received separate receivers for the company's Georgia lines. Fink's appointment had come from the United State Circuit Court for Eastern Tennessee; the Georgia receivers had been tendered by the Superior Court of Fulton County, Georgia. The jurisdictional dispute led quickly to a bizarre procession of orders and counterorders. The superior court demanded that Fink surrender the Georgia; Fink refused adamantly, and the circuit court backed his stand by posting U.S. deputy marshals along the road to protect it. Meanwhile merchants began to shift their trade to other lines, improvements had to be delayed and workers discharged, and a general demoralization of business seemed imminent. Not until May 1, 1885, was a compromise reached and the Georgia suit dismissed. Other suits against the company continued and led to some attachments of property.[51]

Similar troubles flared up elsewhere. The rival Western & Atlantic refused for a time to handle certain East Tennessee freight, charging similar discriminations against the latter.[52] Another suit questioned the validity of the consolidated mortgage's lien on the Knoxville & Ohio. It was disclosed that through some mysterious manipulation the Seney syndicate had not retired the $500,000 in

[50] *Railroad Gazette*, XVII (1885), 14, 31; *Chronicle*, XL (1885), 60. Seney's position on the funding scheme is unclear. He seems to have acquiesced in it since he would still retain control of the company, but I can find no overt evidence on the point. The banking representatives asked that seven places on the 15-man board be given to the bondholders, and Seney agreed to this.

[51] For this tangled story, see "Receiver's Report," 14–15; *Railroad Gazette*, XVII (1885), 46–47, 63, 79, 96, 239, 255, 287.

[52] *Railroad Gazette*, XVII (1885), 96.

K. & O. bonds from proceeds of the East Tennessee mortgage. Rather the K. & O. bonds had simply been transferred to the Metropolitan Bank as collateral for a loan to the syndicate. On the books the bonds had been formally canceled and the mortgage discharged of record; yet they remained in existence, and Seney offered no explanation. The court agreed that the East Tennessee held a valid claim for $1,800,000 advanced to complete the road and buy the old bonds. It ordered a sale of the K. & O. to satisfy that claim.[53]

The East Tennessee board blanched at the news. An open sale might permit the L. & N. or Kentucky Central to acquire the K. & O. and throw a competing line directly into Knoxville. To avert such a dangerous threat to the balance of power, the East Tennessee arranged a compromise. In lieu of the indebtedness it would accept $2,400,000 in Memphis & Charleston stock, $200,000 in Cincinnati & Georgia bonds, and $600,000 in East Tennessee debentures. To pay for these securities the K. & O. would issue $2,000,000 in new 6 per cent bonds. The East Tennessee would in turn deposit the Memphis road's stock and the Cincinnati & Georgia bonds as security for its own 5 per cent consols. The K. & O. would remain under East Tennessee control, and no sale would take place.[54]

The presence of the Memphis & Charleston stock in the deal prompted another unexpected disclosure. The large block of stock supposedly purchased for the East Tennessee to resolve the last crisis had never been taken by the company because of its financial difficulties. Dissatisfaction among the minority holders over the lease had never been thoroughly squelched, and the East Tennessee's troubles gave it new opportunity to bloom. Anxious to complete the transaction before any major reorganization of the East Tennessee took place, Brice and Thomas resolved to use this discontent to their own advantage. As officers of the Memphis road they informed the East Tennessee in March, 1885, that they considered the lease void and would file suit to have it annulled.[55]

In this instance the Brice-Thomas faction held the equity cards, and Seney had no choice but to submit to the purchase or leave the road independent in now unfriendly hands. As the suit progressed Brice spoke confidently of its success and declared that under any arrangement the road "will be operated for the benefit

---

[53] *Ibid.*, 159.   [54] *Ibid.*, 478; *Chronicle*, XLI (1885), 102.

[55] This dispute can be traced in *Railroad Gazette*, XVII (1885), 191, 510, 638, and *Chronicle*, XL (1885), 363, XLI (1885), 155, 189, 356.

of all its security holders without discrimination or preference." Meanwhile he nursed negotiations for a sale to the East Tennessee along to a successful conclusion. Formal consummation of the deal on September 24 brought cries of betrayal and yet another round of lawsuits from the minority holders opposed to the sale. But the suits went down to defeat, and the stock went to the East Tennessee in exchange for the proceeds from $1,200,000 of the new K. & O. bonds. The Brice-Thomas faction did no harm to their own interests in the trade, receiving something less than 50 for a stock that sold at between 34 and 38 during the past few months.

While the intricate maneuvering continued behind the scenes, Fink labored diligently to bring order out of chaos. Even before the financial crisis he had warned vainly against letting the road run down. As receiver he undertook improvement of the line as rapidly as his meager resources would allow. During the receivership he had only net earnings to use for his work. The continuing furor over the funding scheme prevented any funds being raised by its provisions, and under such unsettled conditions Fink hesitated to ask the court for authority to issue receiver's certificates. During his eighteen months as receiver Fink spent $662,148 on betterments and equipment, including $85,248 for changing the road to standard gauge.[56]

In terms of performance the road fared poorly during both 1885 and 1886. Gross earnings fell 11.5 per cent in 1885 and 9.5 per cent in 1886 from the 1884 level, and the high operating ratio imposed by Fink's improvement policy caused net earnings to drop 30.0 per cent and 19.2 per cent for the two years. A fierce rate war on the western lines between November, 1884, and February, 1885, severely crippled business on the Memphis & Charleston. No sooner had that war terminated than the L. & N. combined with the trunk lines to slash rates against the Virginia, Tennessee & Georgia Air-Line. The fight dragged on until mid-July, with the East Tennessee ruthlessly using its advantage of not having to service its funded debt. To drum up new business Fink resorted to gimmicks such as a special "Gospel Train" between Macon and Atlanta with reduced round-trip fares. In noting this novelty one acerbic observer needled the company for its rate policies: "Perhaps some of the managers of other Southern companies indulge in the hope that the officers of the East Tennessee may be led to attend the

[56] East Tennessee, Virginia & Georgia Railroad, "Final Report of the Receiver," July 1, 1885 to June 30, 1886, 8–9, Bureau of Railroad Economics. For the gauge change, see Taylor and Neu, *American Railroad Network*, 79–81.

meetings themselves, and may thereby become convinced of the sin of the course in continually cutting rates." [57]

Reorganization Achieved: Exit Seney

By autumn of 1885 the funding scheme still remained in limbo. The various bondholders had not come to terms among themselves or with Seney. The Clearing House Association grew weary of the delays and arranged to sell their $1,500,000 in consols and a lesser amount of income bonds to a syndicate reportedly not identified with the company earlier. But the initiative still rested with Seney. He planned to send his lawyer to the annual meeting in November with proxies for a majority of the stock. Those proxies would be used to elect an entirely new board of his own choosing and free of the Brice-Thomas group. He would remove Thomas, who as president constituted his main obstacle, and take charge of the reorganization. [58]

The plan was simple and sound, but it did not take into account the ingenuity of Brice and Thomas. At the November meeting the latter pair stunned the assemblage by declaring that the company's secretary had failed to furnish a certified list of stockholders. How, therefore, could the stockholders know who was legally entitled to vote? George Holt, Seney's attorney, countered that Central Trust had provided a proper list, but Brice blithely pointed out that the list did not show the stockholders of record three months before the meeting. Despite Holt's furious protests, the election was suspended and the meeting adjourned until March. Outflanked and outraged, Nelson Robinson denounced the proceedings as illegal and filed suit to enjoin any transfer of stocks until after the election. [59]

His efforts came too late. On January 1 interest on the new funded coupon bonds fell due, and the Brice-Thomas group knew the company lacked the funds to pay them. The position of the two parties had now become perfectly clear. Whatever his original feelings on the funding scheme, Seney now supported it because he could keep the property out of the bondholders' hands. Thomas, on the other hand, had come full circle. Having helped draft the funding scheme, he now wished to dispose of it and force

[57] *Railroad Gazette*, XVII (1885), 394.
[58] *Ibid.*, 750; *Chronicle*, XLI (1885), 174–75, 306.
[59] *Railroad Gazette*, XVII (1885), 750; *Chronicle*, XLI (1885), 578.

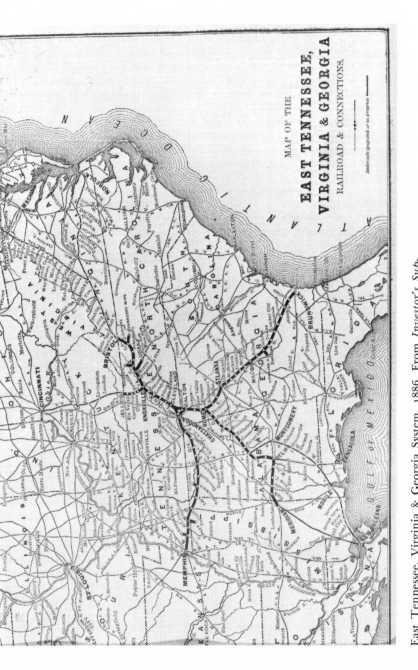

East Tennessee, Virginia & Georgia System, 1886. From *Investor's Supplement, Commercial and Financial Chronicle* (Dec., 1886), 45

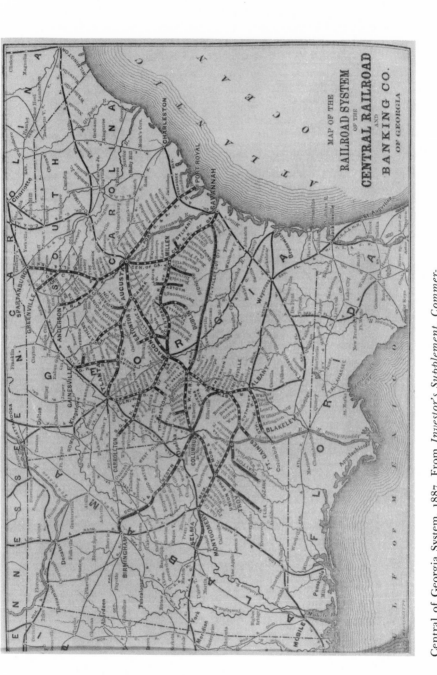

Central of Georgia System, 1887. From *Investor's Supplement, Commercial and Financial Chronicle* (Nov., 1887), 26

a foreclosure under the consolidated mortgage. In the ensuing reorganization he and Brice could wrest control of the company
from Seney or persuade him to retire gracefully and avoid a pro-
tracted fight. Failure to meet the January interest payments would
allow a foreclosure before the March meeting.

The Brice-Thomas strategy worked to perfection. The East Tennessee failed to pay its interest, and the funding scheme was declared a failure. In desperation Robinson hurried to Europe for a
conference with Robert Fleming, head of the foreign bondholders.
The Scotsman offered little solace for Robinson's dilemma. The
foreign interests wanted a genuine reorganization of the company
and an end to the bickering. While they did not entirely trust
Brice and Thomas, they had even less regard for Seney. Gloomily,
Robinson submitted to the inevitable. In short order the bondholders formed a reorganization committee composed of Fleming;
McGhee, now president of the Memphis & Charleston; George
Warren Smith of Kountze Brothers; E. W. Corlies, vice-president
of the Bank of America; Frederick D. Tappen, president of the
Gallatin National Bank; and Frederic P. Olcott, president of Cen-
tral Trust.[60]

The new committee pushed their plans along briskly. They obtained from the court a final foreclosure decree setting May 25 as
the date of sale, but as they formulated their reorganization
scheme, new opposition arose. A group of income bondholders,
learning that the new plan would force them to make heavy sacrifices, filed suit to block the proceedings. Their charges were savage
and provocative. They accused the East Tennessee managers of
fraud and mismanagement and of using their offices to wreck the
company and profit from its reorganization. They insisted that
conditions within the company had been misrepresented and demanded a new trustee in place of Central Trust. The income
bondholders organized rapidly and energetically, but they could
not carry the courts. In May their petition was denied and the sale
ordered.[61]

Analysis of the final reorganization plan yields two interesting
observations. First of all, the plan's provisions reveal clearly just
how much drastic surgery was required to recapitalize the system

---

[60] *Railroad Gazette,* XVIII (1886) , 31, 84, 102; *Chronicle,* XLII (1886) , 60,
124.

[61] *Railroad Gazette,* XVIII (1886) , 118, 222, 255, 358; *Chronicle,* XLII
(1886) , 430, 631. Some of the income bondholders committee's circulars are in
Baker Library.

on a sounder basis. The plan called for a new $20,000,000 consolidated mortgage at 5 per cent and three classes of stock: first and second preferred and common. The basic stipulations for each class of security holder were as follows: consolidated-mortgage holders would receive 60 per cent of their holdings in new consols and 50 per cent in first preferred stock; Cincinnati & Georgia divisional bondholders would get 48 per cent in new consols and 62 per cent in first preferred; income bondholders would pay a 5 per cent assessment and receive second preferred at par for their bonds and first preferred for the amount of assessment; preferred stockholders would be assessed 6 per cent in return for new common at par for their old stock and first preferred for the amount of assessment; present holders of common would pay a 2.4 per cent assessment and receive 40 per cent of the face value of their old common in new common stock. For the cash assessment they would receive new second preferred.[62]

As Table 8 shows, the new plan slashed total capitalization by 11.4 per cent and funded debt by 53.4 per cent. It did increase an already large equity by 29.5 per cent, but under the circumstances it is hard to see how that could have been avoided. Even in the new plan Seney's lavish watering came home to roost. More important, the plan made woefully inadequate provisions for future capital needs, although its authors satisfied themselves that it was satisfactory in this respect. As Daggett has pointed out, nearly 60 per cent of the $2,500,000 allocated for improvements would be needed to liquidate outstanding car trust obligations.[63]

A second observation drawn from the plan is the unqualified extent to which the bondholders triumphed over the junior security holders. Without exception every class except the consol holders made a heavy sacrifice. The harshest lot of all fell upon the common stockholders, who saw 60 per cent of their stock wiped out in addition to the assessment. Preferred stockholders and income bondholders were levied heavy assessments and accepted junior securities in the exchange. Cincinnati & Georgia bondholders paid no assessment but suffered a loss in interest rate from 6 to 5 per cent and allowed a majority of their bonds to be converted into equity with less certain returns. The consol holders, on the other hand, lost nothing in interest and could possibly earn more on the first preferred if prosperity returned. More important, they ac-

[62] These provisions in more detail can be found in *Chronicle*, XLII (1886), 186–87.

[63] Daggett, *Railroad Reorganization*, 156–57.

TABLE 8. Comparison of the East Tennessee's capital structure before and after the reorganization plan of 1886

Before reorganization	Amount	After reorganization	Amount
Bonds		*Bonds*	
Prior lien bonds	$ 7,325,000	Prior lien bonds	$ 7,325,000
Consol. bonds and coupons	16,385,966	New consol. 5's	12,675,000
Cin. & Ga. Div. bonds	2,040,000		
Debenture bonds	687,000		
Total interest-bearing bonds	$26,437,966	Total interest-bearing bonds	$20,000,000
Income bonds	16,500,000	Income bonds	none
All bonds	$42,937,966	All bonds	$20,000,000
Stock		*Stock*	
Preferred	16,500,000	1st preferred	11,000,000
Common	27,500,000	2nd preferred	18,500,000
		Common	27,500,000
Total stock	$44,000,000	Total stock	$57,000,000
Total capital	$86,937,966	Total capital	$77,000,000

SOURCE: *Chronicle*, XLII (1886), 652–53.

quired virtual equity control of the company as well. A key provision of the plan allowed the holders of first preferred stock to elect a majority of the board for five years or until two consecutive 5 per cent dividends were paid on such stock. For that period, at least, the consol holders would call the tune on policy.

Despite this overt favoritism, the plan appeared to be a splendid solution to many observers. The *Chronicle* noted that "the plan is on the whole an excellent one and has the exceeding merit of clearness and simplicity." [64] Later a close student of railroad reorganization went even further in his praise:

> But on the whole the reorganization plan was an excellent attempt to solve a difficult problem. It proceeded on a sound principle, *it laid the burden on the proper parties,* it avoided a funding of current liabilities, and even in respect to the volume of securities it accomplished a much needed reform.[65]

The plan was, however, much more than that. Whatever its financial merits, it was a masterpiece of partisan calculation. It enabled the Brice-Thomas faction to drive the Seney interests from the field once and for all. By demolishing the equity power base on which Seney depended and transferring control to the bondholders via the first preferred provision, it left the Seney interests without a leg to stand on. And Seney knew it. Shortly after the bondholders purchased the road for $10,250,000 on May 25, Seney offered to sell out to Brice and Thomas. His last tenuous hope, the income bondholders, had been thwarted in their efforts, and the foreign bondholders naturally supported the new plan.

By June the deal had been completed, and $4,000,000 in East Tennessee securities went to Brice and Thomas. Together with the $5,500,000 in consols already in their possession, they had sufficient power to control the reorganization and name a majority of the new directors. They had accomplished their objective with no loss and even a potential gain to themselves. Well might they crow over the results of the enterprise. There remained now only the suspicious foreign and junior holders to dispute their will.[66]

The final defeat of Seney ended the long and bitter struggle, at

[64] XLII (1886), 652.

[65] Daggett, *Railroad Reorganization,* 157. The broad nature of Daggett's approach and his lack of information on the infighting doubtless prevented him from evaluating the plan in the terms given here. The italics are mine.

[66] *Chronicle,* XLII (1886), 663, 728; *Railroad Gazette,* XVIII (1886), 391, 412, 616–17.

least for a time. The first board of the reorganized company, elected June 30, 1886, retained seven incumbents, including Brice, Thomas, McGhee, Shethar, Lyman, and Sanford. Jay Moss, an Ohio associate of Brice and Thomas, took a seat, and the other places went to representatives of the foreign and junior holders. Thomas resumed the presidency, and Fink returned as vice-president.[67]

Once free of internecine warfare, the East Tennessee management returned to pressing questions of strategy. Informed that the Danville planned to build a line into Knoxville, they offered to sell that company the Morristown branch instead.[68] To speed the physical restoration of the system, they issued in December the remaining $1,500,000 of consols.[69] But the intrigue was not yet done. The threatened Danville line into Knoxville served to reopen vital questions about the relationship between the two systems. The complex struggle taking place within the Danville's management soon drew the close attention of Brice and Thomas. Their growing involvement in that affair could only have momentous implications for the East Tennessee future.

Vague and contradictory rumors soon flourished. Would the two systems be united under the Terminal, or were Brice and Thomas merely fishing in troubled waters to weaken a dangerous rival? Only the insiders knew for certain, and their lips remained frustratingly sealed. One of them, McGhee, a man deeply committed to the East Tennessee in developmental terms, had mysteriously begun to sell heavily in both first preferred and the new consols.[70]

[67] Henry V. Poor, *Manual of Railroads for 1886* (New York, 1886), 956. Shethar is erroneously listed as the president here.

[68] *Railroad Gazette,* XVIII (1886), 621.   [69] *Ibid.,* 839.

[70] See the transaction receipts for Dec., 1886, and Jan., 1887, in McGhee papers.

Chapter VI

"Conservatism" Challenged
The Central of Georgia, 1880–1886

Decline of the Wadley Regime

The lease to the Nashville, Chattanooga & St. Louis proved a fleeting thing. During the negotiation Cole lost his own company to Newcomb, who hoped to acquire the newly leased Central as well. But Wadley and his board feared no rival more than the powerful L. & N. Upon hearing of Cole's defeat the Central directors voted promptly to rescind the lease.[1]

The menace of the L. & N. was a major problem for Wadley's administration. The policy of systematic expansion under former president E. D. Standiford had suddenly become a whirlwind under Newcomb. Having penetrated Alabama and western Florida, the L. & N. wanted desperately to find a reliable route through Georgia to the coast. During the winter and spring of 1880 Newcomb lured Wadley, Joe Brown of the Western & Atlantic, and Porter Alexander, now president of the Georgia, into lengthy conferences in Savannah and Atlanta. While rumors of an impending gigantic combination raced about the state, Newcomb charmed and bullied the Georgia roads into a ten-year working agreement on rates, fares, and scheduling. All traffic from the west to the Atlantic seaboard would be pooled, a joint office would be opened in Atlanta, and traffic would be interchanged among the systems wherever possible. Before leaving Georgia, Newcomb also persuaded Alexander to leave the Georgia and become first vice-president of the L. & N.[2]

While the agreement temporarily eased the pressure, it did not lull Wadley into carelessness. He knew Newcomb would continue his efforts to acquire the Central or some other major Georgia road. At the same time there were other problems besides the L. & N. The return of prosperity in 1880 swelled Central earnings but put an intolerable burden upon its rolling stock. Wadley wanted a large increase in equipment, and he wanted it purchased

---

[1] *Chronicle*, XXX (1880), 143.

[2] *Ibid.*, 384, 420–22, 493; *Central Report*, 1880, 7; *Railroad Gazette*, XII (1880), 135, 201, 211, XIII (1881), 314; Augusta *Chronicle and Constitutionalist*, May 7, 1880.

out of net earnings. After paring dividends for so long he consented to 6 per cent in 1880, but the pressure of new equipment and improvements inclined him toward a cut in 1881. To worsen matters, the state legislature passed an act creating a railroad commission cloaked with extensive rate-making powers. Hereafter the lament over a squeezed profit margin would become a regular feature of annual reports.[3]

Friction within the management over Wadley's personal domination grew rapidly. By 1880 it began to crystallize around the dividend issue. From 1873 to 1879 the Central paid a total of only 6.5 per cent in dividends even though net earnings had remained reasonably stable except for one or two depression years. In defense of this policy Wadley persistently argued that surplus funds should be used for betterments, retiring old obligations, and placing new acquisitions on a firm basis. But this explanation failed to appease those stockholders anxious for income. The heart of the matter lay in the Southwestern lease with its guaranteed dividend. During that same period Southwestern holders received 49 per cent in dividends, and the gap could not be closed. Under the terms of the lease, Wadley's policy of deferring or reducing annual dividends in favor of reinvestment meant that the Central could not make up for lost dividends without giving Southwestern holders an 80 per cent share of those dividends. And every passed dividend on the Central saw another 7 per cent go to the Southwestern.[4]

The accession of General Jeremy Gilmer, Alexander's brother-in-law, to the Central board in 1880 provided a center for opposition to Wadley. Gilmer's feud with Wadley was of long standing and had led to his ouster from the board in 1875. His relationship to Alexander especially disturbed Wadley because of Alexander's new connection with the L. & N. In response the aging president agreed to the appointment of a vice-president to shoulder some of the burdens and managed to get William G. Raoul, his son-in-law, for the post. Raoul, a capable and talented railroad man, believed firmly in Wadley's policies; in the eyes of many he was being groomed as the heir apparent.[5]

While mutinies simmered beneath him, Wadley pushed his expansion strategy forward. The spring of 1881 brought an unexpected opportunity to lease the Georgia Railroad. That company, though still prosperous, fully appreciated its precarious position.

[3] *Central Report*, 1880, 5–6, 9–10.
[4] *Ibid.*, 1882, 17. For terms of the lease, see chap. 3 above.
[5] *Ibid.*, 1880, 8–9.

Surrounded by three ambitious systems, the L. & N., the Central, and the Danville, Charles Phinizy, the Georgia's president, had no desire to see his road become a pawn in their rivalries. The simplest means of becoming profitably neutral, he reasoned, would be a lease to one of the contending systems. Early in the winter he let it be known that the Georgia would consider leasing proposals. All three competitors snapped at the bait, but Wadley, pleading regional loyalty against outside combinations, quickly got the inside track. As negotiations continued, Central stock soared from 110 to 121 and Georgia from 115 to 143.[6]

Then Wadley ran afoul of complications. For one thing, the recent Georgia constitution flatly prohibited the Central from owning any other competing railroad. That could be skirted by some legal gerrymandering. More important, Wadley met strong opposition from some of his own directors. Their attitude over incurring new obligations infuriated Wadley, who took it as nothing more than greed and timid obstinacy. He was certain that control of the Georgia would clinch the Central's position in the state, but a board meeting rejected his resolution. Walking away from the meeting with some friends, Wadley blistered the air with a string of oaths. If the directors would not relent, he swore, he would lease the Georgia himself! [7]

On his own initiative Wadley nursed the negotiations along. On April 1, he obtained a 99-year lease for himself, Moses Taylor, New York banker Samuel Sloan, and John H. Fisher of the South Carolina Railroad. The terms were stiff. Wadley agreed to pay an annual rental of $600,000, all taxes except the charter tax on net income, and all interest on the jointly controlled Western of Alabama. The rental would guarantee Georgia holders a minimum 10 per cent dividend, and the lease did not include the company's bank. In return he gained control over the 641-mile Georgia system, which included large holdings in the Atlanta & West Point, Rome, and Port Royal & Augusta railroads.[8]

To force his recalcitrant directors into line Wadley then offered the L. & N. a half-interest in the lease. That company responded eagerly, and within ten days Wadley and Alexander signed an

<hr/>

[6] *Chronicle*, XXXII (1881), 334, 396.   [7] Cumming, *Georgia Railroad*, 90.

[8] *Ibid.*, 89; unidentified clippings, Raoul Scrapbook, II, 48; *Chronicle*, XXXIII (1881), 420, 551; *Railroad Gazette*, XIII (1881), 314. Technically the syndicate bought nominal control of the South Carolina, leased the Georgia to that road, and then transferred the lease to Wadley on May 7. A copy of the lease to Wadley is in the Emory University Library.

agreement. The Central directors, duly alarmed, quickly came to terms. On June 1 Wadley assigned the other half of the lease to the Central. By his action Wadley succeeded in uniting the Georgia roads against "foreign invaders." He had long argued that Savannah and Charleston should work together for mutual advantage rather than continue as bitter rivals. To implement this policy further he leased the Port Royal & Augusta outright to the Central and joined Taylor and Sloan in purchasing a controlling interest in the Atlanta & West Point.[9]

Debentures and Division

The new and expensive acquisitions aroused yet another dispute between Wadley and his detractors. In 1881 discontent burst into open rebellion. To compensate for the dividends they claimed to have lost, the dissatisfied directors put forth a plan to create a special 40 per cent dividend by issuing certificates of indebtedness to the stockholders. To do this the board would also have to issue another 32 per cent in debentures for the Southwestern. The thought of creating $4,600,000 worth of new debt with a charge of $315,000 per year appalled Wadley, but he found himself blocked by a majority of the board. Behind the scenes key members of the L. & N.'s management had acquired substantial holdings of Central stock in anticipation of the certificates, and Alexander personally urged Wadley to issue the certificates. Reluctantly he signed the certificates and then hastened in his annual report to defend himself from the inevitable charge that he had merely watered the Central's stock.[10]

Above the furor of the debenture issue there loomed the basic clash between developmental and opportunistic interests, southern style. This classic struggle, characteristic of most important roads in the section, rarely achieved such transparency or found so clear-cut an issue as it did within the Central. In Wadley one can see mirrored the primary qualities of the territorial, developmental attitude. He stood above all for local control, which very often meant domination by a small clique. To retain that control he took care to reward his stockholders while always keeping his eye on the long-range implications of policy. He would not water the

[9] *Railroad Gazette,* XIII (1881) , 568; Cumming, *Georgia Railroad,* 90.
[10] *Central Report,* 1881, 8–9; *Railroad Gazette,* XIII (1881) , 323.

stock or weaken its capital structure; indeed, to protect the property from curious outsiders, he took care to undervalue it.

This tightly knit local control lay at the heart of the "conservative" policy practiced by Wadley and other presidents. Its foremost tenet was dedication to long-term goals. The company should be run as a safe investment, and stockholders were expected to acquiesce in ploughing back a large proportion of net earnings for betterments and additions to capital equipment. A large reserve fund should be accumulated for any unforeseen disaster. The road should be managed as a local concern with its stock widely scattered and tightly held, making it difficult for "outsiders" to accumulate large blocks. Listed only on local exchanges and with its price kept low, the stock would probably attract little attention from speculators. Any bullish tendency might cause a substantial amount to change hands. Outsiders might then enter the management and wreak havoc in two ways: by discarding the careful developmental strategy in favor of one geared to short-run profits and by overthrowing the stranglehold of local control and reducing the road to a mere component of some larger system. In the eyes of the "conservatives," either path would wreck the company and destroy the service it performed for city and state alike.

To the Wadley faction the debentures marked the first step down that path to destruction. The anti-Wadley groups scoffed at such talk. The retorted that a constant undervaluation of the property made all the stockholders suffer. They received inadequate dividends despite good earnings, and the price of their stock remained depressed. While many stockholders accepted Wadley's "conservatism," they could not always reconcile it with their hunger for dividends. After all, a safe investment was supposed to pay regularly, and many public institutions held the stock as part of their endowment.

The articulate Alexander, around whom the anti-Wadley forces coalesced, rejected the old policies out of hand. Representing a younger generation with different ideas about rail enterprises, he mocked the incumbent management unmercifully: "They claim truly to represent 'the old policy,' and to be 'conservative,' if conservatism means to buy the management of a good road cheap and to keep it for yourself." He portrayed himself as champion of the "long suffering stockholders, at whose expense the Central railroad management had come to be regarded as a family heirloom." [11]

[11] See Alexander's letter in Savannah *Morning News,* Dec. 21, 1886. Though the letter is a partisan tract, it presents an accurate statement of the opposing viewpoints.

These words came much later in the long struggle, but the attitude they express was there from the start. Around these polarized viewpoints would develop a power struggle lasting over seven years. On the surface it began with the debenture dispute, but resentment toward Wadley and his policies had been accumulating for several years. It is important to note that two distinct issues become paramount, for their interrelationship and imbrication served to confuse observers and participants alike and thoroughly muddle the conflict in retrospect. The first issue was the developmental versus opportunistic conflict as manifested in the debenture debate. The second concerned the sensitive question of local control versus outside influence.

As will later become clear, the chain of events tied these issues inextricably together and made individual positions nebulous to the casual observer. Many long-time advocates of local control opposed Wadley on the dividend question; yet gradually the "large dividend–high stock price" attitude became firmly associated in the public mind with outside influence. As a result the "conservatives" found themselves solidly together on one point but badly divided on the other. The debenture triumph represented a victory for the more opportunistic "conservatives," but unfortunately it had been achieved with the support of men representing the "foreign" L. & N. As the factions grew more fragmented, well might the average stockholder sigh in despair as he attempted to decipher exactly what each group stood for.

In broad terms the anti-Wadley forces who gathered about Alexander included members of his large family who were long-time stockholders, long-standing enemies of Wadley, some of Savannah's younger financiers, disenchanted stockholders, and the L. & N. faction.[12] They insisted that even the certificates did not provide dividends large enough to reflect the Central's true earning power, and they soon advanced a new scheme. A further dividend could be declared on the earnings of the Ocean Steamship Company, either by distributing that company's stock to Central holders or by issuing certificates of indebtedness upon it. Since it was a separate company owned by the Central, the courts might consider it outside the Southwestern lease and immune from division with stockholders of that road.[13]

When the rebels broached the idea to Wadley in December, the

[12] The L. & N. people apparently sold their certificates and reinvested the proceeds in Central stock (see E. C. Anderson to W. W. Gordon, July 9, 1881, William W. Gordon papers, Southern Historical Collection).

[13] *Railroad Gazette,* XIII (1881), 734.

old president exploded at the suggestion. He had always kept Ocean's lucrative net earnings separate from the Central's earnings and used them primarily as a betterments account. In this respect the opportunists had a point: the Central itself profited from its affiliate in many ways, but Central stockholders got no return from Ocean. During the period 1879–81 Ocean's net earnings averaged nearly $241,000 with fixed charges of less than $50,000. Even allowing a substantial sum for improvements and contingency, there remained a healthy residue for dividend purposes. But as president of Ocean, Wadley dominated its five-man board much as he dominated the Central. He would not allow this crucial betterments and expansion fund to be devoured by another opportunistic ploy for income.[14]

In rebuttal Wadley argued that the proposal simply watered the stock by converting $795,000 worth of assets into debentures. The Central could ill afford such an extra burden. Short crops had hurt business, and the cost of labor and materials mounted steadily. "We are going in two directions," he noted, "declining with our gross earnings and increasing with our expenses." He predicted that gross earnings would drop $250,000 to $300,000 for the fiscal year 1882. His aim was true: earnings on the main system declined by about $258,000. Yet he managed to pay an 8 per cent dividend.[15]

The Alexander faction flatly denied the watering charge and accused unfriendly newspapers of distortion. Alexander insisted that he did not propose any division of assets. He wanted no bond, debenture, or fixed obligation of any kind on either company. He and his supporters wanted simply a certificate of indebtedness on the *net earnings* of Ocean *after* paying all fixed charges, interest, sinking funds, marine losses, and a surplus contingency fund.[16] While still a controversial plan, it bore little resemblance to the description given it in the Georgia press, and one suspects that the misunderstanding extended to many stockholders as well. For their part the procertificate group accused Wadley's supporters of

14 *Chronicle*, XXXIII (1881), 715.

15 *Railroad Gazette*, XII (1880), 593, 747.

16 See Alexander's letter in undated Macon *Telegraph and Messenger* clipping, and undated Savannah *Morning News* clipping, Raoul Scrapbook, II, 54. The Alexander plan specifically called for Ocean to issue the Central a certificate paying the latter 7 per cent a year *if* Ocean earned that much after meeting the obligations listed in the text. In precise figures the first $150,000 after all expenses would go to a reserve fund. Any excess up to $245,000 would go to the Central as a dividend.

trying, in Gilmer's words, "to depreciate the stock for sinister & party purposes." [17]

Lacking support in the press, the rebels rapidly gained equity strength. Wadley still possessed too much strength to be displaced as president, but the board could be realigned. The Alexander syndicate promptly put up its own slate of candidates pledged to issuing the Ocean certificates. The stockholders assembled on January 2, 1882, ripe with expectation. Persistent rumors of a fight for the presidency bore no fruit, but the rebels demonstrated their strength by placing four men on the Central board: Alexander; Charles Phinizy, Augusta banker, president of the Georgia, and a close friend to Alexander; and two Savannah financiers, Robert Falligant and Malcolm McLean. Some of the incumbents, including Gilmer and E. C. Anderson, were known to favor the Alexander proposal. But Wadley retained his post, as did Raoul.[18]

The center of attention then shifted to the Ocean board. There the new Central directorate left Wadley the presidency but filled the other four places with Alexander and his brother Felix, Anderson, and Phinizy. After hearing a petition protesting any certificate proposal, the new Ocean board passed a resolution to issue the necessary certificate to the Central. The document was drawn up and presented to Wadley on February 7. Objecting that it was bad policy and might also be illegal, the old president refused to sign and promptly resigned the Ocean presidency. Anderson replaced him and readily signed the certificate, but the next day a group of pro-Wadley stockholders filed suit to enjoin issuance.[19]

The restraining order touched off a savage war of words. Virtually every major newspaper in Georgia opposed the certificates, but their reasoning and degree of moderation varied considerably. The main question still revolved around whether or not the Alexander position represented a sincere concern for the Central's welfare. Was it a genuine attempt to make the company's dividends reflect its true earning power, or was it simply a raid for the benefit of speculators and outside interests? This last point had come to assume increasing importance. The pro-Wadley forces succeeded

[17] Jeremy Gilmer to Alexander, July 2, 1882, Alexander papers.

[18] *Railroad Gazette,* XIV (1882), 13, 29, 559; Savannah *Morning News,* Jan. 3, 1882; see also undated clipping in W. W. Gordon Scrapbook, VI.

[19] *Railroad Gazette,* XIV (1882), 89–90, 93, 103; *Chronicle,* XXXIV (1882), 177. A detailed account of the whole episode together with copies of the relevant official correspondence, petition, restraining order, and the proposed certificates can be found in the unidentified clippings in Raoul Scrapbook, II.

all too well in tying the Ocean controversy to L. & N. influence. On that ground most of the Georgia press castigated Alexander for trying to wreck the Central and deliver it into foreign hands.

The Macon *Telegraph and Messenger* proved the most implacably hostile journal. Dismissing Alexander's group as "speculators and brokers who are operating for an immediate profit without regard to ultimate damage or benefits to the road," it assailed the scheme with one blistering editorial after another. In seeking to refute the plan from every conceivable angle, the editor pronounced his judgment in vivid language: "If it is finally carried out, the Central will have been financially raped by the Alexander party, and the bastard progeny of this forced embrace should be kicked and spurned by every legitimate man and institution in the country." [20]

The more moderate Savannah *Morning News* also opposed the certificates but reminded its readers that "General Alexander occupies too prominent a position in railroad circles to be willing to recklessly jeopardize his reputation merely for the sake of a speculation." While praising Wadley and his record with the Central, the paper admitted the validity of some of the complaints against him. Without hesitation it recounted the major grievances against the Wadley regime.[21] First of all, for three years it paid no dividends even though earnings totaled 27 per cent above all expenses. Secondly, the board approved a resolution instructing the Central bank not to accept the company's stock as loan collateral, thus forcing some holders to sell out at less than 40 when the stock was intrinsically worth much more. Moreover, the directors persistently unnerved investors by making gloomy predictions about the property's future.

The charges also included foreign policy as well. The management had tried to lease the road to a weak foreign syndicate, the Cole system, for a paltry 6 per cent. Through lack of foresight it bought a large amount of Western of Alabama income bonds at par and interest when careful buying could have obtained them for less than twenty cents on the dollar. Most damning of all, the board had allowed the Macon & Brunswick to pass into rival hands, which promptly built a road from Atlanta to Macon that directly paralleled the Central's line.

Each of these criticisms pinpointed a genuine weakness in the

[20] Jan. 26, 1882.
[21] Savannah *Morning News*, Feb. 16, 1882, and undated clipping in Raoul Scrapbook, II, 63.

Wadley administration and the "conservative" viewpoint it represented. But sick and tired as he was, Wadley still wielded enormous influence in Georgia. His reputation as the Central's postwar
savior would not die easily, and his two trump cards, the charges
of wrecking and outside influence, held infinitely more emotional
appeal than sober recitations of poor managerial judgment. As one
reporter sagely observed of Wadley, "that gentleman's name alone
is a tower of strength." [22]

The injunction brought the conflict to a standstill. As the case
plodded toward the Georgia Supreme Court, both factions
searched for a way out of the deadlock. It soon became apparent
that confidence in the Alexander plan was slipping. In mid-
February, Alexander abruptly called for a conference, and after a
long meeting at the Screven House he offered a compromise. The
Ocean certificate should not be subdivided among Central stockholders as originally planned, he declared, for then the Southwestern holders might get their slice. Instead it should be kept intact
by the Central as a reserve fund to guarantee Central holders a 9
per cent dividend in poor performance years and a bonus 10 or 11
per cent dividend in good years.[23]

But the tide had turned. The wavering incumbent directors who
had sided with Alexander now pledged to abandon the attempt,
and reluctantly the Alexander faction followed suit. The hostile
Macon press rejoiced at Alexander's Waterloo and sneered, "We
are simply astonished that anyone after the Screven House conference, should have been willing to follow a leader . . . armed only
with a Quaker gun." [24] That judgment was unduly harsh and misleading. Stripped of its emotional camouflage the dispute reflected
a genuine conflict over policy, with both sides having powerful
ammunition in their arsenal. The temptation to herald the
triumph of the Wadley faction as a victory of sound business policy over mere opportunism only leads to the same trap that ensnared so many contemporaries. The fact that the "conservative"
policy had served the Central well in the past did not preclude serious errors of judgment by its executors. Nor did it mean that
same policy would continue to serve the company's best interests
in a rapidly changing social and economic environment.

Though this battle was lost, the war went on. Alexander's sup-

[22] Unidentified clipping, Raoul Scrapbook, II, 63.

[23] *Ibid.*, II, 54; *Railroad Gazette*, XIV (1882) , 156.

[24] Macon *Telegraph and Messenger,* Feb. 18, 1882, and undated clipping in
Raoul Scrapbook, II, 67.

porters continued to buy Central stock, and Wadley's own position grew weaker. Fresh rumors of his impending retirement flourished as his health declined. Raoul had already shouldered most of his responsibilities, and even his supporters talked of replacing him if they could agree upon a suitable candidate. In June his long-time New York ally Moses Taylor died and was replaced on the board by E. H. Green of the L. & N. Wadley eyed his accession with grim suspicion.[25]

The Fight for the Presidency

By the spring of 1882 it had become obvious that there would be a fight for control in January. As both camps weighed their prospects, serious problems emerged. Even if Wadley's health improved, many of his supporters had already sold their stock and probably could not be induced to buy again. If he retired, the first question was who would take his place. The obvious choice—and Wadley's—was of course Raoul, but he posed problems. John Gresham, a Wadley supporter, neatly summed up the reservations: "I regard him as the best practical RR man in sight. . . . But whether he could take charge of a great corporation like this, or whether the stockholders would be willing to risk him, I cannot tell." As an alternative Gresham could suggest only W. W. Gordon.[26]

The rebel camp had difficulties of its own. As Gilmer viewed matters, Alexander held the key to the situation. No one wanted an open war for the presidency; all held Wadley in great esteem personally, and it would only hurt the company's stock. But Wadley had made clear his desire to rid the Central of L. & N. influence, and to achieve that end he wanted Raoul to succeed him. He knew he could trust Raoul to carry out his wishes; for that reason, Gilmer feared, he might stand for reelection. If the old lion won and got his own board elected, then he could resign and have them elect Raoul in his place. And he just might win.[27]

To minimize risk Gilmer suggested a compromise plan. Wadley realized that Raoul could not win election on his own. "I am inclined to think," he wrote Alexander, "that Mr. W. would agree to

---

[25] *Railroad Gazette,* XIV (1882), 364, 382; undated clipping in Raoul Scrapbook, III, 9.

[26] Gresham to W. W. Gordon, April 15, 1882, Gordon papers.

[27] For this analysis, see Gilmer to Alexander, July 2, 1882, Alexander papers.

'a compromise or amicable adjustment' that retained Raoul as V.P. & made you President." True, the plan would saddle the board with Raoul, "with his sins of commission and omission— merits & demerits all of which are *great*." But the board could put up with Raoul if Alexander became president, and Wadley might be appeased by retaining him in office "with the hope of succession." Alexander agreed and resigned his post with the L. & N. Shortly afterward the scramble for proxies commenced.[28]

Then fate intervened. Wadley had gone to Saratoga Springs for some rest. There on August 10 he succumbed to an apoplectic stroke. The hastily reassembled board promptly elected Alexander in his place, but the hope of compromise had vanished. Raoul could now go for the presidency on his own by casting himself as Wadley's personally groomed heir apparent. He lacked sufficient votes on the present board, but he could make a rough fight of it in January. In public Raoul maintained an inscrutable silence, but he had made his decision. Even before Alexander's election he wrote a confidant:

I regard this as the most critical epoch in the history of the Central . . . and I believe we ought to have an able and conservative board next January. . . . It may turn out that between now and January that a fair opportunity will be offered for successfully opposing the policy inaugurated by a majority of the present board, which you as well as nearly all the members of the old board truly deplored.[29]

The confusion imparted by Wadley's sudden death was reflected in one journal, which mentioned Alexander as the old president's likely successor on one page and Raoul on the next. In December the air cleared swiftly. Raoul resigned as vice-president to campaign openly for the presidency. He denounced the current board as a tool of the L. & N. and proclaimed himself the true disciple of the Wadley tradition. Though his decision surprised no one, it left the Alexander forces in an awkward position. Raoul had a powerful and emotional theme to play on—that of L. & N. domination. He could evoke memories of the late, lamented titan, dwell touchingly upon his visions of a great Georgia corporation owned and operated by Georgians, and easily link himself to that vision. Chauvinism it might be, but it made potent campaign medicine, and Raoul knew it. To get his message across he sent agents into

[28] *Ibid.; Railroad Gazette,* XIV (1882) , 399, 416, 433.
[29] *Railroad Gazette,* XIV (1882), 510, 530, 559; Raoul to W. B. Johns[t]on. August 24, 1882, Raoul Letter Books

the hustings via horse and buggy to contact the small stockholders.[30]

Behind the façade of emotion and rhetoric, however, lay the two familiar issues of policy differences and outside relationships. The Wadley "conservatism" appealed strongly to smaller stockholders and those who considered the Central a native corporation devoted to the commercial aspirations of the state. Ironically, Raoul was a native of Louisiana while Alexander's family had been rooted in Georgia since the late eighteenth century. Despite his nativity, Alexander's meteoric railroad career had given him the somewhat unjust reputation of representing not so much investors as speculators. He had come up a little too fast and moved a little too quickly. He trafficked with men of large affairs, financiers like Newcomb who had fingers in many pies and no deep personal loyalty to any of them. He spoke for a generation of operators free of regional allegiances and brimming with plans for projects on a hitherto undreamed-of scale.

In his previous associations with the Georgia and L. & N. roads, Alexander had helped steer those companies down new paths. He was an unabashed exponent of new strategies and chafed at the shackles of past policies. In his haste to dismantle what he believed to be obsolete policies, he exerted the same marvellously quick and precise judgment that had characterized his fine military career. That very brilliance dismayed his critics, who distrusted his glib facility for manipulation. Ignoring his genuinely fine managerial talent, they tended to see only a career steeped in ambiguous and therefore suspicious financial legerdemain. That he possessed such a reputation is beyond dispute. The Griffin *News* put the matter baldly: "There can be no doubt that General Alexander is the candidate of the speculators and Captain Raoul of those persons who desire a good, safe, and profitable investment." [31]

Such objections usually crystallized in the charge that Alexander, if elected, would run the company more in the interests of outsiders than in those of natives. This accusation implied in part that "foreign" interests, involved in several vast projects, would manage the Central only as a small compartment of their large affairs and, if necessary, sacrifice the road and its minority holders whenever broader considerations demanded it. In part, too, the charge reflected another basic factor lurking behind the election

---

[30] *Railroad Gazette*, XIV (1882), 759; Atlanta *Constitution*, Jan. 2, 1883.
[31] Undated clippings in Raoul Scrapbook, III, 21–23.

rhetoric: the fiercely conflicting commercial aspirations within the state. On one level Georgians worried about meeting the competition of neighboring outlets and distant markets. On a second level, Savannah, Macon, Columbus, Atlanta, Augusta, and smaller communities vied with each other for commercial supremacy as they had always done. From that perspective Georgians cared less about outside domination than about which interests and locales within the state would benefit from the chosen management.

Under these circumstances the Alexander forces worked against difficult odds. They could not very well deny their L. & N. ties, but they did minimize them. They stressed Wadley's alliance with the L. & N. and his realization that to survive the Central must work harmoniously with neighboring systems. They defended their advocacy of the Ocean certificates when Raoul supporters resurrected the issue. They obtained from Albert Fink, the Trunk Line Commissioner, a glowing testimonial to Alexander's ability. His words are worth quoting as an indication of the "new" or "liberal" thinking in railroad management endorsed by Alexander and thoroughly alien to the "conservative" mind:

> I would consider it a great mistake of the stockholders . . . if they should not re-elect . . . Alexander. . . . His high character and his ability as a railroad manager, and his peculiar acquaintance with the Southern railroad system should, I think, make his services invaluable to the company. . . . It is the short-sightedness and arbitrary policy that has so much prevailed with railroad managers in the past, that has led to so many difficulties with the people, resulting in hostile legislation and in reduced dividends. The full force of this ruinous policy has not yet been felt. I always considered General Alexander peculiarly qualified, while guaranteeing the interests of the companies with which he has been connected, to act upon broad and liberal views, to secure the good will of the people with whom he has to deal, and thereby advance the interest of the railroad companies more than by arbitrary methods.[32]

No company election had ever raised such intense excitement. Normally sedate Savannah talked of nothing else, and the rest of the state gave new developments the breathless coverage usually reserved for political imbroglios. At first Alexander seemed assured of victory, but Raoul cut relentlessly into his lead. Then a stunning reversal occurred. The block of stock held by the L. & N. interests, about 6,250 shares, suddenly fell under a cloud of doubt.

---

[32] Fink to Alexander Lawton, Dec. 13, 1882, Alexander papers. For the Alexander faction's defense of the Ocean certificates, see the circular from E. M. Green, dated Dec. 7, 1882, Gordon papers.

Circumstances within the dissension-riddled L. & N. had caused nearly all the Central shares to be concentrated in the hands of Edward H. Green. In truth, however, the stock appears to have belonged to his wife, Hetty, the notorious "Witch of Wall Street." The jovial Green thus had no voice in disposition of the stock, for Hetty Green always kept her own accounts separate from her husband's and was not inclined to let marital sentiment interfere with business matters.[33]

It had been bandied about for some time that the L. & N. or "Cisco" stock was wavering, and that someone from the Raoul camp might obtain it. The precise facts never became clear, but apparently the "someone" was Senator Joe Brown of Georgia, long-time president of the Western & Atlantic, a close friend of Raoul's, and a solid devotee to the principle of defending local enterprises against outside interests. Only a week before the election he approached Hetty Green with his offer. At first it was rumored that Brown had purchased the shares outright, but the story proved false. Brown merely bought the Green proxies for Raoul, or in the contemporary euphemism, "paid a bonus for the privilege of voting them in this election." [34]

Transfer of the stock took place only three days before the election. News of the switch hit the Alexander camp like a thunderclap and plunged it into gloom. The ever-optimistic Alexander, who had been confident of victory from the first, now telegraphed a supporter, "The case is hopeless. The Cisco shares are against me. I regret it more for my friends than myself." Still he did not concede defeat. Stockholders and proxies representing 66,379 of the Central's 75,000 shares assembled in Savannah, by far the largest number ever voted in a company election. Voters waited patiently outside the bank building to cast their ballots, and wagers on the outcome could be heard everywhere. The crowd kept the

[33] See the undated clipping in Raoul Scrapbook, III, 23. This contemporary rumor concerning the role of Hetty Green has been verified by Mrs. Elizabeth Hilton, Alexander's granddaughter. In a 1963 interview she informed me that her grandfather never referred to the election without labeling Hetty Green as the direct cause for his defeat.

[34] Atlanta *Constitution*, Jan. 2, 1883. The Green stock was known popularly as the "Cisco" stock because it was held in the name of J. J. Cisco & Company. It seems clear that Brown did not buy the stock outright because Hetty Green still owned it in 1886 and would play a vital role in another election. See also Raoul to Percy Pyne, July 8, 1884, Raoul Letter Books.

poll open a full hour past the six o'clock closing time, but the Alexander men glumly conceded defeat early in the afternoon.[35]

The final results made the decisive effect of the Cisco stock painfully evident. About ten days before the election Alexander was reported to have a lead slightly in excess of 2,000 shares. The final tally gave Raoul 35,295 votes to Alexander's 31,084, or a margin of 4,211. The difference figures out very close to the 6,250 transferred shares. In the final analysis, then, Raoul owed his victory not to his beating of the bushes but to the shifting allegiance of the despised "foreign" interests. By this superb piece of irony, almost wholly unnoticed and unappreciated at the time, the reign of local interests and "conservatism" was preserved at least for a time.[36]

Raoul's victory won general applause throughout the state. Newspapers in Atlanta, Albany, Columbus, Macon, Griffin, and even tiny Eatonton praised the triumph of local "conservatism" and promptly put forth their demands on the new regime. No community on the line hesitated to remind the new president of its role in securing him his office, and each expected to be rewarded with new facilities, better service, and more favorable rates and schedules. Like any politician assuming office, Raoul had his backlog of obligations. The unanimous support tendered him at first would not likely endure once he began to make decisions that could not possibly please all his supporters.[37]

"Conservatism" Reasserted

The Raoul sweep brought with it a new slate of directors, all of them dedicated to the Wadley philosophy. Besides Raoul himself, only Anderson and Green, who had run on both tickets, survived the election. Once free of election rigors the board faced serious and complex problems of policy. In general these problems fell into the following broad categories: meeting continued threats by

[35] Clippings describing the election can be found in the Raoul and Gordon Scrapbooks, and the Alexander Scrapbook, presently in my possession. See also *Railroad Gazette*, XV (1883), 14–15.

[36] A complete proxy list for the election can be found in the Raoul Letter Books. Alexander in 1886 recalled the irony in Raoul's dependence upon the Green stock (see the undated Atlanta *Constitution* clipping in Raoul Scrapbook, III, 37).

[37] For a sample of these diverse reactions to the election, see the undated clippings in Raoul Scrapbook, III, 8, 24.

"foreign" interests; formulating strategy for growth; protecting the system from growing competition and the restrictions imposed by the state railroad commission; and harmonizing policy differences within the management and with the stockholders. In their response to these problems the Raoul management found it necessary to modify some of the traditional Wadley precepts. On the whole, however, the Raoul regime fully lived up to its expectations as inheritor of the "conservative" mantle.[38]

As might be expected, Raoul continued to resist encroachment from outside interests. During his four-year tenure he mastered the art of sounding the alarm against invaders. The first challenge came during his first year in office. Jay Gould's interest in eastern connections for his Missouri Pacific had led him to investigate the Central as well as the East Tennessee. Unlike the latter system, however, Gould found no financial bedfellows with whom to dicker. He could only gain access by stock control, and by August, 1883, rumors asserted confidently that he had done so. It was reported that he would scoop up the L. & N. as well and put Alexander in charge of both systems.[39]

The rumor proved utterly false, but not so the threat. Gould's presence helped stir Raoul and Joe Brown's Western & Atlantic into a defensive alliance specifically designed to protect Georgia roads against outside competition. Brown first tried to persuade the state to sell the W. & A. to the Central. When that failed he met with Raoul to draw up a seven-year mutual defense pact. The roads would of course remain separate organizations, but they would be run as one system in every way possible. Common rates would be made on all points to both lines and preferences given on assignments, contracts, and other matters. On through traffic each would exert its influence for the benefit of the other. It would be called the Georgia Associated Traffic Lines, and Brown minced no words about its purpose. It was intended to meet "combinations of Northern syndicates, which threaten to swallow all the roads of the South. . . . The contract just made puts it where no northern syndicate by purchasing a majority of the stock of any

[38] Raoul made his adherence to the "conservative" tradition quite explicit in his own writings. Good examples abound in his letter books, but perhaps the best single statement of his attitudes can be found in *A Letter Written by Wm. G. Raoul to Hon. F. H. Colley, in Reply to a Letter from Major Campbell Wallace* (Savannah, 1885) , copy at Bureau of Railroad Economics.

[39] *Railroad Gazette*, XV (1883) , 627; New Orleans *Picayune*, Sept. 17, 1883. Gould actually did get onto the L. & N. board.

one of the roads mentioned can control it as against the others." [40]

Brown proposed the alliance to counter all outside rivals: Gould, the L. & N., East Tennessee, and Danville. But for good reasons he bore down hard on the East Tennessee in public. That company, after all, had just paralleled both Georgia roads in connecting its main stem to the Macon & Brunswick. It was known to be negotiating with Gould, and its leading figures were involving themselves in the new Danville syndicate. The alliance in a sense represented the last stand of determined local interests against the rapidly proliferating interterritorial systems. Raoul boasted characteristically that

Georgia is the only Southern State that has thus far been able to retain ownership and control of any considerable portion of her railroads; and those roads which are usually regarded as composing the Central system, are the only ones in which the people of the State have control or own any considerable interest.[41]

The desire to keep the stock within the state, widely scattered, and attractive to institutional as well as individual investors was a fundamental tenet of the Wadley tradition. Raoul held it firmly as an article of faith. Shortly after taking office he reassured a large stockholder:

I agree with you also very fully . . . about the desirability of the stock of our Georgia Companies being distributed throughout the country among Georgians. The history of all railroads has been that where this was the case, it has been honestly managed and free from stock manipulation that usually results in damage to the property and small stockholders, and it would certainly be a great satisfaction to me if the control of the Central could always remain in the hands of our own people.[42]

Raoul's devotion to the principle went well beyond mere lip service. He bought a block of Southwestern stock to "get myself on record . . . as a larger stockholder than I had heretofore been." He actively discouraged holders from selling because of fluctuations in the price. These fluctuations he blamed largely on "outside parties who speculate in it, to hammer it down . . . to aid some speculative scheme." To eliminate this pernicious influence he sought

---

[40] Railroad Gazette, XV (1883), 677, 681, XVII (1885), 47; Railway World, XXVII (1883), 1072.

[41] Raoul to Colley, 38. The alliance threatened to cause a rupture of relationships between the Central and East Tennessee (see Raoul to Joseph Fay, Dec. 20, 1883, Raoul Letter Books).

[42] Raoul to U. B. Harrold, Jan. 29, 1883, Raoul Letter Books.

ways of driving the speculators out. Hearing that Hetty Green wished to sell her large block of shares, Raoul tried desperately to organize a syndicate to take it.[43]

His reasoning was simple and revealing. Purchase of the Green stock would take a major speculative block off the market, which in turn would reassure small investors, enhance the market value, and help stabilize the administration. Raids could be curbed more effectively, and the company's credit would doubtless improve. A more stable administration could better plot "far reaching plans which cannot be entered into by an administration of doubtful tenure." The syndicate would not even hold the stock permanently but would gradually parcel it out in small lots to Georgians. For various reasons Hetty Green chose not to sell, and the plan was dropped. Within a short time Raoul would dearly regret the lost opportunity, for the Green stock was destined to haunt him once again.[44]

In pursuing expansion strategy Raoul moved cautiously. His policy was to limit new acquisitions and construction to feeder lines. Especially did he feel the necessity of attaching the important through line feeders before other companies got them. In the old days these independent lines served the Central well; now they had fallen under the control of rival systems and diverted their traffic from Savannah. To regain this business the Central must either capture the remaining arteries or build new ones.[45]

Accordingly, Raoul concentrated on the smaller lines. He purchased the narrow-gauge Gainesville, Jeffersonville & Southern, the East Alabama, and other small roads. He extended branches of the Southwestern, furnished aid to South Carolina roads under Central influence, and made extensive additions to the Columbus & Western, a budding auxiliary system centered in eastern Alabama. To tighten the Central's hold on roads already in its sway he arranged a series of internal leases. In all, however, he added only about 118 miles to the system proper in four years.[46]

[43] Raoul to Percy Pyne, June 7, Dec. 24, 1883, July 8, 1884, and Raoul to Fay, Dec. 20, 1883, *ibid.*

[44] Raoul to Pyne, July 8, 1884, *ibid.* This letter is another good exposition of the "conservative" philosophy.

[45] *Savannah Times,* June 6, 1885; *Railroad Gazette,* XVII (1885) , 382.

[46] *Central Report,* 1886, 8–10; *Chronicle,* XXXVI (1883) , 559, XXXVII (1883) , 233. The actual mileage of the system proper was 1,150 in 1883 and 1,403 at the end of 1886 (see Poor, *Manual for 1884,* 440, and *Manual of Railroads for 1889* [New York, 1889], 566) . Of this 253-mile difference, 135 miles involved no expansion. The estimate of mileage for Ocean Steamship was

Raoul's cautious expansion policy reflected in part his own conservatism and in part another problem: his bitter feud with the state railroad commission. Few difficulties absorbed more of his attention than the fight against rate regulation. The dispute extended well beyond rates, for in a real sense the commission's position struck at the very heart of "conservative" policy. One commissioner in particular, Campbell Wallace, a railroad man of considerable experience and a champion of low rates, antagonized Raoul by his close attention to the Central's affairs.

In June, 1885, Wallace published an open letter that constituted a virtual indictment of "conservative" policy. He charged the Raoul administration with employing all sorts of fraudulent and deceptive tactics to undervalue the company's capital account and earnings performance. In particular he listed the following items: the Central had misrepresented its capital account by using 80 per cent of a $5,000,000 bond issue to acquire railroads and steamships outside the state; the company imposed an undue charge on its capital account by paying too high a rent for certain leased roads, notably the Southwestern; to make net earnings appear lower than they actually were, the Central improperly charged expenditures for rails, depots, rolling stock, and other equipment to operating expenses; the Central's annual reports seriously underestimated net earnings, claiming for example to have earned only 1.18 per cent in 1884 when it actually earned at least 10.5 per cent; the rates charged by the Central prior to 1879, when regulation first commenced, were so abnormally high that the company could not bear the same rate of reduction as roads charging more reasonable rates; and the Central misrepresented the earnings of the Georgia Railroad.[47]

Wallace also raised other issues, including a blistering attack on the 1881 certificates of indebtedness. Stung by the accusations, Raoul prepared a lengthy rebuttal that clarified the sharp differences between president and commissioner over what constituted proper policy. Some charges Raoul categorically denied; others he

---

arbitrarily increased from 250 to 300 miles, and the 85-mile Mobile & Girard was added to the system by lease. It had long been controlled by the Central, however, and the lease represented only a more secure holding arrangement. For a statement of other roads in which the Central had an interest, see Poor, *Manual for 1883*, 458–59, and *Manual of Railroads for 1887* (New York, 1887), 983.

[47] These charges and Raoul's reply to them are detailed in *Raoul to Colley*, *passim*.

tried to show to be fallacies in Wallace's logic. He flatly rebuked any notion of misrepresentation in capital accounts. While admitting the accuracy of Wallace's *descriptions,* he defended his course as sound policy, dwelling especially upon charging improvements to operating expenses. In justifying his method he quoted a Supreme Court decision which deemed such an accounting procedure as *"the most conservative and beneficial for the Company."* [48] In each case he dismissed Wallace's objections as symptomatic of a philosophy unsuited to "conservative" management.

Despite the vehemence of Raoul's protests, he did not sweep away Wallace's main points. Indeed he could not, for they were born of significant differences over policy. Raoul's "conservatism" left little room for effective regulation. In making the company's long-term objectives paramount, it presupposed a laissez-faire environment where only competitive circumstances and the will of the company dictated the rate schedule. "Conservative" accounting methods doubtless served the company well, but they also made it impossible to determine any fair basis for a commission to formulate just rates. Throughout his tenure Raoul insisted that the prevailing commission tariffs offered too low a rate of return, and by his own ledgers he was correct. But neither Wallace nor the other commissioners would accept those accounting methods as an honest basis for figuring profit. Nor would they adhere to the notion that the company's welfare should transcend the public interest.[49] Seldom has the clash of public and private interests unfolded so clearly.

To oppose the commission Raoul resorted to more than public rhetoric. He handed out passes to newsmen to create a favorable sentiment against the oppression of the Railroad Commission.[50] He meddled extensively in state politics and tried to mobilize the press in an effort to elect legislators willing to modify the law.[51] He

---

[48] *Ibid.,* 17. The italics are Raoul's.

[49] In *ibid.,* 37, Raoul went so far as to accuse Wallace of bad faith: "Both Major Wallace and myself occupy positions of responsibility toward the citizens of Georgia—I as the agent of a limited number entrusted with the management of their collective property. He as one of the selected officers of the state to administer a law affecting the rights and property of many. . . . Under the specious plea of protecting the people, he is seeking the applause of those who are using the railroads, while he must know that the price he is paying for that applause is the sacrifice of over eight millions of dollars of property belonging to women and children of Georgia, who are defenseless against the spoilation."

[50] See the correspondence for 1884 in Raoul Letter Books.

[51] Raoul to Fay, Dec. 20, 1883, *ibid.*

promoted unity among the various lines in the state to resist lowering of rates.[52] In service of his cause he did not hesitate to wield the Central's great political and economic power effectively. For campaign purposes key members of the Central's board kept an updated list appraising the attitude and record of each Georgia legislator on the railroad question.[53]

The secretive nature of conservative policy frustrated not only public officials but stockholders as well. While approving the president and his policies in general, holders got from Raoul little information upon which to evaluate their investment. His reports were spare and unrevealing, his accounting methods arcane, and his data incomplete. He refused to issue monthly earnings reports and treated the national financial journals with suspicion.[54] Like Wadley before him Raoul seemed firmly convinced that the less people knew about the company the better. Anxious to keep outsiders ignorant of the road's true worth, he left his shareholders equally in the dark.

Like Wadley, too, Raoul tended to be arbitrary and somewhat heavy-handed. He incurred some rancor with his policy of localizing traffic at Savannah. While in principle he agreed that the board should seat representatives "of points at other than the terminal points of its line," in practice he presided over a board overwhelmingly dominated by Savannah interests.[55] And that board remained solidly entrenched during his reign. Only two changes in personnel took place in four years, one of them being the replacement of E. H. Green by a more suitably conservative New Yorker, J. B. Duckworth.

Central Performance under Raoul

At first glance the Central seemed prosperous enough under Raoul's administration. Mindful of the shareholder's sensitivity to dividends, he paid them regularly: 8 per cent in 1883, 6 per cent in 1884, 5 per cent in 1885, and 4 per cent in 1886. In declaring the

---

[52] Raoul to Henry Fink, March 10, 1884, *ibid.* In seeking to form a unified front against a drop in rates, he told Fink: "I will wire . . . parties urging them to protest rates. I think we should all cooperate to prevent demoralization."

[53] A copy of this report is in the Gordon papers.

[54] See *Chronicle*, XLIII (1886), 622.

[55] Raoul to Harrold, Jan. 29, 1883, Raoul Letter Books.

TABLE 9. Selected data on operations of the Central of Georgia and Southwestern railroads, 1880–1886

9-a Central

Year	(1) Gross earnings (1000's)	(2) Rate of increase in gross earnings (%)	(3) Net earnings (1000's)	(4) Rate of increase in net earnings (%)	(5) Ratio of net to gross earnings (%)	(6) Interest and rentals [a] (1000's)	(7) Rate of increase in interest payments (%)	(8) Ratio of interest payments to net earnings (%)	(9) Operating ratio (%)
1880	$2,346	—	$1,163	—	48.0	$355	—	30.5	52.0
1881	2,762	.177	1,087	−.065	37.3	363	.023	33.4	62.7
1882	2,504	−.093	807	−.258	29.9	658	.813	81.5	70.1
1883	2,606	.041	972	.204	35.3	711	.081	73.1	64.7
1884	2,320	−.110	835	−.141	31.3	708	−.004	84.8	68.7
1885	2,322	.001	793	−.050	30.4	929	.312	117.2	69.6
1886	2,426	.045	1,104	.392	39.0	929	.0	84.1	61.0

9-b Southwestern

Year	(1) Gross earnings (1000's)	(2) Rate of increase in gross earnings (%)	(3) Net earnings (1000's)	(4) Rate of increase in net earnings (%)	(5) Ratio of net to gross earnings (%)	(6) Lease rent and other fixed charges (1000's)	(7) Rate of increase in fixed charge payments (%)	(8) Ratio of interest payments to net earnings (%)	(9) Operating ratio (%)
1880	$845	—	$375	—	44.4	$353	—	94.1	55.6
1881	946	.120	302	−.195	32.0	353	.0	116.9	68.0
1882	935	−.012	240	−.205	25.7	353	.0	147.1	74.3
1883	1,031	.103	344	.433	33.4	353	.0	102.6	66.6

1884	916	−.112	194	−.436	21.3	357	.013	184.0	78.7
1885	947	.034	197	.015	20.8	357	.0	181.2	79.2
1886	976	.031	245	.244	25.2	357	.0	145.7	74.8

9-c Net earnings of Ocean Steamship Company [b]

Year	Net earnings
1880	$214,298
1881	301,122
1882	341,645
1883	457,948
1884	486,989
1885	378,908
1886	469,451

Sources: Calculated from data in Appendixes V and VI and *Annual Reports of the Central Railroad and Banking Company of Georgia*, 1880–87.
[a] These figures do not include Southwestern lease rent.
[b] These figures do not include deductions for fixed charges.

substantial 1883 payment he anticipated the railroad commission's reaction by noting almost apologetically that much of the company's surplus earnings came from property outside the railroad—especially Ocean Steamship.[56] His defense proved futile, however, for the commission lowered rates the following year. Never again did Raoul pay so high a dividend.

Beneath the surface, however, the Central's performance displayed a tendency toward stagnation, if not decay. As Table 9 shows, gross earnings remained sluggish and erratic while net earnings positively declined.[57] Interest payments increased little, but the draining effect of the 1881 certificates manifested itself clearly in the abrupt upward spurt shown in column 8. The squeeze was getting worse, too, for by 1886 Raoul began to accumulate a floating debt born largely of expenditures for expansion.[58] The high operating ratio bears eloquent testimony to Raoul's adherence to "conservative" policy and supports the charge that his administration misrepresented net earnings by including capital expenditures in operating expenses. During the period 1870–82 the operating ratio under Wadley had averaged 61.4. In four years under Raoul it averaged 66.0.[59]

Taken as a whole, the evidence in Table 9 indicates clearly that even in the early 1880's the Central was finding it increasingly difficult to pursue the "conservative" strategy and still find enough surplus to pay the dividend rate Central holders had come to expect. It seems that Raoul was correct in arguing that only the Ocean Company's earnings kept the parent company from a drastic reduction in its dividend payments. The Southwestern remained a drag on Central earnings, as did nearly all of the new acquisitions. Only once during the period 1872–86 did that road's net earnings exceed the payments required under the lease, and there was no reason to expect any substantial improvement.

Part of the Central's troubles could be traced to normal fluctuations such as the poor cotton crop of 1884, but natural causes alone could not adequately explain the whole situation. Predictably Raoul blamed the poor earnings performance almost entirely

[56] *Railroad Gazette,* XV (1883), 712; *Chronicle,* XXXVII (1883), 423.

[57] For an analysis of earnings and capital behavior for southern roads in general during this period, see Klein and Yamamura, "Growth Strategies."

[58] *Central Report,* 1886, 10; Raoul to Percy Pyne, Feb. 4, 1884, Raoul Letter Books.

[59] Calculated from data in Appendix VI. Part of this rise, of course, reflected increased costs and declining or stagnant earnings.

upon the low tariffs imposed by the commission. In return Raoul was accused of withholding earnings to pay for the branch roads in South Carolina and elsewhere. He denied the charge vehemently and insisted that the unusually low 2 per cent semiannual dividend in 1885 was all the company could afford, even with its outside investments included. The squeeze of rising costs and declining rates had already prompted Raoul to cut all wages on the Central by 10 per cent earlier in the year.[60]

The Central's disappointing performance under Raoul's "conservative" regime left its dark imprint on the stock as well. The price stood at 100 when he assumed office. After the election it edged steadily downward, reaching 73 in June, 1886. In view of Wadley's efforts to keep the stock depressed, the decline might have appeared expected and even contrived. Perhaps Raoul did try to push the price down; if so he did it secretly. In August, 1886, he wrote a board member and close associate that "I have been uniformly of the opinion that the stock is worth more than par, and the fact that a few years of depressed business or rates involved an unsatisfactory dividend is no cause for such a decline in the stock as has followed." [61]

Despite the decline, Raoul kept a firm grip on the stock. He retained the support of the Cisco stock, and his campaign to keep the equity scattered among small local investors continued successfully.[62] As Table 10 (p. 172) indicates, over two-thirds of the equity in Georgia roads of the Central system lay in the hands of the Georgians. But the situation soon began to change rapidly. After dropping to a low of 69 during the summer of 1886, Central began to climb sharply. By early August it reached 94 and showed no signs of slowing down. Someone was buying and buying heavily. The obvious questions harried the Central management: who and why?

[60] Raoul to Pyne, Dec. 24, 1883, Raoul Letter Books; *Railroad Gazette*, XVII (1885) , 63, 382; *Chronicle*, XXXIX (1884) , 653.
[61] Raoul to J. J. Gresham, August 6, 1883, Raoul Letter Books.
[62] Raoul to Percy Pyne, Dec. 1, 1883, *ibid.*

TABLE 10. Distribution of stock in the Central of Georgia, Southwestern, Georgia, and Atlanta & West Point railroads in 1885

Aggregate capital stock	$18,035,600
Owned in Georgia	12,782,500

Amount held by persons owning:	
a. More than 1,000 shares	$ 2,839,600
b. Between 500 and 1,000 shares	1,916,800
c. Between 100 and 500 shares	5,831,500
d. Between 50 and 100 shares	2,818,500
e. Less than 50 shares	4,629,200
Stock owned by women, children and	
charitable organizations:	$ 8,456,600
Number of non-Georgia stockholders	715
Number of Georgia stockholders	4,235

SOURCE: *A Letter Written by Wm. G. Raoul to Hon. F. H. Colley in Reply to a Letter from Major Campbell Wallace*, (Savannah, 1885), 36.

Chapter VII

The Politics of Consolidation

By the winter of 1887 the Terminal stood upon the threshold of a new era. With the holding company now dominant a fresh burst of expansion seemed inevitable. For two years the Terminal's ambitious management ranged far and wide in search of new domains, "apparently ready," in the words of one dissuaded observer, "to buy anything in the railroad line south of the Potomac." [1] At the height of its power the company possessed three major systems with an aggregate mileage of more than 8,500 miles.

The process of consolidation bore a curiously tortured logic that merits close study. It proceeded down an uncertain path pocked by severe conflicts between opportunistic and developmental objectives. The road to progress, never lucidly defined by the management, often veered dangerously into bitter personality clashes. Every step of the journey witnessed a new round of internecine warfare as ambitious or frustrated participants tried to seize control for their own purposes. By 1888 the Terminal had reached its zenith; yet it hovered uneasily upon the brink of disaster.

Acquisition of the East Tennessee

The reorganization of the East Tennessee augured a beginning rather than an end to parlor intrigue. When the dust settled, the Brice-Thomas syndicate owned 60,000 of the crucial 110,000 first preferred shares. Having disposed of Seney, the syndicate could content itself with control of the East Tennessee system and thereby circumscribe its southern commitment, or it could reach out for additional profits by peddling the 60,000 shares to the highest bidder. By choosing the latter alternative the syndicate could go in two directions: it could sell out entirely and withdraw, or it could use the sale as a lever to enter the purchasing company. The first choice would terminate their southern venture; the second would deepen it.

[1] *Railroad Gazette*, XIX (1887), 42.

For Brice and Thomas, the logic of the situation pointed toward extending their commitment. They had already plunged too heavily into sequential investments to loosen their hold on the railroad. McGhee, too, had a large financial and personal stake in the region drained by the East Tennessee, as did several of his associates. On that basis the syndicate agreed that an extension of their commitment was the proper course—assuming a suitable transactional profit could be obtained on the sale of the shares.

Once that agreement was made, however, harmony vanished abruptly. Two prospective buyers expressed interest in the syndicate's stock: the Terminal and the Norfolk & Western. As expected, McGhee and his cohorts argued vigorously in favor of the Norfolk system. They had long believed that such a combination offered the most natural and profitable future for the East Tennessee system.[2] In simple competitive terms the Norfolk was an indispensable ally and the Terminal a dangerous rival. The developmental position of the company could best be served by strengthening the existing Virginia, Tennessee & Georgia Air-Line, which would be jeopardized and possibly broken by any association with the Terminal.

Brice and Thomas thought differently. They reasoned that access to the Terminal would be easier and more profitable. Their involvement in the recent Terminal turnover offered them a ready entrance to the new management, whereas they had no such influence in the Norfolk. The Terminal men were, in short, familiar associates amenable to sharp bargaining, while the more conservative Norfolk syndicate offered no such congenial familiarity. In addition, the expansive and flexible financial structure of the Terminal promised more leeway for transactional profits than the somewhat staid, economy-minded Norfolk. In developmental terms Brice and Thomas could even argue that alliance with the Terminal would help abate competition with the Danville.

While the private dialogue progressed, public rumor favored the Norfolk connection as anticipated by the original traffic agreement.[3] But the Norfolk management moved too cautiously and deliberately for the impatient Brice and Thomas. The Terminal proved more responsive to their overtures, and by early January, 1887, negotiations moved into the final stages. Using the Norfolk's interest as a wedge, the two financiers tried to extract par for their

[2] This preference is clearly evident in McGhee's correspondence. For one example, see McGhee to Brice, Jan. 19, 1887, McGhee papers.

[3] See *Chronicle*, XLIII (1886) , 683, 718.

preferred. Their audacity drew the admiration of W. T. "Harry" Walters, who jokingly asked McGhee to inform them that "if they get 100 for preferred they'll be worth so much I'll have to *hate* them."[4]

The prospects appeared promising. On January 13 the Terminal appointed a committee to negotiate the purchase.[5] At first the committee rejected the par offer but within a few days it came to terms and proposed a complicated settlement geared to please all parties concerned. The final plan contained these provisions: the 60,000 shares of East Tennessee preferred would be purchased at par for $4,400,000 cash and $1,600,000 in Terminal common; Scott would buy 40,000 shares of Terminal common from Grant Schley of Moore & Schley at 40 or slightly below market price, these shares to be used for the East Tennessee transaction; an additional 5,000 shares of East Tennessee first preferred would be acquired from two other parties in exchange for 10,000 shares of Terminal common; Scott would sell the Terminal all his holdings below the first mortgage in the Washington, Ohio & Western Railroad for 5,000 shares of Terminal common; and Terminal capitalization would be increased from $24,000,000 to $40,000,000, with part of the new issue going to retire all outstanding Danville stock by exchanging four shares of Terminal for one of Danville.[6]

At first glance the over-all agreement seems strangely diverse and unrelated. In actuality each provision was predicated upon the others, most notably upon the first one, and subject to cancellation should the East Tennessee purchase fall through. The cement that bound them together was the need to satisfy all participants. In all $8,500,000 in cash would be needed to handle the deal. To raise this money the Terminal issued the same amount of 6 per cent collateral trust bonds. These were taken by the First National Bank on behalf of a syndicate including Brice, Thomas, Inman, Scott, John D. Rockefeller, Moore & Schley, and others.[7]

At each stage the negotiators nicely observed the proprieties. Since his firm was handling the transaction, Moore resigned as Terminal director on January 19 and did not return to the board

[4] W. T. Walters to McGhee, Jan. 11, 1887, McGhee papers. See also the undated letter following this one.

[5] Terminal Directors' Minutes, Jan. 31, 1887. The committee consisted of Logan, Rutherfurd, Pace, Emanuel Lehman, and George Stone.

[6] *Ibid.,* Jan. 17 and 19, 1887; *Chronicle,* XLIV (1887), 91, 119; *Railroad Gazette,* XIX (1887), 42, 52.

[7] *Ibid.* A copy of this mortgage is in the Bureau of Railroad Economics.

until February 8.[8] The rights of Brice and Thomas in certain East Tennessee subsidiaries, specifically the yet unfinished Mobile & Birmingham Railroad, received careful delineation. A special general meeting on February 10 ratified all arrangements, increased the number of Terminal directors from thirteen to sixteen, and elected Scott, Brice, and Thomas to the board. Similarly several Terminal figures moved onto the East Tennessee board.[9]

The Terminal had added an important system to its stable at a stiff price. Along the way numerous participants, especially Brice, Thomas, Moore & Schley, Scott, and McGhee, collected handsome transactional profits. For a short time McGhee found himself stranded awkwardly aboard the deserted vessel of Norfolk & Western ambitions. Several parties within the Terminal demanded that he resign from the East Tennessee because of alleged connections to the Norfolk, but McGhee refused, and Brice and Thomas backed him. Of the Norfolk's last gambit he said simply, "They had the opportunity . . . and failed for want of prompt action at the critical moment." [10]

The entire deal echoed again the fateful clash of opportunistic and developmental goals. In consummating their negotiations Brice and Thomas effectively scuttled the long-awaited merger of those geographically natural allies, the Norfolk and the East Tennessee. Though arguing to the contrary, they paid little heed to the company's long-term objectives. Rather they simply accepted the most lucrative offer regardless of its implications for the future. That same attitude would continue to prevail within the more permissive atmosphere of the Terminal itself.

The Norfolk, too, profited from its experience. The reluctance to invest precipitously in existing systems soon persuaded the company to construct its own extensions, most of them to the northwest instead of southward. As for the Terminal, it inherited a dilemma that consolidation alone could not erase. By absorbing a parallel line the holding company had merely internalized its awkward competitive situation. Under any guise the Danville and East Tennessee made strange bedfellows. How would the company reconcile the conflicting interests of the two systems. A reporter for the *Railroad Gazette* spotted the anomaly at once. "The stock has brought a good price and the sellers are undoubtedly satisfied," he

[8] Terminal Directors' Minutes, Jan. 19, Feb. 7, 1887.

[9] Terminal Annual Meeting Minutes, Feb. 10, 1887; *Chronicle*, XLIV (1887), 184, 212.

[10] McGhee to Brice, Jan. 19, 1887, McGhee papers.

noted tersely. "Whether it will prove a good bargain for the purchasers, and what they will do with the road so acquired is another question." [11]

Fall of the Raoul Regime

While the fate of the East Tennessee hung in the balance, a similar crisis engulfed the Central. The sudden spurt in the company's stock baffled Raoul and his colleagues. The president himself seemed sanguine about the mystery. Early in August he confided to a close associate:

There is something more in it than a brokers move, and whether it is a determined effort to buy a control and manage the road in the interest of the controlling party, or whether it is an opinion that the stock is selling too low, and the purchase is made as an investment with a view to making money out of its legitimate operations, I am not able to tell. . . . I am inclined to think it is the latter.[12]

Within a short time it became clear that outside interests were trying to get control of the Central. Though the main source of buying was pinpointed in New York, the identity of the purchasers remained a closely guarded secret. As the price of Central stock floated upward the rumor mills churned furiously, but not until November did curious eyes turn toward the Terminal as a likely backer of the movement.[13]

Every rumor contained a small enough seed of truth to be misleading. Even in retrospect the veil of secrecy can scarcely be penetrated, and events must be deduced or theorized. With this limitation conceded, a probable story can be fitted together. The syndicate seeking control of the Central included men identified with the Terminal, East Tennessee, Norfolk & Western, and other systems. Although acting independently of these companies, their long-range goals extended well beyond the Central itself and derived from shifting conditions within the larger companies.

By their own admission the brothers Calhoun originated the syndicate. Noting the depressed state of Central stock (Pat Cal-

[11] XIX (1887), 42.

[12] Raoul to Gresham, August 6, 1886, Raoul Letter Books. For representative stock quotations, see *Chronicle,* XLIII (1886), 159, 395, 543, 666.

[13] For speculation on the backers, see *Railroad Gazette,* XVIII (1886), 600, 605, 732, 784; Savannah *Morning News,* Dec. 8, Dec. 12, 1886; Augusta *Chronicle,* Dec. 25, 1886; unidentified clippings in Raoul Scrapbook, III, 39.

houn described it as being "kicked around in the seventies") , the brothers decided to invest in a large block. Within a short time they interested other financiers in the stock, notably Isaac L. Rice, E. E. Denniston of E. W. Clark & Company, Harry Hollins, and certain ambitious Savannah brokers. To protect their venture and ensure a friendly management, the syndicate determined to oppose the reelection of Raoul. Only one candidate could muster enough support to dethrone the president: Porter Alexander. Early in the game they offered him the post on their ticket.[14]

Alexander needed little persuasion. He still smarted from his earlier defeat, and he wanted the Central back. He accepted the offer on condition that the financiers buy enough stock to assure victory. They agreed and the campaign began, with Alexander's candidacy formally announced in November. Already Raoul sensed the coming storm. On November 1 he issued a circular soliciting proxies for the coming election. The notice made no reference to the brisk stock movements and in fact declared that the board knew of no desire to change the company's management.[15]

The resulting campaign strongly resembled a replay of 1883. The basic issues had not changed; they had in fact intensified. Predictably Raoul responded to the threat by retiring behind the familiar barricades of local control and "conservative" management. His supporters denounced the unknown buyers as "wreckers" and ridiculed Alexander as the unwitting pawn of brokers and speculators. They dredged up the yet smoldering embers from 1883 and rekindled their bitter import. As the tool of "Eastern speculators" Alexander would be but a puppet for "foreign" interests. The voice of Georgia's interests would forever be lost in the Central's affairs, and its reputation as a sound investment would be ruined.[16]

Unlike the previous campaign, however, the Raoul tactics proved inept and heavy-handed. During his entire tenure Raoul had "poor mouthed" the Central's condition, citing poor earnings, the profit squeeze induced by rising prices, and the low rates im-

---

[14] This version follows closely the account given by the Calhouns themselves in Savannah *Morning News,* Jan. 3, Jan. 4, 1887. There is no reason to doubt their account as far as it goes. Its shortcomings are essentially those of omission.

[15] See the circular and the unidentified clipping in the Alexander papers. Though Alexander had not yet formally announced his candidacy when the circular appeared, indication of strong opposition to the incumbent management was widespread in Savannah.

[16] For typical examples see Savannah *Morning News,* Dec. 5, Dec. 8, Dec. 14, 1886, and Augusta *Chronicle,* Dec. 25, 1886. A rebuttal by Alexander can be found in Savannah *Morning News,* Dec. 21, 1886.

posed by the Commission. Under the guise of these forces he explained both the low dividend rate and falling stock prices. Then, on December 1, he startled observers by declaring a semiannual dividend of 4 per cent. Whatever Raoul's intentions, the unexpectedly large declaration seemed an obvious and ill-timed bid for votes. One suspicious Augusta editor noted that "the people are already enquiring how Mr. Raoul can declare a four per cent semiannual dividend after the dullest season in railroad history when, for the past four years only two per cent has been declared." [17]

If that were not enough, Raoul committed a blunder of even greater consequence. Like his mentor, Wadley, he tended to be highhanded and arbitrary. His rather skimpy reports withheld as much information as they offered, and he staunchly refused to issue monthly earnings reports despite repeated requests. The stockholders had grown accustomed to his justification of such acts as necessary to protect the company from invasion. But now, in the heat of battle, he overreached himself. Knowing that Raoul had already started gathering proxies, the Alexander forces went to the Central's offices and asked for a list of the company's stockholders. On Raoul's order the cashier refused to give out the list.[18]

Outraged by this ploy, Alexander's attorneys filed suit to have the books laid open for inspection. The court as expected upheld the right of any stockholder to examine the company books so that he might confer with his fellow holders on questions of policy. Then Raoul's lawyers appealed the case to the supreme court, which would not convene until January 10 or a full week after the election. For this hollow victory Raoul paid a dear price, for his tactics offended many stockholders.

In contrast to these bumbling tactics, the Alexander camp waged a smoothly efficient campaign. They hammered away at the cliquishness of the Raoul management and especially its refusal to give out information. On that score the refusal to open the stockholder list played right into their hands. An Alexander circular asked why the list had been refused:

To perpetuate their control by preventing us from correcting false reports and presenting to you the reasons why a change of management is not only desirable but necessary for the protection of your interests.

[17] Augusta *Evening News*, Dec. 2, 1886. See also Savannah *Morning News*, Dec. 2, 1886.

[18] For this episode, see the relevant clippings in the Alexander papers; *Railroad Gazette*, XVIII (1886) , 879; Savannah *Morning News*, Dec. 2, Dec. 3, 1886.

Will you endorse by your vote a policy of concealment? . . . Come to the election . . . confer with your associates and vote your stock in person.[19]

Alexander's long-time advocacy of full information on the company's affairs naturally won him the support of the national financial journals. The *Chronicle* tendered him its hearty endorsement.[20]

As the struggle progressed, the issues refined themselves into slogans. Raoul persisted in dismissing the strength or appeal of the opposition. "The question at issue, so far as I can discern it," he proclaimed, "is whether the management shall continue to be what may be termed a Georgia management or become what may be properly designated a New York management." [21]

Alexander vigorously denied the implications of this charge. "The issue . . . is not whether the management of the road shall be a Georgia management or a New York management," he countered, "but whether or not it shall be managed in the interests of the stockholders." [22] To another reporter he iterated the slogan that embodied the theme of his campaign: "The issue was at the first of this contest: Shall Central railroad stock be slaughtered any longer?" By "slaughtered" Alexander meant the constant undervaluation of the stock, the suppression of important data about the company's affairs, and the occasional efforts to depress the share price. He cited one instance of the board advising a stockholder to sell "if the stock ever saw eighty again." [23]

Beyond the level of campaign propaganda lay some deep-rooted issues of long standing. The virulent attacks against Alexander were directed not so much at him personally as at his faceless supporters. Many of Alexander's detractors conceded the honesty of his intentions but doubted his ability to deliver what he promised. One editorial summarized a common fear about the men behind Alexander: "They . . . have centered upon General Alexander simply for the purpose of controlling his influence and that of his friends. Any other man would suit their purposes just as well and when he comes to the head of the Central . . . it is expected that he will carry out whatever plan the real parties . . . suggest." [24]

As election day neared, excitement throughout the state surpassed that of political campaigns. At the Central's annual meet-

[19] Undated clipping in Alexander papers.   [20] XLIII (1886), 622–23.
[21] Savannah *Morning News*, Nov. 27, 1886.   [22] *Ibid.*, Dec. 2, 1886.
[23] *Ibid.*, Dec. 2, Dec. 4, Dec. 21, 1886; undated Atlanta *Constitution* clipping in Raoul Scrapbook, III, 37.
[24] Unidentified clipping in Raoul Scrapbook, III, 39. See also Augusta *Chronicle*, Dec. 25, 1886, and Savannah *Morning News,* Dec. 16, 1886.

ing on December 22 the agenda excluded anything of more than routine interest as both sides avoided any test vote.[25] Despite the intense rivalry, little ill feeling developed between the two factions. Both professed complete confidence in victory. The Raoul strategy, as always, was to rely upon the small holders. He had cornered proxies from most of the long-time Wadley supporters outside Savannah, and he confidently expected most of the yet unpledged shares within the city to go his way. He also expected Hetty Green to cast her ballot for him.[26]

He was wrong on nearly every count. Sensitive to the importance of the Green stock, the Alexander forces moved hastily to obtain it. As early as November they approached her in New York. Sharp-eyed, tight-lipped, and ascetic, clad in her familiar black costume, the "Witch" welcomed her guests with a shrewd, appraising glance. Inherently suspicious of any transaction on which she lacked full information, she pressed the syndicate for details. Central stock then stood near 100. At the appropriate moment, Alexander produced a check for $736,000 and offered it to Hetty for her 6,400 shares. That figured out to 115. Her wrinkled face cloaked in a frown, Hetty shook her head. She wanted 125. The syndicate balked and broke off negotiations. Hetty waited placidly; she knew they would be back.[27]

And back they came with a new offer. The syndicate would take her stock at 125 on the day after the election and regardless of the result if Hetty would vote it for Alexander. As security they would give her a written contract and collateral. Hetty smiled. This was not a cash transaction, she explained quietly; in that case she must have 130. Exasperated, the syndicate came to terms at 127½ and closed the deal. Word of the coup spread quickly through Savannah, but the Raoul forces remained unruffled. Their faith continued to rest in the unpledged stock.

The crowd of voters that descended upon Savannah surpassed even the record turnout of 1883. They flooded into hotels and rooming houses and spilled into the streets wrapped in hot debate

[25] *Railroad Gazette,* XVIII (1886), 894.

[26] Savannah *Evening Press,* Jan. 3, 1887; Charleston *News and Courier,* Jan. 10, 1887.

[27] New York *Times,* Jan. 5, 1887; *Railroad Gazette,* XVIII (1886), 803, 824; *Chronicle,* XLIII (1886), 607. There is no satisfactory biography of Hetty Green. Two popular accounts are Boyden Sparkes and Samuel T. Moore, *Hetty Green: The Witch of Wall Street* (New York, 1930), and Arthur H. Lewis, *The Day They Shook the Plum Tree* (New York, 1963).

over the issues. On election day Alexander arrived an hour early in order to cast his votes first. It was a shrewd move. By 10 A.M. a crowd of voters had queued up along the sidewalk by the bank. For nearly five hours Alexander rattled off his proxy lists, and when he had finished some of his supporters cast their votes. The endless stream of tallies soon affected the less committed standees, and a general lunge for the bandwagon commenced. At 3:15, when the first vote for Raoul was cast, Alexander had 40,145 votes, a clear majority. He finished with 41,666 to Raoul's 27,773. Of the Central's 75,000 votes 69,439 had been cast.[28]

As a victory celebration engulfed the Screven House, the winners immediately proclaimed that the road would be run in the interests of the stockholders and not some distant syndicate. A policy of strict economy would be introduced, the first target of which would be a refunding of the Central's debt at lower interest rates. There would be no bitterness or hard feelings between the new regime and the departing directors, and in fact the transition proceeded smoothly and cordially.[29]

For all the platitudes, the significance of the election escaped no alert critic. Few disputed the opinion of the New York *Times* that Alexander's election was "considered a 'scoop' of the road by New York capitalists." Alexander himself admitted that New York financiers held 25,000 shares. Nor did the source of the General's backing remain a mystery. The *Times* stated the matter succinctly:

That some agreement has been entered into between Gen. Alexander and the managers of the Terminal Company is a fact beyond dispute, though what the terms of the agreement are cannot yet be authoritatively stated. There can hardly be any doubt, however, that the final result will be the merging of the Richmond and Danville and the Georgia Central systems.[30]

Such a merger puzzled some observers. The *Railroad Gazette* pointed out that the alliance would be of more benefit to the Dan-

---

[28] *Railroad Gazette*, XVIII (1886), 824, 896; Savannah *Morning News*, Jan. 3, Jan. 4, 1887; undated clipping from Savannah *Daily Times*, Alexander papers.

[29] Savannah *Morning News*, Jan. 3, Jan. 4, Jan. 5, 1887. John Calhoun asserted that "we expect to run it [the Central] purely in the interest of stockholders and of the state of Georgia." It is noteworthy that one editor speculated that "it may be that the prospective early refunding of the Central's six and seven per cent bonds was the inducement which brought Mr. Hollins into the movement" (see Charleston *News and Courier*, Jan. 10, 1887).

[30] Jan. 4, 1887. See also *Chronicle*, XLIV (1887), 33, 59, and *Railroad Gazette*, XIX (1887), 14.

ville than the Central. The latter derived much of its profit by hauling freight to Savannah and sending it north from there by its steamships. Any alliance with the Danville could only mean a diversion of this traffic northward by rail on the Danville and a subsequent loss of business for the steamships. A minor incident on January 5, when the Central mysteriously surrendered part of its South Carolina traffic to the Danville, further heightened suspicions.[31]

The question of conflict of interest bore seeds destined to sprout bitter controversy. For the moment, however, it remained an opaque speculation. In plumbing the depths of intrigue behind the election, even the most astute observer had not touched bottom. They succeeded in establishing a rough connection to the Terminal but could not differentiate among the diverse interests within that company. The election had in fact strained various relationships within and without the holding company. John Inman and his brother Samuel had favored Raoul. When defeat became apparent, they maneuvered cautiously for some place in the victorious syndicate. The victors themselves had exerted strong pressure upon Savannah financial interests to back Alexander. One erstwhile Raoul supporter, John Garnett, was induced to switch allegiances by the promise of a place on the Alexander ticket. In the end most of the young brokers and all of the city banks except the Central and a few private houses followed the winning banner, though many of them postponed their decision until the last possible moment.[32]

Even at the brink of success the Alexander syndicate divided dangerously. One faction had gone to Raoul with an offer to switch their support if he would allow them to name seven of the Central's directors. When Raoul declined the proposition they returned to the fold and supported Alexander.[33] These random for-

---

[31] *Railroad Gazette*, XIX (1887), 8; Savannah *Morning News*, Jan. 5, 1887. For other reactions to the election, see the Atlanta *Constitution*, Jan. 4, 1887, and Columbus *Daily Enquirer*, Jan. 4, 1887.

[32] W. W. Gordon to Raoul, March 31, 1892, Gordon papers; Savannah *Morning News*, Jan. 4, 1887. With regard to the notion of "coevals" mentioned in chap. 1, it is interesting to note that three of the new directors on the Alexander ticket were the sons of former directors who had all supported "conservative" policy. A brief survey of the new directors can be found in Savannah *Morning News*, Jan. 4, 1887.

[33] Raoul to C. W. Brewster, June 2, 1890, Raoul Letter Books. This was Raoul's version of the story. For a contrary report, see Savannah *Evening Press*, Jan. 3, 1887.

ays indicated only too well that thoughts of more than just possession of the Central lay behind the syndicate's operations. For the
moment their purpose and direction could be neither fathomed
nor predicted. Only one fact could be stated with any degree of
confidence: the Central had embarked upon a new era, the most
salient feature of which could only be further change. The last tat-
tered vestiges of the territorial era were hastening to oblivion.

The Sully Policy

As president Sully presided over a board no less splintered than its
predecessor. Once in control of the Terminal, the mosaic of interests that had secured his victory quickly lost cohesion. The return
of Brice, Thomas, and Scott to the management virtually guaranteed a clash between representatives of the East Tennessee and
those of the Danville. For his part Sully wished to assuage both
camps by promoting a nonpartisan policy. To do this he would
have to persuade those directors deeply involved in the rival systems to make the Terminal their primary concern. In other words,
they must now come to accept the holding company as their developmental investment rather than a speculative vehicle for their
other interests. To achieve this Herculean task Sully had few allies. On the new board only Rice, Dow, Wanamaker, and Stone
stood aloof from previous factional disputes.

To implement this strategy Sully pursued a variety of tactics.
Administratively he reorganized the existing structure to fit the
company's new role. Henry Fink assumed the vice-presidency in
charge of operations for both the Danville and the East Tennessee
with headquarters in New York. The general manager, traffic manager, and other officers also took on new responsibilities for both
systems. Only the Georgia Pacific remained outside this administrative umbrella; for various reasons it continued to be treated as
an independent property. More important, Sully pushed to separate the Danville's administration from that of the Terminal.
Headquarters of the Danville was returned to Richmond, and that
system received its own president.[34]

On the question of expansion Sully tempered ambition with a

[34] *Richmond Terminal Report,* 1887, 7–10; Terminal Directors' Minutes,
Dec. 6, 1887; *Railroad Gazette,* XIX (1887), 207–8, 295; *Chronicle,* XLV
(1887), 857. Presidency of the Danville was offered first to Inman, who
declined. Scott then took the post (Terminal Directors' Minutes, Dec. 9, 1887).
Sully also wished to house the officers of all subsidiary systems in one building.

strict eye for economy. The only fixed charges on the holding company consisted of $510,000 annual interest on the recently issued collateral trust bonds. Hopefully this would be met by dividends on the East Tennessee preferred alone. To tighten the Terminal's financial position Sully recommended that certain unprofitable securities be sold off and specific limits be placed upon future betterments and construction expenditures. Neither proposal met with approval. The statement on betterments especially alarmed Fink, who had already warned the board that "in some cases it seemed to me that the economy was being pushed to the extreme verge and even beyond the limits of safety" on the Danville. Despite his efforts, the Danville's operating ratio never exceeded the low range of 49.6 to 57.0 per cent during the period 1886–92.[35]

In justifying the formation of so vast and centralized a system Sully articulated with unusual clarity the rationale behind interterritorial expansion. His words merit close study, for they represent the thinking of his peers:

The underlying principle which actuated the Board of Directors in bringing into your ownership this extensive system has been the belief that the consolidation of . . . these roads must result in great economies, in less competition, and also enable the roads within the system to devote their attention to furnishing better facilities for the public . . . instead of wasting their energies and resources in senseless competition at competing points, or reckless invasions into each others territory.

As long as the statutes of the different States authorize any combination of men, responsible or irresponsible, to build a road to or from any place, even to the extent of paralleling an existing line, so long will it be necessary to protect invested capital, by consolidating in one ownership, as far as possible, the lines traversing a country so sparsely settled as that covered by the Terminal lines.[36]

Thus ran the credo of interterritorial developmental policy. In theory it sounded like the wise application of order to a chaotic situation. In practice it stumbled badly over one exasperating dilemma after another.

Factionalism Reasserted

Though Sully gained reelection in December, 1887, his authority was clearly on the wane. Throughout the first year of his tenure he

---

[35] Terminal Directors' Minutes, March 23, 1887; *Railroad Gazette*, XIX (1887) , 207–8; *Chronicle*, XLIV (1887) , 401.

[36] *Richmond Terminal Report*, 1887, 4.

watched the perimeter of his influence shrink before successive eruptions of factionalism. The first executive committee, composed of Sully, Brice, Logan, Inman, Pace, Scott, Stone, and Lehman, harbored a profusion of goals and little sympathy for the president's plans. Scarcely had the new management organized when John Wanamaker resigned. In his place came Edward Lauterbach, a well-known corporation lawyer who had negotiated the recent purchases of both Danville and East Tennessee stock.[37]

As Sully struggled to perfect his grand design, a host of problems confronted him. Foremost among these was the question of rate adjustment. If the East Tennessee and Danville systems were to be truly integrated, a carefully equitable tariff would have to be devised. At the moment East Tennessee rates sharply undercut those on Terminal-controlled roads, a situation that barred any sizable interchange of traffic under the provisions of the recently passed Interstate Commerce Act. Unwilling to lower its own rates, the Terminal board instructed Fink to work out a new tariff schedule for the East Tennessee.[38]

The rate problem opened the door to another delicate question: the diversion of East Tennessee through traffic from Norfolk to the Terminal roads. For the Danville faction, headed by Scott, acquisition of the East Tennessee by the Terminal logically presumed a transfer of through traffic currently passing over the Virginia, Tennessee & Georgia Air-Line. To achieve that end Scott introduced a resolution to instruct the Terminal's general manager to take all necessary steps for the diversion.[39]

The East Tennessee faction immediately protested. Though not a member of the Terminal board, McGhee asked both Scott and John Inman to preserve the Air-Line. He renewed the logic of geography by arguing that "it is impossible to divert it, or any considerable portion of it to the . . . Danville . . . as that line is unknown to the shipping public. Even if it could be diverted at once, it would be impossible for the . . . Danville System, with its inadequate facilities at West Point and its small steam ship service to handle it." The Air-Line had been the fruit of twenty years of hard

[37] Terminal Directors' Minutes, March 2, Nov. 11, 1887; *Railroad Gazette*, XIX (1887), 151, 819; *Chronicle*, XLV (1887), 821. Lauterbach was discreetly absent from the meeting and did not vote on his own gratuity of $25,000 for conducting the negotiation.

[38] Terminal Directors' Minutes, March 31, 1887. The East Tennessee also had a reputation for tolerating employees with questionable ethics on financial matters (see W. T. Walters to McGhee, Dec. 23, 1887, McGhee papers).

[39] Terminal Directors' Minutes, March 31, 1887.

labor, McGhee pleaded; to destroy it thoughtlessly would result in serious injury to the East Tennessee's (and Memphis & Charleston's) business "and will not confer any corresponding benefits to the . . . Danville." McGhee spoke as an investor heavily loaded with securities of all classes in the Tennessee roads. His colleagues, Brice and Thomas, also had large holdings in East Tennessee and joined the protest. Despite their opposition the campaign to disrupt the alliance proceeded cautiously. Small amounts of traffic were shifted, and some Air-Line agencies abolished along the East Tennessee line. The Terminal avowed its intention to stop all East Tennessee contributions to the Air-Line's expenses.[40]

The Air-Line controversy remained a festering sore within the Terminal. On matters of financial policy disagreement ran equally deep. Sully's attempt to steer a conservative course foundered on the rocks of factional ambitions. To meet the Terminal's obligations Sully had to rely upon dividends received on its Danville and East Tennessee stock, but neither seemed inclined to declare. Both companies preferred to retain their cash for construction and other purposes. After considerable effort he finally wrung 3 per cent from the Danville and 4 per cent from the East Tennessee.[41] Elsewhere, however, his policies consistently met defeat. He disagreed with Scott over the proper handling of the Danville's long moribund debentures. Scott wanted to fund the debentures with new Danville consolidated fives, and to achieve that end he agreed to pay a substantial portion of the unpaid interest. Despite Sully's opposition the plan was approved, and shortly afterward Sully reluctantly declared a 2.5 per cent dividend on the Terminal's own preferred stock.[42]

As the autumn of 1887 waned Sully grew progressively gloomier over his prospects. His position as president gave him little power other than as mere executive agent for the board anyway; yet he inevitably bore the brunt of every criticism heaped upon the Terminal management. Vulnerable to assault and helpless to create or even sway policy, his only refuge lay in obtaining a board sympa-

[40] McGhee to Inman, June 30, 1887, to E. B. Thomas, August 4, 1887, and to Robert Fleming, August 5, 1887, McGhee papers.

[41] An injunction to block payment of the dividend was denied (see *Railroad Gazette*, XIX [1887], 445, 462) .

[42] *Chronicle*, XLIV (1887) , 752. Details of Scott's refunding plan can be found in *ibid.*, XLIV (1887) , 435. Not all factional disputes involved Sully versus the representatives of one of the major roads. For a policy split between Brice and McGhee and Inman, see McGhee to Inman, Jan. 9, 1888, McGhee papers.

thetic to the interests of the holding company itself. That prospect grew discouragingly remote. The current board showed no desire to shake free of their commitments to the operating systems, and the tiny band of directors loyal to Sully dwindled steadily.

In December, Sully gained reelection and managed to put on the ticket R. T. Wilson, William Rockefeller, and Rosewell P. Flower. He pinned his hopes for the future on the support of this trio, but his illusions were quickly shattered. All three declined to serve, and in their place came Lauterbach for a full term, James Swann (Inman's partner), and Jay Moss. The new executive committee consisted of Inman, Scott, Brice, Thomas, Logan, Lehman, and Stone.[43]

Origins of the Georgia Company

A cloak of mystery shrouded the birth of the Georgia Company. Organized in the spring of 1887 under a North Carolina charter, it was obviously intended as a holding company modeled after the Terminal. Upon an authorized capital of $16,000,000 the company issued $12,000,000 in stock and $4,000,000 in 5 per cent bonds. As collateral for the bonds the directors deposited 40,000 shares of Central of Georgia stock and $415,000 in cash assessed from the purchasing syndicate.[44] The Georgia Company's charter limited the uses to which the bonds could be put. The company could buy, guarantee, or endorse the securities of any railroad in North Carolina and adjoining states, and it could operate and lease roads as well. It could engage in the "business of transportation," but it was specifically forbidden to construct any railroad.[45]

[43] Terminal Directors' Minutes, Dec. 20, 1887, Jan. 21, 1888; *Chronicle*, XLV (1887), 857; *Railroad Gazette*, XIX (1887), 819, 836.

[44] David Schenck Diary, May 31, June 12, 1887; *Chronicle*, XLV (1887), 210, 792.

[45] *The Richmond and West Point Terminal Railway and Warehouse Company, Plaintiff, against John H. Inman and Others, Defendants* (New York, 1892), 11–13, 51–53, archives of the Southern Railway Company; hereafter cited as *Terminal vs. Inman*. This summons and complaint comprises the most valuable single source for the entire Georgia Company episode. It forms the basis for the account given by E. G. Campbell, *The Reorganization of the American Railroad System* (New York, 1938), 97–104, though he does not cite it in his footnotes. The version in Daggett, *Railroad Reorganization*, 162–78, is based upon the secondary reports in contemporary journals. A third account in Stover, *Railroads of the South*, 247–49, is drawn largely from Campbell and Daggett and the contemporary journals.

The founding syndicate comprised a large and intriguing lot of individuals and banking houses. Since the company was incorporated by subordinate employees serving as "dummy" officials, a complete roster of the participants cannot be pieced together. A list of known participants and the firms they represented is summarized for convenience in Table 11.

A survey of the parties involved makes the complexity of interests and goals painfully clear. The syndicate included most, but not necessarily all, of the men who had backed Alexander in the fight for the Central's presidency. It was no surprise, therefore, that the Central stock pooled for that fight became the primary asset of the new company.[46] Sully's presence betrayed a strong connection to the Terminal and seemed to confirm the suspicion that Alexander's election meant control of the Central by the holding company. But the situation was by no means that simple. Not all of the syndicate members were interested in the Terminal, and the presence of the Clarks and their friends, all deeply interested in the Norfolk & Western, suggested a faction antagonistic to the Terminal in developmental terms. Nor did all the participants agree upon objectives or policies. Small wonder, then, that the new company aroused considerable speculation in financial circles.

In a series of conferences the syndicate announced that no important changes in the Central's management would take place, though Hollins assumed the vice-presidency. Instead the syndicate turned its attention to financial tactics. The 40,000 shares of Central stock were duly deposited as collateral for the Georgia Company bonds. At the same time 60,100 of the Georgia Company's 120,000 shares were deposited as a voting trust, with the remainder placed in a pool for sale. Under this arrangement the syndicate set out to market the $4,000,000 in bonds and the undeposited stock. Despite the earnest efforts of every firm involved and circulars that painted the prospects of the Central in glowing colors, the sale went poorly. Only a handful of bonds were sold before the bankers withdrew them, and the stock attracted no purchasers.[47]

---

[46] David Schenck Diary, May 31, June 12, 1887. Schenck, a lawyer with no access to inside information, noted that "it would seem that some stupendous scheme is concealed under this simple corporation. . . . Mr. Rice intimated that the Company had the Georgia Central in view, but I am inclined to believe it is the Balt & Ohio scheme revived." For the rumor that the Terminal was about to acquire the B. & O., see *Railroad Gazette*, XIX (1887), 162–63.

[47] *Terminal vs. Inman*, 13–16; *Chronicle*, XLV (1887), 792; *Railroad Gazette*, XIX (1887), 490, XIX (1887), 14. A clipping of an advertisement for the Georgia Company bonds, placed by August Belmont & Co., can be found in

TABLE 11.   Participants in the Georgia Company syndicate

Participant	Firm represented
1. H. B. Hollins	H. B. Hollins & Co.
2. Fernando A. Yznaga	"
3. Frederick Edey	"
4. Bernard J. Burke	"
5. August Belmont Jr.	August Belmont & Co.
6. Walther Luttgen	"
7. Emanuel Lehman	Lehman Brothers
8. Mayer Lehman	"
9. Meyer H. Lehman	"
10. Sigmund M. Lehman	"
11. Philip Lehman	"
12. John Inman	Inman, Swann & Co.
13. Robert W. Inman	"
14. James Swann	"
15. Bernard S. Clark	"
16. William Kessler	Kessler & Co.
17. Edward Kessler	"
18. Gustav E. Kissel	"
19. Simon Wormser	I. & S. Wormser
20. Isador Wormser	"
21. Jacob Scholle	Scholle Brothers
22. William Scholle	"
23. James Seligman	J. & W. Seligman
24. Jesse Seligman	"
25. Charles Blum	Blum & St. Goar
26. Frederick St. Goar	"
27. Alfred S. Heidelbach	Heidelbach, Ickelheimer & Co.
28. Isaac Ickelheimer	"
29. Alfred Lichtenstein	"
30. Edward W. Clark	E. W. Clark & Co.
31. Edward W. Clark, Jr.	"
32. Clarence H. Clark, Jr.	"
33. Edward E. Denniston	"
34. J. Milton Colton	"
35. Sabin W. Colton	"
36. Harold M. Sill	"
37. Isaac L. Rice	No firm
38. John C. Calhoun	No firm
39. Patrick Calhoun	No firm
40. Alfred E. Sully	No firm

SOURCE: *The Richmond and West Point Terminal Railway and Warehouse Company, Plaintiff, against John H. Inman and Others, Defendants* (New York, 1892), 3–6, in archives of Southern Railway Company.

The attempt to dispose of the bonds on no other basis than the potential of the Central marked the Georgia Company as a purely opportunistic scheme. It conducted no business and did not even

the archives of the Southern Railway Company. A contemporary report that the bonds were all taken by a foreign syndicate at 95 was incorrect (see *Chronicle,* XLV [1887], 210).

bother to issue the usual bromides of intent. The purpose of the company was quite simply to sell its securities at a profit and realize a handsome reward on the original investment in Central stock. So far the syndicate had failed miserably in their speculation, but new plans were under way. Why bother to sell the company's securities piecemeal? Why not sell the whole lot to a captive buyer, and what more likely prospect than the dissension-riddled Terminal?

Centrifugal Forces

By the winter of 1888 the citadels of conflicting interests had effectively destroyed Sully's hope of winning complete authority for the Terminal over its component parts. On the Danville, Scott assumed full authority and brooked no interference from the Terminal management. The dispute over refunding the Danville debentures furnished an instructive example. The decision to exchange the debentures for new consols had been made when several members of the Danville board were out of town and without any approval from the Terminal board, which owned 86 per cent of the Danville's stock. Despite these circumstances Scott brazenly refused Sully's request to examine the proceedings of the Danville board, and Sully could find no support for his protest.[48]

A similar affair occurred on the Georgia Pacific. That road had been built by the Richmond & Danville Extension Company, the stock of which was owned mostly by the Terminal and its friends. In constructing the road the Extension Company issued both first-mortgage bonds and second-mortgage income bonds. High construction costs, disappointing earnings, and a perennial floating debt prevented holders of the income bonds from gaining any income. In March, 1888, a committee of income bondholders offered to exchange their 6 per cent bonds and accrued interest for an equal amount of 5 per cent securities, half of which would be fixed mortgage bonds and half income bonds. The arrangement would add $95,000 to the Terminal's fixed charges (exclusive of the Georgia Pacific bonds held by it), and for that reason Sully opposed the plan. Once again, however, his negative vote was overridden and the plan approved.[49]

48 Terminal Directors' Minutes, Jan. 21, 1888.

49 *Ibid.*, March 29, 1888; *Chronicle*, XLVI (1888), 320. A clipping on the settlement can be found in the archives of the Southern Railway Company. The income bondholders committee was headed by John A. Rutherfurd, J. C. Maben, and Joseph Bryan.

On the East Tennessee, Brice and Thomas established their authority no less effectively than Scott had on the Danville. Distrustful of the Georgia Company's ambitions for the Central, the East Tennessee management pushed an aggressive expansion program that also proved profitable to themselves. To finance new growth the company authorized a $15,000,000 first-extension mortgage on June 1, 1887. Of this amount only $5,140,000 was actually issued, with $2,500,000 going to Brice and Thomas, $1,500,000 to John Inman, $2,000,000 to the First National Bank, and the rest in scattered lots. During the next three years most of this money went to purchasing new feeder and connector lines.[50]

At the same time Brice and Thomas arranged to have the East Tennessee acquire certain roads in which they held large personal interests. Foremost among these was the unfinished Mobile & Birmingham, acquired by Brice and Thomas only a couple of years earlier. With a fine disregard for legal technicalities and without any specific sanction from the Terminal, the two financiers used their dual position as buyers and sellers to complete a transaction foreshadowed in the Terminal's purchase of East Tennessee preferred. The East Tennessee paid $810,000 for a majority of the road's stock and agreed to endorse a new $3,000,000 bond issue to complete the line.[51]

The Brice-Thomas syndicate also succeeded in persuading the Terminal to purchase the stock of the Asheville & Spartanburg and complete its hold on that long-unprofitable road. Brice tried to have the East Tennessee acquire the Georgia Midland Railroad as well, but here he met sufficient resistance to drop the matter. In these transactions and some of the acquisitions covered by the extension mortgage, notably the small Walden Ridge Railroad, Brice and Thomas worked closely with the firm of Moore & Schley. As a member of the Terminal board John Moore served as a valuable ally to the East Tennessee interests.[52]

The lines of East Tennessee autonomy from the Terminal radiated in every direction. At the top Brice and Thomas had effec-

---

[50] McGhee to Robert Fleming, August 11, 1887, McGhee papers; Harrison, *Southern Railway*, 686–89. For Brice's explication of the mortgage, see *Chronicle*, XLV (1887), 304.

[51] *East Tennessee Report*, 1888, 6–12; *Chronicle*, XLIV (1887), 681, XLVI (1888), 678. For background on the Mobile & Birmingham, see Harrison, *Southern Railway*, 886–92.

[52] *Railroad Gazette*, XIX (1887), 358, 411, XX (1888), 62. For the history of the Asheville & Spartanburg, see Harrison, *Southern Railway*, 366–92.

tively nullified Sully's efforts to bring the system into harmony with the Danville. Within the system they retained the support of the influential second-preferred holders in England simply because, as McGhee noted, "they are the only parties who can protect the East Tenn Property." At the same time they kept firm grip upon such important subsidiaries as the Memphis & Charleston through the cooperation of McGhee and other loyal allies. For their pains these allies received a twofold reward: protection of their often heavy investment in the East Tennessee and the authority to dispense largess to their friends whenever possible. Despite this policy, the interminable battle against the minority holders of the Memphis road continued in the courts.[53]

The Central, though not formally a Terminal property, also posed grave problems for Sully. The large Terminal interest in the Georgia Company and the dangerous competitive position of the Central system naturally engaged his close attention. To Sully's profound displeasure Alexander regarded the aggressive East Tennessee as a threat and responded with an expansion plan of his own. He let contracts to complete a controversial extension to Birmingham, extended other Alabama feeder lines, and put the Central's South Carolina roads into better shape. To pay for these projects he created a new $5,000,000 issue of 5 per cent collateral trust bonds, which increased the Central's funded debt by 50 per cent.[54]

In fashioning his expensive policy Alexander tried to compromise with the East Tennessee. After reorganizing some of the Central's South Carolina roads into a new company known as the Port Royal & Western Carolina, he offered to swap the latter to the East Tennessee for its Brunswick line. Neither road profited its owner, but the trade would materially reduce the arena of competition between the systems; for that reason it could not help but improve relations. But the East Tennessee showed no interest in lessening tensions. It continued instead to develop Brunswick and completed a survey for extending the road to Jacksonville to vie for the Florida trade. Thomas even urged that a feeder line to Savan-

[53] *Railroad Gazette,* XIX (1887), 692; McGhee to Fleming, August 11, 1887, McGhee papers; *Chronicle,* XLV (1887), 613. A fairly common example of this largess can be seen in this extract from McGhee to H. S. Chamberlain, Jan. 24, 1887, McGhee papers: "Am holding back an order for steel rails for Memphis & Charleston until you are ready to bid for them. We shall want a thousand tons and I hope to keep them for you."

[54] For the Central's expansion, see *Chronicle,* XLIV (1887), 653, XLV (1887), 744–46, XLVII (1888), 285–87; *Railroad Gazette,* XIX (1887), 206, 240, 357, 390, 444, 595.

nah receive serious consideration and did not even bother to mention the proposed swap in his annual report. Alexander's response to this threat was to seek a traffic alliance with the Florida-based Plant system.[55]

The centrifugal thrust of these rising tensions swamped the few feeble strides toward cohesion inaugurated by Sully. In addition, the fluidity of alliances within the Terminal management thwarted any attempt to form a stable coalition in support of his policies. And no one figure proved more elusive than John Inman. Shifting nimbly from faction to faction, he kept a sympathetic hand in every scheme. He participated in the purchase of the Danville, the East Tennessee bond issue, and the Georgia Company. During the fall of 1887 he was rumored to have purchased 10,000 shares of Central stock.[56] So adeptly had he covered all fronts that no one (including perhaps Inman himself) knew for certain what stand he would take in a managerial crisis.

That crisis was clearly forthcoming. In Savannah, Alexander warned the absent Alexander Lawton of its mood. After noting that the Georgia Company had given him a free hand to run the Central, he added: "I think there is only one man who is watching me with hostile designs & that is Sully. He at least is disposed to interfere & criticize but he has lost all his influence & power on the board & the majority of it . . . is *now hard at work* . . . to turn him out of the Terminal." [57]

The Fight for the Presidency

Despite the antagonism between the East Tennessee and Danville factions, the movement to oust Sully came from neither of them. Rather it originated with part of the Georgia Company group headed by August Belmont, Brice, Hollins, and the Clarks. Concluding that the East Tennessee faction posed the greatest threat to their interests, they determined to remove not only Sully and Logan but Brice and Thomas as well. With their influence gone the Terminal could be persuaded to acquire the securities of the

---

[55] *East Tennessee Report*, 1888, 7–9; *Chronicle*, XLV (1887), 643, 853; *Railroad Gazette*, XIX (1887), 708.

[56] *Railroad Gazette*, XIX (1887), 519.

[57] Alexander to Lawton, March 22, 1888, Lawton papers. The italics are Alexander's.

Georgia Company, and a profit on that speculation could at last be realized. The interests of the Danville and the Central could be harmonized within the Terminal, and perhaps the East Tennessee could be once again reconciled with the Norfolk & Western, a matter of no small concern to the Clarks.[58]

On that basis Rice and Hollins persuaded a reluctant Porter Alexander to stand for the Terminal presidency if they succeeded in driving Sully out. The campaign opened early in March when Rice, E. W. Clark, and William Libbey released a newspaper card calling for a general stockholders' meeting. The card alleged that the Terminal had been forced to borrow money to pay its January dividends on preferred stock and interest on its collateral trust bonds despite the fact that both the Danville and the East Tennessee showed substantial increases in earnings.[59]

Sully, as expected, found his position untenable. At a stormy directors' meeting on April 5 he resigned his position. In a letter to Rice's committee he gave the opposition movement his endorsement. "Several times during the past year," he noted, "I was tempted to call a meeting of the stockholders with a view to deciding as between a majority of the directors and myself as to certain measures which I deemed clearly against the best interests of the Terminal stockholders, but which were adopted against my earnest opposition." A week later, however, he appeared before the Terminal board to inform them that he had no interest in the current fight and would take no part in it.[60]

After accepting Sully's resignation with unseemly haste, Brice calmly marshaled his forces for the counterattack. He offered a resolution, approved unanimously, to resist any effort to transfer control of the Terminal to another company. Together with Stone and Lauterbach he drew up a circular refuting the charges made by Rice's committee and accusing it of trying to subvert the Terminal to the Georgia Company. The circular also pointed up the Clarks' relationship to the Norfolk & Western. Efforts to favor this system, the board insisted, had severely cut into traffic on the East Tennessee and other Terminal roads; now the attempt to discredit the management succeeded only in creating confusion, depressing security values, and demoralizing employees. The board urged

[58] R. T. Wilson to McGhee, March 22, 1888, McGhee papers.
[59] Alexander to Lawton, March 22, 1888, Lawton papers; New York *Times*, March 12, 1888; Richmond *Dispatch*, March 21, 1888.
[60] Terminal Directors' Minutes, April 5, April 12, 1888; Richmond *Dispatch*, March 21, April 4, April 6, 1888.

upon stockholders the importance "in times of depression of uniting all interests in support of their properties and securities." [61]

That same day Emanuel Lehman abruptly resigned his position as a Terminal director, saying that he refused to be associated with the present management and would support the opposition. In his blast he accused the board of running the Terminal in the interests of the East Tennessee. Reports singling out Alexander as the opposition candidate soon emerged openly, and on April 13 the rebels published a card demanding a general meeting of the company on May 31. According to the Terminal's charter, such a call could be made at any time by holders of 10 per cent of the company's stock.[62]

The eruption of an open struggle for power threw the board into confusion. Inman especially hesitated to take a position. In March, R. T. Wilson confided that "I think he probably regrets the move but still he will have to follow his interests." [63] Unfortunately, it was not entirely clear where his primary interests lay. Inman had large stakes in both Terminal Company systems and the Georgia Company. To protect all his investments he needed to find some way of reconciling the dispute. By the same token, his diversity of interests rendered him a likely choice for the Terminal presidency. He alone among the incumbents could unite the badly divided factions. Despite some reservations the board elected him unanimously on April 16. At the same meeting the directors agreed to hold a general meeting on May 31.[64]

Inman's election caught the rebels by surprise. The incumbents had charged the Rice committee with trying to dump the Georgia Company on the Terminal; yet both Inman and his partner James Swann were members of the Georgia Company board, and two of Inman's brothers sat on the Central's board. As the Terminal candidate he obviously represented the board's interests and supported their position, but he also owned the second largest piece of the Georgia Company. It was known that Inman, a bull in the cot-

[61] Terminal Directors' Minutes, April 5, April 6, 1888; New York *Times*, April 7, 1888. A copy of the circular is in the archives of the Southern Railway Company. For the Rice committee response, see New York *Times*, April 8, 1888.

[62] Terminal Directors' Minutes, April 6, 1888; New York *Times*, April 7, April 13, 1888; *Chronicle*, XLVI (1888), 449. Lehman's resignation was at first tabled and was not accepted until April 30.

[63] Wilson to McGhee, March 22, 1888, McGhee papers.

[64] Terminal Directors' Minutes, April 16, 1888; *Railroad Gazette*, XX (1888), 262; *Chronicle*, XLVI (1888), 511; New York *Times*, April 18, 1888; Richmond *Dispatch*, April 22, 1888. That Inman had definitely cast his lot can be verified in Inman to McGhee, May 23, 1888, McGhee papers.

ton market, had suffered heavy losses in a recent collapse of cotton prices, and some observers wondered what role these losses played in his maneuvering. What was his game? What stakes did he have in mind? Charming and genial as always, the chameleon promoter masked his every intention.[65]

Once assured of a meeting and thus an election, the Rice committee unveiled its proposed board and then issued its own circular to refute the one issued by the Terminal board.[66] In it the Rice committee ridiculed the plea of the incumbents that much of the responsibility for current policy belonged to the previous board, elected in December, 1886. Thirteen of the sixteen directors had served on both boards, and the fount of power had in no way changed. In the quest for information on Terminal affairs, the pamphlet sneered, "we are at a loss to know whether to apply to Messrs. Scott-Thomas-Brice-Stone-Lauterbach of the old board or Messrs. Scott-Thomas-Brice-Stone-Lauterbach of the new board." [67]

On the heels of this circular the Rice committee unleashed its most devastating attack. It published a blistering and detailed indictment of the policies pursued by the Terminal management. Seldom in the nebulous world of nineteenth-century economic development have the savage conflicts between developmental and opportunistic motivations been so clearly exposed and dissected. To be sure the exact motives of the participants can never be unearthed, for they involved verbal agreements and transactions of the sort that never find their way to paper. Only rarely, in the heat of battle, did the details of such episodes slip free of their closets. As a window into the complex motivations of decision makers, then, the Rice committee charges deserve close scrutiny.[68]

[65] Richmond *Dispatch*, April 22, 1888.

[66] New York *Times*, April 24, 1888. The proposed board consisted of Belmont, Hollins, Rice, Libbey, Alexander, E. W. Clark, Emanuel Lehman, Rudolph Keppler, Robert Colgate, H. Van Rensselaer Kennedy, Frederick N. Lawrence, John Hone, Jr., W. S. Gurnee, F. H. Lovell, Thomas Janney, and Alfred Lee Tyler.

[67] William Libbey, E. W. Clark, and Isaac L. Rice, *To the Stockholders of the Richmond and West Point Terminal Railway and Warehouse Company* (n.p., n.d.) , 7, copy at Bureau of Railway Economics. The changes in the Terminal boards of 1887 and 1888 were as follows: Moss replaced Dow; McGhee replaced E. D. Christian; and Swann replaced Rice. Earlier John Hall had replaced H. M. Flagler, who was elected in December, 1886, but never qualified for the board.

[68] This pamphlet, entitled *Points on Which Information Will Be Desired at the Next General Meeting* . . . (n.p., n.d.) , can be found in the archives of the Southern Railway Company. It was also reprinted in full in *Chronicle*, XLVI (1888) , 579–81.

First of all, the committee probed into the Terminal's purchase of the East Tennessee first preferred. Why, they asked, had the Terminal purchased all 65,000 shares when 55,001 would have sufficed for a majority? And why were so many other deals tied into the purchase? The committee suggested that the Terminal directors who negotiated the East Tennessee purchase themselves held large interests in the outstanding minority of the Danville's stock. In approving the acquisition of all 65,000 East Tennessee shares, they included a stipulation that the Terminal also buy up all outstanding Danville stock at a price of about 200 or twice the market value.

To gain further support the Terminal also agreed to buy the entire stock and income bonds of the Washington, Ohio & Western for $500,000 in Terminal stock. That long-moribund property was owned by Scott and some of his associates on the Terminal board. Another inducement to the purchase lay in the obvious boon to holders of Western North Carolina securities. If the East Tennessee succeeded in diverting traffic to the Danville, it would be via the Carolina road and promised prosperity for its minority holders.

The supreme irony, duly underscored in the pamphlet, was that the Terminal did not even acquire effective control of the East Tennessee despite its costly outlay. A clause inserted in the collateral trust deed enabled Brice, Thomas, and Scott to return to the Terminal board to "protect" their interests. Later, in the supplemental mortgage of September 30, 1887, the Terminal's entire equity in the Danville stock was pledged as security for the bonds. As a result the Terminal management could not wield effective authority over either of its major systems. The committee asserted that within a year the Danville and East Tennessee factions had agreed to divide power among themselves, and the Terminal holders were left to shift for themselves.

As part of this plan the systems refused to issue dividends so that the Terminal could meet its expenses. Instead earnings would be devoted to construction, advances to other companies, and other tactical necessities. When the Terminal board convened to provide money for a dividend on its own preferred stock, Scott not only refused to declare a dividend on Danville stock but demanded immediate payment of $75,000 allegedly owed to the Danville by the Terminal for four years. The embarrassed Sully had to borrow $125,000 (which Scott refused to loan the Terminal), and his board declined to reprove the Danville president for his intransigence. Later, when interest fell due on the Terminal bonds, Sully endured a similar rebuff from the East Tennessee board and was forced to borrow to avoid default.

In general, then, the Terminal had failed abysmally to unite or even subdue its subordinate companies. In the process, however, substantial transactional profits went to the participants, and the Rice committee listed them with ruthless efficiency. Brice and Thomas sold their Mobile & Birmingham road to the East Tennessee for a tidy profit and then had the latter road guarantee the bonds necessary to complete the line. In fact, the committee alleged, advances by the East Tennessee to the Mobile road constituted a major reason for the company's inability to find money to pay dividends. Joining with John Moore and his colleagues in Moore & Schley, Brice and Thomas sold the diminutive Walden Ridge Railroad to the East Tennessee, tried unsuccessfully to unload the Georgia Midland as well, and planned an expensive extension through the pine barrens from Jesup to Jacksonville. The extension mortgage was passed largely to serve these projects without any apparent approval of the Terminal company.

The committee found equal free-lancing on the Danville. They attacked the conversion of the Virginia Midland and Georgia Pacific income bonds into fixed charge bonds.[69] These acts, pushed through during Sully's absence, added a new burden of fixed charges to the Danville on roads whose earning records had been notoriously poor. In the committee's eyes, the only explanation could be found in the personal holdings of Terminal directors in the income bonds. The same reasoning applied equally to the funding of the Danville's debenture bonds. Two other transactions, the purchase of minority stock in the Asheville & Spartanburg and the guarantee of certain bonds on a hotel, came in for sharp review by the committee. In almost every instance a common theme emerged: the unilateral action of select members of the Terminal executive committee without either formal approval or ratification by the entire board.

The matter of the leased lines posed another thorny issue. In attempting to dump the Terminal, the Danville leased all the holding company's important roads and transferred its most valuable assets to the Danville treasury. When the scheme failed, it was assumed that the leases and transfers would be voided and all properties returned to the Terminal's control. The transfer of assets did take place, but for unexplained reasons the roads remained

---

[69] For final disposition of the Georgia Pacific bonds, see Terminal Directors' Minutes, April 13, 1888, and Inman to McGhee, April 14, 1888, McGhee papers.

leased to the Danville. In that capacity they were kept under Scott's authority, and the Rice committee charged that certain Terminal directors profited personally from the leases. Moreover, the Danville had advanced over $1,600,000 or over 16 per cent on its own stock to the leased lines, creating yet another excuse for not declaring a dividend from which the Terminal might benefit.

The most intriguing charge, however, concerned a land syndicate headed by Brice and Thomas. Here the narrow line between opportunistic and developmental motivation received its clearest exposition, as did the relationship between investment in the railroad and in sequential enterprises. Brice, Thomas, E. J. Sanford, E. R. Chapman of Moore & Schley, and some of their friends owned extensive tracts of mineral lands in Tennessee and neighboring states. One of these fields nestled in a ravine of the Cumberland Mountains and was accessible only through Coal Creek Gap. To haul the coal from these fields the Knoxville & Ohio had built a Y-shaped spur line through the gap extending four miles south and one mile north. On the northern end another three-mile road, known as the Coal Creek & New River Railroad, was constructed to reach more distant mines. The Coal Creek road belonged to the East Tennessee-dominated Knoxville & Ohio, which left its operation in the firm grasp of the Brice-Thomas syndicate.

The syndicate did not own all the mines in these fields, and therefore wished to drive out its competitors. It issued orders to the East Tennessee superintendent not to furnish cars to the rival owners or haul any coal from them. With a backlog of orders for the coal and no way of moving it, the operators petitioned the Interstate Commerce Commission for relief. The Commission upheld every article of the complaint and dismissed the defense as feeble evasion, but discrimination continued under a different guise. Such practices, the Rice committee charged, benefited individual pockets at great cost to the railroads involved. The coal of the petitioners, if carried, would have gone over the East Tennessee, Western North Carolina, and other Terminal roads. Refusal to move it cost the company thousands of tons of cargo, and the committee wondered how many other similar instances existed.[70]

The committee also probed into certain other questionable financial practices such as the sudden dumping of 29,564 shares of Terminal common on the market during the summer of 1887 and the sum of $824,601 lost by the company in trying to support the

---

[70] For disposition of the case, see *Second Annual Report of the Interstate Commerce Commission* (Washington, D.C., 1888) , 139–40.

market during the great Terminal speculation in 1882. The Rice committee's pamphlet told an overwhelming tale of factional conflict and financial opportunism. In so far as relevant evidence exists to verify the charges, they appear to be accurate in almost every instance. No satisfactory refutation of them was ever made. Nowhere had the Terminal's failure been catalogued so thoroughly and the competence of its management condemned so trenchantly. On this basis alone the Terminal stockholders could scarcely deny the urgency of the rebel's demand for a change in management. Unfortunately the small Terminal holder counted for little in the battle.

The scorching tract evoked howls of protest among the wounded on Wall Street; yet within a few days the conflict lapsed into mysterious silence. Both sides radiated confidence and claimed to have on hand enough votes to triumph. Movements in Terminal stock remained curiously normal and even slow at times. A game of bluff, the New York *Times* sneered: "That Richmond Terminal contest for control is lost, strayed, or stolen." [71]

On May 13 the Rice committee suddenly announced its candidate to be not Alexander but F. B. Clarke, a veteran manager in the Vanderbilt system. No one proffered a reason for the switch. The rebels put forth their proposed policy in four main points: a thorough physical and financial examination of the Terminal properties; the promotion of harmony among the systems; an end to purchases of any securities in which Terminal directors held personal interests; and operation of all systems without discrimination. Still the suspicious *Times* dismissed the contest as a power struggle between the Rice faction and the Brice faction. "It is believed that a good deal of stock will not be represented at the meeting," the paper scoffed, "as it is in the hands of persons who are more interested in the material welfare of the road than in any partisan struggle for control. The contest does not rise above that level." [72]

Sporadic bursts of allegation enlivened the final week, but the meeting convened in a strangely apathetic atmosphere. Though well-attended, it proceeded at a pleasantly brisk pace. Rice represented his party on the floor, and Lauterbach the incumbents. At every turn Rice rose dutifully to present his criticisms and Lauterbach amiably parried the charges or had them voted down.[73]

[71] May 8, May 9, May 11, 1888.
[72] May 14, May 18, May 20, 1888; Richmond *Dispatch,* May 22, 1888.
[73] The account of the meeting is drawn from Minutes of the General Meeting of the Richmond & West Point Terminal Railway and Warehouse Company,

In this fashion the proceedings moved rhythmically toward the balloting. Rice submitted the questions detailed in the pamphlet issued by his committee. Lauterbach countered with a set of answers drafted by a committee of himself, Inman, Brice, Scott, and Rutherfurd. For the most part the replies consisted of mere denials, pointed digressions, and a careful sidestepping of the real issues involved.[74] After consuming an hour with his reply Lauterbach read Inman's report for the previous seven months. Upon a motion by John Branch resolutions were introduced approving the conduct of the present management and condemning the actions of those who had forced the meeting. The vote on these resolutions offered the first show of strength between the rivals: the resolutions carried by a 298,006 to 94,645 margin. Lauterbach, Stone, and Logan cast the entire winning vote, and Rice and Libbey the negative ballots.

Lauterbach quickly wrapped up the loose ends. He nominated Inman for the presidency and won by the same margin, as did John Calhoun and Walter S. Chisholm, who were nominated to fill the seats vacated by Sully and Lehman. Over Rice's objection Lauterbach then submitted a code of bylaws drawn up by the directors and asked their approval sight unseen. The motion carried by the usual margin. A final resolution calling for Sully and Lehman to resign their positions in all Terminal subsidiaries also passed easily.[75]

After a fifteen-minute recess the meeting adjourned. Over the Ballard House's empty hall, littered with rumpled paper and disarrayed chairs, might well have hung the haunting refrain uttered by Brice early in the campaign. "All this row about holding an election to oust the present Directors is like a prairie fire," he noted affably. "It looks like a tremendous affair; but don't you shut your eyes for half a minute while you're watching it, for before you open them again it'll all be gone." [76]

Next day the *Times* reported rumors of a bull movement in Terminal common.[77]

May 31, 1888, in archives of the Southern Railway Company, and Richmond *Dispatch,* June 1, 1888.

[74] The replies are printed in the account in Richmond *Dispatch* June 1. 1888. See also Terminal Directors' Minutes, May 29, 1888.

[75] New York *Times,* June 1, 1888; *Chronicle,* XLVI (1888), 699; *Railroad Gazette,* XX (1888), 376.

[76] New York *Times,* April 6, 1888.   [77] June 2, 1888.

Chapter VIII

A Beast with Many Heads

THE ousting of Sully and defeat of the rebels ensured that factionalism would continue to prevail within the Terminal. More important, it suggested that the Terminal would remain a vehicle for opportunistic ambitions rather than a device for effective developmental control. The recent election—indeed the company's entire history—had demonstrated the Terminal's need for thorough integration. To a large extent Sully's policies reflected a basic concern for the welfare of the holding company and its stockholders. But he failed to appreciate fully that the Terminal was a horse capable of being harnessed to many different carts. It had, after all, originally been created by the Danville to serve the parent road either by providing feeder lines or by eliminating dangerous competition. From this perspective the Terminal mattered only insofar as it promoted the Danville's designs; it was a means to an end, not an end in itself. Small wonder, then, that its stock should be considered a plaything of speculators.

And therein lay the awkward dilemma created when the Terminal turned the tables on the Danville. The successful revolt of the Terminal stockholders depended ultimately upon more than a mere change of control: to be complete it required a change in investment strategy as well. But this latter change never took place, for the new board never rose above the level of partisan interests. As long as the Terminal board consisted of men deeply involved in individual railroad systems, especially those owned by the Terminal, how could they resist the temptation to manipulate the holding company to suit their own particular needs?

No semblance of physical or financial integration occurred, apparently for three broad reasons. First of all, it suited the opportunistic desires of the financiers to retain the complex structure studded with numerous kinds of securities. The more tangled the web of intercompany relationships, the more possibilities there were for the imaginative manipulator to devise opportunities for transactional profits. Secondly, the task of complete financial integration would be an enormous one. At its peak the Terminal possessed holdings in over sixty different railroad companies. To acquire complete or even near-complete equity control over all of them would require a huge outlay of capital.

Finally, any attempt to forge a thorough integration would encounter serious social and legal problems. Often the Terminal's indirect and sometimes tenuous control of a property derived from either legal prohibition or social restraint. It might be recalled that the Terminal itself was created specifically to skirt just such a restraint. The existing social environment, in short, might well discourage even the most sincere advocate of developmental consolidation. Especially did it handicap an enterprise like the Terminal. To own relatively parallel systems meant inevitably to favor one over the other if they were to be operated separately; and the prevailing social, legal, and political atmosphere demanded that they be operated separately, to preserve "competition" and avoid "monopoly."

Under these conditions control of the Terminal had been maintained by a fragile coalition between representatives of the rival systems, who successfully polarized power within the company. Each faction ran its own system and both used the Terminal to further their designs. In this setting Inman assumed the Terminal presidency. He would find the office no less comfortable than his predecessor. Though he possessed more personal power and influence than Sully, the task of composing radically diverse interests remained beyond his grasp. No longer could he stand aloof from the conflicts within his board. The ordeal of struggle would force him to commit himself and, once having done so, incur enemies.

During the autumn of 1888 the last phase of the Terminal's checkered history commenced. It would be characterized by bitter clashes over policy at three separate levels: between Inman and the East Tennessee and Danville factions, between representatives of the two factions, and between the Terminal management and minority stockholders in roads owned by the holding company. These minority holders, writhing in discontent under Terminal rule, found their cause aided immeasurably by the divisiveness already inherent within the Terminal board.

Purchase of the Georgia Company

Late in October, 1888, the *Railroad Gazette* announced that the Terminal had "startled the financial world by obtaining control of the Georgia Central System." The deal involved a purchase of 120,000 outstanding Georgia Company shares at $35 a share or $4,200,000 in all from the Hollins-Lehman syndicate. Skeptical observers recalled that during the election campaign these same Terminal directors had bitterly castigated their opponents for wanting to buy this same stock. Naturally critics insisted that the transaction reflected some secret bargain struck during the heated spring campaign, and the facts did little to refute them. Since the acquisition became the most publicized and controversial episode in the Terminal's history, it deserves careful examination.[1]

On October 22 nine members of the Terminal board convened for a special meeting. Conspicuously absent were Inman and John Calhoun. Both sent letters explaining their absence and asking that it be specifically noted. At the meeting Emanuel Lehman—he who had mysteriously deserted the incumbents to join the rebels—confronted the board with an offer to sell the Terminal all outstanding Georgia Company stock as well as the $4,000,000 in collateral trust bonds issued by it. Since the price of $35 a share included control of the $400,000 cash assessment paid in by the Georgia Company syndicate, the actual price would be reduced to slightly under $31 per share.[2]

At first glance the proposal seemed tempting. The price could by no means be considered extravagant for 40,000 shares of Central stock which marketed for prices ranging from 110 to 130 during 1887 and currently rested around 115. Its original price had probably ranged between $4,400,000 and $5,000,000, and some might consider control of so powerful a system as the Central cheap at that price.

But the bonds were the real snake in the garden. They constituted a first lien on the Georgia Company stock, which meant that any purchaser of the stock would either have to guarantee interest on the bonds or buy them as well. The bonds had nothing to do with the Central system itself and had no reason beyond the speculative for even existing. But exist they did, and they would require an annual interest of $200,000 to keep the Central stock out of the bondholders' hands. If the Terminal wished to take them up as well, the price for control of the Central would mushroom to over $8,000,000.

[1] *Railroad Gazette*, XX (1888) , 705. See also *Chronicle*, XLVII (1888) , 499.
[2] Terminal Directors' Minutes, Oct. 22, 1888; *Terminal vs. Inman*, 18–20. The directors at the meeting were Wormser, Moore, Lauterbach, Scott, Thomas, Hall, McGhee, Moss, and Chisholm.

TABLE 12.   Holders of Georgia Company
stock participating in the sale to the Richmond
Terminal, October 26, 1888

Name	No. of shares
H. B. Hollins & Co.	21,812
August Belmont & Co.	7,200
E. W. Clark & Co.	18,000
H. B. Hollins & Co. for	
E. P. Alexander	2,175
Inman, Swann & Co. for	
E. P. Alexander	4,154
Inman, Swann & Co.	15,592
Isaac L. Rice	7,634
Emanuel Lehman	24,379
Gustav E. Kissel	18,754
Total shares	119,700 [a]

SOURCE: *The Richmond and West Point Terminal
Railway and Warehouse Company, Plaintiff, against
John H. Inman and Others, Defendants* (New York,
1892), 61.
[a] The remaining 300 shares were acquired by
the Terminal from an unknown party or parties
shortly afterward.

At that lofty price the Central would not be worth having. Yet
at the meeting the directors voted, without prior committee investigation, to accept Lehman's proposal. Moore, Hall, and Chisholm were instructed to draw a plan for financing the acquisition
and arranging all details. On October 26 eleven directors, exclud-
ing Inman and Calhoun, reassembled to approve the final contract. The terms were simple. The Terminal agreed to purchase
the entire Georgia Company stock at $35 a share and to buy from
August Belmont & Company $1,000,000 of the bonds at 95 plus ac-
crued interest. The company further pledged either to purchase
the remaining $3,000,000 worth of bonds or to have the Danville
guarantee interest upon them. As security for the pledge they deposited $250,000 with Belmont.[3] Table 12 lists the holders of Geor-
gia Company stock participating in the sale.

Having made its decision, the Terminal faced the awkward
problem of finding money for the purchase. It had committed itself to a minimum outlay of more than $5,000,000 at a time when

[3] Terminal Directors' Minutes, Oct. 22, Oct. 26, 1888. A copy of the contract
is in *Terminal vs. Inman,* 54–62. The directors present at the meeting were
Logan, Rutherfurd, Stone, Wormser, Moore, Lauterbach, Scott, Brice, Thomas,
McGhee, and Chisholm.

it allegedly possessed less than $14,000 in ready cash. Sully's recent frustrations in obtaining money to meet current obligations attested to the Terminal's marginal liquidity. Nevertheless the board appointed a committee consisting of Inman, Thomas, and Scott to come up with a financial plan to handle the purchase and pay off other outstanding debts. Mindful of the need to complete the transaction in short order, the board reconvened on November 7 and voted Inman a free hand to borrow the necessary funds from any source and on any terms he deemed suitable.[4]

Everything proceeded on schedule. Inman formed a syndicate, largely within the company, to advance the necessary cash for the stock and $1,000,000 of the bonds. On November 20 the stock was formally transferred, and within three weeks the bonds had been acquired. In completing the transaction Inman unquestionably exposed himself to charges of conflict of interest, not only in the stock sale but in the matter of the bonds as well. On behalf of the Terminal he had purchased $500,000 of the bonds from his own firm, Inman, Swann & Company. The board ratified his action, and a general meeting of the company on December 13 unanimously approved all acts and transactions. Such approval should not be taken too seriously, however, for the Terminal annual meetings consisted of little more than large blocks of stock controlled by the board itself and represented by proxy. After the special election of 1888 no annual meeting transcended a purely *pro forma* level.[5]

Immediately after the meeting the Terminal board decided not to purchase the remaining Georgia Company bonds but rather to have the Danville guarantee interest on them. There the matter rested until May, when the Danville board notified the Terminal that it refused to endorse the bonds. No reason was given for the refusal. On May 29 the Terminal authorized Lauterbach and Pat Calhoun, the latter recently elected to the board, to make all arrangements for purchasing the remaining bonds outright. Later

[4] Terminal Directors' Minutes, Oct. 26, Nov. 7, 1888; *Terminal vs. Inman,* 18–21.

[5] Terminal Directors' Minutes, Nov. 13, Dec. 8, 1888; Terminal Annual Meeting Minutes, Dec. 11, 1888; Inman to McGhee, Nov. 8, Nov. 13, 1888, McGhee papers; *Terminal vs. Inman,* 21–22, 63–64; *Railroad Gazette,* XX (1888), 779; *Chronicle,* XLVII (1888), 625. The pattern of attendance for annual meetings can be seen in the minutes of the meetings. Terminal Annual Meeting Minutes, Dec. 9, 1890, for example, show that no preferred stock and only 200 shares of common were represented in person, while 33,108 preferred and 462,950 common were represented by proxy.

Inman joined the committee, and by mid-June the trio drafted a remarkable arrangement for acquiring the bonds.[6]

By the spring of 1888 the Central had itself run into serious financial problems. An ambitious extension project known as the Savannah & Western had consumed most of the company's ready cash and given rise to a sizable floating debt. To relieve that debt and provide funds for completing his project, Alexander proposed issuing $18,000,000 in bonds on the Savannah & Western system with the Central guaranteeing interest on them. Lacking funds to purchase the Georgia Company bonds, Inman and his colleagues decided to borrow the money from the Central and to utilize the new Western bonds in a complex transaction.[7]

Inman proposed to borrow $3,000,000 from the strapped Central through an elaborate shuffling of securities. Hollins & Company agreed to purchase $5,000,000 worth of the new Western fives at 95 *if* the Terminal agreed to conclude the purchase of the Georgia Company bonds at 95 from a syndicate headed by Inman, the brothers Calhoun, Swann, and Simon Wormser. The Central then loaned the Terminal $3,500,000 for the Georgia Company bonds, which were deposited as collateral for the loan. In addition, the Central agreed to pay Hollins & Company and E. W. Clark & Company $25,000 each "for their claims arising out of negotiations or intended negotiations by them of said Savannah and Western Railroad Company's bonds and otherwise." Since the Terminal originally wished to pay only 94 for the Georgia Company bonds, the Central paid the holding company an additional $25,000 as compensation for the difference in price.

When the smoke had cleared, the Terminal possessed the Georgia Company's entire stock and all but $553,000 of its bonds.[8] The sorely pressed Central had delivered over to the Terminal $3,500,000 of the Western bond proceeds. So short of cash was the Central that its board refused to approve the loan unless the Terminal cashed the notes immediately. On approval by the Terminal board, Inman, Swann & Company formed a syndicate to cash the loan and carry the Terminal's notes given for the purchase of the

---

[6] Terminal Directors' Minutes, Dec. 14, 1888, May 8, May 29, 1889; *Terminal vs. Inman*, 23–25.

[7] The account that follows is derived from Terminal Directors' Minutes, June 19, June 27, 1889, and *Terminal vs. Inman*, 25–29. Copies of the relevant documents involved in the transaction are in *Terminal vs. Inman*, 65–71.

[8] In Sept. the Terminal board declined an offer by August Belmont to sell these bonds at 97½ (see Terminal Directors' Minutes, Sept. 13, 1889) .

Georgia Company. The carrying of this loan enabled Inman and his associates to profit not only on their sale of the Georgia Company but on the transaction itself.

The problem of providing a plan for permanently financing the acquisition fell to a committee composed of Inman, Scott, and Thomas. During the winter of 1889 Inman announced a new $24,300,000 blanket mortgage for this and other purposes. Of this amount $5,000,000 was set aside for the Georgia Company transaction and sold to a syndicate headed by Inman, Swann, John C. Calhoun, Kessler & Company, Maitland, Phelps & Company, and other parties who had been involved in the prior transactions. The price was about 85 less commission. In summary, the Terminal saddled itself with an additional fixed charge of about $384,000 a year not counting the interest already paid on short-term notes. The only income it received would be the dividends declared on the 40,000 shares of Central stock, and these never exceeded $320,000 a year. The net loss to the Terminal, then, would amount to at least $64,000 a year.[9]

The obvious conflicts of interest involved were indisputably illegal, for Section 1122 of the Virginia Code specifically stated that "no member of the board shall vote on a question in which he is personally interested otherwise than as a stockholder."[10] Yet, as Table 13 shows, the directors' meetings that considered and ratified the crucial transactions never possessed a legal quorum, if the known interested parties are excluded as the law required.

Aside from legal problems, there remains the fundamental question of why the other Terminal directors acquiesced in so palpably fraudulent a deal. Later it would be charged that the disinterested directors were largely ignorant of the Central's affairs, that Inman and his friends convinced them of the company's great worth by gross misrepresentations of its condition, and that the directors approved the deal on the basis of this misinformation. A crucial part

[9] *Ibid.*, April 12, May 6, 1889; *Terminal vs. Inman*, 28–29; *Railroad Gazette*, XXI (1889), 135, 366; *Chronicle*, XLVIII (1889), 209, 261, 764, XLIX (1889), 115–16. A copy of the mortgage is in the archives of the Southern Railway Company.

[10] Virginia General Assembly, *The Code of Virginia* (Richmond, 1887), chap. 47, sec. 1122. This act was originally passed with slightly different wording in 1837 (see *Acts of the General Assembly of Virginia* [Richmond, 1837], 68). In *Terminal vs. Inman*, 38, it was alleged that Inman, Swann, Wormser, and the Calhoun brothers owned about 20 per cent of all the Georgia Company securities sold to the Terminal. Their collective profit can be reckoned accordingly.

TABLE 13. List of directors present and voting at selected Richmond Terminal directors' meetings considering the purchase of Georgia Company securities

Date of meeting	Purpose	Directors voting
October 22, 1888 [a]	Approve purchase of Georgia Company stock	(9) Chisholm, Hall, Lauterbach, McGhee, Moore, Moss, Scott, Thomas, Wormser [b]
October 26, 1888 [a]	Arrange details to complete transaction and provide funding	(11) Brice, Chisholm, Lauterbach, Logan, McGhee, Moore, Rutherfurd, Scott, Stone, Thomas, Wormser [b]
November 7, 1888 [a]	Inman authorized to borrow money for purchase on any terms he deems suitable	(11) J. Calhoun,[b] Chisholm, Hall, Inman,[b] Lauterbach, Logan, McGhee, Moss, Rutherfurd, Scott, Swann [b]
June 19, 1889 [c]	Plan to use loans from Central of Georgia to purchase Georgia Company approved	(9) J. Calhoun,[b] Hall, Inman,[b] Lauterbach, McGhee, Moore, Scott, Swann,[b] Thomas

SOURCE: Minutes of the Directors' Meetings of the Richmond & West Point Terminal Railway and Warehouse Company.
[a] Nine votes were needed for quorum.
[b] This director was known to be personally involved in the transaction and therefore was legally disqualified from voting.
[c] Ten votes were needed for quorum.

of Inman's campaign involved not only ballyhooing the Central's merits but underscoring its threat as a rival as well. Specifically, the Inman syndicate warned that unless it was controlled, the Central would extend feeders deeper into the territory worked by the Danville and open a competition that could seriously injure the latter system.[11]

It may well be true that busy financiers like Brice and Thomas knew little about the actual physical and financial condition of the Central, and on that basis Inman and his friends may have done a superb job of promotion. But by the same token it seems highly implausible that these same experienced financiers could be ignorant either of the personal motivations behind the promotion or the size of the transactional profits involved. The negotiations consumed several months and received widespread publicity; moreover the close attention given the Georgia Company during the recent election campaign surely disclosed the nature of the company to the Brice-Thomas faction.

While the available evidence does not yield a conclusive explanation for their acquiescence, it does suggest a probable one. In retrospect, the Georgia Company deal appears to be the price paid by the incumbent factions for retaining control of the Terminal. In accepting the presidency Inman doubtless exacted some compensation for his powerful support. Perhaps the factions figured that continued undisturbed reign over their systems was worth admitting Inman to a share of the spoils. Certainly they envisioned no change in existing lines of power once Inman took charge. Even more important, every member of the board had too lucrative a stake in the Terminal to risk losing hold of the management. Whether it be a Brice or Scott making large transactional profits, a McGhee protecting a developmental investment as well as pursuing opportunistic gains, or a Lauterbach defending the substantial fees he collected as general counsel for the company, the incumbents preferred concession to outright war.[12]

Even in circles ignorant of the guerilla warfare within the Terminal, the transaction roused unanimous suspicion. The objections centered primarily upon strategy. The acquisition could scarcely fail to benefit the Terminal. It assured the Danville of a

---

[11] *Terminal vs. Inman*, 39–45.

[12] The firm of Hoadley, Lauterbach & Johnson became the Terminal's general counsel on Jan. 7, 1888 (see Terminal Directors' Minutes, Jan. 7, 1888). For examples of Lauterbach's fees, see *ibid.*, Dec. 12, 1890, which notes the firm's annual retainer at $10,000.

southern connection and seemed to eliminate the threat posed by the Norfolk & Western. But what did the Central stand to gain? Alexander had apparently brought prosperity to that system, and any significant change could hardly be for the better.[13] The *Chronicle* noted that everything depended upon the motives of the Terminal management:

Where various pieces of road, all under separate and distinct ownership, are connected and brought together so as to form a harmonious and complete system under one management, the operation is clearly beneficial to the public and to all concerned. The effect of such an arrangement is to reduce cost, furnish cheaper and better service, economize time, and in various other ways add to the value and usefulness of the roads. But when the object is to control competition, the matter may wear a different aspect.[14]

In financial terms the *Railroad Gazette* pinpointed the critical issue more precisely. Though not yet fully aware of the Terminal's intricacies, it recognized nevertheless that the danger of the company lay in its very nature. The Terminal was "a financial concern which controls railroads by ownership of a majority of their securities. The Pennsylvania and other roads have done the same thing in the past, but the difference is that the Pennsylvania is a railroad while the Richmond & West Point is not. This gives the operations of the last named company a more distinctly financial character." [15]

The Quest for Integration

As Terminal president, Inman confronted the monumental task of integrating the company's discordant systems. His attempt proceeded along two distinct levels, the physical and the financial. The first involved the consolidation of the roads into one unified system and the elimination of intersystem competition; the second required the Terminal to gain absolute control over the systems possessed by it and rid the managements of conflicting interests. In essence the task demanded that each system's sense of individual identity be erased in practice if not in theory. Upon this difficult quest hinged the Terminal's fate.

The basic tactics in each case seemed clear to Inman and his al-

---

[13] *Railroad Gazette*, XX, (1888), 704–5.   [14] XLVII (1888), 486–87.
[15] XXI (1889), 29.

lies. Physical integration must be achieved by unifying the administrations of the three systems and by compelling their operating officers to work out common policies. Financial integration could be approached by buying up the outstanding securities of all three major companies. Two advantages would derive from this tactic: it would offer holders of these securities a tempting transactional profit, and it would either remove their influence from the Terminal management or (if they chose to exchange their securities for those of the Terminal) transfer their primary allegiance from the individual system to the holding company. Even if the tactic succeeded, however, one serious problem remained: the minority holders in each railroad controlled by the individual systems. To their hostility Inman could oppose only a tedious and interminable spate of legal actions.

In shouldering these problems Inman found more support on his board than Sully had garnered, but he needed a power base from which to operate. Sully's mistake in defending the holding company had been to wander helplessly into the cross fire between the powerful leaders of the two major systems. For his part Inman began with the leverage wrought by the addition of the Central, but he had no intention of stopping there. To retain power he would have to side with one of the warring factions in order to best its rival, and circumstances gradually dictated that it be the Danville. The implementation of his policies and the obstacles confronting them can best be understood by first considering developments within each of the three systems.

The Ordeal of the East Tennessee

Not surprisingly, the East Tennessee posed the thorniest problem for Inman. Its representatives on the Terminal board could be considered the president's most dangerous adversaries, and the holding company's control over the system was tenuous to an extreme. That control, it will be recalled, rested in the hands of the first preferred stockholders for five years or until two successive 5 per cent dividends upon first preferred has been declared. The East Tennessee board had blandly declared a 4 per cent dividend in 1887 despite loud protests from the minority holders. Arguing the injustice of allowing $6,500,000 worth of first preferred to dictate policy to $45,000,000 of second preferred and common, they demanded a 5 per cent declaration for 1888 and an additional 1 per cent paid retroactively for 1887. Even if the board did not relent, the priority of the first preferred would expire by 1891, and even a semblance of control would vanish.[16]

Before the matter came to a head, the Terminal made one last effort to rid itself of friction by selling its interest in the East Tennessee to the Norfolk & Western. The latter's interest had never lapsed, and dispute within the Terminal had lost none of its bitterness. Scott remained convinced that traffic must be diverted from the Norfolk to the Danville, while McGhee argued adamantly that such a course would be ruinous. In fact, despite Scott's strenuous efforts, little diversion of traffic had occurred, largely because the Danville connection was inferior to the Norfolk in terms of service, convenience, and facilities.[17] During the spring of 1888, therefore, Inman renewed negotiations with the Norfolk. By July the matter had gone far enough for Inman to yield the bargaining to a committee composed of Scott, Thomas, and Chisholm. Discussion continued until August, when it broke down for what proved to be the last time.[18]

Ostensibly the failure was attributed to a difference over price, but the Norfolk's reluctance went much deeper. President Kimball's private explanation deserves examination, for it reflects a strategy radically different from that pursued by the Terminal management.[19] Kimball conceded the intrinsic value both of the East Tennessee and of the alliance. His board, however, had been pursuing a careful developmental policy for some time and was reluctant to risk any major move without the most thorough investigation. In addition, a shift in the Norfolk's basic traffic pattern rendered the Air-Line less vital to the company. "There was a time," Kimball observed, "when the through business of our line constituted a very large proportion of our total business, but that time has passed and now the through business forms but a very small proportion, and we think it would be better for us to risk the loss of our entire through business rather than to assume obligations without a thorough and careful investigation."

The East Tennessee could be made a valuable road by develop-

---

[16] *Chronicle,* XLVI (1888), 708, XLVII (1888), 200, 353.

[17] For Scott's position, see Scott to McGhee, June 7, 1888, McGhee papers.

[18] Terminal Directors' Minutes, July 24, 1888; *Chronicle,* XLVII (1888), 63, 81, 140.

[19] The following is based upon F. J. Kimball to McGhee, August 4, 1888, McGhee papers. See also *Chronicle,* XLVII (1888), 482–83.

ing its resources, Kimball added, but it would require large expenditures, and the Norfolk refused to commit itself without assurance of a *"permanent* alliance," which it could not obtain because of the uncertain tenure of the first preferred's control. A lease might be possible but promised legal resistance from minority holders. For these reasons Kimball declined to buy the stock, apologizing to McGhee for "our way of looking at the matter, which you may consider too conservative and cautious." The Norfolk would continue its conservative policy of stressing local development and retiring from highly competitive through business wherever necessary.

The importance of local development did not go entirely unnoticed in Terminal councils. In November, 1888, the company appointed Logan a committee of one to promote "immigration into the territories adjacent to our lines" and voted him a fund of $25,000 for that purpose. Two weeks later, however, the resolution was mysteriously repealed and expunged from the minutes.[20] It never came up again. Later that same winter E. J. Sanford emphasized to a sympathetic McGhee that "there is no doubt but that local development is the big feature to be looked after with railroad enterprises at this time in the South." [21] In its annual reports the East Tennessee continued to pay obeisance to the primacy of local development, but in practice most of its financial resources went to acquire new roads whose immediate value lay in expanding the East Tennessee's field of battle for through traffic.[22]

Unable to dispose of the East Tennessee profitably, the Terminal management perceived two alternative means of preserving its control over the system: a lease or the outright purchase of all classes of East Tennessee securities. Since the lease offered the cheapest and most immediate solution, Inman tried it first. Scott drew up and the board approved an elaborate lease designed to keep possession of the system for ninety-nine years.[23] Even a cursory glance showed the lease to be tainted with impropriety if not outright fraud. It kept actual control of the company in the hands of the first-preferred holders for an inordinate length of time and utterly ignored the spirit of the 1886 reorganization plan. It also stifled any chance for junior holders to gain any benefits from

20 Terminal Directors' Minutes, Nov. 21, Dec. 8, 1888.
21 Sanford to McGhee, Feb. 7, 1889, McGhee papers.
22 For an example of this obeisance, see *East Tennessee Report,* 1889, 9–10.
23 Terminal Directors' Minutes, Oct. 3, 1888.

their stock, since the dividend proviso openly favored first-preferred holders.[24]

Some of the minority holders refused to bow. No sooner had the lease been signed than they filed suit to enjoin the Danville from operating the East Tennessee, to enjoin the latter from ratifying the lease at its annual meeting, and to restrain the Terminal from voting its first preferred at the East Tennessee meeting.[25] The decisions on the suit dealt the Terminal a setback. The court denied the application for a receiver and upheld the Terminal's right to vote its stock, but it struck down the lease as violating Tennessee statutes against the combination of competing roads.[26]

Their appeal denied, the Terminal board withdrew the lease and switched to the more prosaic tactic of buying up additional East Tennessee stock of all classes. Inman's chief technique was to exchange Terminal common for the outstanding shares. In the autumn of 1889, for example, he acquired nearly 20,000 shares of East Tennessee first preferred in return for Terminal common at a rate of one East Tennessee preferred to three and a quarter shares of Terminal common. At the same time he induced McGhee to swap 4,300 shares of East Tennessee second preferred for an equal number of Terminal common. The effect was to increase the Terminal's capitalization rapidly without significantly strengthening the company's hold over the East Tennessee. As late as January 1,

[24] *Chronicle*, XLVII (1888), 381, 410, 472; *Railroad Gazette*, XX (1888), 695; Harrison, *Southern Railway*, 685–86; Daggett, *Railroad Reorganization*, 161–62. The provisions of the lease were as follows: the duration would be 99 years; the East Tennessee would receive as rental 33⅓ per cent of its gross earnings for the first four years, 35 per cent the next five years, 36 per cent the next five years, and 37 per cent thereafter; the Danville guaranteed that this percentage would be sufficient to pay all fixed charges and a guaranteed 5 per cent dividend on the first preferred. Any remaining net income would then belong partly to the junior holders.

[25] The specific charges of the complaint are summarized in *Chronicle*, XLVII (1888), 532, 663–64, and *Railroad Gazette*, XX (1888), 744, 778. A rebuttal to the charges by those junior holders in favor of the lease can be found in a circular entitled, "To the Second Preferred and Common Shareholders of the East Tennessee, Virginia & Georgia Railway Co.," Nov. 19, 1888, archives of Southern Railway Company.

[26] *Railroad Gazette*, XX (1888), 795, XXI (1889), 135. The strength of local feeling against Terminal control is evident in the fact that Inman demanded and received a change of venue on grounds that "from prejudice and local influence the company would not be able to obtain justice in the Chancery Court at Knoxville or any other State Court" (*ibid.*, XXI [1889], 135).

1891, the Terminal owned $8,783,200 of the East Tennessee's $11,000,000 first preferred, but only $6,536,000 of the $18,500,000 second preferred and $5,888,000 of the $27,500,000 common.[27]

Moreover, the East Tennessee board in 1889 declared a second 5 per cent dividend on the first preferred, and with it came a loss of the voting monopoly enjoyed by those shares.[28] Inman and his associates knew that "friends" of the Terminal possessed or influenced enough of the second preferred and common to assure control over the system, but that control depended upon the good will of such "friends" as Brice and Thomas. By declaring the dividend the East Tennessee men had strengthened their own voice in Terminal councils and remained a potentially dangerous center of opposition to Inman's policies.

While the struggle for control proceeded, the East Tennessee pursued a vigorous expansion policy that further complicated its relationship with the Terminal. In less than two years the company brought nearly 900 miles of road under its control. Foremost among these acquisitions were two key components of the Erlanger system, the Alabama Great Southern and the Cincinnati Southern. Possession of these roads gave the East Tennessee an unbroken route from Cincinnati through Chattanooga to Meridian, Mississippi, where it connected with lines reaching New Orleans, Vicksburg, Shreveport, and points west. By leasing the Louisville Southern the East Tennessee gained entrance into Louisville, while purchase of the Cincinnati, Selma & Mobile provided a lateral connecting link between the Alabama Great Southern and the Mobile & Birmingham. By 1891 the East Tennessee system embraced 2,576 miles of road, with the six spokes of its cart wheel extending into Louisville and Cincinnati, Bristol, Brunswick, Mobile, New Orleans, and Memphis.[29]

27 *Richmond & West Point Terminal Railway & Warehouse Co.: Statements of Securities Issued and Outstanding of Railroad Properties Owned and Controlled,* Jan. 1, 1891, Statement B, archives of Southern Railway Company. For the details on the Terminal's purchases of East Tennessee securities, see Terminal Directors' Minutes, July 19, Sept. 17, Nov. 14, 1889; *Chronicle,* XLIX (1889), 374; *Railroad Gazette,* XXI (1889), 622. A significant amount of this stock was carried by such firms as Inman, Swann and Moore & Schley.

28 *Railroad Gazette,* XXI (1889), 671; *Chronicle,* XLIX (1889), 453.

29 Terminal Directors' Minutes, Nov. 14, 1889, Feb. 3, May 21, 1890; *Chronicle,* L (1890), 276, 519, 560, 662, 834, and LI (1890), 21, 51, 290; *Railroad Gazette,* XXII (1890), 222, 275, 349; Henry V. Poor, *Manual of Railroads for 1892* (New York, 1892), 217.

Inevitably the expansion program proved expensive. Part of the burden fell upon the East Tennessee and part upon the Terminal. To pay for some of the additions the company issued the remaining bonds of the 1887 first-extension mortgage. Finding these securities inadequate and somewhat inflexible, the East Tennessee replaced them with a $15,000,000 general mortgage in 1890. In acquiring the Erlanger roads the East Tennessee persuaded the Terminal and the Danville to share the burden. A $6,000,000 mortgage known as the Cincinnati Extension mortgage was issued jointly in 1890 by the East Tennessee and Danville, with the Terminal guaranteeing interest by endorsement. A substantial portion of these bonds were taken by Terminal men at a price of about 87½. For the rest of the issue Inman resorted to private inducements; Henry Plant, for example, agreed to take $500,000 of the bonds on the understanding that his Southern Express Company would get the express business on the new acquisitions.[30]

Expansion provoked an equally serious problem in the realm of equipment and improvements. The failure of the 1886 reorganization plan to provide adequate capital for these needs had already begun to plague the East Tennessee management. The rapid growth of fixed charges made it virtually impossible to set aside any significant portion of net earnings for this purpose. Accordingly, Thomas in 1888 authorized an issue of $6,000,000 in 5 per cent equipment and improvement bonds, arguing in his report that "the best managed railroad companies have found the plan of funding all expenditures for additional equipment and improvements yearly, instead of relying upon surplus earnings, the most satisfactory to the stockholders." Despite some objection to both the veracity and logic of Thomas's justification, the issue was approved.[31]

The expansion program sharply increased the East Tennessee's funded debt. From the $20,000,000 debt of the 1886 reorganization the figure soared nearly 87 per cent to $36,960,000 by 1891. The constant addition of new mileage muddled the total-earnings figures enough to conceal the fact that net earnings were not keeping pace with spiraling fixed charges. Even so, symptoms of a stagnating financial situation began to appear. Interest charges grew from

[30] Harrison, *Southern Railway*, 687–91. For the Plant deal, see McGhee to Thomas, Dec. 23, 1889, and McGhee to Inman, Dec. 23, 1889, McGhee papers.

[31] *East Tennessee Report*, 1890, 6; *Chronicle*, XLVII (1888), 181; *Railroad Gazette*, XX (1888), 549; Harrison, *Southern Railway*, 691–92; Maitland, Phelps & Company to McGhee, Sept. 13, 1888.

$1,103,835 in 1888 to $1,889,982 in 1891, an increase of over 71 per cent. In contrast both gross and net earnings went up only about 54 per cent even though tonnage carried increased nearly 72 per cent. Data on earnings and cost per ton-mile further revealed the pattern of a dwindling profit margin: between 1886 and 1891 the former declined 23 cents from $1.14 to 91 cents while the latter declined only 10 cents from 71 cents to 61 cents.[32]

In part the sluggishness of East Tennessee earnings signified a failure of the management's long-proclaimed policy of local development. Between 1887 and 1891 through tonnage on the system increased more than 86 per cent, but local tonnage went up less than 72 per cent. During that same period the proportion of local tonnage to through tonnage actually declined slightly from 78 per cent to 76 per cent. To some extent these figures reflected the addition of new lines with relatively undeveloped territories. On the other hand, as the shortage of funds for equipment and improvements eloquently attested, the choice of a growth strategy over a developmental one inevitably meant a telling neglect of the latter.

The expansion rationale assumed a steady growth of business upon the new lines to justify their cost, but such growth did not take place. The Mobile & Birmingham never earned its fixed charges, and its deficit, which was not included on the East Tennessee ledger, mounted every year. The Erlanger roads barely held their own, but the Louisville Southern ran constantly in the red.[33]

The most conspicuous trouble spot in the system was not an expansion road at all but rather the long-feeble Memphis & Charleston. In an effort to bolster its two weakest roads, the Memphis line and the Georgia Pacific, the Terminal formed a traffic alliance with Jay Gould in 1889. Under this pact the Memphis road would exchange traffic with the Missouri Pacific at Memphis while the Georgia Pacific could connect with the Iron Mountain road at Arkansas City. Partly for that reason the Terminal board expanded from sixteen to eighteen members that year and elected George Gould along with Pat Calhoun.[34] In spite of high hopes and glow-

[32] All figures calculated from data in Appendixes III and IV or in company annual reports for the years listed. For contemporary analyses of the East Tennessee's financial condition, see *Chronicle*, L (1890), 436–38, LI (1890), 290–91.

[33] *Chronicle*, L (1890), 436–38, LI (1890), 290–91.

[34] Gould was also elected to the executive committee. He resigned as director in Feb., 1890, but was reelected that Dec. (see Terminal Directors' Minutes, Jan. 1, May 28, June 19, 1889, Feb. 3, May 21, 1890). For the alliance, see *Chronicle*, XLVIII (1889), 190, 730.

ing predictions, however, the interchange at Memphis never amounted to much. The business given to the Missouri Pacific did increase, but the traffic received rose only slightly and actually declined after 1890.[35]

As a result the Memphis road continued to decay. An alarmed McGhee tried to get the Terminal to buy the road outright and improve it, but Inman showed no interest. By the end of 1890 the road was borrowing money from the East Tennessee to meet its interest payments, and the latter company was in no mood to lend. After a sharp exchange with Thomas, McGhee advanced the money out of his own pocket, but prospects for the coming year looked bleak. "The amount of money which will be required to provide interest on the first of July is rather appalling," he noted wearily in May, 1891. A few days later he issued strict orders to his treasurer to "remit all monies on hand and future receipts to Financial Agents in New York. No exceptions will be made of any bill against the Company, unless you owe your bank, in which case you will pay that account." [36]

To a lesser degree the entire East Tennessee system felt the pinch. Both 1888 and 1889 had been banner earning years, but a fateful downturn commenced about halfway through the following year. During the fall of 1890 a brief but severe panic tightened the money market and left most of the Terminal roads squeezed for cash. Earnings on the East Tennessee system declined largely because of rising costs. For the calendar year 1890 gross earnings on the system rose nearly 18 per cent, but operating expenses went up almost 41 per cent. The result was a drop in net earnings of more than 16 per cent. When the downward trend continued into 1891, the board reluctantly lowered the dividend on first preferred from 5 to 2 per cent.[37]

As the pinch worsened, the East Tennessee developed a bothersome floating debt. The heavy load of obligations incurred during the recent burst of expansion now made itself felt. By the summer of 1891 Thomas and his board were scrambling to keep their system solvent, and prospects looked anything but encouraging.

---

[35] Samuel M. Felton to McGhee, Sept. 26, 1891, McGhee papers. See also the enclosed letter from Henry Fink to Felton, dated Sept. 23, 1891.

[36] McGhee to Inman, Oct. 5, Dec. 3, 1890, to Thomas, Dec. 29, Dec. 30, 1890, to Felton, May 20, 1891, and to H. C. Wilton, May 26, 1891, *ibid.*

[37] McGhee to Wilton, Nov. 19, 1890, and to R. C. Payne, Jan. 7, 1891, *ibid.*; *Chronicle*, LII (1891), 182, LIII (1891), 692–93.

The Central Revolts

Once free of the Terminal election intrigue, Alexander initiated a bold expansion plan designed to seal the Central system off from competition. His ambition crystallized into two projects: completion of the Columbus & Western to Birmingham and construction of a through line linking the Columbus & Western to Savannah. He completed the first project by July 1, 1888. The Central's entry into Birmingham gave it access to the rich coal and iron regions in northern Alabama and promised a lucrative traffic in subsidiary goods. It also provided direct connections to Memphis, Kansas City, and points north. To feed the new line Alexander bought a small Alabama road and pushed extensions on two other Central branches.[38]

But the Birmingham line meant little if it did not have an efficient route eastward to Savannah. This was the purpose of the second project, the Savannah & Western. The present route east of Columbus contained a cumbersome dogleg. The new line would route traffic down to Americus and then across a nearly straight 180-mile stretch to Eden. Despite a divided opinion within his board Alexander pushed the work along. By September he had formally consolidated the new road with the Southwestern, Columbus & Western, Mobile & Girard, Montgomery & Eufaula, East Alabama, and Eufaula & Clayton into the Savannah & Western.[39]

Then came the purchase of the Georgia Company by the Terminal. The elaborate nuances of that transaction marked the beginning of serious financial difficulties for the Central. The system was already laboring from its sluggish performance during Raoul's administration, and Alexander's expansion program put an additional financial burden on the company. To complete the Columbus & Western and provide capital for other projects the Central issued $5,000,000 in collateral trust bonds in 1887. The following year Alexander planned to bond the Savannah & Western for a similar amount to finish work on that line. Confronted by its growing obligations and the same squeeze on profits that affected

---

[38] Alexander to Lawton, March 22, 1888, Lawton papers; *Chronicle,* XLVII (1888), 226, 274–75, 285–86; *Railroad Gazette,* XX (1888), 229, 245, 481, 564, 613.

[39] *Chronicle,* XLVII (1888), 50, 218, 274, 285, 410; *Railroad Gazette,* XX (1888), 343, 465, 597.

other southern roads, the Central board had little margin for error. It would need all the capital it could muster.[40]

Unfortunately it could not use all its available capital, for the Georgia Company deal quickly deranged Central finances. The company had placed its first issue of collateral trust bonds with Drexel, Morgan & Company, which took an option on the second batch as well. Shortly after the Georgia Company fell into Terminal hands, however, Drexel, Morgan abruptly declined to handle the first issue and surrendered their option on the second. With the bonds suddenly in limbo the Central soon accumulated a large floating debt, and Alexander reluctantly cut back some of his commitments.[41]

The need for money led Alexander to propose a comprehensive $18,000,000 mortgage on the Savannah & Western. He contemplated an immediate $5,000,000 issue to take up the floating debt and provide for further construction. At this point the Georgia Company transaction intervened. Money badly needed for the Central's debts went instead on loan to the Terminal. At the same time the Central borrowed $1,000,000 in London and reloaned it to the Terminal for six months, pending sale of the Savannah & Western bonds. For this money the Central paid a rate (including commission) of 8 per cent; yet it charged the Terminal only 5 per cent. As a result of these transactions only a part of the bond proceeds ever reached the Central, and the floating debt mounted steadily.[42]

The Central's financial woes unmasked a complex web of antagonistic relationships. Most minority holders distrusted Terminal control, and the Georgia Company deal only further inflamed their hostility. To fasten his hold on the Central, Inman ensconced both Calhouns and his own brothers, Samuel and Hugh, on the board. To appease the minority holders he invited W. W. Gordon, Hugh Comer, and Jacob Rauers, all long-time Wadley and Raoul supporters, to take seats. The peppery Gordon agreed and persuaded the others to accept, but he watched Inman's every

40 *Chronicle,* XLVII (1888) , 410.

41 *Ibid.,* XLVII (1888) , 410, 664; *Railroad Gazette,* XX (1888) , 660, 809.

42 W. W. Gordon to John Inman, Oct. 28, 1889, Dec. 29, 1889, Gordon papers. Inman actually offered the Central a choice: it could sell the bonds at 94 and loan more than $2,000,000 of the proceeds to the Terminal, or it could sell them at 90 to a syndicate headed by Inman and keep all the proceeds for its own debts. For details of the Savannah & Western mortgage, see *Chronicle,* XLVIII (1889) , 729, XLIX (1889) , 240.

move with a wary eye. Despite a very cordial relationship with Alexander, the minority trio saw quickly that the General had been reduced to a figurehead. "The fact is A. has no power," Gordon complained to Walter Chisholm, "and the power behind the throne is Pat Calhoun. That power is not always wisely used and I see no good in helping to inspire confidence in a crowd who are feathering their nests—and run the property solely for that end." [43]

Despite every assurance to the contrary, Inman and the Terminal virtually ignored the Central board. Important decisions were made in New York and implemented without even bothering to notify the southern directors. Two of these decisions that especially rankled the minority concerned the six-month loan to the Terminal at a loss of 3 per cent interest to the Central and the sudden appointment of a new general manager for the system without even consulting its board. Gordon harangued Inman by mail with no success. In less than a year he gave up in disgust. Before the election of 1890 he informed Inman:

When we consented to serve . . . we understood that Central RR affairs were to be managed by the Central RR Board of Directors and did not understand that its functions were confined to the support of and cooperation in the policy of the Terminal Company. . . . I and my friends insist that the other Directors should not decide matters of importance . . . without the knowledge of and consultation with the local Directors. We have asked you for assurances . . . which you have not given. On the contrary your letter in reply states that the Terminal Co. wants Directors in the Central RR Co. "willing to support the general policy which the Board of Directors of the Terminal Co. may settle upon." While this radical difference of opinion exists . . . we must respectfully decline to be re-elected.[44]

Gordon put the matter to Chisholm more bluntly: "Inman . . . wants a 'dummy' board. I dont propose to play 'dummy' for anybody. . . . The past year has convinced me that unless CRR affairs are managed differently a smash up is inevitable in the near future. The owners of the stock held by the Terminal Co. are simply working the finances of the road to make money for themselves and the property will bleed to death." [45]

The departure of the trio marked the last effort at harmony be-

[43] Gordon to Chisholm, Dec. 21, 1889, Gordon papers; *Railroad Gazette,* XXI (1889), 31.

[44] Gordon to Inman, Jan. 2, 1890, Gordon papers. For elaboration of this complaint, see *ibid.,* Oct. 28, Dec. 21, Dec. 29, 1889.

[45] Gordon to Chisholm, Jan. 2, 1890, Gordon papers.

tween the Terminal and the Central's minority holders. From that point the relationship grew progressively more acrimonious as the minority holders stoutly resisted every policy imposed by the Terminal management. Between the antagonists and charged with the impossible task of reconciling their conflicts stood the hapless Alexander. Though his management continued to win public praise, his position steadily worsened.[46] Unable to influence or deflect Terminal policymaking for the Central, he had to shoulder the minority holder's wrathful objections to that policy. The result was persistent disgruntlement at all levels of management and a state of drift in company affairs.[47]

Inevitably the strain began to show on the company's ledgers. A large floating debt had by 1889 become a permanent companion despite every effort to reduce it. The regular 8 per cent dividend could not very well be cut because the Terminal would not stand for the loss of income, to say nothing of possible discredit thrown upon the whole Georgia Company deal. Expenses were pared to the bone, service curtailed on some lines, and new construction done as cheaply and quickly as possible. By early 1890 the deteriorating physical plant and a soaring accident rate on the system had become noticeable.[48]

To meet the widening gap between income and expenses the Central resorted to a new $13,000,000 first mortgage designed to retire the outstanding "tripartite" bonds of 1872, call in the 1881 certificates of indebtedness, and pay off the current floating debt of over $2,000,000.[49] As Table 14 reveals, gross earnings on the main system continued to rise during the period 1888–91, but net earnings declined steadily, and interest charges mounted. This additional burden of debt only made matters worse in the long run and, as the figures indicate, scarcely helped reduce the floating debt in the short run. By 1890 the squeeze had become so tight that the Central transferred a $600,000 sinking fund for retirement of Ocean Steamship bonds to its own surplus fund in order to meet its obligations and still pay dividends. To supplant the fund the Central issued a new $1,000,000 bond issue to call in the old Ocean securities.[50]

The financial difficulties of the Central and the recalcitrance of its minority holders prompted the Terminal board to entrench its

[46] See, for example, *Chronicle*, XLIX (1889), 527–28.
[47] *Railroad Gazette*, XXII (1890), 348.   [48] *Ibid.*, XXII (1890), 129–30.
[49] *Chronicle*, L (1890), 800, LI (1890), 571.
[50] *Ibid.*, LI (1890), 720; *Railroad Gazette*, XXIII (1891), 870.

TABLE 14.   Selected financial data on the Central of Georgia main system, 1888–1891

Year	Gross earnings (1000's)	Net earnings (1000's)	Interest and rentals [a] (1000's)	Dues & accts. (1000's)	Operating ratio (%)
1888	$2,698	$1,217	$1,586	$2,038	56.5
1889	2,926	1,132	2,116	2,481	64.9
1890	3,267	1,016	1,881	3,989	72.3
1891	3,171	970	2,069	5,602	75.4

SOURCES: Calculated from company annual reports and figures given in Poor, *Manual of Railroads*.
[a] Figures include all obligations rather than the main system alone.

authority more securely. Inman received approval to buy more of the Central's outstanding stock, but he could not rely upon that costly and time-consuming process alone. Under pressure from his board he determined in January, 1891, to formulate a lease of the road. By June he had the document ready for ratification. The Central would be leased to the Georgia Pacific (which was in turn leased to the Danville) in order to skirt the restrictions of the state constitution. It would run for ninety-nine years and pay a guaranteed 7 per cent dividend on the stock, with all profit or loss accruing to the Danville.[51]

The lease proved a palliative but by no means a cure for the clash of interests within the Central. The minority holders cheerfully accepted the guaranteed dividend but remained dubious about the extent to which the Terminal would stand behind the lease. In a carefully thought-out statement Raoul noted that the lease made no practical difference in terms of control but warned that it left the minority holders unprotected. "There is no security for the lease," he observed, "the road leasing and the road guaranteeing being practically irresponsible parties financially, and if it be convenient to run the physical condition of the Central down, overload it with debt, and throw up the lease, it strikes me the Stockholders would be helpless." [52]

In fact the lease produced virtually no change in the over-all situation. Alexander continued to promote expansion both by con-

[51] Terminal Directors' Minutes, Feb. 5, Dec. 23, 1890, Jan. 21, April 22, 1891; *Chronicle*, LII (1891), 462, 862; *Railroad Gazette*, XXIII (1891), 205, 400.
[52] Raoul to Messrs. Denmark, Adams & Adams, August 20, 1891, Raoul Letter Books. This lengthy letter is an excellent statement on the practical effects of railroad consolidation.

struction and acquisition, but that policy produced more weaknesses than strengths.[53] The new roads could not pay their way at once and faced growing competition not only from other through lines but from a burgeoning network of new local lines as well. In 1891 Alexander unhappily acknowledged the difficulties wrought by interterritorial ambitions:

These four years have witnessed an unprecedented activity in railroad building in the territory served by this Company, its own prosperity being often the stimulus of other roads built to attract its business over shorter routes, or to other ports and lines. Under these circumstances this Company has been forced to occupy and develop the territory tributary to it, for itself and to control its own feeders. . . . As the . . . new roads built and acquired . . . are all of them branches and extensions into new territory, and necessarily enjoy much less business than our trunk lines and other established branches, it is naturally to be expected that the consolidated earnings of the system per mile would be diminished.[54]

By 1891 the Central, despite its impressive mileage total, no longer dominated the region as it once had done, and its owners no longer resided in the state. Its once proud low debt–equity ratio had evaporated as the funded debt neared $15,000,000, or twice the capital stock. Though the company still paid good dividends, it was becoming apparent that they were not actually being earned. And the floating debt continued to swell. So bad had the situation become that late in the year the company was forced to borrow some $4,200,000 at short-term rates to meet its obligations.[55]

The Danville and Its Millstone

Unlike its sister systems the Danville did not pursue expansion on a grand scale. Nevertheless it experienced financial difficulties of equal magnitude. The long-awaited interchange of traffic with the East Tennessee never materialized, and friction continued to mar the relationship of the two systems. Thwarted by his alleged "friends," Scott turned to his "enemies." He formed an alliance with the Atlantic Coast Line and by its provisions gained access to

[53] See, for example, *Chronicle,* LI (1890) , 721, LII (1891) , 761, 939; *Railroad Gazette,* XXIII (1891) , 400, 418.

[54] *Central of Georgia Report,* 1889, 9; 1891, 13. For a specific example of this heightened competition, see *Chronicle,* LIII (1891) , 754.

[55] *Chronicle,* LIII (1891) , 256, 674, 713; *Railroad Gazette,* XXIII (1891) , 809.

Norfolk. For a time he dickered with Harry Walters over purchasing the Coast Line roads for the Terminal, but the negotiations soon lapsed.[56]

Scott was in fact losing interest in the Danville. His involvement had rarely transcended the level of transactional profits, and opportunities for such gains appeared to be shrinking. As Terminal president, Inman naturally wished to use the Danville as a power base against the East Tennessee interests on the board, and Scott's authority gradually diminished. Moreover, Inman genuinely desired to unify the Terminal properties under one management, and this was difficult work for which Scott had neither heart nor talent. In December, 1889, he surrendered the Danville presidency to Inman; within another year he disappeared from its board and that of the Terminal as well. George Stone also resigned from both boards and was replaced on the Danville by John Calhoun.[57]

Having strengthened his position in the Danville, Inman moved to tighten the system. Scott had already leased the Georgia Pacific and thereby fastened that road's heavy deficit to the Danville. Unawed by the Georgia Pacific's enormous debt, Inman wanted to extend the road deeper into the Yazoo Delta. His plan brought him into direct conflict with the roads controlled by R. T. Wilson and Collis Huntington. When war between the rival interests threatened, McGhee, who had a stake in both systems, intervened to plead for compromise. "The Wilson-Huntington combination is a strong one," he warned Inman, "and will not sit by and see their territory recklessly interfered with without an effort to make reprisals." In face of such powerful opposition Inman came to terms, and except for the important Central lease in 1891, the Danville confined its expansion almost exclusively to branch extensions. Later it even leased a branch of the Virginia Midland to Huntington's Chesapeake & Ohio.[58]

In part the Danville did not expand vigorously simply because it could ill afford any such policy. During the period 1888–91 both

[56] Terminal Directors' Minutes, June 5, 1888; *Chronicle*, XLVI (1888), 828, XLVII (1888), 81, 531.

[57] Terminal Directors' Minutes, May 6, June 19, Dec. 17, 1889; *Chronicle*, LI (1890), 788; *Railroad Gazette*, XXI (1889), 844.

[58] *Railroad Gazette*, XXI (1889), 16, XXIII (1891), 173; *Chronicle*, XLVII (1888), 745; McGhee to Inman, Nov. 7, 1889, Jan. 23, 1890, McGhee papers. The Georgia Pacific lease provided that the Danville would guarantee to *advance* payment on the Pacific's fixed charges and taxes. This advance would then become part of the Pacific's floating debt and a preferred charge on income ahead of the income bonds.

gross and net earnings increased steadily on the main system, as did the amount of freight carried. The funded debt rose surprisingly little, and fixed charges therefore revealed no sharp upward trend. Behind this superficially favorable appearance, however, lay some serious financial weaknesses. The impressive earnings record was maintained by slashing operating expenses and neglecting or deferring needed expenditures on improvements and equipment. The operating ratio dropped consistently from 57 per cent in 1888 to 49.6 per cent in 1892.

Like the East Tennessee, the Danville chose to meet its equipment needs through new security issues rather than attempt to provide for them out of earnings. Accordingly the company executed a 5 per cent $2,500,000 equipment mortgage in 1889 and another 6 per cent issue for $2,000,000 in 1891.[59] It seems clear that the Terminal played no small role in urging this policy upon its subsidiary. As owner of nearly all the Danville's stock the Terminal depended heavily upon its dividends for income. After a four-year abstention the Danville resumed dividend payments of 3 per cent in 1887. Prompted by the Terminal's need for cash, the Danville upped its dividend rate to 10 per cent in 1889 and maintained that level for three years despite the pressing need for equipment and improvement funds.

The most serious weakness of the Danville concerned not the main system but the auxiliary system. Without exception every one of the Danville's auxiliary roads lost money consistently. As Table 15 eloquently testifies, none of these lines managed to pay their way during the relatively prosperous decade of the 1880's. In many cases these losses reached substantial sums. By far the worst of the lot was the Georgia Pacific, whose fixed charges exceeded net earnings by nearly $900,000 in 1890, more than $1,500,000 in 1891, and over $500,000 in 1892 and 1893.

Since the Danville operated most of these roads by lease, it accounted for these obligations by making advances to the various companies. In theory this advance remained an asset since the subsidiary roads were expected to repay it; in practice there existed little hope of these struggling lines ever achieving solvency without a drastic financial reorganization. Nor did it help when a company like the Charlotte, Columbia & Augusta, which had never paid a dividend in its corporate existence, inexplicably declared a 9 per

[59] *Railroad Gazette*, XXIII (1891), 490, 506; Harrison, *Southern Railway*, 103–4.

TABLE 15. Results of operations on auxiliary roads controlled by the Richmond & Danville Railroad, 1881–1891

Road	1881	1882	1883	1884	1885	1886	1887	1888	1889	1890	1891
Georgia Pacific	na	na	na	na	na	na	x	x	x	x	x
Western North Carolina	na	na	na	na	x	x	x	x	x	x	0
Washington, Ohio & Western	na	na	na	na	na	na	na	x	x	x	x
Virginia Midland	x	x	x	x	x	x	x	0	x	x	x
Charlotte, Columbia & Augusta	x	x	0	x	0	x	0	0	x	x	x
Columbia & Greenville	0	x	0	x	0	x	x	x	x	0	x

SOURCES: Calculated from figures obtained in company annual reports and Poor, *Manual of Railroads*.
na: No data available.
x: Net earnings failed to meet all fixed charges and obligations.
0: Net earnings exceeded all fixed charges and obligations.

cent dividend in 1889. Doubtless it was more than coincidence that the declaration came at a time when the parent company badly needed money.

In this way the Danville's funded debt remained unaffected (except for the equipment issues), but the floating debt swelled ominously. In June, 1891, the company's dues and accounts totaled some $3,295,073 and advances to leased lines another $5,657,712. The Danville report attempted to blame the luckless Georgia Pacific for this showing, but in truth the entire auxiliary system had become a millstone around the company's neck. After the panic of 1890 the Danville came increasingly to share the need for ready cash. Like its sister systems, it had swept the cupboard bare and found no relief.

The Search for Order Revisited

The financial woes and internal discontent of the three Terminal systems beset the parent company as well. Inman continued to grope for solutions to the problems of integration. In his annual reports he painted a rosy picture of harmony and successful unification, but reality belied his optimism.[60] Realizing that physical integration could not be easily achieved, he tried to enforce cooperation among the three systems. When the systems continued to cut rates against one another in spite of all pleas to the contrary, the Terminal in September, 1889, passed a series of sharp resolutions. Since all three major systems belonged to the Southern Railway & Steamship Association, the parent company ordered all three presidents to obey the rate regulations set forth by the Association. No deviations would be allowed unless approved by either the Association president or Inman, and any officer caught violating the order would be immediately dismissed. Fink of the East Tennessee, Alexander of the Central, and T. M. R. Talcott of the Danville were ordered to formulate a set of principles governing rates and relations among the systems.[61]

The report of the three officers was dutifully submitted, but apparently little change took place. The annual meeting in 1889 explicitly approved a resolution calling for a policy of harmonizing the three systems. In April, 1890, the Terminal board went so far

---

[60] See, for example, *Richmond Terminal Report*, 1889, 3, 8–9, 11; 1890, 4–5.
[61] Terminal Directors' Minutes, Sept. 13, 1889.

as to decree that all maps published by the company should show all three systems rather than each one separately. The most significant step came in December when the board established a committee to look into the question of a common traffic manager for the three systems. Nevertheless, the bickering among systems could not be quelled. On December 23 the board passed yet another set of resolutions ordering the subsidiary roads to adhere to the Association's rate and traffic policies.[62]

Part of the Terminal's difficulty in enforcing its will derived from the structure of its authority. In practice the Terminal board appointed a standing committee to compose the slate of candidates for each subsidiary company election.[63] Naturally the different factions in the parent company management took care to entrench themselves on the boards of those companies in which they held large interests. As a result the conflicts within the Terminal tended to exist in like proportion on the major subsidiary boards with the notable exception of the Central, where Inman carefully established directors loyal to him.

The presence of a powerful and antagonistic minority there hampered Inman's effectiveness, however, and gave rise to frequent complaints about the responsiveness of the Central board to the Terminal's wishes.[64] In large measure the Central lease was devised to eliminate this difficulty, but it failed because the problem went much deeper. It concerned not only the hostility of the Central minority holders but the hardening factional lines within the Terminal. The Brice-Thomas faction resented the Central not only for the trouble it caused but for the leverage it gave Inman in the power struggle. With the help of the Calhouns, Inman was moving rapidly to solidify his position, and he tied his own destiny to the successful integration of the Terminal systems. In the summer of 1891 he took an important if largely symbolic step toward this end by transferring the headquarters of both the Terminal and the Danville to Atlanta. Significantly, Pat Calhoun assumed the post of Terminal vice-president in charge of the Atlanta office.[65]

[62] *Ibid.*, Sept. 17, 1889, April 17, Dec. 12, Dec. 23, 1890; Terminal Annual Meeting Minutes, Dec. 10, 1889.

[63] See, for example, Terminal Directors' Minutes, Nov. 14, 1889.

[64] See, for example, *ibid.*, Dec. 23, 1890, Jan. 21, 1891.

[65] *Ibid.*, August 12, 1891; *Chronicle*, LIII (1891), 96; *Railroad Gazette*, XXIII (1891), 504, 587. For one hint of the widening rift in the Terminal, see Gordon to Chisholm, Nov. 21, 1889, Gordon papers.

Differences over financial policy formed another source of discontent within the Terminal. The expansion policies pursued by the subsidiary companies and by the Terminal itself quickly outran the financial resources of the 1889 blanket mortgage. Inman's reliance upon exchanges of stock as an expansion device caused the Terminal's capital stock to mount rapidly. When in 1890 it became necessary to sell another portion of the 1889 bonds to meet the large floating debts on each system, the board approved a plan allowing each holder of 100 Terminal shares a $1,000 bond plus twenty shares of fresh common for $1,200. The new issues increased the Terminal's outstanding capital stock to $70,000,000, a figure that startled more than one veteran manipulator within the company.[66]

To tighten the reins the board unanimously ratified a resolution to prohibit any further increase in the company's stock unless approved by a majority of the common holders.[67] The resolution did not so much curb future expansion as it prevented a broader dispersal of Terminal stock to the point where certain factions, notably Brice and Thomas, no longer wielded their former power. As a check on Inman's freewheeling activities, therefore, it represented a conscious partisan tactic. A policy of integration, however vaguely defined, could only win the approval of smaller holders and conversely throw the partisan interests of the Brice-Thomas faction in a bad light. In announcing the Central lease Inman had added: "The process of amalgamating the properties into one is gradually going on. . . . We hope to lease the East Tennessee in the same way later on. This will simplify traffic matters very much and enable us to retire many expensive men." [68]

By 1890 the Terminal appeared to have reached the zenith of its power. It boasted a total mileage of 8,883, second in the nation only to the sprawling Atchison system. Fortified by an encouraging sale of the new bonds, Inman phrased his annual report in exuberant tones. "The position of your company is stronger than at any

[66] Terminal Directors' Minutes, May 21, 1890; *Chronicle*, L (1890) , 736.

[67] *Ibid.* The resolutions actually allowed an alternative: approval by the majority of common holders or right of the holders to purchase the new issue on a pro rata basis. Later the board passed a resolution stating that "any action contemplated by the Board of any of the Companies owned or controlled by the Terminal involving the creation of additional capital, bonded or other fixed indebtedness for the building, purchase, or lease of additional roads be referred to the board . . . of the Terminal or its executive committee for reconsideration before the adoption thereof" (Terminal Director's Minutes, Dec. 12, 1890) .

[68] *Railroad Gazette*, XXIII (1891) , 296.

previous period of its history," he boasted. "It is now entirely free from all floating indebtedness; it has a cash surplus in bank of $526,762.82, loaned on demand $343,009.50, and unpledged securities of the market value of $3,050,000.00." While freely admitting that "large sums of money have been required" to unify the system, he insisted that the Terminal had now "acquired a controlling voice in all the important railroads necessary to perfect the system it undertook to form." Any further expansion "can be done gradually and at the convenience of your company. It now commands the situation." [69]

On paper his argument looked impressive, and even the *Chronicle,* whose attitude toward the Terminal had always wavered between admiration and distrust, admitted that the company seemed prosperous. Curiously, no one noted the fact that the Terminal's apparent solvency derived entirely from the proceeds of the recent bond sale, which cleaned up the most pressing obligations and put some cash in the company's treasury. Certainly no proof yet existed that the huge system could pay its way.

The Terminal remained in fact a largely unknown quantity despite all the publicity it had received. For one thing, its legality had never been fully tested in the courts. More important, it had never demonstrated its economic or administrative feasibility. Constant expansion coupled with inadequate and misleading bookkeeping had so far thoroughly blurred its performance record. It was hard to judge its effect upon the performance of the older systems, much less measure the impact of new mileage. The Terminal's rapidly expanding capitalization put a severe strain upon its earning power, and its labyrinth of interrelated leases, holdings, and obligations rendered the whole structure perilously vulnerable to some sudden slump in earnings across the systems or even at a few key points.

Though not apparent to the casual observer, the Terminal could collapse like a house of cards if the wrong wind blew hard enough. And the ever-widening gap between rising costs and declining rates seemed an ill omen; gross earnings continued to mount steadily, but net earnings lagged well behind. "Transportation rates in the South have not been so badly demoralized as in the West," the *Chronicle* observed, "but business there, too, has to be done at low average rates, and moreover, this average is steadily declining." [70]

[69] See *Richmond Terminal Report,* 1890, 1–7; *Chronicle,* LI (1890), 853–54, 878.

[70] LI (1890), 854.

Despite the cheery tones of Inman's report, the Terminal had by no means banished its financial difficulties. The contraction of 1890, which plummeted stock prices to their lowest level since the crisis of 1884, further aggravated the situation. Terminal stock declined to 15 and at that price attracted Jay Gould, who bought nearly 15 per cent of the company's stock and promptly won election to the board along with his son George, Russell Sage, and Sidney Dillon. At the same time a growing discontent with both the Inman and Brice-Thomas factions forced Inman to accept two largely independent newcomers, Abram S. Hewitt and R. T. Wilson, as well as another less disinterested party, Henry Plant. The missing faces consisted largely of Inman's supporters: Lauterbach, Rice, Chisholm, Hoadley, and Johnson.[71]

The effect of the 1890 election was to fragment the board even more, especially as Gould moved onto the executive committee and increased his role in company affairs.[72] Conversely the presence of the Gould crowd alarmed the nonaligned investors who already distrusted the existing factions. The wheels of intrigue spun furiously as the new year proceeded. Inman's position grew progressively weaker, and the financial situation darker. To the public the Terminal presented a brave and confident front as that part of the press influenced by it churned out a host of panegyrical pamphlets and accounts about the systems and the regions traversed by them.[73] That front could not be maintained indefinitely, however, and in August it crumpled unexpectedly before a devastating onslaught.

---

[71] *Ibid.*, LI (1890), 637, 654–55, 788, 828, 878; Julius Grodinsky, *Jay Gould* (Philadelphia, 1957), 578. It was rumored that Gould was about to go onto the Central board as well and had designs upon adding the whole Terminal system to his domain (see New York *Times*, Dec. 19, 1890, and *Chronicle*, LII [1891], 280). Chisholm, who served as Plant's watchdog on the Terminal board, died late in 1890, and it is probable that Plant simply took his place.

[72] Terminal Directors' Minutes, Dec. 23, 1890. The executive committee consisted of both Goulds, Thomas, Moore, John Calhoun, Brice, and John Hall.

[73] For a sample of this literature, see *Railroad Gazette*, XXIII (1891), 414; Henry E. Colton, *The East Tennessee, Virginia & Georgia Railway System; Its Resources* (n. p., 1890); and *The Richmond and Danville System and the Wonderful Country It Runs Through* (n.p., n.d.). Both pamphlets can be found at the Bureau of Railroad Economics; the Colton tract is also in the Lawson-McGhee Library. For a good example of the conscious use of public media for propaganda purposes, see E. J. Sanford to McGhee, Nov. 14, 1888, McGhee papers.

Chapter IX

The Old Order Passing

THE prevailing weaknesses within the Terminal persisted despite every effort to dispose of them. As financial problems intensified and dissension worsened, news of the turmoil began to leak to the press. Sensational accounts of malpractices within the company and its possible impending bankruptcy hurt the Terminal's already crippled credit just when it most needed funds. Within a year the company and all three subsidiary systems succumbed to receivership, and the ensuing legal and financial wreckage further confused an already snarled situation. From the different attempts to untangle the Terminal's difficulties emerged two alternative courses of action: a reorganization of the properties by integration or an atomization of the system into its component parts.

The Herald Attack

The public indictment of the Terminal broke with unexpected fury on August 8, 1891, when the New York *Herald* published a lengthy exposé of the company's affairs. Intrigued by the recent decline in Terminal securities, the newspaper obtained a copy of an extensive financial analysis of the company by F. J. Lisman, a New York broker. So startling were Lisman's conclusions that the *Herald* felt obliged to give both Inman and Thomas an opportunity to correct errors. After surveying the report for two days Thomas declined comment and shunted the reporter to Rutherfurd. He in turn denounced the report as riddled with errors but pleaded lack of time to point them out. Inman, too, insisted that the report contained numerous errors and asked for a delay of publication. He agreed to study the report but would not promise an answer. Annoyed by the hedging, the *Herald* went ahead with publication and included an offer to print any rebuttal the Terminal officers chose to submit.[1]

The article minced no words. Using the various companies' own

[1] New York *Herald,* August 8, 1891.

figures as given in their annual reports, it explored the Terminal's labyrinthian financial structure and itemized the following conclusions about it:

1. It was evident that "the system is so vast and complicated that the average investor is utterly unable to form any idea of its financial status for himself."

2. The liberal dividends paid regularly by Terminal subsidiaries had seldom been earned.

3. The total floating debt on the three Terminal systems increased more than $13,750,000 during the past year.

4. The Danville earned only about 2 per cent on its stock even though it paid a 10 per cent dividend; as a result it incurred a deficit exceeding a million dollars.

5. This shortage was converted into an illusory profit by dishonest bookkeeping that concealed heavy losses on the Danville auxiliary lines.

6. To help pay its exorbitant dividends the Danville apparently resorted to selling off some of the securities listed among its assets.

7. The Central had not recently earned its 8 per cent dividends and had lately incurred a striking increase in its funded debt.

8. The East Tennessee system could only barely pay its way, and most of its auxiliary lines showed serious deficits.

While the charges may have erred in some details, their substance was accurate. The response to them was curiously feeble and unconvincing. Inman and Alexander rushed immediate replies to the paper. Inman did not even deny the charges but retorted lamely that "when the detailed reports now in preparation are completed . . . it will be seen that the statements which have been made are misleading, and the Richmond Terminal Company and its separate divisions are entirely solvent." Alexander replied more vigorously and frankly, but he too ignored the main issues. The Terminal board elected to make no formal statement but allowed each officer to explain matters to security holders at his discretion.[2]

The *Herald* exposé did nothing to ease the Terminal's financial crisis. Inman now discovered that he could find no buyers for the company's bonds, and short-term credit proved equally difficult to obtain. By mid-September he admitted the existence of floating

[2] For Inman's and Alexander's replies, see *ibid.*, August 10, 1891, and *Chronicle*, LIII (1891), 224; for the board's action see Terminal Directors' Minutes, August 12, 1891.

debts amounting to $530,000 on the Terminal, $3,200,000 on the Danville, $3,800,000 on the Central, and $1,400,000 on the East Tennessee. The executive committee, he added bravely, had been meeting all week to perfect a plan for handling the debts. But no concrete plan emerged. Inman himself formed a syndicate to deal with the Danville debt, and Thomas did likewise for the East Tennessee. Through the efforts of John Calhoun the Central staved off disaster by negotiating two short-term loans, one for $3,500,000 from Speyer & Company and the other for $700,000 from Mutual Life.[3]

In October rentals and interest payments totaling some $600,000 fell due on the Danville and Central systems. Inman claimed these charges could all be met by earnings from the two systems, but more than one observer noticed that he had just sold a block of 4,000 shares of Baltimore & Ohio stock acquired by the Terminal in the summer of 1890. Confronted with the obvious charge, Inman denied any relationship between the stock sale and the interest payments. He sold the stock, he explained, because the company received an unusually good offer of 97 for it. This explanation seemed strange to those suspicious onlookers who recalled that Inman had originally paid 102 for the stock.[4]

Inevitably the financial dilemma hardened factional lines. The Brice-Thomas faction grew progressively more hostile to the Central lease. They noted sullenly that junior holders of the Central reaped healthy dividends regardless of income while the East Tennessee had cut its dividend from 5 to 2 per cent. The only concession made by the Terminal to the East Tennessee was the purchase of about $230,000 of the latter's bonds to help relieve the floating debt.[5]

Small wonder, then, that Brice and Thomas soon agreed that Inman's star had set. Rumors to that effect soon emblazoned the wide publicity given the Terminal's woes. In mid-November, Inman found it necessary to denounce reports that the Terminal had lost control of the East Tennessee. "There is," he insisted, "no friction between the East Tennessee and the Richmond Terminal

[3] Terminal Directors' Minutes, Nov. 11, 1891; *Chronicle*, LIII (1891), 408, 641, 713; *Railroad Gazette*, XXIII (1891), 810. The East Tennessee helped ease its financial squeeze by selling equipment bonds in Dec. (see *Chronicle*, LIII [1891], 922, and *Railroad Gazette*, XXIII [1891], 908).

[4] Terminal Directors' Minutes, June 18, 1890, and Nov. 6, 1891; *Chronicle*, L (1890), 703, 874, LIII (1891), 475; *Railroad Gazette*, XXIII (1891), 718.

[5] Terminal Directors' Minutes, Dec. 4, 1891.

interests." Shortly afterward, however, the Terminal board decided to postpone the election of officers in all subsidiary companies until the holding company held its own meeting. For all the denials, it seemed more and more likely that there would be a showdown between the divergent interests at the December annual meeting.[6]

Emergence of the Olcott Committee

For his own part Inman held a hand that grew progressively weaker. Publication of the Danville report revealed the system's weaknesses with painful clarity. Moreover, it was well known that part of the Danville's troubles could be traced to the East Tennessee's recent policy of diverting through traffic from the Danville to a rival line. Nothing better illustrated the practical effects of the Terminal's internecine warfare. In that company's report Inman again defended his policies. He insisted again that the Terminal owed no floating debt and that all systems were paying their way. The floating debts he blamed upon "the general financial condition of the past year, coupled with attacks upon the credit of your company, and the effort in Georgia to pass hostile laws intended to injure your system of roads." [7]

The unsettled state of Terminal affairs prompted some of the preferred holders to form a committee to protect their interests shortly before the December meeting. Anticipating some such move, Inman tried to steal a march by sponsoring an investigation of his own. With the board's approval he solicited proxies for reelection by announcing that he had formed a committee of distinguished financiers to inquire into the company's financial condition and perfect a plan of adjustment. The ploy bought Inman time. He gained reelection along with the incumbent board as a temporary management until the committee submitted its plan, at which

[6] *Chronicle,* LIII (1891), 713, 754.

[7] *Ibid.,* LIII (1891), 878; *Railroad Gazette,* XXIII (1891), 890; Harrison, *Southern Railway,* 35. The reference to "hostile legislation" doubtless refers to the debate over the Olive bill, which was designed to prohibit such combinations as the Terminal on the grounds that they destroyed competition. Not surprisingly, most railroad men bitterly opposed the bill and debate over it raged in the Georgia press. Some representative clippings from the debate can be found in the Alexander papers and the Raoul Scrapbooks.

time the stockholders would vote upon the plan and elect a permanent management.[8]

The committee represented a desperate gamble by Inman to
bring his antagonists to bay; unfortunately for him it did not succeed. For one thing the personnel of the committee aroused suspicion. Two of its members, Eckstein Norton and Jacob Schiff, had
long been associated with the Terminal's two most powerful rivals,
the L. & N. and the Norfolk & Western. A third member, William
Salomon of Speyer & Company, was a close associate of Schiff. The
remaining members, Charles S. Fairchild and Louis Fitzgerald,
were presidents of trust companies. None of the financiers held
any substantial interest in the property over which they had been
granted broad power. Under the leadership of Norton and Schiff
the L. & N. and Norfolk systems had developed a close alliance;
some critics, therefore, naturally questioned the wisdom of placing
the Terminal's fate in hands so closely tied to its adversaries.[9]

Even more important, the committee's work thoroughly unmasked the lines of dissension with the Terminal management.
Under the strain of financial disruption the Brice-Thomas faction
assumed the role of atomizers, willing to dismantle the holding
company to protect their influence over the East Tennessee.
Inman by contrast defended the policy of integrating the three systems, and in that sense he represented what might be called the
unifiers. For the unifiers any division of the property back into its
separate components invited disaster, especially at a time when
southern railroads had fallen under the influence of a handful of
powerful systems. Against so imposing a trend toward consolidation, any attempt to disassemble the Terminal could only weaken
each system's competitive position.

Yet the Brice-Thomas faction proposed to do just that. They
feared that the committee might push through some comprehensive plan of reorganization and permit the unifiers to implement
their policies by gaining control of the individual systems. For this
reason the committee insisted upon postponing elections in all
subsidiary companies until a more permanent management for the
Terminal had been established. Faced with possible loss of control

[8] Terminal Directors' Minutes, Nov. 24, Nov. 25, 1891; Terminal Annual
Meeting Minutes, Dec. 8, 1891; *Chronicle*, LIII (1891), 804, 846, 881; *Railroad
Gazette*, XXIII (1891), 870, 890; New York *Sun*, August 20, 1892.

[9] See the caustic editorial in *Railroad Gazette*, XXIII (1891), 880. Inman
served as a director for the L. & N. from 1885 to 1891.

to outsiders, Brice and Thomas objected vigorously and flatly refused to cooperate with the committee unless it first allowed the East Tennessee to hold its delayed election and reelect the present board. On this issue they won most of the Terminal board to their side. When Brice introduced a resolution authorizing the Terminal to vote its East Tennessee stock for the incumbent board, only Henry Plant and the Calhoun brothers, the most determined unifiers on the board, voted against it.[10]

Confronted by the board's resistance, the committee could do nothing. The basic plan it proposed demanded heavy sacrifices from parties singularly unwilling either to make them or concede any of their power. On December 16 the committee acknowledged the hostility of the Terminal board and abandoned its task. The failure of the Schiff-Norton committee resulted in the creation of a new committee headed by Frederic P. Olcott, president of the Central Trust Company. Olcott had been offered a place on the original committee but declined to serve because he thought the terms of the Schiff-Norton plan too stiff. Stockholders representing about 240,000 shares asked Olcott to form a committee to work out a new financial plan.[11]

The Olcott committee developed momentum rapidly. In short order Frederick D. Tappen of the Gallatin National Bank, Oliver H. Payne, William H. Perkins of the Bank of America, and Henry Budge of Halgarten & Company joined Olcott. The committee canvassed openly for support of the preferred stockholders' committee as well, but the going would be rough. The East Tennessee election took place, and both factions remained solidly entrenched on its board. Once free of that danger, Brice and Thomas renewed their struggle against that other obstreperous Terminal appendage, the Central.[12]

The Central Controversy

The tactics of the atomizers took two forms: the attempt to disengage the East Tennessee from Terminal control and an effort to

[10] Terminal Directors' Minutes, Dec. 15, 1891. The position of the committee is stated in their circular dated Dec. 18, 1891, a copy of which is in the archives of the Southern Railway Company.

[11] Terminal Directors' Minutes, Dec. 28, 1891; *Chronicle,* LIII (1891) , 922.

[12] *Chronicle,* LIII (1891) , 922, 969, LIV (1892) , 34; *Railroad Gazette,* XXIV (1892) , 16.

abort the Central lease or at least bring that company's management to heel. The first dividend payments under the Central lease fell due in December, and the Brice-Thomas faction was in no mood to pay. At the December 15 Terminal directors' meeting Brice noted that the Georgia Pacific would require large advances to meet these payments and observed pointedly that "these obligations were subsequent in point of time and in point of lien to other engagements of the Danville." He pushed through a resolution directing the Danville executive committee to look into some possible "readjustment" of the relationship between the companies.[13]

The purpose of the move was clear enough. With money tight and every system pinched for cash, the Central lease became an intolerable onus, especially to those who had not shared in the Georgia Company largess. Moreover, by late 1891 the dangers posed by the financial interdependence of the Terminal systems began to dawn upon its creators. The fall of one system could wreak havoc in every corner; all the more reason then to shed unwanted burdens like the Central. So reasoned the Brice-Thomas group, and for the moment fate appeared to favor their efforts. Inman fell ill with the grippe and attended no meetings for nearly two weeks.

Unhampered by Inman, Brice moved quickly. He obtained from the Terminal board authority to borrow some of the company's securities to aid the Danville in meeting its obligations. But he had no intention of using them for the Central. Instead the Danville executive committee concocted an unitemized claim against the Central for $844,000 and refused to make the lease payments until the claim was settled. Later the courts would dismiss virtually the entire claim as a trumped-up evasion of the lease obligations, but it served another purpose as well. The Danville wished to borrow certain securities from the Central to help meet its obligations, and the executive committee fully expected the Central's cooperation. They did not get it, however, and the old problem of control over the subsidiary lines flared anew. The claim was designed to coerce the Central into surrendering the desired securities, 4,995 shares of New England & Savannah Steamship Company.[14]

---

[13] Terminal Directors' Minutes, Dec. 15, 1891.

[14] *Ibid.*, Dec. 21, 1891. Unless otherwise stated the account that follows is drawn from the pamphlet *Decisions of the U.S. Court for the Southern District of Georgia* (Savannah, 1892), 31–52, a copy of which is at the Bureau of Railroad Economics. Most of the relevant court decisions and the correspond-

The position taken by the Danville baffled Alexander and the Georgia directors. The lease provided for arbitration of all differences, but Thomas, speaking for the Danville, demanded that the steamship stock be turned over as collateral for what he termed "advances." "If the Central railroad officers will render us the assistance which we think we have a right to expect of them," he added sharply, "advances will be made." Alexander retorted that the payments were not an advance but an obligation, and that he could not legally surrender the securities outright. With the terse comment, "am willing to do anything legal," he offered to put the stock in escrow pending arbitration, but the Danville rejected his offer.

As the prospect of formal default on the lease reared, a sense of crisis engulfed Savannah. Failure to honor the lease would permit Speyer & Company to call their loan to the Central and virtually destroy the company's credit. The minority holders reacted with predictable venom to the apparent renege and hoped that it would break the lease. Supported only by Swann and the Calhouns, Alexander anxiously awaited word from Inman. To the press he remained a model of patience, saying only that "the issue is so simple . . . that I think there is really some misunderstanding in New York which only needs to be cleared up." Despite his denials, however, rumors persisted that the crisis derived from the split between the Inman and Brice-Thomas factions.[15]

Finally, on December 31, Inman stepped forward. He summoned a special meeting of the Terminal and Danville boards and persuaded them to accept Alexander's offer. Reluctantly Thomas telegraphed Alexander to place the stock in escrow pending arbitration and ordered all payments met. Alexander hailed the announcement as a final settlement of the dispute, but in fact it was only a prelude. The incident rankled Central minority holders, who felt that the Danville had already abused the financial stipulations of the lease. For their part the Brice-Thomas faction deeply resented the obstinacy of the Central board and demanded the ousting of those directors not amenable to Terminal direction. In

---

ence about the default is reprinted here along with a commentary by the counsel for the Central minority holders. For judical comments on the validity of the Danville's claim, see *ibid.*, 37, 45–46. Much of the decision and correspondence is also reprinted in Atlanta *Constitution*, June 9, 1892.

[15] *Railroad Gazette*, XXIV (1892), 33; Savannah *Morning News*, Dec. 30, Dec. 31, 1891. This newspaper provides considerable information on the crisis and captures the mounting excitement in Savannah commercial circles; see the issues for the period Dec. 25, 1891, to Jan. 1, 1892.

particular they wanted to drive out the Calhouns, who had long since come to be regarded as their worst antagonists.[16] Since the Central election was slated for January 4, the issue came swiftly to a head. Both Samuel Inman and E. M. Green resigned from the board, leaving two vacancies. At a crucial meeting of the Terminal board on January 2, Brice, as chairman of a nominating committee, submitted a list of proposed directors for the Central that omitted both Calhouns. In defense of the move he explained that a fee for John Calhoun's services in obtaining the Speyer loan had not yet been fixed; by leaving the brothers off the board Calhoun might be paid "more speedily and more liberally than if he was retained on the board." In addition Brice added that the Terminal in its present condition needed full power over its subsidiaries. The refusal of the Central board to deliver the steamship stock only stressed the need for a responsive board. He then moved that his report and the proposed board for the Central be accepted.[17]

Pat Calhoun immediately offered a substitute resolution by which any proposed Central board would be explicitly designated as temporary pending the election of a permanent management for the Terminal. John Calhoun then delivered a lengthy explanation of the negotiation for his fee.[18] He disclaimed any strong interest in the final sum and denied that his presence on the board would influence the decision in any way. Brice countered with additional reasons for his recommendations and called for a vote on the Calhoun resolution. It went down to a 7 to 3 defeat with only the Calhouns and Swann supporting it.[19] By a vote of 8 to 3 the directors adopted the Brice report, with the same three directors opposed.

At that point Pat Calhoun tendered the resignation of his firm as general southern counsel for both the Terminal and Danville. To the pleas of Swann and others that he reconsider he turned a deaf ear, arguing that he could no longer defend as counsel a set of policies he personally opposed. The adoption of the Brice report rendered him helpless to fight those policies within the company;

[16] Savannah *Morning News*, Jan. 1, Jan. 3, 1892; Terminal Directors' Minutes, Dec. 31, 1891; *Decisions of the U.S. Court*, 43–45. For specific examples of Danville abuse of Central finances, see *ibid.*, 52–60.

[17] The following scene is taken from Terminal Directors' Minutes, Jan. 2, 1892.

[18] According to Calhoun the fee was to be fixed by three arbitrators, one selected by the Central, one by the Danville, and the third named by the two thus chosen.

[19] Wormser abstained, and Inman was not present at the meeting.

therefore he would attack from without. To the press he accused the Danville of trying to wreck the Central and referred to the lease episode as a "disgraceful default." More trenchantly, he accused the Terminal board of duplicity in their rough handling of Inman's reorganization committee. The members of the board, he insisted, "have broken faith with the very stockholders who elected them and repudiated their pledge to co-operate with a committee . . . through the use of whose names the directors secured proxies for their own temporary election." [20]

Calhoun's outburst inevitably touched off a war of words. As expected, Alexander denied that the ouster of the Calhouns involved anything more than personality or that it had anything to do with the fight between Inman and the Brice-Thomas faction. But a Savannah paper reported that "the belief is general that as the Calhouns and Inmans are very intimate the dropping of the Calhouns means a victory over Mr. Inman and his ultimate retirement from the Terminal presidency." [21]

Despite the semblance of triumph, the election settled nothing. The uncertain tenure of the Terminal board together with its imperative need for a reorganization plan prevented it from wielding effective power. In Georgia the Central's affairs continued to pitch fitfully on a sea of controversy. Competitively the company's position had become demoralized. Its connection with the Terminal had deeply antagonized some connecting roads and local commercial interests. "There seems to be quite a deep-seated feeling in Savannah against the Central under its present management," observed Joseph M. Brown of the Western & Atlantic, "the people considering that it is really hostile to Savannah and desires to build up the Virginia ports." [22] During the winter of 1892 that hostility marched steadily toward another fateful clash.

Reorganization and Resistance

The web of intrigue that permeated Terminal affairs throughout 1892 derived from a scramble to protect vested interests in the face

[20] Savannah *Morning News,* Jan. 3, 1892.

[21] *Ibid.,* Jan. 4, 1892; *Railroad Gazette,* XXIV (1892), 31. For the new Central board, see *Chronicle,* LIV (1892), 78.

[22] The Central's competitive position is discussed in Brown to J. W. Thomas, Feb. 5, Feb. 6, and Feb. 29, 1892, and to D. Miller, Jan. 16, 1892, Joseph M. Brown Letter Books, Emory University Library. The quotation is taken from the Feb. 29 letter.

of impending financial reorganization. The necessity for such a reorganization had long been obvious and had virtually dictated the course of events within the company since the autumn of 1891. The need for reorganization by no means assured what form the plan would take, however, and it was this vital issue that defined the basic differences between the atomizers and the unifiers. In broad terms the former group believed that their interests in a given system could best be protected by cutting that system loose from the Terminal and running it on its own merits. In contrast the latter group argued that survival of their system (and thus their investment) depended upon harmonizing the systems into one efficient company. From these differences emerged a new round of factionalism within the company that was further complicated by the desire to sacrifice as little as possible under the terms of whatever plan prevailed.

The factional schism soon extended beyond the Inman and Brice-Thomas coteries. The Olcott committee drew the support of several Danville security holders headed by William E. Strong of Work, Strong & Company. Two other familiar groups, the First National Bank syndicate and William Clyde and his friends, also renewed their involvement in the company. Unlike the other groups, their interests centered not in the subsidiary systems but in the Terminal itself and specifically in the preferred stock created after the turnover of 1886. There also existed organizing bands of minority holders in both the East Tennessee and the Central systems. Finally, the list of interested parties included those institutions, firms, and individuals who had extended credit to the Terminal or its subsidiary systems. Often the membership of these groups overlapped sufficiently to frustrate any attempt at a more precise delineation.

Even so cursory a survey, however, reveals one striking fact: an overwhelming majority of the contestants cared less about the Terminal than about the systems it controlled. Part of the explanation lay in the peculiar history of the Terminal as a holding company, which powerfully influenced the investment attitude of virtually all participants. While the boundary between opportunistic and developmental investment often appears ambiguous, it seems clear that despite all efforts to the contrary nearly all the prominent Terminal figures continued to treat the holding company as a speculative engine while reserving their developmental commitment for the individual systems. The opportunistic impulses of such men as Clyde, Inman, Brice, Thomas, McGhee, and Logan have been made clear in previous episodes, and the McGhee papers furnish an especially instructive example. His surviving financial records show only occasional transactions in East Tennessee securities but frequent and rapid turnovers in Terminal stock. On the basis of what little evidence is available for other figures, it may be surmised that McGhee represented the norm rather than the exception. Yet Terminal securities totaled some $91,565,000 of the approximately $394,500,000 in securities of all kinds in the Terminal system.[23]

From January to March maneuvering within the company proceeded in anticipation of the forthcoming Olcott plan. The long-deferred Danville election finally took place early in March; both warring factions remained entrenched, and Inman retained the presidency, though he asked to be relieved of his duties as soon as possible.[24] On the Terminal board itself significant changes occurred. Strong took the seat vacated by the death of John Hall, and John C. Maben, a veteran southern promoter and friend of Clyde, replaced Henry Plant, who resigned.[25] All the factions joined forces to raise over $5,000,000 for taking up the Danville's floating debt until the reorganization plan was perfected.[26]

The Olcott Plan

On March 1 the Olcott plan was made public. At first glance it appeared to confront the major problems in both letter and spirit. The prevailing condition of system-oriented investors naturally favored the cause of the atomizers, who demanded that the Terminal be abolished and its systems returned to separate control. The Olcott committee forthrightly disputed this viewpoint. It noted that the systems had not integrated or even cooperated harmoniously but had instead retained their own organizations and

[23] *Chronicle*, LIV (1892), 464–65; Poor, *Manual for 1892*, 509.

[24] Terminal Directors' Minutes, Jan. 4, Jan. 8, 1892. Like the other boards, the Danville directors were explicitly told that their position was a temporary one pending the reorganization. Inman himself specifically asked to be relieved "certainly not later than the day on which the members of the comm. shall put into operation the plan that may be agreed upon by them."

[25] *Ibid.*, Dec. 21, Dec. 23, 1891; *Railroad Gazette*, XXIII (1891), 171, 922. Strong actually replaced A. J. Rauh, the Terminal's treasurer, who filled Hall's seat as a "dummy" director.

[26] *Chronicle*, LIV (1892), 29, 120; *Railroad Gazette*, XXIV (1892), 34.

continued to compete with each other. Under such an arrangement surplus earnings in one system could not be applied to losses in another, and no systematic financial policy could be formulated. The committee concluded, therefore, that "the only adequate remedy which can be adopted is to unite the several corporations . . . in one system, under one management, and to consolidate their obligations." [27]

The committee proposed to consolidate the Terminal, Danville, and East Tennessee properties. Neither the Central nor the Erlanger roads would be included, but the Terminal's interest in both would be made subject to a new mortgage. For the new company the plan called for issuing $170,000,000 of new 4 per cent bonds, $70,000,000 of preferred stock, and $110,000,000 of new common. Basically the new bonds would be exchanged for old bonds and the new common for old preferred and common, with most of the preferred being used to sweeten the trades. By this arrangement the committee estimated that fixed charges on the new system would be reduced from $9,474,837 to about $7,660,000. Enough new bonds and preferred would be sold to raise $14,588,640 in cash to pay off outstanding equipment trusts, floating debts totaling $6,310,000, and other miscellaneous expenses. [28]

The merits of the plan were obvious enough. It unified the systems both physically and financially, it reduced the burden of fixed charges, and it promised to clean up all outstanding indebtedness. Such an integration under one management seemed to assure an orderly transition to an efficient operating company. [29] Unfortunately certain serious defects stood out with equal transparency. For one thing, the plan woefully underestimated cash requirements. It allotted $10,000,000 in new bonds for acquiring additional property but made no provision for improvements or betterments. With incredible myopia the committee pro-

---

[27] *Richmond and West Point Terminal Railway and Warehouse Company: Plan of Reorganization Dated March 1st, 1892* (New York, 1892), 2, hereafter cited as *Olcott Plan*. A copy of the plan is in the archives of the Southern Railway Company. The full plan is reprinted in *Chronicle*, LIV (1892), 487–92.

[28] For the cash provisions, see *Olcott Plan*, 22. The figures on fixed charges and floating debts are in *ibid.*, 2–3. The fixed charges did not include the following: taxes, which were included under operating expenses; interest on securities owned by component corporations of the system; and the Central and Alabama Great Southern roads.

[29] A favorable report on the plan is in *Chronicle*, LIV (1892), 464–65.

nounced the properties to be "in a fair physical condition" and claimed that the plan made due allowance for betterments. But no such provisions could be found in the report.[30]

An equally serious defect concerned the exchange ratios between old and new securities. Stuart Daggett has noted of the plan that "as between the bonds and the stock it altogether favored the latter. It levied no assessment, it compelled no subscription to new securities, and in three cases only did it announce an intention of reducing the nominal value of the stockholders' holdings." [31] While true as far as it goes, Daggett's observation does not go far enough. Not only the favoring of the stock but the specific exchange provisions baffled most observers. The ratios paid no apparent heed to the market prices of the various securities involved. For example, the plan allotted Terminal sixes currently quoted at 96, and Atlanta & Charlotte sevens listed at 120, each 120 of new fours and 40 of new preferred. Similar examples abounded elsewhere on the list and prompted a perplexed Daggett to admit that "the principle which determined the various ratios of exchange is more difficult to discover. It was not that of equivalence of return." [32]

It most assuredly was not. The reason for the strange pattern of allocation lay not in the mathematics but in the politics of the situation. If simple justice required that equity be rendered with fine impartiality, the practical circumstances demanded that the plan suit those influential parties whose support would be needed to implement it. No plan that failed to appease the predominant factions would have much chance of winning acceptance; accordingly the committee took great pains to please the parties that counted. The most conspicuous example concerned the Terminal preferred. It currently sold for 65, but most of it still belonged to the powerful First National group. In the plan, therefore, it received 100 in *bonds* and 20 in preferred. Similarly the East Tennessee first preferred received 30 in *bonds,* 50 in preferred, and 50 in common.

---

[30] *Olcott Plan,* 3.

[31] Daggett, *Railroad Reorganization,* 173. The plan compelled no subscription but offered holders of the Terminal fives a chance to subscribe to the cash fund on the following terms: each holder of 100 shares of stock and each holder of $10,000 of bonds could subscribe for $1,600 of the proposed fund, for which he would receive $2,000 in new fours and $700 of new preferred (*Olcott Plan,* 27). The syndicate guaranteeing the subscription is given in *Chronicle,* LIV (1892), 486.

[32] Daggett, *Railroad Reorganization,* 172. The comparative figures are taken from a contemporary critique of the plan in *Railroad Gazette,* XXIV (1892), 230.

First-mortgage sixes on the debt-riddled Georgia Pacific brought 110 in bonds and 50 in preferred, and even Terminal common was marked for 10 in preferred and 100 in common.[33]

In trying to make its proposal attractive the Olcott committee undercut one of its most important premises: a scaling down of the company's obligations. For purposes of exchange it would replace $137,488,386 in old bonds with $133,946,955 of new ones. Of course the new bonds would effect considerable saving on interest rates, but the liberal issue of stock would increase the company's over-all capitalization. Under the plan $57,853,579 in new preferred would supplant $19,180,800 in old, and $105,160,654 in new common would replace $111,278,779 in old common. Another $18,235,800 in bonds and $6,382,530 in preferred would be sold to raise the necessary cash. The total capitalization of the proposed company would be $350,000,000, but no adequate provision was made for improvements or for some miscellaneous bonds still outstanding. By any measure the plan failed to reduce the company's obligations sufficiently to put it on a sound basis. It had done more rearranging than reorganizing, and for that reason deserved its label as a conservative plan.[34]

The primary victims of the plan were the underlying bondholders, who usually fared no better in the allotment than holders of more speculative securities. As one journal noted, "it seems strange . . . that for the best secured bonds of the old companies, and which naturally are held by the most conservative investors, it is proposed to issue their assumed equivalent partly in the *stock* of the proposed new company." [35] These bondholders, though possessing a substantial aggregate of the outstanding securities, lacked either the cohesion or the influence to voice their protest within the councils of power. They could protest only by rejecting the plan; for the committee the more pressing problem involved some sort of reconciliation among the organized contending factions.

Such a compromise proved impossible for the Olcott committee or anyone else to achieve at the moment. Though some of the committee's members had little or no interest in the Terminal, the plan still originated within the company and therefore could not avoid the charge of partisanship. So diffused had authority within

[33] The complete exchange ratios are in *Olcott Plan,* 23–26.

[34] All figures calculated from *ibid., passim.*

[35] *Railroad Gazette,* XXIV (1892), 230. Later the *Gazette,* XXIV (1892), 394, described the plan as "one of the most disreputable ever proposed by respectable financiers."

the Terminal become and so diverse were its participants that its affairs trembled on the brink of managerial anarchy. Despite the presence of numerous powerful and talented personalities, no leader emerged to cope with the rival groups and their deep mutual suspicions. All the leading figures had been too deeply implicated in the company's past dealings, and none seemed capable of transcending the fierce jealousies engendered by the struggle. The result could only spell doom for the Olcott plan and another bout of intramural combat.

The Central Receivership

While the Olcott committee perfected its plan, a disastrous blow struck the Terminal on another front. The patience of some Central minority holders had at last reached its breaking point. Early in March, Mrs. Rowena Clarke of Charleston, owner of 50 shares of Central stock, filed suit in the Macon Circuit Court to annul the lease. The complaint alleged that the lease violated the Georgia Constitution, that the lessees had not managed the property properly, and that the proposed Olcott plan would be detrimental to Central holders. She asked that a permanent receiver be appointed, that the lease be annulled, and that the Terminal be enjoined from voting or otherwise using its 42,200 shares of Central stock.[36]

The suit touched off a complex chain of events, one effect of which was to remove the Central from Terminal reorganization plans pending settlement of the litigation. The case fell under the jurisdiction of Judge Emory Speer, who was no stranger to railroad circles. He had for some years held a pass from the East Tennessee, and he had long been friendly with such "conservative" Georgians as Raoul, Gordon, and Comer. At first all parties to the contest seemed to regard Speer as eminently suitable for the difficult task of protecting all interests. In time, however, he would become engulfed in controversy over his handling of the case.[37]

Speer moved with disarming alacrity on the suit. On the very night the complaint was filed he issued an order appointing Alex-

[36] *Chronicle,* LIV (1892), 443.

[37] McGhee to E. B. Thomas, July 11, 1887, McGhee papers; clipping from Macon *Telegraph* in Raoul Scrapbooks, III, 46. In the letter cited here McGhee noted of Speer that "the East Tenn Company has a great deal of litigation in his district and I think it important to give him a pass."

ander temporary receiver of the Central without even notifying the company's officers. So surprising was the receivership that it bewildered parties on every front: some thought it a friendly suit instigated by the Olcott committee, while McGhee, who was privy to Terminal affairs, believed the Calhouns had done it behind the holding company's back. News of the Clarke suit caused a sharp break in Terminal securities prior to the first hearing on March 14. At that session A. O. Bacon, an antirailroad legislator, intervened in the case with a lengthy bill. His indictment broadened both the dimensions and bitterness of the charges. He flatly accused the Terminal of fraud and wrecking and charged that all its roads involved in the lease were insolvent. On these grounds he demanded that the lease be voided and the Terminal barred from voting its shares.[38]

Sensing the importance of the case and the bitterness it reflected, Speer continued the case until March 24 when Circuit Judge Don A. Pardee could join him on the bench.[39] On that day, Pardee read the joint decision. In it the justices agreed that the Terminal's holding of Central stock violated the Georgia Constitution and therefore prohibited the company from using its stock to influence the Central's management. To assure the Central of a management loyal to its interests, the court ordered a special election to be held on May 16 and barred the Terminal from voting its stock. But the court offered no ruling on the lease itself and sidestepped the charges of mismanagement. Instead it appointed Alexander and most of the incumbent board as receivers.[40]

The decision seemed to promise return of the Central's management to the minority holders. The Terminal confirmed this impression by announcing even before the decision that it would neither intervene in the proceedings nor resume operation of the Central after the temporary receiver had been discharged, and it did not appeal the decision. Unfortunately the minority holders found themselves badly divided on the question of who should take charge of the company. The minority holders and creditors alike agreed that Alexander had outlived his usefulness, a conclu-

[38] Charles Leonhardt to McGhee, March 5, 1892, McGhee papers; *Railroad Gazette*, XXIV (1892), 199–200; *Chronicle*, LIV (1892), 485; clippings in Raoul Scrapbook, III, 47.

[39] For one example of this bitterness, see the letter from Tom Branch in Augusta *Chronicle*, March 23, 1892.

[40] The decision is reprinted in *Decisions of the U.S. Court*, 11–15, and in *Chronicle*, LIV (1892), 560. See also *Railroad Gazette*, XXIV (1892), 258.

sion to which Alexander himself finally came. Taking the receivership appointment as a vindication, he resigned immediately after
the hearing.[41]

Alexander's departure culminated a dispute over his succesor
that strained more than one friendship of long standing. Discus-
sions over the selection kindled strong hopes in Gordon to follow
in his father's footsteps as president of the Central. Raoul promised to support his candidacy and Speer seemed sympathetic, but
the creditors from Speyer and Mutual Life balked. Preferring either Raoul or Charles Phinizy, they abruptly settled upon Comer
as a compromise choice. The decision surprised Raoul, who had
faithfully pressed Gordon's candidacy, and it outraged Gordon
himself to the point of rupturing his relationship with both
Comer and Raoul. Gordon bluntly accused Raoul of bad faith.
"Both you and Comer knew that it had been a lifelong aspiration
of mine to be at the head of the Central," he complained bitterly.
"My latent feeling on the subject was fanned into a flame by Speer
and you and Comer. . . . I think Comer's conduct incapable of
defense." [42]

Such division among the minority holders did not augur well
for a swift reorganization of the Central. Comer inherited a difficult financial position characterized by a soaring floating debt and
rapidly declining earnings.[43] While the financial interests haggled
over a plan of reorganization, he set on foot a policy designed to
pare expenses and win back customers lost during the turmoil of
recent months. The May 16 election took place as scheduled and
returned a board sympathetic to Comer's policies; among those
who lost their seats were Maben, Swann, and Alexander. The new
board promptly announced that no June dividend would be declared. Comer managed to restore cordial relations with some of
the Central's local competitors, but business in general was beginning to decline.[44]

On the legal front Comer made some headway. Early in June,

[41] *Decisions of the U.S. Court,* 15; *Railroad Gazette,* XXIV (1892), 237–38,
255; W. W. Gordon to Raoul, March 28, 1892, Gordon papers.

[42] Gordon to Raoul, March 28, March 31, 1892, Gordon papers; Raoul to
Gordon, April 7, 1892, Raoul Letter Books. Raoul's support of Gordon is made
quite clear in "Memorandum handed Mr. Beaman as he left to attend Central
receivership case at Macon," March 21, 1892, Raoul Letter Books. Beaman was
one of the Speyer representatives.

[43] For Comer's first report, see Atlanta *Constitution,* Nov. 5, 1892.

[44] *Chronicle,* LIV (1892), 684; *Railroad Gazette,* XXIV (1892), 378; Atlanta
Constitution, May 31, 1892.

Speer decided the Central-Danville case in favor of the former road and ordered the steamship stock returned to it. Comer then filed suit asking for a receiver for the Danville on the grounds that the latter company owed the Central $2,459,670 and was currently insolvent. The Terminal countered by appointing a former vice-president of the New Jersey Central to examine the accounts between the Central and the Danville. Predictably the investigation showed the Central to owe a substantial sum to the Danville. Once more both parties retreated to the courts in search of satisfaction.[45]

In June, 1892, the Central's position remained precarious. It continued to battle the Terminal over the status of both the lease and the latter company's 42,200 shares of Central stock. Meanwhile the Central's temporary receivership seemed headed irretrievably toward a permanent financial receivership as default on the July interest appeared unavoidable. Raoul himself grew progressively gloomier over the company's prospects. "The stupidity and recklessness of the management for the past five years have very seriously embarrassed the property," he moaned that June. "While the present management is honest, capable and energetic, and while I know of my own knowledge that it is straining every nerve in the interests of the stockholders, it is impossible to predict with certainty what success it will have in dealing with the serious problems that confront it." [46]

The Road to Stalemate

The Olcott committee set April 14 as the time limit for deposits under its plan. As might have been expected, Terminal securities came in relatively quickly but underlying securities did not. Hopefully the committee extended the deadline first to May 6 and then to May 16, but it soon became apparent that the plan was in deep trouble.[47] In addition to its obvious inequalities, the plan suffered from the power struggle within the Terminal. For the moment the Brice-Thomas faction held power, but their authority remained tenuous. The executive committee appointed on March 11, 1892, consisted of Brice, Thomas, Moore, Maben, Swann, Strong, and

---

[45] Atlanta *Constitution*, June 8, June 9, 1892; *Chronicle*, LIV (1892), 924, 965; *Railroad Gazette*, XXIV (1892), 437–38.

[46] Raoul to Mrs. George D. Wadley, June 15, 1892, Raoul Letter Books.

[47] *Chronicle*, LIV (1892), 486, 643; *Railroad Gazette*, XXIV (1892), 306, 340, 360.

George Gould, but already rumors hinted that the entire East Tennessee group was about to exit in favor of the First National Bank syndicate. Any such arrangement would have to be predicated upon an understanding with Thomas, who held the largest single commitment in the East Tennessee.[48]

External evidence appeared to bear out the rumors. On March 16 Inman at last resigned the Terminal presidency and was made director in place of Wilson. In his place came Walter Oakman, the familiar operational executive of the First National group. Oakman also assumed the Danville presidency and replaced Thomas as board chairman and Samuel M. Felton, Jr., as president of the East Tennessee. The series of changes gave the First National full administrative authority over the Terminal system. At the same time the Olcott committee added Harris Fahnestock and J. Kennedy Tod to their number, thus cementing their connection with the First National syndicate. Brice and Thomas vigorously denied rumors that they opposed the committee's work. "We are doing all we can to support the efforts of the committee," Thomas insisted, "and are in hearty accord with all they have done." Brice himself took time off from Senate duties to take an active role in the reorganization.[49]

Despite these maneuvers the plan failed, largely because the underlying bondholders would not support it. Even the conservative *Chronicle*, which had supported the plan, admitted in its obituary of the committee that "it is perhaps no surprise that they have failed to inspire public confidence in their plans, for the effort made has been reformation from within and hence reform has been sought without removing the cause of the embarrassments." [50] Immediately after the announcement virtually the same group of investors that had originally appointed Olcott's committee held another meeting. Composed primarily of interests holding Terminal common and various underlying bonds, the

[48] Terminal Directors' Minutes, March 11, 1892; Leonhardt to McGhee, March 15, 1892, and to C. M. McClung, March 15, 1892, McGhee papers. Of the First National group Leonhardt observed: "if they do take an active interest . . . it must be with considerable concessions to them, for I believe they never go into anything without . . . full control."

[49] Terminal Directors' Minutes, March 15, March 16, 1892; *Olcott Plan*, 3; Leonhardt to McGhee, March 19, 1892, McGhee papers; *Railroad Gazette*, XXIV (1892), 218, 236; *Chronicle*, LIV (1892), 561.

[50] LIV (1892), 866. See also *Railroad Gazette*, XXIV (1892), 380, and New York *Sun*, May 17, 1892.

group appointed Clyde, Thomas, and Strong as an advisory committee of three to protect their interests.[51]

The demise of the Olcott plan greatly increased the danger that the Terminal properties would be dismantled. The First National syndicate wished to keep the systems intact but lacked both a plan and unified support for doing so. Clyde's interests, which straddled Terminal common and Danville bonds among other holdings, still bore a strongly opportunistic stamp. Thomas still possessed considerable capital and influence but tended to exert it toward a breaking up of the systems. Many of the underlying bondholders also took an atomistic stand, with security holders in each system believing that the weakness of the other system (and the holding company) accounted for the current state of financial chaos. Even during the Olcott committee's undertaking one group of East Tennessee holders filed suit unsuccessfully to prevent consolidation with the Danville under the reorganization plan.[52]

Backed by the new committee, Thomas acted first. He announced that the East Tennessee would not be included in any new reorganization and promptly submitted a plan for the Danville alone. The Thomas plan proved considerably more severe than the Olcott plan. It called for abolishing the Terminal and replacing it with an operating company whose cash needs would be provided by a 10 per cent assessment upon its new common.[53] When a stockholders' meeting showed no interest in implementing the plan, Thomas suggested that a committee of fifteen be appointed to consult with the committee of three; later this advisory committee was enlarged to seventeen, with Strong as chairman.[54]

At first the committee tried to kindle interest in the Thomas plan, but a group of banking interests led by the First National syndicate outflanked them. In a bid to hold the Terminal systems together the bankers asked Drexel, Morgan & Company to undertake the reorganization work. Hearing of this petition, the advisory committee dropped the Thomas plan and joined somewhat reluctantly in the request. Morgan expressed interest in the prospect and sent one of his railroad experts, Georgia-born Samuel Spencer, on a tour of the Terminal properties with Oakman and

[51] *Ibid.*   [52] *Railroad Gazette*, XXIV (1892) , 305, 420.

[53] *Ibid.*, XXIV (1892) , 380. There is a good brief description of the Thomas plan in Daggett, *Railroad Reorganization*, 174.

[54] See New York *Sun*, August 20, 1892.

other officials. For his part Oakman tried to ease Morgan's task by softening his stand in the dispute with the Central.[55]

During the summer of 1892 the need for a solution to the Terminal's woes grew more urgent than ever. The economic horizons in the South were fast darkening, and earnings across the entire Terminal system were slumping rapidly. Unable to meet coming interest payments and harassed by hostile litigation, the Terminal, Danville, and East Tennessee all went into the hands of friendly receivers. Oakman remained as receiver of the Terminal, but Clyde dominated the Danville suit and managed to install his cohorts, Huidekoper and Reuben Foster, as coreceivers. On the East Tennessee, Thomas predictably held sway. He filed suit himself and had Henry Fink and McGhee appointed receivers. To preserve the securities loaned by the Terminal to the Danville, the holders of the Danville's floating debt were persuaded to carry it for another two years if necessary.[56]

The receiverships relieved some of the immediate financial and legal pressure, but only at a cost of further decentralization of authority. To effect their reorganization Morgan's agents would now have to deal separately with the systems and the men in control of them. Moreover the receiverships spurred the formation of new bondholders' committees as default was made on different issues. To be sure most of these committees worked with the advisory committee and tended to support the Morgan efforts, but any such harmony might vanish abruptly once concrete figures were proposed.[57]

The bitter partisanship enshrouding Terminal affairs left a deep imprint upon the Morgan agents. They came speedily to the conclusion that no settlement would placate all interests; therefore the only feasible course was a "blind pool." Morgan would at-

[55] Terminal Directors' Minutes, August 10, 1892; *Chronicle*, LIV (1892), 888; Atlanta *Constitution*, June 10, 1892; *Railroad Gazette*, XXIV (1892), 420. For Spencer's tour, see Atlanta *Constitution*, May 28, May 31, 1892; Knoxville *Tribune*, June 3, 1892; *Dow Jones Co. Bulletin*, June 17, 1892.

[56] Terminal Directors' Minutes, August 10, 1892. For the Terminal receivership, see *Chronicle*, LIV (1892), 1048, and *Railroad Gazette*, XXIV (1892), 484, 494, 644; for the East Tennessee, *Chronicle*, LV (1892), 21, 100, and *Railroad Gazette*, XXIV (1892), 501, 504; and for the Danville, *Chronicle*, LIV (1892), 983, 1010, and *Railroad Gazette*, XXIV (1892), 482, 484. Interestingly, the Danville receivers moved the company's general headquarters from Atlanta back to Washington.

[57] For examples of these committees, see *Chronicle*, LV (1892), 21, 216; *Railroad Gazette*, XXIV (1892), 590, 608.

tempt the reorganization only if the major parties agreed in advance to accept whatever terms were imposed. Specifically he wanted the following concessions: prior deposit of a majority of each class of Terminal stock and bonds; the placing of all litigation under Morgan control; and the resignation of all receivers in favor of a Morgan selection, presumably Spencer. Such a course would protect Morgan from any single interest or group desiring to thwart the reorganization. It would also prevent undue speculation while the work proceeded.[58]

Obviously a "blind pool" could only be repugnant to veteran manipulators like Clyde, Brice, and Thomas. The latter two men reluctantly agreed to the terms, however, leaving only Clyde in dissent. Although he had signed the invitation to Morgan along with the other members of the advisory committee, he had no heart for Morgan's intervention. According to one story Morgan summoned Brice, Thomas, and Clyde to his office to discuss the matter. Clyde arrived last, reclined on the long sofa in the partners' room, and listened while Morgan outlined his terms. When Morgan had finished, Clyde replied puckishly, "Well, Mr. Morgan, I've bought Richmond Terminal at 7 and 8 and sold it at 15 twice in the last few years. I see no reason why I shouldn't do it again. So I fear I cannot join with the others in asking you to deal with the property." [59]

Whether or not the story is literally true, it characterizes both the men and the situation well. The assumption of Morgan, his First National associates, and their supporters was that the Terminal could be preserved intact only by transforming it into an enterprise geared to sound operational efficiency. But such a change would sharply reverse the Terminal's historical role as a speculative plaything. The goal of converting the holding company from an opportunistic investment to a developmental commitment had long been sought in vain. Morgan concluded logically that such a transition could not take place as long as the company's major investors remained speculators at heart and limited their developmental commitment to the individual systems or related enterprises. The fierce partisanship engendered by these centrifugal forces could not be resolved from within; order would have to be

[58] The Morgan position is formally stated in the letter quoted in both the *Railroad Gazette,* XXIV (1892), 504, and New York *Herald,* June 29, 1892.

[59] This scene is given in Frederick Lewis Allen, *The Great Pierpont Morgan* (New York, 1949), 92–93.

imposed from without and on terms that fitted the needs of the company rather than the individuals controlling it.

For these reasons Morgan declined to undertake the reorganization without Clyde's cooperation. In his refusal he stated bluntly that Clyde "declines to give us any assurance, and our conversation with him leads us to doubt his loyalty to any reorganization plan whatever." The announcement touched off a round of controversy in which Clyde was alternately blamed for subverting the reorganization and praised for refusing to surrender his interests sight unseen. As usual Clyde stoutly defended his stand but won few adherents.[60]

The withdrawal of Morgan returned Terminal affairs to a stalemate. While admitting that Wall Street "favors almost any kind of settlement, because it fears the effect on the market of the collapse of the Terminal Company," the hostile *Railroad Gazette* predicted a breakup of the Terminal systems and applauded the prospect.[61] Other observers voiced their dismay over the apparent hopelessness of the company's future. There seemed in truth nothing to anticipate beyond a resumption of hostilities. As Stuart Daggett put it, "the field was left to the disputes between members of the Richmond Terminal family." [62]

---

[60] Morgan's refusal and Clyde's defense can be found in *Chronicle*, LV (1892), 23; *Railroad Gazette*, XXIV (1892), 504; New York *Herald*, June 29, 1892; New York *Evening Sun*, June 29, 1892. For a defense of Clyde, see Boston *Commercial Bulletin*, July 2, 1892.

[61] XXIV (1892), 230, 494.   [62] *Railroad Reorganization*, 175.

Chapter X

Out of Many, One

Disputes within the Terminal family dragged on for six tedious months. At the end of that period Clyde found no alternative but to relent and acquiesce in a new invitation to Drexel, Morgan. The return of Morgan produced the first serious efforts at reorganizing the Terminal since the failure of the Olcott plan. To the labyrinthian ledgers of the Terminal systems Morgan sent the brilliantly analytical mind of Charles H. Coster. From his ingenious calculations and the detailed report of Samuel Spencer on the physical condition of the various roads would emerge the plan Morgan presented to his clients. As expected it brought a mixed reception from the interests involved and general approval from most observers. Two broad problems eluded the shrewd calculations of the Morgan men: the thorny reorganization of the Central and the severe deepening of the economic depression during 1893. Both would have an influence on the final phase of the Terminal's history.

The Only Open Place in Town

Clyde had clearly outflanked both Morgan and the First National interests in securing the Danville receivership. After Morgan's withdrawal he moved quickly to secure control of the Terminal. In August he gained a seat on the board vacated by the death of Sidney Dillon, and soon afterwards he persuaded the Strong advisory committee to acquiesce in his leadership. That committee had by its own admission virtually served as the Terminal board in recent months. When the Morgan plan fell through, Strong appointed a subcommittee composed of himself, Maben, and George Stone to reopen negotiations with Morgan. Increasingly, however, the committee's members fell under Clyde's sway and in so doing abdicated all hope of reconciling the diverse interests impartially.[1]

[1] Terminal Directors' Minutes, August 10, 1892; *Chronicle*, LV (1892), 59; *Railroad Gazette*, XXIV (1892), 538. The Strong committee explicated its

Not all the Terminal interests approved Clyde's activities. The First National interests, supported by some minor factions, continued to nurse the Morgan negotiations along. Several stock and bond holders' committees arose in opposition to Clyde's leadership, the most important of which was headed by Alexander E. Orr. In general the Orr committee wished to oust Clyde, elect an independent board favorable to reorganization, and pursue the Morgan intervention. Yet its efforts were by no means free of partisanship. Pat Calhoun belonged to its ranks, and it was widely rumored that parties sympathetic to Morgan were buying Terminal securities to support the reorganization party.[2]

Basically Clyde opposed immediate reorganization because it would interfere with his speculative plans. He had forced the Danville receivership largely by playing on the fears raised by the Central's suit against the Danville. To profit from his position he needed first to gain control over the Terminal management and then to find ways of booming the company's stock without producing a workable reorganization plan. The first objective could be achieved by dominating the special meeting to elect a Terminal board on September 15; the second could be attained by resurrecting the Georgia Company episode.

As it turned out, the two fitted nicely together. The Strong subcommittee on reorganization admitted that it could not make any headway until past scandals had been unearthed and righted:

This Sub-Committee found it impossible to . . . make any reliable estimate as to the earning power of this property in the future, upon which earning power alone any plan of reorganization, no matter by whom it shall be attempted, must ultimately be based, without first determining how much of the present embarrassment of the Company is due to inherent defects or weakness in the property itself, and how much is due to vicious or bad management. . . . It was necessary for the Sub-Committee first to ascertain what, if anything, could be recovered from any person or persons who have wronged the Company in the past. . . . It has already found matters of such magnitude and importance as to compel it to suspend negotiations for reorganization until it can more fully investigate the past.[3]

***

position in a circular reprinted in the New York *Sun,* August 20, 1892. For attacks on the committee, see New York *Times,* August 22, 1892 and the circular published by the committee chaired by Alexander E. Orr. Copies of both circulars can be found in the archives of the Southern Railway Company.

[2] *Chronicle,* LV (1892) , 298. See also the circular issued by the Orr committee.

[3] New York *Sun,* August 20, 1892.

The investigation provided both a potent campaign weapon and a bullish pressure on Terminal securities as talk of a suit to recover the Georgia Company losses began to spread. In the forthcoming election the opposition to Clyde would be a slate of candidates put up by the Orr committee. To gain his majority Clyde and his supporters bought every proxy in sight and outstripped the Orr faction in both money and resourcefulness. Shortly before the election Oakman received permission to file suit for recovery of $7,500,000 allegedly lost in the Georgia Company transaction. For a time the contest warmed up as Calhoun denied Clyde's accusations and charged that the Danville's embarrassment derived from the costly leases made during Clyde's own tenure as Terminal president.[4]

As usual the heat of battle produced little light, and victory went to the biggest battalions. Clyde's successful gathering of proxies enabled his ticket to defeat the Orr slate 400,122 to 169,888. On the investigation issue Calhoun tried to diversify the membership of the inquisitorial body. He offered a resolution to appoint a five-member committee to examine the company's past affairs. Three of the members would be named by the Strong committee and two by Orr's group. By the same 400,122 to 169,888 margin Calhoun's resolution was replaced by one simply calling for the newly elected board to conduct the investigation. That board included only four incumbents, George Gould, Maben, Rutherfurd, and McGhee, and both Gould and McGhee promptly declined their seats. The new members were Strong, Stone, Bryan, Robert G. Erwin, Alexander Van Nest, Thomas F. Ryan, George Blagden, C. A. Low, William H. Goadby, John N. Hutchinson, Edwin Packard, Thomas L. Manson, Jr., and R. S. Hayes.[5]

Despite his lopsided victory, Clyde did not possess full control. Orr's committee remained in opposition, and behind its efforts was a syndicate known to be sympathetic to Morgan intervention. Known popularly as the Whitney-Elkins syndicate and led primarily by W. C. Whitney and Thomas Fortune Ryan, the group al-

---

[4] Atlanta *Constitution*, Sept. 19, 1892; *Railroad Gazette*, XXIV (1892), 636, 678. For Calhoun's position, see New York *Times*, August 21, August 28, 1892, and New York *Evening Post*, August 23, 1892.

[5] Terminal Annual Meeting Minutes, Sept. 15, 1892; *Chronicle*, LV (1892), 463; *Railroad Gazette*, XXIV (1892), 716, 736; Richmond *Times*, Sept. 16, 1892; Richmond *Dispatch*, Sept. 16, 1892; Atlanta *Constitution*, Sept. 19, 1892; Macon *Telegraph*, Sept. 21, 1892; *Journal of Finance*, Sept. 16, 1892. Erwin represented the Plant interests after Plant left the board.

ready owned about 80,000 shares of Terminal common and was still buying; in time it would be joined by Harrison M. Twombly, a Morgan associate. Ryan, Hayes, and Manson represented this stock on the new board, and the new executive committee, consisting of Clyde, Strong, Stone, Maben, Ryan, Hayes, and Bryan, clearly reflected the split. On the other hand Thomas threw his support behind Clyde in the election. While that alliance might not last long, it gave Clyde strong additional backing for the moment.[6]

On this somewhat tenuous basis Clyde took command. Publicly he promised to preserve the Terminal system intact and to produce a new plan in short order. Early in October rumors spread of a new plan based upon one class of stock and a stiff assessment on present stockholders. A board meeting on October 7, however, denounced all such stories as "fakes." After the meeting Maben denied that any plan had been formulated, much less approved, and said that a thorough investigation would first have to be made. "We cannot be expected to reorganize the Richmond Terminal system in a month," he added. "We could not use the Olcott committee report as it was not accurate." [7]

By the end of October no plan had appeared, and observers grew increasingly skeptical over the prospects. No palpable progress had been made, and factionalism continued to rule Terminal affairs. While Clyde dragged his heels the company's stock fluctuated upon every rumor or false step.[8] So far the only positive step taken by Clyde was to push the Georgia Company investigation. The directors authorized Oakman to press the suit in late October and appointed an investigating committee composed only of directors who had not served during the period under scrutiny.[9]

With appropriate fanfare Oakman instituted proceedings. On November 21 he received a court order to secure cancellation of the Georgia Company sale contract. To the long list of participants in the transaction he sent letters offering a stern choice: the guilty parties could undo the deal by taking back the Georgia Company securities and returning the money paid for them by the

[6] Terminal Directors' Minutes, Oct. 20, 1892; Atlanta *Constitution*, Sept. 19, 1892; *Journal of Finance*, Sept. 16, 1892; New York *Evening Post*, Feb. 3, 1893.

[7] *Journal of Finance*, Sept. 30, Oct. 6, 1892; *Daily Investigator*, Oct. 7, 1892; *Wall Street Daily News*, Oct. 8, 1892.

[8] See *Wall Street Journal*, Oct. 7, Oct. 13, 1892; *Journal of Finance*, Oct. 24, Oct. 27, 1892; Chicago *Herald*, Nov. 16, 1892.

[9] Terminal Directors' Minutes, Oct. 7, Oct. 20, 1892.

Terminal, or he would sue for recovery.[10] Not unexpectedly the offer brought no takers, and on December 17 Oakman filed suit in the New York Supreme Court. The suit produced spectacular publicity and carefully worded denials from most of the defendants.[11]

It did not bring spectacular results. From the beginning some stockholders and observers alike dismissed the suit as a bluff and marveled at Clyde's gall in charging others with the responsibility for the Terminal's bankruptcy. On a more serious level Clyde quite possibly intended the suit as a counterweight in the Terminal's complex litigation with the Central. Harry Hollins, who had taken charge of the Central's reorganization, held a large block of Terminal fives which might be exchanged for the Central stock held by the Terminal in a compromise settlement. Whatever Clyde's intentions, the suit served several purposes; it buoyed Terminal stock, it applied pressure to his opponents, and it helped distract attention from his inability either to reconcile the dissonant factions or to produce a viable reorganization plan. But it reaped for the Terminal none of the financial rewards advertised by its advocates and became in the end little more than an informative dialogue between the pot and the kettle.[12]

By December, Clyde had reached the end of his tether. He had produced nothing and was running short of excuses. Meanwhile the ranks of his adversaries swelled steadily. He could never hope to appease the underlying bondholders, who were hostile to any plan converting their holdings even partially to stock, and the per-

[10] For the order and Oakman's offer, see *Railroad Gazette*, XXIV (1892), 891; New York *Herald*, Nov. 26, Dec. 1, 1892; New York *Sun*, Nov. 27, 1892; Macon *Telegraph*, Nov. 22, 1892; *Wall Street Daily News*, Nov. 28, 1892.

[11] The suit itself is contained in *Terminal vs. Inman*, 1–71, as quoted in chap. 8 above. Of the newspaper accounts the most detailed is probably New York *Evening Sun*, Dec. 17, 1892. For other pertinent and often overlapping accounts, see New York *Evening Post*, Dec. 17, 1892; New York *Mail and Express*, Dec. 17, 1892; New York *World*, Dec. 18, 1892; Philadelphia *Press*, Dec. 18, 1892; New York *Tribune*, Dec. 18, 1892; *Manufacturers Record*, Dec. 23, 1892; *Chronicle*, LV (1892), 938, 1078. A copy of the legal brief filed by John and Robert Inman, Swann, and Bernard S. Clark denying the charges is in the archives of the Southern Railway Company. For denials by other defendants, see New York *Commercial Advertiser*, Dec. 20, 1892; Macon *Telegraph*, Dec. 21, 1892; Augusta *Chronicle*, March 8, 1893; Baltimore *American*, March 14, 1893; Columbia (S.C.) *Weekly Register*, March 21, 1893; *Chronicle*, LVI (1893), 972; and *Railroad Gazette*, XXV (1893), 197.

[12] *Journal of Finance*, Oct. 10, Oct. 28, 1892; New York *Evening Post*, Oct. 4, 1892.

sistent string of interest payments due on junior liens increased the danger that the system might be dismembered. The stagnating financial and economic situation intensified the demand for some reorganization amidst fears on Wall Street that a general collapse of the Terminal and its components might deal the market a fatal blow. Affairs on the Danville deteriorated alarmingly as earnings diminished and complaints over its service rose.[13]

Things were no better on the East Tennessee. As holder of much of the floating debt, Thomas took virtually everything of value in the company's treasury as collateral. General poverty and a poor crop prevailed along most of the company's lines, and no reduction in expenses could be foreseen. Fink confessed that "we are unable to carry any farther, the so-called 'economy.' In fact, we will have to make extraordinary expenditures to make up for past economies." [14] By November the company could no longer meet interest on all its general mortgage bonds, and within a month the floating debt crept up to $2,000,000. So far Thomas had staved off disaster, but the uncertainty of financial conditions rendered the sluggishness of reorganization efforts intolerable. As early as August a despairing McGhee diagnosed the situation astutely:

It is now evident that a reorganization is necessary. It is also evident that several years may in all probability elapse before that can be accomplished. In the meantime a panic may occur and General Thomas may not be so flush of money as he is at present. The present President of the Company could do nothing to protect the collateral and the burthen might be thrown upon us [the receivers].[15]

The situation impressed itself no less forcibly upon Thomas himself, who grew progressively impatient with Clyde's dawdling. The only apparent solution lay in cooperating with those interests striving to bring Morgan back and to keep the two systems together. Accordingly the East Tennessee board surrendered a ma-

---

[13] For the position of the Danville's underlying bondholders, see their circular dated Nov. 7, 1892, in the archives of the Southern Railway Company. For attempts to keep the system together by meeting interest on underlying bonds, see *Chronicle*, LV (1892) , 23, and *Railroad Gazette*, XXIV (1892) , 522. Examples of the Danville's difficulties can be found in Atlanta *Constitution*, Nov. 19, Nov. 29, 1892.

[14] McGhee to Fink, July 12, 1892, and Fink to McGhee, August 26, 1892, McGhee papers.

[15] McGhee to Fink, August 19, 1892, *ibid*. See also Fink to McGhee, Nov. 2, 1892 and McGhee to W. L. Bull, Dec. 22, 1892, *ibid.;* and *Journal of Finance*, Oct. 29, 1892.

jority of its seats to the Terminal at the November 22 election, with Thomas and Brice dominating the remaining places. At the same time Thomas returned to the Terminal board in place of the resigned George Gould and added his voice to those already clamoring for a reorganization from the outside. In response Clyde tried once more to present a "house" plan in late December, but nothing materialized.[16]

By January, Clyde had expended his evasions. Financial conditions remained threatening, earnings continued to decline, and unpaid interest mounted steadily. Dissension within the ranks had only grown worse during Clyde's tenure and showed no signs of abating. It had become painfully evident to all that only some powerful outsider could gain the confidence of all factions and preserve the Terminal system. Under the circumstances Morgan was the only feasible "outsider" for the job, and he would have to be approached quickly if disaster for all classes of security holders was to be avoided.

Beset by these pressures, Clyde could only relent. On February 2, he joined Stone, Strong, Maben, and Ryan in signing a letter to Morgan asking that his firm again take up the task of reorganization. In the key paragraph the five financiers assured Morgan that they were "willing to do all in our power to give you full control of the reorganization as suggested in your letter of June 28 and to advise our friends and the security holders generally to deposit their securities without requiring the assurances customary in such cases." Olcott sent a separate letter approving the offer and affirming his own cooperation.[17]

Morgan accepted the offer conditionally, pleading somewhat ingenuously that "since our correspondence of last summer we have not kept ourselves advised as to the Richmond Terminal situation." The news of Morgan's acceptance caused a mild bullish trend in Terminal securities, and for the first time in more than a year confidence that a genuine reorganization would take place was restored.[18] Publicly the press clothed Clyde's coming to terms with all the trappings of a statesmanlike compromise. In the inner

[16] Terminal Directors' Minutes, Nov. 22, 1892; *Chronicle*, LV (1892), 856.

[17] Copies of the correspondence are in *Chronicle*, LVI (1893), 207; New York *Morning Advertiser*, Feb. 3, 1893; Macon *Telegraph*, Feb. 3, 1893; and *Railroad Gazette*, XXV (1893), 120.

[18] *Ibid.*; New York *Herald*, Feb. 3, Feb. 4, 1893; New York *Evening Post*, Feb. 3, 1893; New York *Commercial Advertiser*, Feb. 3, 1893; New York *Times*, Feb. 4, 1893; *Wall Street Daily News*, Feb. 6, 1893.

circle the matter was seen in a different light. With sardonic glee Morgan partner Charles H. Coster, who would do more than any other single person to fashion the final plan, described the surrender. "They were like the man who came home at daybreak," he remarked. "His wife asked him why he had bothered to return at all. He replied: 'I would not have come, but every other place in town was closed.' "[19]

Reorganization of the Central

The Speer decision and the Central's suit against the Danville proved but the opening salvos of a long and bitter battle.[20] The Terminal could not simply abandon its large holding, of course, and the lease remained unjudged and unenforced. More important, the ambiguity of the Terminal's large block of Central stock complicated any attempt to reorganize either of the companies. Reorganization was definitely in order for the Central by the summer of 1892. As predicted, the company defaulted on its July interest payments, and the court, upon application by the creditors, appointed Comer sole receiver. The floating debt, primarily in the form of the Speyer and Mutual loans, hovered around $5,000,000 and remained the road's most pressing obligation.[21]

During the summer it became readily apparent that despite Comer's presence real control belonged not to local "conservative" interests at all but rather to diverse and opposing sets of creditors, each with his own plan for reorganization. Speyer & Company assembled a plan that reduced fixed charges sharply by paring down the company's capitalization several million dollars. After reorganization Speyer envisioned a possible lease of the system to the L. & N. on good terms; but the plan encountered implacable opposition from those security holders who would be forced to make heavy sacrifices under its provisions. Foremost among the objectors was the familiar figure of Harry Hollins, whose firm held few Central securities but retained substantial holdings in Southwestern securities.[22]

To thwart the Speyer plan Hollins formed a committee com-

[19] Quoted in John K. Winkler, *Morgan the Magnificent* (New York, 1930), 128–29.

[20] See the correspondence reproduced in *Chronicle*, LIV (1892), 1010, LV (1892), 22–23.

[21] *Railroad Gazette*, XXIV (1892), 522, 538.

[22] Atlanta *Constitution*, Sept. 24, 1892; Macon *Telegraph*, Sept. 26, 1892; New York *Sun*, Sept. 30, 1892.

posed of himself, Emanuel Lehman, Phinizy, E. E. Denniston, E. Rollins Morse of Boston, Frederick M. Colston of Wilston, Colston & Company of Baltimore, and James T. Woodward, president of the Hanover National Bank. Drawing upon support from several other banking firms interested in the Central, the committee took up the Speyer loan and promised to produce a reorganization plan of its own.[23]

The news brightened financial circles in Georgia considerably, but the committee soon faced some stiff problems. Nearly $2,000,000 of the floating debt still had to be taken up, and the dilemma of the Terminal's stock remained unsolved. Hostile legislation was being introduced into the Georgia legislature, and in South Carolina, Governor Ben Tillman threatened legal action against the Central for willfully bottling up Port Royal. Even worse, the long-awaited receiver's report by Comer and Superintendent George D. Wadley painted a gloomy picture of the company's present condition and future prospects. Comer noted that the effects of depression had further widened the gap between falling income and rising expenses, while Wadley, in a detailed survey of the Central's physical condition, concluded that over $5,000,000 would have to be spent on improvements over the next three years if the road was to be run economically. Where that sum would come from no one could imagine, but the need would not make the task of reorganization any easier.[24]

The attempt to stifle the adverse legislation, a bill introduced by A. O. Bacon and aimed specifically at combinations like the Terminal, brought a host of worried southern railroad men to Atlanta for the hearings. Clyde himself came down and presented a telling argument before the Senate committee.[25] For that brief moment Terminal and Central interests stood together; afterward the conflict between them was renewed in earnest. Hollins's first efforts at a reorganization plan bogged down because his committee took too sanguine a view of the Central's earning capacity and because he could find no way to gain control of the stock owned by the Terminal. By December, 1892, the committee had scrapped its original plan and contemplated a more drastic one, not unlike the

[23] *Ibid.; Chronicle,* LV (1892), 503, 544–45; *Railroad Gazette,* XXIV (1892), 737, 778; Atlanta *Constitution,* Sept. 23, 1892; Macon *Telegraph,* Sept. 29, 1892.

[24] Atlanta *Constitution,* Oct. 17, Nov. 5, Nov. 27, 1892; Macon *Telegraph,* Oct. 17, Nov. 28, 1892; New York *Post,* Nov. 30, 1892.

[25] For this affair see Terminal Directors' Minutes, Dec. 30, 1892; Atlanta *Constitution,* Dec. 8, Dec. 9, 1892; New York *Sun,* Dec. 9, 1892. After the hearings the Georgia Senate unanimously rejected the Bacon bill, which had passed the House 115 to 0.

odious Speyer plan, to scale down fixed charges. By December, too, the committee found itself on the defensive in its relations with the Terminal.[26]

The provisions of the revised Hollins plan were announced shortly before Christmas. Based upon an issue of $40,000,000 in new bonds and $25,000,000 each of new common and preferred, the plan called for exchanging two shares of new common for one share of old. The terms seemed clearly prejudicial toward the Terminal, whose holdings would be reduced to a minority and placed behind the preferred for dividend purposes. Since the committee did not consult the Terminal while preparing its plan, Oakman predictably threatened legal action unless the holding company's majority position was recognized and its rights were protected. Oakman's stance posed a formidable obstacle for any reorganization effort, and the Danville added further insult by obtaining an attachment against the Central for $1,213,405 for money allegedly expended during the lease. An attempt at mediation by Jacob Schiff, who had joined the Hollins committee, only provoked a rancorous correspondence with Oakman.[27]

Hopefully the Hollins committee pressed their plan and even renewed negotiations with the L. & N. over a possible lease, but the difficulties multiplied rapidly. An attempt to set the plan in motion by foreclosing on the recently matured "tripartite" bonds was met by a countersuit staying the proceedings as hostile to the interests of the junior security holders. Another suit dissolved the Port Royal lease and ordered the Central to surrender the property. A committee of Southwestern holders announced their suspicion of the Hollins plan, and eight different suits asked judgments against the Central's certificates of indebtedness.[28]

The most devastating blow, however, came directly from the Terminal. Early in April, Oakman filed suit asking that the deci-

---

[26] Atlanta *Constitution*, Dec. 10, 1892; New York *Post*, Nov. 30, 1892; *Wall Street Daily News*, Dec. 1, 1892.

[27] *Ibid.; Chronicle*, LVI (1893), 82; *Railroad Gazette*, XXV (1893), 40; *Wall Street Daily News*, Jan. 14, 1893. The Schiff-Oakman letters illustrate the bitterness engendered by the controversy. They are reprinted in full in a circular to Terminal stockholders dated Jan. 19, 1893, in the archives of the Southern Railway Company. A partial reprinting and paraphrase can be found in New York *Sun*, Jan. 20, 1893.

[28] *Chronicle*, LVI (1893), 578, 972; Atlanta *Constitution*, Jan. 21, 1893; Savannah *Evening Press*, March 30, 1893; Philadelphia *Evening Telegraph*, April 24, 1893; Macon *Telegraph*, May 10, 1893. Some observers attributed the suit staying the tripartite foreclosure to parties working with Drexel, Morgan & Company.

sion in the Clarke suit be reversed, that the Terminal be allowed to vote its Central stock and participate in the reorganization, and that Comer be discharged as receiver. In a series of spectacular and venomous outbursts, the Terminal's counsel, Henry Crawford, bluntly accused Judge Speer of conspiring with the present management throughout the past year. Insisting that Speer's conduct and decisions were without legal precedent, Crawford further alleged that the judge had approved the Hollins plan in advance and then used his influence to compel acceptance of it by dissenting security holders.[29]

After a round of sensational hearings Circuit Court Judge Howell E. Jackson gave the Terminal virtually everything it wanted. He completely reversed Speer's decision, dismissed the Clarke suit, and restored voting rights to the Terminal's Central stock.[30] The weight of Jackson's decision successfully killed the Hollins plan, and within three weeks the committee conceded. It was then evident that the Terminal would play a major role in the Central reorganization, a fact confirmed by the appointment of R. S. Hayes as coreceiver of the company in October. During the next months the burden of reorganization fell largely into the hands of Ryan and Thomas, but their work went on for well over a year before reorganization was accomplished. Throughout this period the uncertainty surrounding the property complicated the Terminal reorganization and caused Morgan, like Olcott before him, to exclude it from his plan.[31]

The Morgan Plan

The major Terminal interests stood by their bargain with Morgan this time. A committee composed of Clyde, Stone, Thomas, Strong,

[29] *Railroad Gazette*, XXV (1893), 328; Augusta *Chronicle*, April 12, 1893; Louisville *Courier-Journal*, April 12, 1893; New York *Sun*, April 13, 1893; New York *Indicator*, April 13, 1893. For Speer's rebuttal to the charges, see Macon *Telegraph*, April 14, 1893.

[30] *Chronicle*, LVI (1893), 972, LVII (1893), 21, 59; *Railroad Gazette*, XXV (1893), 506, 513; Savannah *Morning News*, July 1, 1893; New York *Sun*, June 29, July 1, 1893. For opposing editorial views on the decision, see Atlanta *Constitution*, July 2, 1893, and Macon *Telegraph*, July 2, 1893. Jackson also declared the receivership invalid under the Clarke decision, but Comer retained his post on the basis of a separate suit not affected by Jackson's decision.

[31] New York *Sun*, July 6, 1893; *Railroad Gazette*, XXV (1893), 558, 758; *Chronicle*, LVIII (1894), 263, 307, 637–38, LX (1895), 1008; Harrison, *Southern Railway*, 557–59.

Maben, and Ryan guided negotiations through the final stages. On April 12 Morgan informed the committee that his firm would definitely undertake the reorganization providing sufficient deposits of all securities were made. "It must be understood," Morgan added, "that we are given full authority to include any of the securities of the Terminal so deposited in the plan when announced, and that each depositor by his deposit gives such authority and his consent that all the terms and provisions of the plan together with assessments on deposited stock shall be discretionary with us." Unblinkingly the committee recommended that all stockholders agree to these terms before the deadline of May 1. A majority of each class of securities was obtained with little difficulty, and on May 23 Morgan released the plan to the public.[32]

Drawn up by a reorganization committee consisting of Coster, George Sherman, and Anthony J. Thomas, the plan took a different tack than the earlier Olcott plan. It emphasized a more severe paring down of fixed charges and stressed the urgency of raising ample capital for improving and modernizing the system. The entire plan, in fact, hinged upon a thorough rehabilitation of the road to make it competitive under existing conditions. "Without ample provision for both present and future," the committee insisted, "no reorganization of these systems can be permanently successful. . . . There is no other basis on which it is worth while seriously to consider the reorganization of these systems." [33]

What were these existing conditions? Essentially they comprised a competitive environment in which profit derived from carrying a heavy tonnage at low rates. To do this profitably a system needed high operating efficiency, which in turn meant using the most modern equipment. The Terminal lines, built largely in an era attuned to a business featuring moderate traffic at high rates, found themselves unable to compete effectively in the new environment. Capital had gone not into modernization and im-

[32] Terminal Directors' Minutes, April 13, 1893; Atlanta *Constitution*, Feb. 6, 1893; New York *Times*, April 11, 1893; Macon *Telegraph*, April 14, 1893; *Railroad Gazette*, XXV (1893) , 310, 348.

[33] *Plan and Agreement for the Reorganization of the Richmond and West Point Terminal Railway and Warehouse Company, Richmond and Danville Railway Company and System* (New York, 1893) , 4, 6, hereafter cited as *Morgan Plan*. Copies of the plan are in the Bureau of Railroad Economics, Baker Library, and the archives of the Southern Railway. It is also reprinted in full in *Chronicle*, LVI (1893) , 874–86. While my analysis is based upon my own study of the plan, it is doubtless influenced by the account in Daggett, *Railroad Reorganization*, 179–85.

provements but into expansion; as a result the systems were saddled with light, obsolete rolling stock, rail of insufficient weight,
ancient and inadequate facilities, and deteriorated roadbeds,
bridges, tunnels, and the rest of the physical plant. In ruthless detail the plan itemized the physical deterioration that attended
years of neglect and "economy." [34]

The indictment took great pains to impress the gravity of the
situation upon the stockholders. "The trouble in the East Tennessee," it noted bluntly, "is largely explained by the fact that, for
some years back, the property and its equipment have been allowed to deteriorate physically, and this has now been followed by
the financial collapse *inevitable* from such a course." [35] The Danville fared no better, and most of the subsidiary lines in both systems received specific and scathing criticisms. Even the newer lines
were in sorry disrepair. The notorious Mobile & Birmingham, for
example, was dismissed with this trenchant comment: "This line is
of no value whatever to the East Tennessee. It is in extremely bad
physical condition in all respects. It has nine miles of trestles, of
which the life is almost exhausted. It has practically no
equipment." [36]

The basic assumption behind this insistence upon physical rehabilitation was the desire to transform the Terminal from a financial, opportunistic enterprise to an operational, developmental
company. Indeed this reasoning lay behind the whole purpose of
the plan and explained why the committee tied the obvious need
to reduce fixed charges so closely to the provision of large sums of
capital for improvements. On this basis, therefore, the committee
approached financial reorganization from the standpoint that "it
is useless to consider any reorganization which continues, as fixed
charges, securities that are not now earning their interest." [37] Earning potential, then, became the primary criterion by which the adjustment of securities proceeded.

The principle of basing fixed charges upon earning capacity was
not original with Morgan. The Olcott plan professed the same
goal but did virtually nothing to implement it. As an "inside"
plan it had been forced to sacrifice economic necessities for political expedience and so accomplished little. While not immune to
the politics of the situation, the Morgan agents, as an "outside"

[34] For remarks on the physical condition of the lines and the necessity for
improving it, see *Morgan Plan*, 4–6, 12, 24–34, 41.

[35] *Ibid.*, 41. The italics are in the original.   [36] *Ibid.*, 31   [37] *Ibid.*, 12.

group, could concentrate more fully upon the economic needs of the company rather than the personal desires of individual interests. It was precisely for this reason that Morgan insisted upon having the leverage he could exert through the "blind pool" arrangement. It is hardly surprising, therefore, that the provisions of his plan were radically different from those of the Olcott plan.[38]

Basically the Morgan plan contemplated issuing $140,000,000 in new 5 per cent bonds, $75,000,000 in preferred stock, and $160,000,000 in common. Of these amounts $96,617,000 in bonds, $56,035,000 in preferred, and $104,349,000 would be required for exchange purposes. The cash requirements were estimated at $23,250,000, of which $12,900,000 would be used to extinguish the floating debts and equipment notes, $8,000,000 for new construction and equipment, and $2,350,000 for reorganization expenses and contingencies. To raise this cash $8,000,000 in bonds would be sold at 85 and $33,333,000 in common at 15. In addition some $11,450,000 would be raised by levying the following assessments per share: Terminal common $12.50, East Tennessee first preferred $3.00, second preferred $6.00, and common $9.00. The assessment followed the proposition that "it is for the stockholders to provide for acquisition or extinction of the floating debts. . . . The first requirement is that the Terminal security holders shall recognize and meet the situation . . . as otherwise, they cannot expect, or reasonably ask, concessions from any Richmond and Danville or East Tennessee bondholders." [39]

Unlike the Olcott plan, the Morgan committee specifically favored the senior bonds and whittled down the stocks and more recent liens. The fundamental approach was to "deal with each particular class of securities on its own merits, having due regard for its relation to all other securities." Accordingly the committee deemed about $74,000,000 worth of bonds and guaranteed stocks adequately secured and left them undisturbed. About $50,000,000 in junior liens, most of them recent issues, were declared inadequately secured and adjusted on the basis of the following rationale:

[38] On these grounds alone it is hard to accept, except in a very superficial sense, the judgment in Campbell, *Reorganization,* 94, that "the [Olcott] plan was substantially that under which the system would finally be reorganized."

[39] *Morgan Plan,* 17. The high Terminal assessment was due, of course, to the fact that the holding company owned virtually all the Danville's stock and large amounts of East Tennessee stock of all classes and was held responsible for its proportionate share of the floating debts.

The general theory of adjustment of disturbed bonds has been to substitute for them the new five per cent bonds to such an extent as is warranted by the earnings and situation of the properties covered by the present mortgages, and the new preferred stock for the remainder of principal. In some cases, where the bonds are on properties of no actual and little prospective earning capacity, a more severe reduction is necessary. In several instances, where the bonds are on properties which are likely to improve more rapidly than other disturbed parts of the system, this fact is recognized, and an extra allowance is made in compensation therefore. Finally, in one or two cases where the bonds are on properties the loss of which would adversely affect the rest of the system, a proper recognition is made of this fact.[40]

By applying this principle rigorously, the committee put forth a markedly different set of adjustment figures than those of the Olcott committee. Of sixty-seven securities adjusted under both plans, the Morgan committee placed a lower valuation on sixty-five, with the other two receiving the same valuation from both committees. The comparative adjustments on a representative sampling of securities, as shown in Table 16, point up the differences clearly.[41]

The intended effect of these adjustments and other provisions already mentioned would be to reduce fixed charges from about $9,900,000 to $6,789,000. A comparison of selected financial provisions in the Olcott and Morgan plans helps illuminate the extent by which the latter surpassed the former in paring down fixed obligations and providing adequate capital for all needs. This is done in Table 17.

As Table 17 indicates, the Morgan plan cut nearly a million dollars from the fixed charges proposed in the Olcott plan. It did this primarily by issuing the preferred stock *instead* of bonds rather than in addition to them. As a result it required $45,147,200 less of bonds for exchange purposes and less of both classes of stock as well. By this means, coupled with the assessment, it proposed to raise nearly $7,000,000 more cash than the Olcott plan while reserving $25,383,000 more in bonds and substantial amounts of the stocks for additions, betterments, and improvements.

All these differences befitted the purpose of the committee to unify the diverse Terminal properties into an efficient operating system. No more than $2,500,000 of the bonds reserved for con-

---

40 *Ibid.,* 10, 23. The undisturbed securities are listed in *ibid.,* 18–19.

41 For a contemporary comparison of the two plans in slightly different terms, see New York *Evening Post,* May 31, 1893.

struction could be issued in any one year, although an additional $3,000,000 could be used for building branches or extensions if the building began within three years after the creation of the new mortgage and if the unanimous consent of the stock trustees was obtained. All property acquired with these bonds would come under the lien of the new mortgage, and no new mortgage or increase in the amount of preferred stock could be issued without the consent of a majority of the existing preferred.[42]

[42] *Morgan Plan,* 12–13. The new company also reserved the right to redeem its preferred at par at any time.

TABLE 16.   Comparative adjustments of selected securities under the Olcott and Morgan plans

Security		Olcott plan			Morgan plan		
		4% bonds	Pre-ferred	Com-mon	5% bonds	Pre-ferred	Com-mon
Terminal	6's	120	40		35	90	
	5's	100	10			70	30
	Preferred	100	20			35	65
	Common		10	100		12½	100 [a]
Danville	6's	120	45		100		
	Deb. 6's	120	30		100		
	5's	100	40		100	5	
	Eq. 5's	100	40		100		
Charlotte, Columbia & Augusta	1st 7's	105	50		100		
	2d 7's	110	50		100		
	6's	105	50		100	20	
Richmond, York River & Chesapeake	8's	120	20		100		
	6's	120	20		100		
Atlanta & Charlotte Air-Line	Pr. 7's	120	25		100		
	7's	120	40		100		
	Inc. 6's	100	40		100		
Northwestern North Carolina	6's	110	40		35	65	
Clarksville & North Carolina	6's	100	40		30	70	
Virginia Midland	Ser. 1 6's	120	45		100 [b]		
	5's	100	40		100		
Charlottesville & Rapidan		100	50		100		
Atlantic, Tennessee & Ohio	6's	100	50		100		

TABLE 16 (*cont.*)

Security		Olcott plan 4% bonds	Pre-ferred	Com-mon	Morgan plan 5% bonds	Pre-ferred	Com-mon
Chester & Lenoir	7's	100	40			100	
Columbia & Green-ville	1st 6's	105	50		100	20	
	2d 6's	100	20			120	
Spartanburg, Union & Columbia	5's	90			30	70	
Georgia Pacific	1st 6's	110	50		90	40	
	2d 5's	60	60			100	
Asheville & Spartan-burg	6's	80	20			40	60
Danville & Western	5's	80	20			100	
East Tennessee	1st 7's	120	35		100		
	1st 5's	105	50		100		
	Consol. 5's	100	50	25	100		
	Ext. 5's	100		20	25	80	
	Eq. 5's	100	20		60	70	
	Cin. Ext. 5's	90		25		125	
	1st Pref.	30	50	50		18	85 c
	2d Pref.		35	65		6	80 d
	Common			60		9	60 e
Knoxville & Ohio	6's	110	40		100		
Louisville Southern	5's	90		25	70	30	
Mobile & Birmingham	5's	100	20			50	50

SOURCES: Olcott and Morgan plans as reprinted in *Chronicle*, LIV (1892), 487–92, and LVI (1893), 874–86.

a On payment of $12.50 per share assessment.

b All six series of Virginia Midland bonds received 100 under the Morgan plan. The Olcott plan allotted them varying combinations ranging from 120 in bonds and 45 in preferred to 100 and 10 in each.

c On payment of $3.00 per share assessment.

d On payment of $6.00 per share assessment.

e On payment of $9.00 per share assessment.

The Morgan plan performed another valuable service in reorienting the Terminal toward developmental goals: it exposed the inconsistent and misleading accounting practices within both systems. Indeed, much of the confusion over the actual financial condition of the Danville and East Tennessee derived from an inability to decipher their books. On both systems, especially the Danville, there developed a tendency to swell net earnings by charging even ordinary maintenance to "construction" accounts instead of operating expenses. The Danville included in this account such items as rails and the *repair* of trestles, and the Louisville Southern went so far as to charge "construction" with $11,000

TABLE 17. Comparison of selected provisions from the Olcott and Morgan plans

Provision	Olcott plan	Morgan plan
1. Proposed bond issue	$170,000,000	$140,000,000
Needed for exchange	141,764,200 ª	96,617,000
2. Proposed preferred issue	70,000,000	75,000,000
Needed for exchange	63,617,470 ª	56,035,000
3. Proposed common issue	110,000,000	160,000,000
Needed for exchange	110,000,000 ª	104,349,000
4. Cash requirements	14,588,640	23,250,000
Bonds sold for cash	18,235,800	8,000,000
Preferred sold for cash	6,382,530	none
Common sold for cash	none	33,333,000
Cash raised by assessment	none	11,450,000
5. Cash reserved for improvements & additions	none	8,000,000
Bonds reserved for same	10,000,000 ᵇ	35,383,000 ᶜ
6. Proposed fixed charges	7,660,000	6,789,000

SOURCES: Olcott and Morgan plans as reprinted in *Chronicle*, LIV (1892), 487–92, and LVI (1893), 874–86.

ª This figure includes allotments for securities not provided for in plan in the following amounts: bonds, $7,817,245; preferred, $5,763,891; common, $4,839,346.

ᵇ These bonds were to be used for additions only.

ᶜ These bonds were to be used for additions, improvements, and extensions.

for *ditching!* Both roads carried numerous worthless accounts in their current assets. The Danville also listed as current assets all the money advanced to its leased lines even though in most cases it could entertain no hope of recovering these funds; on June 30, 1892, these advances totaled $7,990,634. Finally, the ledgers of both companies contained serious omissions. For example, the committee belatedly discovered that the Danville had outstanding about $1,200,000 in car trust notes which neither the company nor the receivers had bothered to record on the books.[43] All these practices the committee declared to be at an end. Henceforth accounts would be cleanly and clearly kept and maintenance properly charged off as operating expenses. Significantly, the plan calculated future net earnings on the basis of a 70 per cent operating

[43] For explication of these abuses, see *ibid.*, 23–33, and Henry V. Poor, *Manual of Railroads for 1893* (New York, 1893), 551. The car trust episode is noted in *Richmond and West Point Terminal Railway and Warehouse Company, and Its Subordinate Companies . . . Plan of Reorganization as Modified* (New York, 1894), 12, hereafter cited as *Modified Morgan Plan*. Copies of the plan are in Baker Library and the archives of the Southern Railway, and it is reprinted in *Chronicle*, LVIII (1894), 385–89.

ratio, a figure higher than any ever recorded for either main system prior to the depression year of 1892.[44]

The terms imposed by Morgan for effecting the reorganization were admittedly stiff. For their services the bankers would receive $750,000 in the new common stock at 15 and $100,000 for expenses. More important, the new stocks would be deposited with three trustees appointed by Drexel, Morgan to be held for five years and any further period until the preferred paid a 5 per cent dividend. During that time the new company would remain under the control of the House of Morgan to ensure unity of purpose and continuity of policy.[45]

In return for this generous fee and surrender of control what did the security holders receive? First and foremost they received a viable plan that promised not only to prevent destruction of their securities but offered the hope of converting them into a sound investment. Secondly they received the backing of one of the country's most powerful banking houses in implementing the plan. The familiar assertion that Morgan's immense prestige and influence was the most valuable commodity offered by his firm certainly rang true in the Terminal reorganization. Many contemporary observers attributed the company's hope of salvation precisely to the fact that Morgan had taken charge of it.[46]

The House of Morgan exerted this influence both internally and externally. In the latter sense it provided funds for the reorganization, helped support the market, arranged for the necessary loans, and most important, restored public confidence in the Terminal properties to a degree that few other houses could have matched. Internally Morgan forced the warring factions to accept a plan in advance of its formulation, and he could do this largely because the plan would be drawn up by an impartial outside observer.

Morgan's ability to win the confidence of the Terminal interests relied on more than mere trust in his abilities and fairness. In drawing up the plan his committee resorted to two shrewd devices

[44] *Morgan Plan,* 37; *Modified Morgan Plan.*

[45] *Morgan Plan,* 11–12. The trustees eventually appointed were Morgan himself, George F. Baker, and Charles Lanier. See *Chronicle,* LIX (1894), 836, 880.

[46] For contemporary analyses of the plan, see Jacksonville *Times-Union,* May 24, 1893; *Chronicle,* LVI (1893), 858–60; *Wall Street Journal,* May 25, 1893; *Wall Street Daily News,* May 25, 1893; New York *Evening Post,* May 25, 1893; Chicago *Tribune,* May 29, 1893; Augusta *Chronicle,* May 30, 1893; New York *Press,* June 13, 1893; Baltimore *News,* June 15, 1893.

to compel acceptance of its terms. First, he anticipated the objections of those interests receiving the harshest treatment by empowering the committee simply to exclude from the plan any road whose security holders raised serious objections. Knowing well how helpless these isolated properties would be if left to fend for themselves, the committee unabashedly waved the scalpel above every negotiation. Secondly, the committee constantly reminded the security holders that the only alternative to the Morgan plan was immediate disaster. Throughout the report it sprinkled warnings that rejection of the plan invited disaster; at one point the committee said of its plan that "the other alternative is a general dissolution of the component parts of the Richmond and Danville and East Tennessee systems—which is now *imminent*. This would be disastrous to *all* interests, and would practically mean the annihilation of the Terminal Company." [47]

To be sure, the plan contained some weaknesses, most of which have been noted by Daggett.[48] While it did reduce the debt-to-equity ratio, it did so by increasing total capitalization about 6 per cent. A more critical flaw concerned the fixed charges. The plan allowed a significant reduction in charges and buttressed it with substantial amounts of cash for improvements and additions. Even so, the committee estimated a surplus of earnings above fixed charges of only $936,000 for 1892 and $211,000 for 1893. So slender a margin of earnings could not possibly support the proposed policy of financing improvements from earnings (at least for awhile), and it certainly offered little hope for dividends on either class of stock. Small wonder, then, that Daggett concluded that "compared with previous fixed charges the plan proposed noteworthy deductions; compared with the earnings of the lines involved it did not go far enough." [49]

As a detached, objective appraisal Daggett's observations seem accurate. The difficulty lay in the politics of the situation, which limited the degree of pruning even Morgan could attempt. Most observers agreed that the plan as stated involved surgery of the most drastic kind, justified only by the urgency of the crisis. Be-

---

[47] *Morgan Plan*, 17. For other examples of such a threat, see *ibid.*, 4, 6–7, 10–12, 41.

[48] *Railroad Reorganization*, 183–84.

[49] *Ibid.*, 184. For various criticisms of specific points, see Brooklyn *Daily Eagle*, May 23, 1893; New York *Daily Investigator*, May 29, 1893; *Bradstreet's Journal*, June, 3, 1893.

yond the clear threat to drop several questionable properties from the plan altogether, it is highly unlikely that the committee could have gone much further than it did. As Table 16 demonstrates, the plan hit the weakest and most speculative securities hardest and seemed designed to purge the new company of its opportunistic elements. Holders of securities in those roads considered expendable were also hit hard and would soon become the shrillest opponents of the plan; they could not very well be asked to sacrifice anything more. The only remaining interests, those holders of securities deemed sound by the committee, did not respond to the plan with unanimous enthusiasm and would doubtless have resented any sizable sacrifice. Since their holdings comprised the most essential components of the proposed system, the committee could least afford to antagonize them as the Olcott plan had done.

In short, it appears that the Morgan plan was a well-conceived compromise between the ideal of what would constitute the best possible financial basis for the new company and the reality of an intricate and complex situation that curtailed possible alternatives. Perhaps it is more instructive to realize how much the plan did achieve than what it failed to achieve. It did offer a satisfactory financial reorganization for a company whose entire history had been marked by financial instability. It put an end to two years of rancorous stalemate that more than once despaired of reaching any workable solution. It swept away over thirty separate corporations and boards of directors, many of them often antagonistic and working at cross-purposes, and replaced them with one operating company under a unified management.

Most important of all, it succeeded in transforming the Terminal properties from essentially speculative to developmental enterprises. In setting up a system geared to operational efficiency, the committee took care to separate financial and operational responsibilities. The latter function would reside in the hands of experienced railroad men acquainted with the territories drained by the system. Financial questions would remain in the hands of the bankers controlling the board, who had little disposition to interfere with the president's operational policies unless they involved large outlays of capital. On the question of local identity the committee was equally adamant:

The new organization must adapt itself to these physical and commercial features, and preserve to each system such a clear degree of *local executive independence* in matters outside of purely financial questions, as shall insure the identification of each property with its territory from which its business is derived.[50]

Complications and Concessions

Part of the urgency surrounding the Morgan plan arose from the stagnating economic conditions. The audacity of Morgan in pushing so complicated a reorganization in the teeth of an impending depression brightened an otherwise gloomy Wall Street. The committee did not hesitate to use the dark economic situation to spur doubtful security holders. It presumed that prompt handling could complete all arrangements before the storm broke. Unable to foresee either the length or the severity of the depression, the committee miscalculated the ability of the receivers to maintain the properties during reorganization. As a result they were forced into concessions and modifications that weakened the plan at its most vulnerable points.[51]

In general the announcement of the plan failed to produce the expected rally in Terminal securities. The reason for this lay partly in the severity of the plan but mainly in the ragged condition of the market as a whole.[52] The anticipated opposition among those securities receiving the stiffest terms developed rapidly and prompted the committee to extend some concessions. By mid-June over 95 per cent of all Terminal securities had been deposited, leaving only the crucial underlying securities. The committee set a deadline of July 8 for the deposit. Faced with this deadline the remaining interests capitulated, the Louisville Southern bondholders being the last to surrender. Foreclosures on the Terminal and the two main systems began in July, with Samuel Spencer becoming coreceiver in each case.[53]

Almost immediately the deepening depression plunged the reorganization work into serious difficulties. Net earnings on the

[50] *Morgan Plan,* 9. The italics are in the original. Obviously this separation of financial and operational responsibility could lead to serious conflicts over policy.

[51] It seems clear that the committee, like many other financiers, anticipated that the general decline of financial and economic conditions would get worse. In *ibid.,* 36, for example, it estimated net earnings for the Terminal systems at $7,000,000 for 1893 compared with $7,800,000 for 1892.

[52] Cincinnati *Enquirer,* May 25, 1893; *Journal of Finance,* May 26, 1893; *Wall Street Daily News,* June 8, 1893.

[53] *Railroad Gazette,* XXV (1893), 444, 474, 514, 558; *Chronicle,* LVII (1893), 61, 105; New York *Sun,* June 28, 1893; *Journal of Finance,* June 22, 1893;

Terminal systems, as on most American systems, dropped sharply, totaling only $5,300,000 instead of the $7,000,000 estimated by the committee. Pessimistically the prediction for 1894 was lowered to $4,250,000. On these figures the committee could hardly hope to carry out its plan. The original assumption had been that the receivers could provide for the interest on all undisturbed securities and still accumulate enough money to handle interest on the readjusted securities. The decline in revenues, however, forced the receivers to default on several of the undisturbed securities without leaving anything for the readjusted securities. Further defaults were averted only by issuing receivers' certificates. In short order the committee found itself confronted with a large floating debt and a mounting pile of unpaid coupons, and the end was nowhere in sight.[54]

The impact of these changes rendered modifications of the plan inevitable. On February 20, 1894, the committee published a pamphlet announcing its proposed modifications. The gist of the report lay in three proposals. The first involved dropping from the plan several of the most burdensome roads. The Memphis & Charleston, Mobile & Birmingham, and both Erlanger roads had already been excluded before February; to this list the plan added seven smaller roads.[55] These omissions reduced the amount of new bonds needed from $140,000,000 to $120,000,000, of preferred stock $75,000,000 to $60,000,000, and of common stock $160,000,000 to $125,000,000. The effect of the over-all modification was to increase the company's capitalization in relative terms. It was clearly stipulated that additional securities could later be issued to reacquire any of the properties excluded from the plan, but not in amounts exceeding the totals of the original plan.[56]

Boston *Herald*, June 18, 1893; Savannah *Morning News,* June 17, 1893; New York *Herald,* May 27, 1893; Baltimore *Sun,* May 30, June 3, 1893; Richmond *Times,* June 6, 1893. For the concessions made by the committee, see *Chronicle,* LVI (1893), 1036–37. The foreclosure timetables are in Harrison, *Southern Railway,* 37–39, 105–6, 692–94.

[54] *Modified Morgan Plan,* 1, 14. For a brief description of conditions in the South, see *Eighth Annual Report of the Interstate Commerce Commission* (Washington, D.C., 1894), 20–24, and Joubert, *Southern Freight Rates,* 66–68.

[55] *Modified Morgan Plan,* 5. The roads excluded were Chester & Lenoir, Cheraw & Chester, Macon & Northern, Asheville & Spartanburg, Richmond & Mecklenburg, Spartanburg, Union & Columbia, and Northeastern of Georgia. The plan also proposed reducing charges on two roads, the Richmond, York River & Chesapeake and the Atlanta & Charlotte Air-Line.

[56] *Ibid.,* 11; Daggett, *Railroad Reorganization,* 185–86.

To ease the immediate crisis, the committee proposed to fund two years' worth of coupons on new bonds exchanged for some securities and to defer interest on other new bonds until 1895 or 1896. In most cases preferred stock would be given in exchange for the unpaid coupons. Thirdly, assessments on both Terminal and East Tennessee common were reduced 20 per cent, and all assessed stocks were allowed one-fourth in bonds and three-fourths in preferred instead of the entire amount in preferred. At the same time the committee granted further concessions to some securities, notably underlying bonds in the Danville system, which resulted primarily in the holders receiving additional preferred.[57]

Through these changes the committee hoped to raise the average earnings of the system while scaling down fixed charges beyond the calculations of the May plan. Assuming that half the new bonds to be sold were disposed of in 1894 and the other half in 1895, fixed charges were now estimated to be $4,100,000 in 1894, $4,700,000 in 1895, and $5,400,000 in 1896. These predictions proved sound. Under the modified plan only $8,000,000 in bonds and $25,000,000 in common would be sold to raise cash, and only about $19,000,000 in bonds would be reserved for construction, additions, and improvements. Of these only $2,000,000 could be used in one year instead of the $2,500,000 proposed in the original plan. Other provisions of the May plan remained unchanged.[58]

The modified plan plainly resembled a child of necessity. Its provisions aggravated the weaknesses inherent in the original in two ways: it left no more surplus for improvements and additions than its predecessor, and it significantly reduced the amount of bonds and cash available for betterments. Moreover, the modifications increased the new company's already high capitalization per mile by the following amounts: bonds, $20,000 to $22,000; preferred, $10,000 in both plans; and common, $25,000 to $26,000. A major reason for this increase lay in the concession of bonds to stockholders for one-fourth of their assessment which, along with the funding of coupons, was labeled "unsound financiering" by Daggett.[59]

Unsound it may have been, but for the moment it worked. Though weakening the plan as a whole, the modifications succeeded in preserving the reorganization through an hour of crisis.

[57] A complete list of modifications of specific securities is in *Modified Morgan Plan*, 7–10; see also *ibid.*, 1, 5.
[58] The financial provisions are given in *ibid.*, 11–14.
[59] *Railroad Reorganization*, 187.

Once again the committee larded its pamphlet with stern warnings that tardy acceptance of the revised plan would lead to its abandonment and disaster for all interests. Whatever its long-term shortcomings, the funding of two years' coupons on some bonds kept charges down until earnings revived. Within less than a month over 75 per cent of the bonds assented to the modifications.[60]

Once past this crisis, the committee began the long chain of foreclosure sales. Not until June 15 did the new Southern Railway Company organize under a Virginia charter with Spencer as the first president. By September 1 the new company possessed properties totaling 4,607 miles and owned bonds in another 184 miles. This did not include its holding in the Central, which still lacked a reorganization plan and a definable future. The voting trust was established on October 15. After two years of bickering and negotiating, the transformation of the Terminal into a unified operating company had been accomplished.[61]

The new Southern Railway profited enormously from the striking revival of business in the South after 1897. Within little more than a decade gross earnings of the company tripled and net earnings doubled. Accordingly it soon began to regain several of the roads excluded from the plan of 1894, acquiring the Alabama Great Southern in 1895, the Memphis & Charleston and Richmond & Mecklenburg in 1898, and the Cincinnati Southern, Northeastern of Georgia, and Mobile & Birmingham in 1899. Only the Central strayed from the fold for any length of time; the Southern disposed of its holdings in the reorganized company in 1907 and did not reacquire the system until 1963. By 1900 the Southern boasted a system of 7,717 miles, an increase of 3,110 miles in less than six years.[62]

Expansion and prosperity did not come without problems. Foremost among these was the familiar problem of modernizing the

[60] Even Daggett admitted that the funding enabled the company to survive until the depression passed. For a discussion of the modifications, see *Chronicle,* LVIII (1894) , 363–64.

[61] The final stages of reorganization can be followed in Harrison, *Southern Railway,* 40–48; *Railroad Gazette,* XXVI (1894) , 613; *Chronicle,* LVIII (1894) , 815, 1036, 1073, 1110, LIX (1894) , 192, 332, 515–16, 836. For relations with the Central, see *Chronicle,* LVIII (1894) , 1034, LIX (1894) , 74, 834.

[62] Daggett, *Railroad Reorganization,* 188–89; Harrison, *Southern Railway,* 70–76. In addition the Southern acquired the Mobile & Ohio and a half interest in the Monon. For reacquisition of the Central, see *Southern Railway Company: 70th Annual Report* (n.p., 1963) , 20.

systems. Despite the expenditure of large sums for improvements and new equipment, the Southern continued to provoke criticism for its imperfect condition and inability to handle the business offered it. Nothing attested to the Southern's physical shortcomings more dramatically than the death of Samuel Spencer in the collision of two passenger trains in 1906. Fairly massive sums of capital continued to flow into improvements during the next decade. Financially the Southern remained sound if not entirely secure. A host of factors conspired to keep the net surplus down: a high capitalization of about $72,000 per mile in the still relatively sparse territories of the South, inadequate facilities that drove the operating ratio as high as 76 per cent, and the old temptation to absorb less prosperous roads into the system. As a result dividends on preferred began in 1897 but remained a mirage for common.[63]

For better or worse the credit for guiding the derelict Terminal properties into a new era belonged to the House of Morgan. The feat of unraveling so intricate and controversial a problem launched Morgan toward his now familiar reputation as "The Doctor of Wall Street." While few if any of the principles contained in the Terminal reorganization were new in themselves, the pattern of the over-all plan and its successful implementation furnished a working model for the torrent of reorganizations occurring after the Panic of 1893. In this respect the Terminal reorganization became a landmark in Morgan's railroad activities. Small wonder, then, that his most laudatory biographer considered it the Master's greatest achievement, a "reorganization which will always stand out as the prime example of his peculiar ability for mastering a bewildering and apparently hopeless situation." [64] If intended as a monument the Southern proved an enduring one. Unlike most of its rivals it remains, more than seventy years after the reorganization, a powerful and independent system.

[63] Daggett, *Railroad Reorganization,* 190–91.
[64] Carl Hovey, *The Life Story of J. Pierpont Morgan* (New York, 1911), 228–29, 232.

Conclusion

The Terminal Experience in Retrospect

IN TERMS of his influence upon the Terminal's reorganization, it is tempting in retrospect to assert that if Morgan had not existed it would have been necessary to invent him. Such a view would over-simplify matters, of course, by implying either that no one else could have solved the Terminal enigma or that it could not have been done in some different manner. Yet the fact remains that the House of Morgan *did* accomplish the reorganization, and it did so after several of the most prominent and powerful houses on Wall Street abandoned the task. Few major banking firms (including Drexel, Morgan) went through the period without some association with the Terminal or its properties. In 1892 most of these firms showed little desire to take charge of the reorganization work or even, in some cases, to participate in the underwriting syndicate. Those that did attempt leadership failed conspicuously, and the Terminal itself contributed no one resembling a commanding figure to rescue it.

Much has been written about the role Morgan played in American economic life during the late nineteenth century. In broad terms the literature has emphasized, often unfavorably, such themes as the accession of banker control and its role in effecting economic concentration, the development of the "community of interest" idea, the stifling of competition, and the heavy tax imposed by the bankers for their services. While the degree of truth or accuracy of these notions in general is not at stake here, the Terminal experience does illuminate them as a specific test case. By the same token the culmination of the Terminal's history in banker control suggests quite a bit about the development of southern railroads as a whole. In short, both problems derive much of their broader significance from that point of convergence where the House of Morgan took command of the Richmond Terminal.

In analyzing the significance of that convergence it is helpful to recall two obvious but easily overlooked points: Morgan did not create the conditions that led to the call for his intervention, and once summoned he preformed valuable services that apparently could not be obtained elsewhere. The first of these points has in large measure been the subject of this book, for the Terminal clearly represented one kind of solution for the problems created by prevailing conditions in the economic environment. The second point becomes more meaningful when discussed within the hypothetical framework suggested in the first chapter and illustrated by the history of the Terminal and its component systems. For the sake of clarity, a brief recapitulation of that framework is useful.

Prior to the Civil War southern railroad development tended to be territorial and the investment motivation behind it developmental. The problems posed by the impact of war profoundly altered the prevailing economic environment, however, and fostered new conditions characterized most obviously by rapid expansion. Expansion brought heightened competition on one hand and internal conflict on the other as local economic interests resisted the movement toward interterritorial systems. Despite all resistance, these trends, aggravated by the depression of 1873, spurred the growth of interterritorial systems designed paradoxically to reduce competition in existing markets and to heighten it in more distant markets enjoying monopoly or near-monopoly status. The result was the coalescing of southern lines into a handful of giant systems that dominated the region's traffic despite a striking proliferation of smaller independent lines.

This pattern of response to the problems of the postwar economic environment produced some profound changes in that environment. Loss of territorial monopolies altered the very basis of profitable operation. Previously the carriers had been content to dominate their territory by hauling a modest traffic at high rates. Confronted with an ever-growing competition, they soon found it necessary to reverse the pattern completely by stressing a heavy tonnage carried at low rates. This in turn required the kind of operational efficiency that only the most modern equipment and facilities could obtain, but no major southern railroad possessed these requirements or the immediate resources to acquire them. At the same time interterritorial competition and the quest for new markets demanded expansion as well. As declining rates and rising costs narrowed the profit margin, the squeeze could be eased only by increased efficiency and a substantial growth in volume. Both modernization and expansion required large sums of capital; for that reason it should not be surprising to find that the men dominating southern railroads after 1880 were experienced not in practical railroad matters but in the mobilizing of capital.

Once in power, however, the financiers faced some difficult problems. The transition from territorial monopoly to interterritorial competition affected the social and political situation no less deeply than it did economic conditions. The rapid development of interterritorial systems inevitably caused a loss not only of local control but of local identity as well. The process of transforming a road from its earlier function as servant of local commercial interests to that of regional giant did not take place without bitter conflicts among the various antagonists. The financiers, usually of a younger generation than the previous managers, seldom possessed strong local ties or loyalties. To the great chess game of commercial rivalry among southern towns they came as self-interested neutrals anxious to profit from the vigorous struggle for supremacy.

In elevating the roads from their local status the financiers paid a heavy price in public resentment. For all their rhetoric to the contrary, the financiers could not conceal the problems posed by the new competitive situation. As the railroads gradually ceased their traditionally primary role as local servants, shippers and other local interests naturally took a less sanguine view of them. Their dependence upon the carriers had not diminished, but their control over them had. The specter of important decisions being made by unsympathetic strangers in distant places began to haunt local interests. If it suited the railroad to favor other commercial centers over their own town by discriminatory rates or new construction or other methods, the local interests were virtually powerless to affect the decision. As the local road became an impersonal regional corporation the power of arbitrating the fight for commercial supremacy passed increasingly from local hands to the burgeoning systems.

Small wonder, then, that disenchantment phased quickly into outright hostility. As local control slipped away, its former wielders and their allies responded vigorously with a series of social and legal actions designed to reverse or at least impede the process. This counterattack concentrated especially upon the two most obvious manifestations of the new situation: consolidation and rates. Restrictions against both were incorporated into state constitutions and statutes, and eventually the regulation of rates was entrusted to vigilant state commissions. Unwilling or unable to view the existing situation as the product of impersonal long-term forces, the guardians of local interests tended to personify the threat to their economic position in the form of the financiers currently shaping policy for the major southern roads. By seizing effectively upon the many overt and palpable abuses of financier control, the guardians succeeded in mobilizing public opinion against not only the individual transgressors but also against the whole pattern of railroad development in the region. They vowed to oust the trend as well as the rascals.

In this sense the financiers were as much creatures as creators of the situation in which they found themselves. Faced with the task of mobilizing capital for both modernization and expansion, they encountered opposition from a formidable array of local interests that ardently wanted the railroads but not on the terms being offered. Their position contained more than one element of irony. Operating in an environment relatively free of social restraint, the financiers confronted a variety of local opponents capable of invoking protective social measures should their cause fail. While the financiers did not lack political influence, the increasing scale of their operations prevented them from wielding it with equal authority in every state penetrated by their roads. The growing body of legislation on the consolidation and rate questions alone bore strong testimony to the fact that every victory by the financiers was achieved at the cost of additional legal restriction upon their activities. The extent to which the financiers managed to delay or evade these restrictions should not overshadow the latter's restraining effect. Even as mere nuisance value the law proved an expensive obstacle for the financier.

Strategically the prevailing economic and social environment posed two broad alternatives to southern railroad entrepreneurs. The limited available capital could be devoted primarily to increasing operational efficiency through modernization, or it could be used mainly for expansion by means of consolidation and construction. The first course was the more conservative in that it contented itself with handling a modest business as efficiently as possible while prudently allotting funds for expansion only when it did not impose a serious strain on the company's capital structure. The second course meant accepting the interterritorial approach completely by diverting virtually all capital into the quest for new markets. Such a strategy would of course deprive existing mileage of funds needed for betterments and result in the construction of new lines with inadequate equipment and facilities. The object was to compete in as many markets and develop as much traffic as possible regardless of the lack of equipment to handle the amount of business offered. Once extensions were built or bought they could gradually be modernized and equipped.

To be sure, these alternatives are theoretical extremes. No railroad manager fastened upon either one and pursued it rigidly; rather the course of a given company followed some variation between the extremes. The important point is that each company had to choose some shade of gray between the alternatives, and that choice powerfully influenced, if it did not dictate, company policy during the period from 1875 to 1893. In retrospect it is apparent that the first alternative was the safest choice for avoiding financial mismanagement and disaster. At the time, however, the pressures born of postwar conditions and the Panic of 1873 rendered the second alternative much more compelling and expedient. As a result most major southern roads pursued some variation of it, and those that did not grew progressively more insecure in their competitive position.

In terms of investment motivation, the first alternative proved to be the more developmental course and the second the more opportunistic. As noted earlier, prevailing economic conditions put an increasingly tighter squeeze on the operational profit margin. The roads best suited to resisting the pressures of steadily rising costs and declining rates were those lines endowed with relatively high efficiency and low fixed charges. The companies allocating most of their resources to expansion soon discovered that the cost of new mileage shoddily built and inadequately equipped simply could not be serviced by the earnings derived from it. Despite their penetration of new markets, the expansion-oriented companies could not compete effectively because of their comparative inefficiency. In many cases this inefficiency spread from newly acquired mileage to the main stem itself as funds badly needed for modernization and equipment were diverted to expansion. And the burden of debt produced by expansion left these roads especially vulnerable to financial disaster.

These conditions help explain the largely opportunistic nature of investment in the expansion-oriented roads. At a time when all southern roads found it increasingly difficult to make operational profits, the interterritorial systems faced the toughest task of all. Yet they required the most capital to implement their basic strategy. Obviously many of the financiers mobilizing this capital could not and did not expect their primary reward to come from long-term developmental goals that were uncertain at best. Quite naturally they turned their attention to profit from the process of expansion. The possibilities of personal gain seemed infinitely greater and more immediate from transactional and manipulative activity than from patient attempts to erect sound, efficient transportation systems. Thus occurred the crucial shift from developmental to opportunistic investment that characterized so much southern railroad activity after 1875.

It is precisely at this point that the Terminal provides insight into what was taking place. The holding company became the most ambitious vehicle devised for furthering opportunistic investment. It represented the opportunistic financier's best answer to the growing squeeze on operational profits. Within its nebulous framework lay manipulative possibilities that spurred fertile minds to new heights of imagination. Superficially the holding company served an important function as a device for promoting expansion. It enabled financiers to skirt legal restrictions against consolidation and provided a means for controlling a large number of lines with a relatively small amount of capital. It even yielded potentially good public relations in that the financiers could defend the company as a necessary instrument for achieving stability, efficiency, and economy of operation.

To the financiers, however, the practical importance of the holding company lay in its speculative versatility. It offered at once a sizable array of new securities eminently suitable for manipulation. At a higher level the vague structure of the company allowed transactional profits to flow freely from the construction, purchase, sale, or lease of any railroad or other property. In fact, the ease with which Terminal management personnel could occupy dual positions as buyers and sellers in a given transaction virtually invited financial abuse, as did the shadowy lines of responsibility between the holding company and its subsidiary properties.

This same vagueness of structure also permitted an appalling complexity of interrelationships to develop among the various component properties. Achieved primarily through a series of leases, these labyrinthian lines of control thoroughly obscured the obligations of the subsidiary roads to each other, to the parent systems, and to the Terminal. Ambiguity characterized the company's administrative hierarchy at every level, and it suited the financiers to perpetuate that condition. For one thing it shielded activities within the company from the prying eyes of outsiders. The persistent reputation of the Terminal as a corporate enigma derived from the inability of bewildered observers to unravel its inner relationships and responsibilities. At the same time it offered the most talented financiers the widest possible latitude for outfoxing their less gifted rivals or the uninformed general investor.

It should be emphasized that this line of development did not flow automatically from the holding company but rather from one particular use of it. As one of the first pure holding companies the Terminal was created for special purposes, and its creators could hardly have been expected to foresee the entire nature of the beast. To a large extent the Terminal experience became an exploration of possibilities, and while opportunism played an important role in its inception it need not necessarily have dominated the company's short life. Other contemporary holding companies like the Southern Railway Security Association, the Atlantic Coast Line, and the Plant Investment Company, though tinged with opportunism, drew their strength from the pursuit of essentially developmental goals.

In contrast the Terminal never outgrew the aura of speculation that surrounded its birth. While no financier could be categorized as exclusively opportunistic or developmental in his southern rail investments, it is apparent that no major figure made any substantial developmental commitment to the holding company itself. If such a commitment was made at all, it went to one of the main systems or even to one of their subsidiary roads. Interest in the Terminal thus tended to gravitate upward from a prior involvement in one of the subsidiaries, and it assumed two basic forms. Passively it sought simply to protect the developmental commitment from any financial aberrations within the Terminal. More actively it sought transactional and manipulative profits through use of the holding company's machinery. In either case the Terminal itself remained an orphan outside the pale of long-term commitment.

The inability to generate any real developmental commitment explains much of the frustration and failure inherent in the Terminal experience. For all the rosy prophesies and boastful claims of its officers, the holding company made very little progress toward unifying and integrating its properties. No unification took place because it suited the financiers in command to leave things pretty much as they were. The much-heralded campaigns for economy and efficiency of operation accomplished nothing because they were at best peripheral goals useful mainly for improving public relations. In fact any successful steps toward integration might seriously jeopardize the Terminal's opportunistic usefulness. No measurable strides toward the creation of a unified and efficient operating system could be made as long as the Terminal remained in the hands of men interested primarily in short-term profits and unwilling to make any substantial developmental commitment.

Obviously the Terminal could not survive indefinitely as an opportunistic facility, especially in an economic and social environment growing steadily more uncongenial to the inefficient operation of railroads. Even before the Panic of 1893 it collapsed beneath the weight of its own history, a harbinger of the fate awaiting similar companies during the coming decades. The Terminal failed because the railroads controlled by it could scarcely support their own obligations, much less sustain the burden of the holding company as well. The ensuing wreckage contained a host of securities radically differing in value and importance to the future of the railroads themselves. Long promoted as a device for achieving unity of interests, the ruined Terminal threatened to effect a general disintegration of its systems. Any hope of preserving the properties intact depended almost entirely upon transforming the company from an opportunistic to a developmental investment.

This in essence was the most important service performed by the House of Morgan. The firm's reorganization plan rested solidly on the assumption that it could succeed only by fashioning as efficient a transportation system as possible out of the ramshackle collection of roads possessed by the Terminal. The plan thus served as a vital bridge in the Terminal's history by providing an orderly transition from its essentially opportunistic past to a hopefully developmental future. Nothing illustrated this intention more clearly than the committee's insistence that fixed charges on each road be revised according to its earning capacity. Other evidence suggests the committee's determination on this point. The plan disposed of the holding company entirely and of over thirty separate boards of directors. In their place the committee installed one operating company staffed by professional railroad men and possessing clear lines of authority over the whole system. The accounting catacombs made possible by the existence of so many different companies lacking uniform bookkeeping procedures were replaced by one set of books kept according to standardized formats. Numerous lesser details followed the same direction.

In this light it is interesting to note that the principal opponents to the Morgan intervention from the beginning were the more opportunistic elements within the company. Part of their resentment doubtless arose from a reluctance to surrender control to "outsiders." Another part, however, may be explained by their unwillingness to extend their commitment to a long-term investment. Once Morgan took charge, most of the opportunists departed speedily; the principal investors who remained did so in a passive role and on a developmental basis. Thomas provides a fascinating example in this respect. After an initial opportunistic investment, the general plunged deeper into East Tennessee affairs until his commitment became so extensive that he could not easily withdraw in the face of impending depression. Moreover, his growing involvement in investments sequential to the railroad made him all the more reluctant to sever his ties with the East Tennessee. By the late 1880's his commitment strongly resembled a developmental one, a fact that did not entirely please the general. As a result his behavior during the ordeal of reorganization followed an erratic course before finally coming to terms with the Morgan approach.

From this perspective, then, the Morgan reorganization ushered the Terminal properties into a new era. Whatever its specific shortcomings, the plan accomplished this vital task faithfully and satisfactorily. The subsequent problems of the Southern Railway belonged not so much to the plan itself as to the complex events that led to the reorganization. Heavy capitalization, inadequate facilities and equipment, lack of modernization that kept operating ratios high, and the difficulty of obtaining ample funds from earnings to provide for improvements and dividends all were problems inherent in the process by which the Terminal systems arose. If Morgan did not adequately solve these problems it was because even he could not reverse forty years of complex historical development. What he could do was ease the Terminal lines as much as possible from beneath the weight of their collective history and start them down a new path governed by different standards and goals.

There remain unanswered several closely related questions implicit in this study: the role of social overhead, the long-standing conflict between social gains and private interest, and the evaluation of the end product in terms of its cost in human and material resources. Satisfactory answers to these questions have long been the despair of economists, historians, and social philosophers alike. Julius Grodinsky, in his intensive study *Transcontinental Railway Strategy, 1869–1893,* concluded in his preface that "the story is typical of a growing industry in its pioneering stage. Competition then and now works itself out in a similar fashion. Some businessmen gain, some lose—but the public benefits. It got the railroads."

The brutal simplicity of this logic is at once disarming and dissatisfying. It bespeaks a helpless acquiescence to the sheer fact of history as sufficient reason for its results. Most frustrating of all, it shuts out alternatives quite naturally by consigning them to the murky realm of "might have been." The rigors and results of unrestrained capitalism in nineteenth-century America continue to be catalogued and dissected. Protests against both the process and product of that development continue to mount but fail to solve the problem of viable alternatives. It would be pleasant to suppose that the Terminal experience suggested some means of penetrating Grodinsky's inexorable conclusion; unfortunately it succeeded only in reinforcing it. Nevertheless it is tempting to pose the obvious questions: Did the public want the railroads? Did it want them at the price paid? Were there any feasible alternatives to the path of economic development taken? But these and other questions like them are another story, perhaps another book.

Appendixes

APPENDIX I. Selected Data from the Richmond & Danville Balance Sheet
(all figures except miles in 1,000's)

Year	Miles	Total assets	Capital stock	Funded debt	Dues and accts.[a]	Interest and taxes	Dividends	Profit and loss[b]
1866	148	$ 7,302	$2,000	$ 1,718	$ 792	$ 224	0	$2,672
1867	148	7,684	4,000	1,902	836	225	0	3,020
1868	148	8,269	4,000	2,612	174	193	0	1,858
1869	148	8,816	4,000	2,681	229	196	0	1,906
1870	148	8,767	4,000	2,582	229	56	0	1,900
1871	148	8,868	4,000	2,491	367	74	0	1,936
1872	148	7,256	4,000	2,510	573	173	0	(55)
1873	148	8,065	4,000	2,485	1,307	129	0	143
1874	148	8,555	4,000	2,478	1,256	221	0	599
1875	148	8,371	4,000	3,593	654	75	0	49
1876	151	8,306	4,000	3,713	508	84	0	(128)
1877	151	8,298	3,866	3,879	458	94	0	(201)
1878	152	8,446	3,866	4,132	261	186	0	(312)
1879	152	8,267	3,866	4,116	198	87	0	(93)
1880	152	8,369	3,866	4,066	238	75	0	124
1881	449	10,097	3,866	4,311	933	75	$116 [c]	910
1882	744	14,048	5,000	5,904	1,846	263	450 [c]	1,034
1883	757	14,385	5,000	6,715	1,477	196	0	997
1884	757	14,778	5,000	7,035	1,202	431	0	1,110
1885	757	17,266	5,000	9,385	850	671	0	1,360
1886	774	19,161	5,000	9,467	1,732	1,430	0	1,531
1887	774	19,536	5,000	10,199	1,756	677	150	1,903
1888	774	21,841	5,000	11,775	1,694	985	150	2,386
1889	774	22,751	5,000	12,141	2,001	1,000	500	2,609
1890	751	25,598	5,000	13,461	3,255	1,110	500	2,771
1891	751	29,631	5,000	14,191	5,747	1,180	500	3,513
1892	750	35,079	5,000	16,361	7,977	1,664	250	4,078
1893	741	35,167	5,000	16,403	7,802	88 [d]	0	4,875

SOURCES: *Richmond & Danville Reports*, 1866–93; Henry V. Poor, *Manual of the Railroads of the United States* (New York, 1867–94).

Data represents only the Danville system proper and does not include roads controlled but operated as separate companies.

a These figures include bills payable and dues and accounts.

b Deficit figures are indicated in parentheses.

c Amount is estimated.

d This figure does not include receiver's account of $999,495. Unpaid accrued interest on the entire system was $2,911,953.

APPENDIX II. Selected Data on Richmond & Danville Operations

Year	Avg. miles oper.	Gross earn.[a]	Net earn.[a]	Net earn. minus i.t. & d.[b]	Operating ratio[c] (%)	Earn. per ton-mile[d] (cents)	Cost per ton-mile[e] (cents)	Tons freight carried[f]	Dividend rate (%)
1866	196	$ 673	$ 285	$ 61	57.7	9.85	6.04	68	0
1867	196	640	280	55	56.2	6.74	3.63	82	0
1868	196	574	219	26	61.8	6.05	3.68	89	0
1869	196	609	257	61	57.8	5.99	3.67	99	0
1870	196	692	224	168	67.5	5.60	3.84	121	0
1871	196	758	334	260	54.6	5.61	2.66	161	0
1872	196	834	364	191	56.4	4.97	2.49	177	0
1873	196	957	447	318	53.3	4.84	2.54	228	0
1874	224	926	328	107	64.6	4.04	2.60	198	0
1875	224	923	323	248	65.0	3.49	2.31	221	0
1876	224	937	438	354	53.7	3.38	1.89	228	0
1877	224	909	293	199	67.8	2.89	1.91	239	0
1878	224	942	311	125	67.0	2.85	1.80	236	0
1879	224	1,099	500	413	54.7	2.42	1.18	308	0
1880	224	1,243	498	423	59.9	2.16	1.28	370	0
1881	224	1,376	647	456	55.9	2.03	.99	406	3
1882	224	1,452	587	(126)	59.6	na	na	470	9
1883	224	1,554	809	613	48.0	na	na	530	0
1884	224	1,576	814	383	48.5	na	na	542	0
1885	755	3,981	1,750	1,079	56.1	na	na	1,452	0
1886	755	3,992	1,871	441	53.1	na	na	1,500	0
1887	755	4,153	1,865	1,038	55.1	na	na	1,672	3
1888	755	4,510	1,941	806	57.0	1.71	1.03	2,243	3
1889	755	5,109	2,279	779	55.4	1.48	1.02	2,402	10
1890	755	5,601	2,489	879	55.6	1.38	.99	2,777	10
1891	755	5,947	2,938	1,258	50.6	1.42	.95	2,970	10
1892	755	5,945	2,997	1,083	49.6	1.36	.93	2,946	5
1893	755	5,146	1,741	1,653	66.1	1.21	.93	3,057	0

Sources: Same as Appendix I.

Changes in accounting methods, realignment of roads included in returns, and alterations caused in change of administrations render accurate and complete data virtually impossible. The above figures pertain to those lines designated in reports as comprising the Danville main stem system. The "auxiliary" system, which includes a host of roads, is not included here.

Na: No data available.

[a] All figures are given in 1,000's and rounded to nearest thousand.

[b] This figure is obtained by subtracting interest, taxes, and dividends from net earnings. Figures are rounded to nearest thousand.

[c] This figure is the ratio of operating expenses to gross earnings.

[d] These are average earnings per ton per mile.

[e] This is average cost per ton per mile.

[f] Figures are given in 1,000's and rounded to nearest thousand.

APPENDIX III. Selected Data from the East Tennessee, Virginia & Georgia Balance Sheet (all figures except miles in 1,000's)

Year	Miles	Total assets	Capital stock	Funded debt	Dues and accts.	Interest and taxes	Divi-dends	Profit and loss
1869	272	$ 7,430	$ 1,943	$ 5,032	$ 455	$ 304	0	na
1870	272	9,777	1,970	5,019	235	318	0	$2,553
1871	272	9,527	1,970	3,581	245	282	0	3,731
1872	272	9,764	1,970	3,890	169	267	0	3,735
1873	272	9,925	1,968	4,192	95	277	0	3,638
1874	272	9,968	1,968	4,205	96	280	$118	3,666
1875	272	9,926	1,968	4,203	113	281	59	3,607
1876	272	9,935	1,968	4,208	106	281	59	3,619
1877	272	10,044	1,968	4,110	296	284	0	3,533
1878	272	9,803	1,967	4,186	185	287	59	3,424
1879	272	10,058	1,967	4,186	300	280	59	3,466
1880	272	10,321	1,967	4,186	457	283	157	3,592
1881	902	82,500	44,000	38,500	na	386	209	436
1882	902	84,608	44,000	38,500	2,108	1,283	0	na
1883	1,023	95,391	44,000	49,020	1,789	1,501	0	(184)
1884	1,023	88,272	44,000	43,264	1,008	1,403	0	(1,000)
1885	1,023	88,758[a]	44,000	40,699	1,951[b]	1,531	0	(421)
1886	1,033	na[a]	57,000	20,000	na	1,467	0	na
1887	1,033	78,958	57,000	20,000	1,423[b]	832	440	535
1888	1,033	79,928	57,000	21,000	1,225[b]	1,104	550	703
1889	1,067	82,063	57,000	23,500	842[b]	1,242	550	720
1890	1,100	94,184	57,000	35,240	1,109[b]	1,367	550	835
1891	1,231	97,351	57,000	36,960	2,834[b]	1,890	550	556
1892	1,265	99,855	57,000	39,000	3,855[b]	1,972	220	(534)
1893	1,265	99,346[a]	57,000	39,000	3,346[b]	1,406	0	(734)

Sources: *East Tennessee, Virginia & Georgia Reports*, 1869–93; Poor, *Manual of Railroads*, 1867–94.
Data represents only the East Tennessee system proper and does not include roads controlled but operated as separate companies. All headings and symbols are the same as in Appendix I.
[a] The company was in receivership.
[b] This figure includes car trust certificates.

APPENDIX IV.   Selected Data on East Tennessee, Virginia & Georgia Operations

Year	Avg. miles oper.	Gross earn.	Net earn.	Net earn. minus i.t. & d.	Operating ratio (%)	Earn. per ton-mile (cents)	Cost per ton-mile (cents)	Tons freight carried	Divi-dend rate (%)
1869	272	$1,053	$ 364	$ 60	65.4 a	na	na	na	0
1870	272	1,279	416	98	67.5	4.41	na	172	0
1871	272	1,285	282	0	78.1	na	na	186	0
1872	272	1,201	367	100	69.5	na	na	172	0
1873	272	1,378	449	172	67.4	na	na	222	0
1874	272	1,111	414	16	62.8	na	na	192	6
1875	272	1,060	342	2	67.7	na	na	187	3
1876	272	994	325	(15)	67.6	1.25	na	198	3
1877	272	1,010	341	57	66.2	na	na	219	0
1878	272	1,022	410	64	59.9	1.71	na	239	3
1879	272	988	368	29	62.5	1.54	na	273	3
1880	272	1,213	436	(4)	64.1	1.75	na	377	3
1881	506	2,118	955	360	54.9	na	na	na	3
1882	902	3,145	1,283	0	59.2	na	na	na	0
1883	902	3,777	1,318	(183)	59.2	1.51	na	1,350	0
1884	1,104	4,173	1,700	297	59.2	1.37	na	1,519	0
1885	1,104	3,694	1,190	(341)	67.8	1.19	.79	1,437	0
1886	1,104	3,778	1,374	(93)	63.6	1.14	.71	1,535	0
1887	1,104	4,368	1,467	195	66.4	1.03	.66	1,947	4 b
1888	1,104	5,110	1,843	189	63.9	.97	.58	2,365	5 b
1889	1,104	5,302	1,927	135	63.7	.91	.56	2,628	5 b
1890	1,104	6,412	2,236	319	65.1	.87	.56	3,229	5 b
1891	1,265	6,719	2,263	(177)	66.3	.91	.61	3,344	5 b
1892	1,265	6,049	1,198	(994)	80.2	.87	.68	3,124	2 b
1893	1,265	5,769	1,518	112	73.9	.85	.60	3,124	0

Sources: Same as Appendix III.
See general note to Appendix II. All headings and symbols are the same as in Appendix II.
a This is an estimated figure.
b This was a dividend on first preferred stock only.

APPENDIX V. Selected Data from the Central of Georgia Balance Sheet

Year	Miles	Total assets	Capital stock	Funded debt	Dues and accts.	Interest and taxes [a]	Dividends	Profit and loss
1866	284	$ 8,422	$4,667	$ 786	$ 184	$ 205	$ 0	$ 285
1867	284	7,740	4,667	786	39	142	27	(5)
1868	284	7,684	4,667	786	46	137	560 [b]	176
1869	284	7,813	4,667	786	113	142	467 [b]	(251)
1870	284	9,279	4,667	789	84	308	467 [b]	130
1871	284	8,871	5,000	789	54	318	500 [b]	93
1872	284	10,392	5,000	1,389	352	616	500 [b]	402
1873	284	14,546	7,500	2,966	380	547	0	112
1874	709	13,692	7,500	3,731	396	599	300 [b]	(143)
1875	709	15,180	7,500	3,872	81	841	0	143
1876	714	14,758	7,500	3,339	201	779	0	(894)
1877	714	14,418	7,500	3,617	342	695	0	(601)
1878	714	14,906	7,500	3,617	457	719	375 [b]	(749)
1879	714	15,151	7,500	3,617	422	712	0	(845)
1880	714	15,317	7,500	3,852	188	707	450	(857)
1881	722	21,770	7,500	8,352	1,990	716	0 [e]	(277)
1882	730	22,663	7,500	9,600	2,270	1,011	600	715
1883	730	22,361	7,500	9,600	1,416	788	600	195
1884	730	22,555	7,500	9,600	2,124	1,066	450	325
1885	708	23,811	7,500	9,600	2,240	1,286	375	(316)
1886	708	23,311	7,500	9,600	3,398	1,286	300	(491)
1887	981	27,984	7,500	14,599	3,190	1,342	600	(984)
1888	1,001	26,697	7,500	14,599	2,038	1,586	600	(726)
1889	1,001	26,954	7,500	14,479	2,481	2,116	600	770
1890	1,001	28,357	7,500	14,479	3,989	1,881	600	808
1891	1,001	27,409	7,500	14,479	5,602 [d]	2,069	563	(432)
1892	1,001	na [e]	7,500	14,479	12,222 [d]	na	0	na [e]
1893	1,001	30,658 [e]	7,500	14,479	11,435 [d]	2,558 [b]	0	(375)

SOURCES: *Central of Georgia Reports*, 1866–93; Poor, *Manual of Railroads*, 1867–94.
Data represents only the Central of Georgia system proper and does not include roads controlled but operated as separate companies. All headings and symbols are the same as in Appendix I.
[a] These figures include rental obligations on subsidiary roads.
[b] Amounts are estimated.
[e] This figure does not include special 40 per cent certificate of indebtedness dividend.
[d] This figure includes car trust and equipment notes.
[e] The company was in receivership.

APPENDIX VI. Selected Data on Central of Georgia Operations

Year	Avg. miles oper.	Gross earn.	Net earn.	Net earn. minus i.t. & d.	Operating ratio (%)	Earn. per ton-mile (cents)	Cost per ton-mile (cents)	Tons freight carried	Dividend rate (%)
1866	151	$1,628	$ 713	$ 509	56.2 [a]	na	na	na	0
1867	284	2,286	911	742	60.6	na	na	na	12
1868	284	2,009	765	68	61.9 [a]	na	na	na	12
1869	542	3,235	1,342	733	57.8 [a]	na	na	na	10
1870	542	3,764	1,299	524	66.5	na	na	na	10
1871	542	3,689	1,455	636	60.8	na	na	na	10
1872	644	3,324	1,186	71	58.4	na	na	na	10
1873	725	3,477	1,121	574	61.7	na	na	na	0
1874 [b]	725	3,100	283	(616)	71.6	na	na	na	4
1875	725	2,878	1,201	360	53.2	na	na	na	0
1876	729	2,601	983	204	57.9	na	na	na	0
1877	729	2,440	842	147	67.3	na	na	na	0
1878	729	2,721	1,123	29	59.1	na	na	na	2.5
1879	729	2,825	1,209	497	57.2	na	na	na	0
1880	729	3,191	1,538	380	52.0	na	na	na	6
1881	729	3,708	1,389	673	62.7	na	na	na	0
1882	729	3,439	1,047	(564)	70.1	na	na	na	8
1883	729	3,637	1,316	(72)	64.7	na	na	842 [c]	8
1884	729	3,236	1,029	(486)	68.7	na	na	1,432 [c]	6
1885	729	3,269	990	(671)	69.6	na	na	1,277 [c]	5
1886	739	3,402	1,349	(237)	61.0	na	na	na	4
1887	739	3,676	1,584	(358)	55.2	1.95	na	na	8
1888 [b]	739	3,785	1,699	(487)	56.5	1.89	.75	1,738	8
1889	706	4,084	1,568	(1,148)	64.9	2.04	1.21	1,329	8
1890	718	4,537	1,293	(1,189)	72.3	1.90	1.43	2,345	8
1891	718	4,332	1,170	(1,462)	75.4	1.53	na	na	7.5
1892 [d]	718	1,853	455	na	66.1 [a]	na	na	na	0
1893	718	3,876	876	(1,682)	87.5	1.25	.96	na	0

SOURCES: Same as Appendix V.
See general note to Appendix II. Gross and net earnings include those lines designated in reports as the Central main stem and the Southwestern system. Deductions for interest and rentals include payments for some auxiliary lines whose earnings are not included here. All other data pertains only to the Central main stem except where noted otherwise. All headings and symbols are the same as in Appendix II.

[a] Figure is estimated.

[b] Fiscal year changed. Figures represent twelve months in each case except 1874, where only nine months of Southwestern earnings are included.

[c] Figure includes both Central and Southwestern.

[d] Figures represent only seven months' earnings.

Bibliography

Bibliography

THE following list is not intended to be complete or comprehensive, and therefore does not include many works cited in the footnotes as references for specific points. This bibliography is rather a compilation of the materials consulted most frequently in this study.

Manuscript Collections

Edward Porter Alexander papers, Southern Historical Collection, University of North Carolina
Alexander-Hillhouse papers, Southern Historical Collection
Edward C. Anderson papers, Southern Historical Collection
Alexander Boyd Andrews papers, Southern Historical Collection
Joseph M. Brown Letterbooks, Emory University Library
Grover Cleveland papers, Library of Congress
Dun & Bradstreet Credit Reports, Baker Library, Harvard Graduate School of Business Administration
Albert Fink papers, Library of Congress
William W. Gordon papers, Southern Historical Collection
Henry W. Grady papers, Emory University Library
Fairfax Harrison papers, Virginia Historical Society
Ingraham Genealogical papers, Library of Congress
Alexander R. Lawton papers, Southern Historical Collection
Thomas M. Logan papers, Southern Historical Collection
Charles M. McGhee papers, Lawson-McGhee Library, Knoxville, Tenn.
William G. Raoul papers, Emory University Library
Richmond & West Point Terminal Railway and Warehouse Company, minutes of directors' and annual meetings and other records, archives of Southern Railway Company, Washington, D.C.
David Schenck papers, Southern Historical Collection
Samuel Spencer papers, Southern Historical Collection

Books

Ackerman, W. K. *Illinois Central Railroad: A Historical Sketch*. Chicago, 1890.

Adams, Charles F. *Railroads: Their Origins and Problems.* New York, 1878.

Adler, Cyrus. *Jacob Schiff: His Life and Letters.* New York, 1929.

Alexander, Edward P. *Railway Practice.* New York, 1907.

Biographical Dictionary of the State of New York. New York, 1900.

Black, Robert C., III. *The Railroads of the Confederacy.* Chapel Hill, N.C., 1952.

Bonbright, James C. *Railroad Capitalization.* New York, 1920.

——, and Gardner Means. *The Holding Company.* New York, 1932.

Brown, Cecil Kenneth. *A State Movement in Railroad Development.* Chapel Hill, N.C., 1928.

Brownson, Howard. *History of the Illinois Central Railroad to 1870.* Urbana, Ill., 1915.

Bryan, John S. *Joseph Bryan: A Memoir.* Richmond, 1935.

Campbell, E. G. *The Reorganization of the American Railroad System.* New York, 1938.

Clark, Thomas D. *The Beginning of the L. & N.* Louisville, Ky., 1933.

Clarke, Malcolm. *First Quarter Century of the Richmond & Danville, 1847–1871.* Washington, D.C., 1959.

Cleveland, Frederick, and Fred Powell. *Railroad Finance.* New York, 1912.

——. *Railroad Promotion and Capitalization in the United States.* New York, 1909.

Clews, Henry. *Twenty-Eight Years in Wall Street.* New York, 1888.

Colton, Henry E. *The East Tennessee, Virginia & Georgia Railway System: Its Resources.* N.p., 1890.

Corliss, Carlton J. *Main Line of Mid-America.* New York, 1950.

Cumming, Mary. *The Georgia Railroad and Banking Company, 1833–1945.* Augusta, Ga., 1945.

Daggett, Stuart. *Railroad Reorganization.* Cambridge, Mass., 1908.

Derrick, Samuel. *Centennial History of the South Carolina Railroad.* Columbia, S.C., 1930.

Dewing, A. S. *The Financial Policy of Corporations.* New York, 1953.

Doster, James F. *Railroads in Alabama Politics, 1875–1914.* Tuscaloosa, Ala., 1957.

——. *Alabama's First Railroad Commission, 1881–85.* Tuscaloosa, Ala., 1945.

Dozier, H. D. *A History of the Atlantic Coast Line Railroad.* Cambridge, Mass., 1920.

Ferguson, Maxwell. *State Regulation of Railroads in the South.* New York, 1916.

Fishlow, Albert. *American Railroads and the Transformation of the Ante-bellum Economy.* Cambridge, Mass., 1965.

Ginger, Ray. *The Age of Excess.* New York, 1965.

Grodinsky, Julius. *Jay Gould.* Philadelphia, 1957.

——. *Transcontinental Railway Strategy, 1869–1893.* Philadelphia, 1962.

Haines, Henry. *Problems in Railway Legislation.* New York, 1911.

Hall, C. C. (ed.). *Baltimore: Its History and People.* New York, 1912.

Hall, Charles (ed.). *The Cincinnati Southern.* Cincinnati, 1902.

Hampton, Taylor. *The Nickel Plate Road.* New York, 1947.

Haney, Lewis. *A Congressional History of Railways in the United States, 1850–1888.* Madison, Wis., 1910.

Harrison, Fairfax. *A History of the Legal Development of the Southern Railway Company.* Washington, D.C., 1901.

Hungerford, Edward. *The Story of the Baltimore & Ohio Railroad, 1827–1927.* New York, 1928.

Johnson, Arthur M., and Barry E. Supple. *Boston Capitalists and Western Railroads.* Cambridge, Mass., 1967.

Johnson, Emory. *American Railway Transportation.* New York, 1909.

——, and Thurman Van Metre. *Principles of Railroad Transportation.* New York, 1918.

Johnston, James. *Western and Atlantic Railroad of the State of Georgia.* Atlanta, 1931.

Joubert, William. *Southern Freight Rates in Transition.* Gainesville, Fla., 1949.

Kerr, John L. *The Louisville & Nashville: An Outline History.* New York, 1933.

Kolko, Gabriel. *Railroads and Regulation.* Princeton, N.J., 1965.

Milton, Ellen Fink. *A Biography of Albert Fink.* Rochester, N.Y., 1951.

National Cyclopedia of American Biography. New York, 1898–1963.

Nixon, Raymond. *Henry W. Grady: Spokesman of the New South.* New York, 1943.

Phillips, U. B. *A History of Transportation in the Eastern Cotton Belt to 1860.* New York, 1913.

Prince, Richard. *Georgia Railroads and West Point Route.* Salt Lake City, 1962.

Ratner, Sidney. *New Light on the History of Great American Fortunes.* New York, 1953.

Ripley, William Z. *Railroads: Finance and Organization.* New York, 1915.

——. *Railroads: Rates and Regulations.* New York, 1927.

—— (ed.). *Railway Problems.* Boston, 1907.

Smith, Robert H. *General William Mahone, Fredrick J. Kimball and Others: A Short History of the Norfolk & Western Railway.* New York, 1949.

Smyth, G. W. *Henry B. Plant.* New York, 1898.

Snyder, Carl. *American Railways as Investments.* New York, 1907.

Sparkes, Boyden, and Samuel Taylor Moore. *Hetty Green: The Witch of Wall Street.* New York, 1935.

Spearman, Frank. *The Strategy of Great Railroads.* New York, 1905.

Stover, John. *Railroads of the South, 1865–1900.* Chapel Hill, N.C., 1955.

Stover, John. *American Railroads.* Chicago, 1961.
Taylor, George R., and Irene Neu. *The American Railroad Network, 1861–1900.* Cambridge, Mass., 1956.
Thomas, Henry. *Digest of the Railroad Laws of Georgia.* Atlanta, 1895.
Thompson, C. Mildred. *Reconstruction in Georgia, 1865–72.* New York, 1915.
Tyler, L. G. (ed.). *Encyclopedia of Virginia Biography.* New York, 1915.
Van Oss, S. F. *American Railroads as Investments.* New York, 1893.
Woodward, C. Vann. *Origins of the New South.* Baton Rouge, La., 1951.
———. *Tom Watson: Agrarian Rebel.* New York, 1938.

Articles

Fish, Carl R., "The Restoration of Southern Railroads," *University of Wisconsin Studies in the Social Sciences and History,* No. 2 (Madison, Wis., 1919).
Holland, James W., "The East Tennessee and Georgia Railroad, 1836–1860," *Publications of the East Tennessee Historical Society,* III (1931), 89–107.
Hudson, Henry, "The Southern Railway and Steamship Association," *Quarterly Journal of Economics,* V (Oct., 1891), 70–94.
Klein, Maury, "Southern Railroad Leaders, 1865–1893: Identities and Ideologies," *Business History Review,* XLII (Autumn, 1968), 288–310.
———, "The Strategy of Southern Railroads, 1865–1893," *American Historical Review,* LXXIII (April, 1968), 1052–68.
———, and Kozo Yamamura, "The Growth Strategies of Southern Railroads, 1865–1893," *Business History Review,* XLI (Winter, 1967), 358–77.
Martin, S. Walter, "Henry Bradley Plant," in Horace Montgomery (ed.), *Georgians in Profile: Historical Essays in Honor of E. M. Coulter* (Athens, Ga., 1958), 261–76.
Potter, David M., "Historical Development of Eastern-Southern Freight Rate Relationships," *Law and Contemporary Problems,* XII (Summer, 1947), 416–48.
Turner, Charles W., "Virginia Railroad Development, 1845–1860," *The Historian,* X (Autumn, 1947), 43–62.

Periodicals, Manuals, and Newspapers

American Railroad Journal
Atlanta *Constitution*
Augusta *Chronicle and Constitutionalist*
Baltimore *Sun*
Bradstreet's Journal

Commercial and Financial Chronicle
Handbook of Financial Securities
Macon *Telegraph*
New York *Herald*
New York *Indicator*
New York *Journal of Finance*
New York *Sun*
New York *Times*
New York *Tribune*
New York *World*
Poor's Manual of the Railroads of the United States, 1867–1895
Railroad Gazette
Railway World
Richmond *Dispatch*
Richmond *Times*
Savannah *Morning News*
Savannah *Evening Press*
Wall Street Daily News
Wall Street Journal

United States Government Publications

U.S., Bureau of the Census. *Historical Statistics of the United States, Colonial Times to 1957.* Washington, D.C., 1960.
U.S., Bureau of Statistics. *Annual Reports on the Internal Commerce of the United States.* Washington, D.C., 1877–93.
U.S., Congress. "Southern Railroads," *House Reports,* 40 Cong., 2d sess., 1868, No. 3, I, 1–130.
Reports of the Industrial Commission. Washington, D.C., 1900–1902.

Railroad Annual Reports [1]

Atlanta & Charlotte Air-Line, 1878–80
Atlanta & West Point, 1869, 1871–73, 1876–82
Alabama Great Southern, 1876, 1880
Central of Georgia, 1838–93
Charlotte, Columbia & Augusta, 1875–76, 1878–80, 1884
Chesapeake & Ohio, 1875–77, 1879–87, 1889–93
East Tennessee, Virginia & Georgia, 1869–93
Georgia, 1872–93

[1] These printed annual reports are listed by railroad to eliminate the needless repetition of long and basically similar titles caused by frequent change of company name.

Louisville & Nashville, 1866–93
Memphis & Charleston, 1869, 1877–81, 1884–88, 1890–93
Mobile & Girard, 1872–79
Mobile & Montgomery, 1876–79
Mobile & Ohio, 1867, 1869–71, 1877–82, 1888–90
Nashville, Chattanooga & St. Louis, 1875–93
Norfolk & Western, 1881–93
Raleigh & Gaston, 1866–78, 1890–93
Richmond & Danville, 1866–93
Richmond & West Point Terminal Railway & Warehouse Company, 1882–92
Savannah, Florida & Western, 1880–85, 1888, 1893
Seaboard & Roanoke, 1867, 1870, 1887, 1890–93
Southwestern, 1869
Virginia Midland, 1875, 1882
Western Railroad of Alabama, 1877, 1879
Wilmington & Weldon, 1869, 1875, 1878–83, 1891–93

Index

Index